Celebrate Freedom

Celebrate Freedom

Three documents are especially important to the United States. These are the Declaration of Independence, the Constitution, and the Bill of Rights. Read parts of these documents. Then answer the questions.

Declaration of Independence, 1776

We hold these truths to be self-evident, that all men are created equal, that they are endowed by their Creator with certain unalienable Rights, that among these are Life, Liberty, and the pursuit of Happiness. That to secure these rights, Governments are instituted among Men, deriving their just powers from the consent of the governed. That whenever any Form of Government becomes destructive of these ends, it is the Right of the People to alter or to abolish it, and to institute new Government . . .

- **What does the Declaration of Independence tell us about American beliefs?**

Constitution of the United States of America, 1789

We the People of the United States, in Order to form a more perfect Union, establish Justice, insure domestic Tranquility, provide for the common defense, promote the general Welfare, and secure the Blessings of Liberty to ourselves and our Posterity, do ordain and establish this CONSTITUTION for the United States of America.

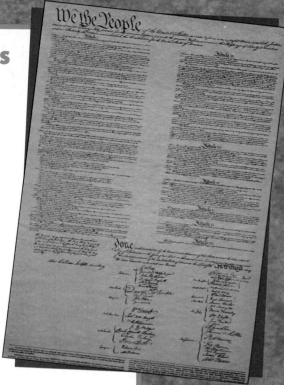

- **The first line of the Constitution is "We the People of the United States . . ." What does this say about whom the document is for?**

Bill of Rights, 1791

The first ten Amendments (changes) to the Constitution are called the Bill of Rights. They include:

- freedom of religion
- freedom of speech
- freedom of the press
- the right to protest peacefully
- the right to bear arms

- **In what ways might Americans peacefully protest?**

Celebrate Freedom

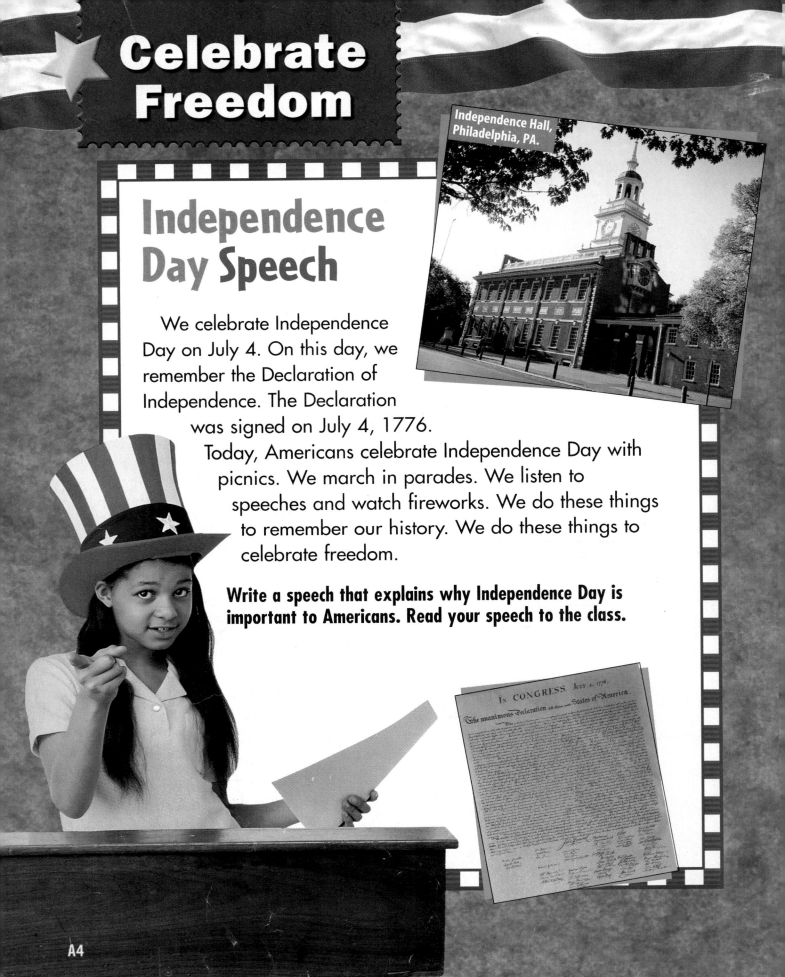

Independence Hall, Philadelphia, PA.

Independence Day Speech

We celebrate Independence Day on July 4. On this day, we remember the Declaration of Independence. The Declaration was signed on July 4, 1776.

Today, Americans celebrate Independence Day with picnics. We march in parades. We listen to speeches and watch fireworks. We do these things to remember our history. We do these things to celebrate freedom.

Write a speech that explains why Independence Day is important to Americans. Read your speech to the class.

Constitutional Word Search

Materials:
- Grid Paper
- Pencil
- Eraser

1 Use words from the United States Constitution to make a word grid. Words can be written in every direction.

2 After you have finished making your word grid, trade papers with another student. See if you can find all of the constitutional words in your partner's grid.

You may include:

Constitution

Union

justice

people

liberty

Celebrate Freedom

Bill of Rights Collage

1. Go through old magazines and cut out pictures that illustrate the Bill of Rights. Choose pictures that show our freedom of speech, freedom of the press, and freedom of religion.

2. Arrange the pictures and paste them onto the paper to create a collage.

3. Beneath your collage, write a paragraph telling what freedom means to you.

Materials:
- Old magazines
- Scissors
- Glue
- Markers
- Construction Paper
- Ruler

The Pledge of Allegiance

I pledge allegiance to the flag of the United States of America and to the Republic for which it stands, one Nation under God, indivisible, with liberty and justice for all.

Pledge to the Texas Flag

Honor the Texas flag.
I pledge allegiance to thee,
Texas, one and indivisible.

History

TEXTS

| 1500 | 1600 | 1700 |

TEXAS

1500s
Native Americans live in Texas; Spanish explorers bring horses and cattle to America.

1681
The first mission in Texas is built near what is now El Paso.

1836
Sam Houston defeats Mexico's General Santa Anna; Texas becomes free from Mexico.

| 1500 | 1600 | 1700 |

NEW SPAIN/ MEXICO

1521
Spain's Hernando Cortés defeats the Aztec; begins New Spain.

1500s
Moctezuma II leads the Aztec Indians.

| 1500 | 1600 | 1700 |

COLONIAL AMERICA/ UNITED STATES

1500s
Native Americans live throughout what is today the United States.

1607
English settlers arrive at Jamestown, Virginia; Powhatan Indians help the English.

1776
The Declaration of Independence tells the world that America is a free country.

A8

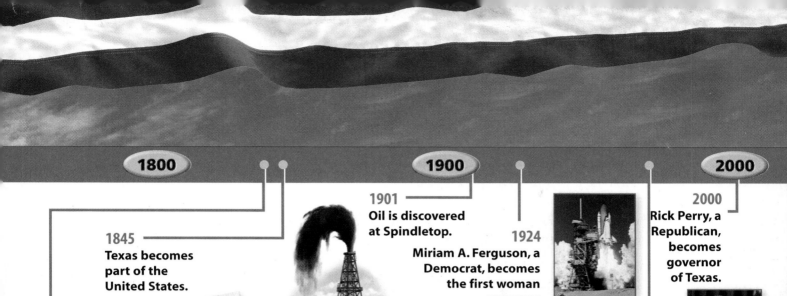

1800   **1900**   **2000**

1845
Texas becomes part of the United States.

1901
Oil is discovered at Spindletop.

1924
Miriam A. Ferguson, a Democrat, becomes the first woman governor of Texas.

2000
Rick Perry, a Republican, becomes governor of Texas.

1981
Space Shuttle *Columbia* is guided by NASA Mission Control in Houston.

1800   **1900**   **2000**

1810
Miguel Hidalgo begins fight against Spain for Mexican independence.

1841
General Santa Anna takes control of Mexico.

1911
Mexican Revolution begins; people vote to make Francisco Madero president.

1990
Writer Octavio Paz receives the Nobel Prize.

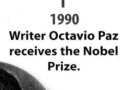

2000
Vicente Fox elected president.

1800   **1900**   **2000**

1865
The Civil War ends; President Lincoln is killed six days later.

1903
Wright brothers make the world's first engine-powered "flying machine."

1955
Rosa Parks works for African American equality.

2001
George W. Bush becomes the 43rd President of the United States.

Geography

Texas is a big place. To see it all would take weeks. Luckily, there are plenty of ways to get around in Texas. Texas has more railroad lines than any other state. Texas has big international airports. Of course, there are roads and highways. In Texas, the best way to get from here to there depends on where you are!

READING CHECK Texas has more of what type of transportation than any other state?

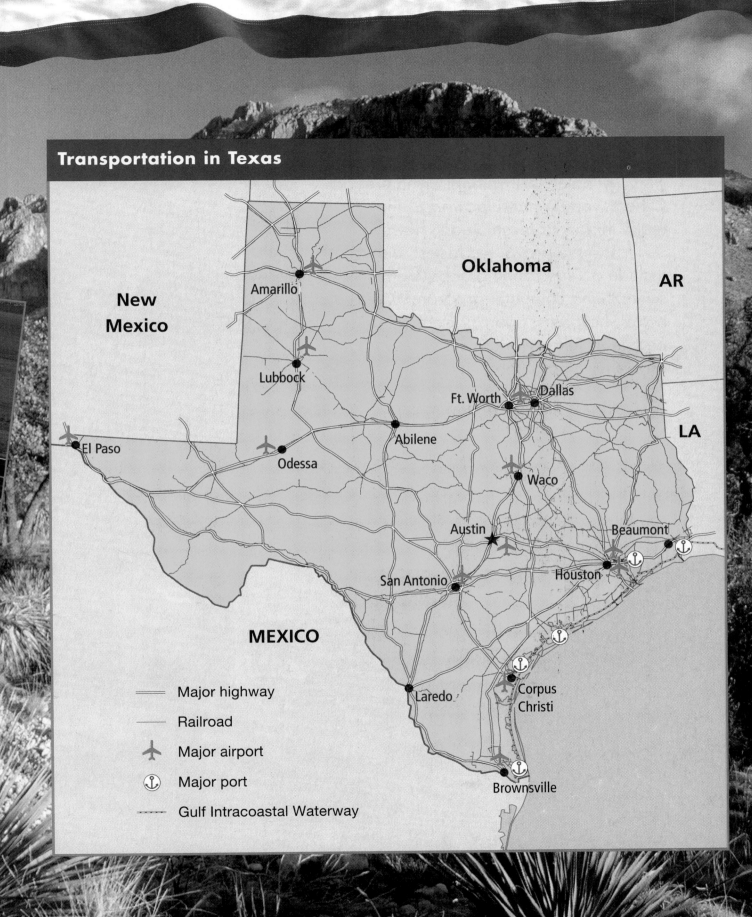

Transportation in Texas

New Mexico

Oklahoma

AR

LA

MEXICO

Amarillo

Lubbock

El Paso

Odessa

Abilene

Ft. Worth   Dallas

Waco

Austin

Beaumont

San Antonio

Houston

Laredo

Corpus
Christi

Brownsville

— Major highway
— Railroad
✈ Major airport
⚓ Major port
---- Gulf Intracoastal Waterway

Economics

There are many types of jobs in Texas. Many people work with oil or natural gas. Others work in *manufacturing*—they make things. In recent years, however, *services* have grown the fastest. Services include a wide range of jobs, from science and computer programming to hotels, hospitals, and dry cleaners. More people in Texas work in services than in any other type of job.

READING CHECK **What is the fastest-growing part of Texas's economy?**

Government

The Texas state government has three branches. There is an executive, a legislative, and a judicial branch. The governor leads the executive branch. The legislative branch is made up of the Senate and the House of Representatives. The Supreme Court and the Court of Criminal Appeals make up the judicial branch.

READING CHECK Who leads the executive branch of Texas government?

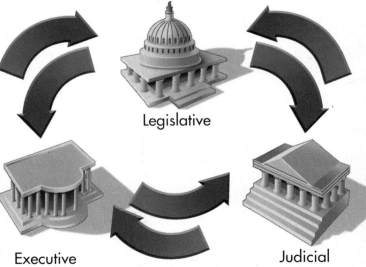

Legislative

Executive

Judicial

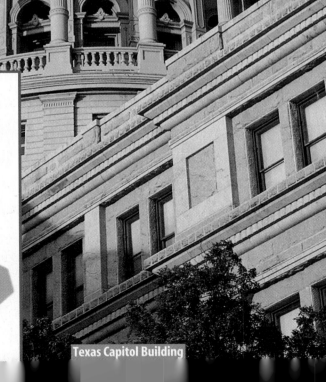

Texas Capitol Building

Citizenship

Suzanna Dickenson survived the Battle of the Alamo in 1836. Her husband and about 200 other Texans died there. They were fighting for Texas's freedom from Mexico. Suzanna helped to care for wounded soldiers. Even after the Mexican army won the battle, Suzanna was very brave. She helped spread news about the Alamo through Texas.

 What battle did Suzanna Dickenson survive?

Culture

The Texas Memorial Museum of Science and History is in Austin. This museum displays things that show how people have lived in Texas. There you can see over 7,500 photographs. The museum has millions of Texas plant and animal fossils. There are also old saddles, art, toys, and more.

READING CHECK What would you like to see at the Texas Memorial Museum of Science and History?

Science, Technology, and Society

The Internet is a powerful tool. It allows people to find information, buy things, and communicate. Because of its ability to connect people, it has been called "the single most important advancement to freedom of speech since the writing of the Declaration of Independence."

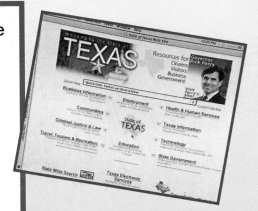

 How does the Internet help us?

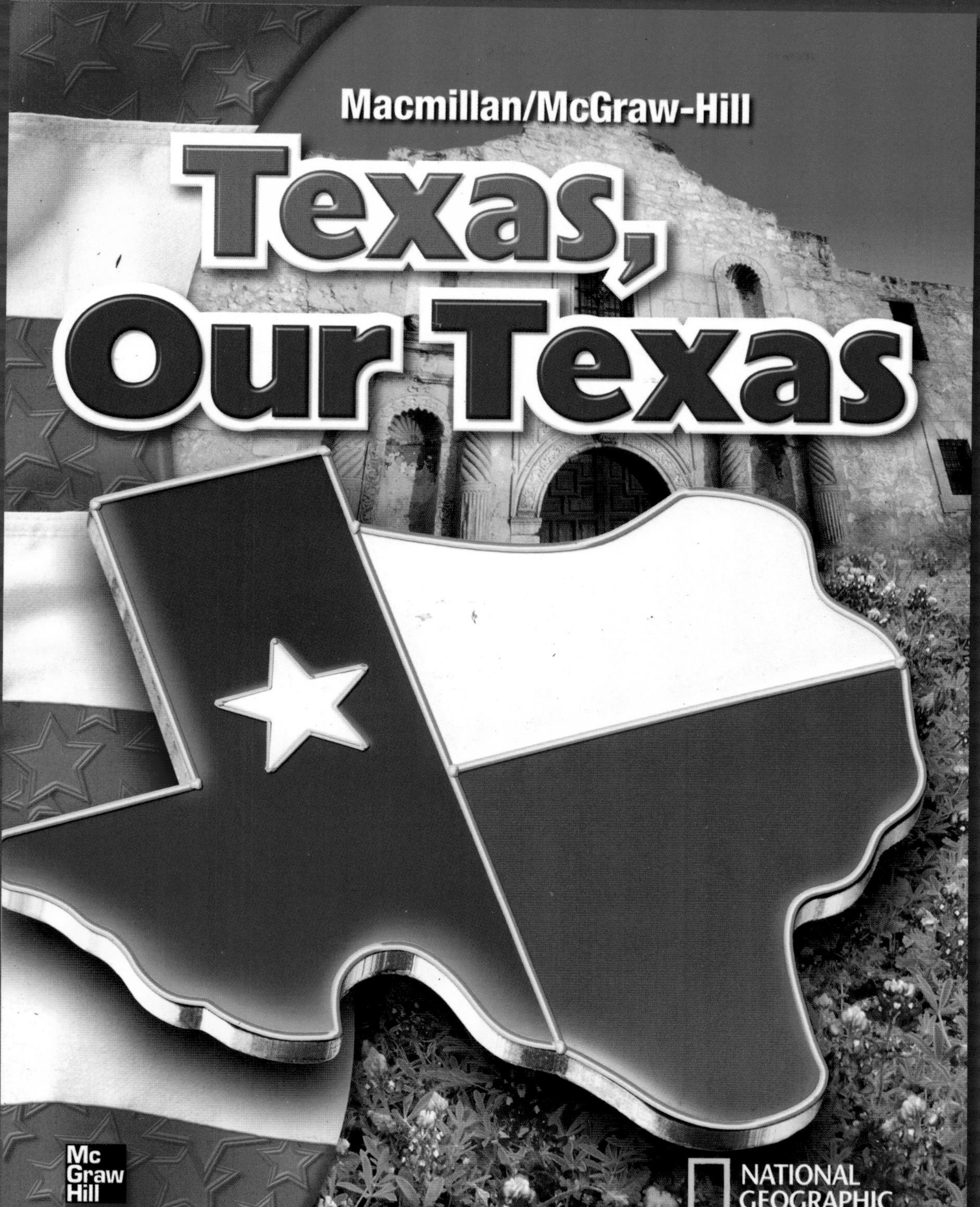

Macmillan/McGraw-Hill

Texas, Our Texas

McGraw Hill

NATIONAL GEOGRAPHIC

BEING A GOOD CITIZEN

In this textbook you will meet special people and learn many important things. On the BIOGRAPHY pages and in the POINTS OF VIEW lessons, you will see eight important words that help define what it means to be a good citizen. These words are listed below. They help us understand how to be better citizens in our home, neighborhood, school, community, country, and world.

★COURAGE★
being brave in the face of difficulty

★FREEDOM★
making choices and holding beliefs of one's own

★HONESTY★
telling the truth

★JUSTICE★
working toward fair treatment for everyone

★LEADERSHIP★
showing good behavior worth following
through example

★LOYALTY★
showing support for people and one's country

★RESPECT★
treating others as you would like to be treated

★RESPONSIBILITY★
being worthy of trust

Macmillan/McGraw-Hill

Texas, Our Texas

James A. Banks

Richard G. Boehm

Kevin P. Colleary

Gloria Contreras

A. Lin Goodwin

Mary A. McFarland

Walter C. Parker

 NATIONAL GEOGRAPHIC

Mc Graw Hill **Macmillan McGraw-Hill**
New York

PROGRAM AUTHORS

Dr. James A. Banks
Russell F. Stark University
  Professor and Director of the
  Center for Multicultural Education
University of Washington
Seattle, Washington

Dr. Richard G. Boehm
Jesse H. Jones Distinguished
  Chair in Geographic Education and
  Director, The Gilbert M. Grosvenor
  Center for Geographic Education
Southwest Texas State University
San Marcos, Texas

Dr. Kevin P. Colleary
Curriculum and Teaching Department
Hunter College
City University of New York
New York, New York

Dr. Gloria Contreras
Professor of Education
University of North Texas
Denton, Texas

Dr. A. Lin Goodwin
Associate Professor of Education
Department of Curriculum
  and Teaching
Teachers College
Columbia University
New York, New York

Dr. Mary A. McFarland
Social Studies Education Consultant,
  K–12
St. Louis, Missouri

Dr. Walter C. Parker
Professor of Education and Chair
  of Social Studies Education
University of Washington
Seattle, Washington

Washington, D.C.

HISTORIANS/SCHOLARS

Dr. Joyce Appleby
Professor of History
University of California, Los Angeles
Los Angeles, California

Dr. Alan Brinkley
Professor of American History
Columbia University
New York, New York

Dr. Nancy Cott
Stanley Woodward Professor of
  History and American Studies
Yale University
New Haven, Connecticut

Dr. James McPherson
George Henry Davis Professor of
  American History
Princeton University
Princeton, New Jersey

Dr. Donald A. Ritchie
Associate Historian of the United States
  Senate Historical Office
Washington, D.C.

TEXAS PROGRAM CONSULTANTS

Betty Ruth Baker, M.Ed.
Assistant Professor of Curriculum
  and Instruction
Early Childhood Specialist
School of Education
Baylor University
Waco, Texas

Dr. Randolph B. Campbell
Regents' Professor of History
University of North Texas
Denton, Texas

Dr. Steven Cobb
Director, Center for
  Economic Education
Chair, Department of Economics
University of North Texas
Denton, Texas

Frank de Varona, Ed.S.
Visiting Associate Professor
Florida International University
Miami, Florida

Dr. John L. Esposito
Professor of Religion and International
  Affairs, and Director of the Center for
  Christian-Muslim Understanding
Georgetown University
Washington, D.C.

READING INSTRUCTION CONSULTANTS

M. Frankie Dungan, M.Ed.
Reading/Language Arts Consultant, K–6
Mansfield, Texas

Antonio A. Fierro
Program Director for the Texas
  Reading Initiative, Region 19
El Paso, Texas

Dr. William H. Rupley
Professor of Reading Education
Distinguished Research Fellow
Department of Teaching,
  Learning and Culture
College of Education
Texas A&M University
College Station, Texas

GRADE LEVEL CONSULTANTS

Autumn Ashley
Fourth Grade Teacher
Franklin Elementary School
Alamo, Texas

Jana Magruder
Education Program Coordinator
The Bob Bullock Texas State
  History Museum
Austin, Texas

Sarah R. Massey, Ed.D.
Institute of Texan Cultures
University of Texas at San Antonio
San Antonio, Texas

Betty McGinnis
Fourth Grade Teacher
Spring Shadows Elementary School
Houston, Texas

Sonya Palmer
Fourth Grade Teacher
Thomas Tolbert Elementary School
Dallas, Texas

Delia Soza
Fourth Grade Teacher
Carman Elementary School
San Juan, Texas

LaNelle Vansau
Fourth Grade Teacher
Central Elementary School
Duncanville, Texas

CONTRIBUTING WRITERS

Dinah Zike
Comfort, Texas

Emily Laber
New York, New York

Linda Scher
Raleigh, North Carolina

RFB&D
learning through listening

Students with print disabilities
may be eligible to obtain an
accessible, audio version of the
pupil edition of this textbook.
Please call Recording for the Blind
& Dyslexic at 1-800-221-4792 for
complete information.

Acknowledgments The publisher gratefully acknowledges permission to reprint the following copyrighted material:
From **The Flute Player, An Apache Folktale** retold and illustrated by Michael Lacapa. Copyright © 1990 by Michael Lacapa. Rising Moon, Flagstaff, Arizona. Used by permission. From **Deaf Smith, Scout, Spy and Texas Hero** by Jo Harper, illustrated by Virginia Roeder. Copyright © 1996 by Jo Harper and Virginia Roeder. Eakin Press, A Division of Sunbelt Media, Inc., Austin, Texas. Used by permission. From **Freedom's Gifts, A Juneteenth Story** by Valerie Wesley, illustrated by Sharon Wilson. Text copyright © 1997 by Valerie Wesley, Illustrations copyright © 1997 by Sharon Wilson. Simon & Schuster Books for Young Readers, New York. Used by permission. From **The Spindletop Gusher, The Story of the Texas Oil Boom** by Carmen Bredeson. Copyright © 1996 by Carmen Bredeson. All Rights Reserved. Millbrook Press, Brookfield, Connecticut. Used by permission.

(continued on page R55)

Macmillan/McGraw-Hill

A Division of The **McGraw·Hill** *Companies*

Published by Macmillan/McGraw-Hill, of McGraw-Hill Education, a division of The McGraw-Hill Companies, Inc., Two Penn Plaza, New York, New York 10121.

Printed in the United States of America
ISBN 0-02-149266-2
4 5 6 7 8 9 071/043 06 05 04 03

Contents

Introduction

Primary Sources

Music

Datagraphics

Exploring Economics

Exploring Technology

History Mystery

MAPS

Social Studies Handbook

The Social Studies Strands are a way of thinking about social studies. Social studies is the study of people and the world we live in. This is a very big subject! One way to think about social studies is to break it into parts. We call these parts strands.

The pie chart on the next page shows the eight strands of Social Studies. Each strand teaches us something about the world. Studying all of the strands together leads to an understanding of our world, past and present. The only thing left is the future. That will be up to you!

The Eight Strands of Social Studies

Economics
Wants and needs, goods and services. Basic human needs are met in a variety of ways.

Citizenship
Rights, responsibilities, pride and hope. Our beliefs and principles help make up our national identity.

Culture
Holidays, traditions and stories. We learn about ourselves and our families through the customs we share and celebrate.

Geography
Location, place, maps and more. People and environments surround us and are ever changing.

Science, Technology, and Society
Inventions, computers and ideas. Technology has changed how people live together in the world

Social Studies Skills
Many special skills are needed to better understand the world around you.

History
Time and chronology, years and dates. Historical figures and ordinary people help shape our lives.

Government
People work to make the laws that influence our lives. People work with citizens to govern.

Thinking About Reading

Your social studies book traces the history of Texas and examines its place in the world today. In order to understand the important facts and ideas presented, it is necessary to read your book carefully. The strategies below describe some of the ways that will help you become an effective social studies reader.

How to Preview, Ask, Read, and Review:

1 **Preview the lesson.** Read the title, headings, and highlighted words. Look at the photographs, illustrations, and maps, and read their captions. Think about what you already know about the topic. Form a general idea of what the lesson is about.

2 **Ask yourself questions before you read and as you read.** For example, you might ask, "What is the lesson telling me about the Battle of the Alamo?"

3 **Read and reread.** Read the lesson carefully. Figure out the main ideas. Reread a sentence or paragraph if it doesn't make sense to you. Look up the meanings of any unfamiliar words.

4 **Review by summarizing what you have read, either aloud or in writing.** Did you find the answers to your questions?

Communities

1

Preview.
The title, the highlighted words, the picture, and its caption tell me this lesson will be about communities in Texas.

2

Ask yourself questions.
One question I might ask is, "What different types of communities will I learn about?"

3

Read and reread.
I carefully read the paragraphs and think about the main ideas. I look up the meanings of *urban* and *rural*.

4

Review.
I will say or write the answers to my questions.

A community is a group of people who live and work together. A community may be just one neighborhood, or it may be made up of several neighborhoods near one another.

Cities are made up of many communities. Have you ever visited or lived in **Houston**? It is the largest city in Texas. Most Texans live in large urban areas such as Dallas, Fort Worth, El Paso, Austin, and San Antonio.

Other Texans prefer rural life. Many families have lived on their farms and ranches for a long time. Small towns are also found throughout rural Texas.

Houston skyline

Use Visuals

Visuals are the pictures, maps, charts, and graphs that appear throughout your book. Visuals provide useful information in a clear, easy-to-study form.

How to Use Visuals

Look closely at the visual. Then ask yourself the following questions:

- What does the picture, map, chart, or graph show?
- How does it help me understand what I have read?
- What information does the caption or label provide?

Study the picture. Then read the caption.

Tip!

★ When looking at graphs, maps, or charts, read the legend or key to find out the meanings of special symbols.

★ Look for objects in the picture that may give additional information.

Cowboys are driving cattle through a busy intersection. Traffic must come to a stop.

The caption tells us that traffic must come to a stop as cattle move through a busy intersection.

Think about the information that is given in the photograph and caption. Then copy and complete the diagram on a separate sheet of paper.

Workers in a clothing factory in Mexico are sewing clothes. Most of the finished product will be exported.

Visual:

Caption Information:

The factory is in Mexico. Most of the clothing will be exported.

Visual Information:

Factory workers are sewing clothing.

Keep in Mind

For more help in reading social studies, keep these strategies in mind:

Reread
Make sure you understand what each sentence means before you read further. Reread any sentences that don't make sense to you.

Look up unfamiliar words
Use the glossary in your book or a dictionary to find the meanings of unfamiliar words.

Summarize
In your own words, briefly describe what your reading is about.

Practice Activities!

1. **Use Visuals** Find an interesting photograph in your book. Write a caption for it.

2. **Create Visuals** Create a visual by making an illustration of something you like. Write a caption for it. Then exchange visuals with a classmate and discuss them.

Context Clues

You can often figure out the meaning of an unknown word by using **context clues**. A context clue can come before, after, or in the same sentence as the unknown word. Using context clues will help you to become a better reader.

How to Use Context Clues

Ask yourself the following questions:

- Are any parts of this word familiar?

- Are there other words, phrases, or sentences in the paragraph that can help me figure out the meaning of the word?

- What information do the other words, phrases, or sentences provide?

- Do the pictures give me any information about the word?

Read the paragraph below. What context clues would you use to identify the meaning of the word *immigrants*?

Tip!

★ Have you heard this word before? Think about how it was used.

★ Write down the context clues you used to find the meaning of the new word.

★ After you find its meaning, use the new word in a sentence of your own to help you remember it.

Today people from almost every country in the world live here. Starting in the 1600s, **immigrants** (IHM ih gruntz) began to arrive. Most immigrants came to this land to find a better way of life.

Context Clue:
people from almost every country in the world live here

Context Clue:
came to this land to find a better way of life

Context Clue:
began to arrive

Try It!

Read the paragraph below about how water is used in Texas. Then copy and complete the chart to find context clues for the word *recreation*.

People use water for **recreation**. The variety of Texas's landscapes offers many opportunities for recreation. Do you like to swim, water-ski, sail, fish, or just float on a raft? You couldn't do any of these things without water.

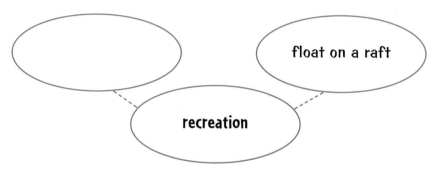

float on a raft

recreation

- What steps did you take to find the meaning of **recreation**?

Keep in Mind

For more help in reading social studies, keep these strategies in mind:

Reread
Make sure you understand what each sentence means. Reread any sentences that don't make sense to you.

Find the main idea
As you read, think about the topic and the main idea in each paragraph or section.

Summarize
In your own words, briefly describe what you are reading about.

Practice Activities!

1. **Read** Look in your book for an unfamiliar word or term. Then look for context clues to help you figure out the meaning of the word.

2. **Write** Choose an unfamiliar word from the dictionary. Write a short paragraph using the new word and one or two context clues.

WELCOME TO Austin

Places and Regions:
The Texas State History Museum is where much of our state's past is recorded and preserved.

Physical Systems:
Hamilton Pool Preserve is one place where the environment is protected.

The World in Spatial Terms:
This aerial photograph shows us the location of our state's capitol.

Uses of Geography
People use computer technology and other tools to make maps.

Human Systems:
Transportation routes, such as roads, are built to carry people and goods to and from the city.

Environment & Society:
The Congress Avenue Bridge is one example of how we change the environment to improve our lives. Mexican free-tailed bats have adopted this bridge as a home.

Using Globes

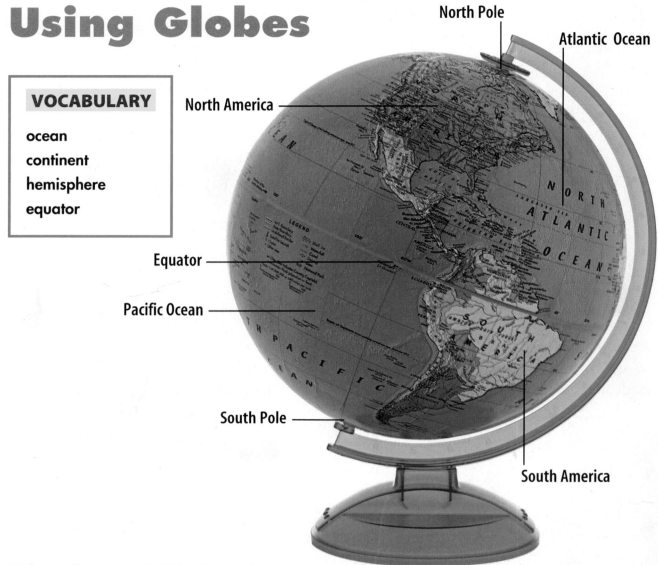

VOCABULARY

ocean
continent
hemisphere
equator

North Pole

Atlantic Ocean

North America

Equator

Pacific Ocean

South Pole

South America

What does a globe show?

- A globe is a model of Earth. Like Earth, a globe is a round object, or sphere. A globe is a useful tool for showing what Earth looks like.

- Globes show the parts of Earth that are land and the parts that are water. Which does Earth have more of, water or land?

- Earth's largest bodies of water are called **oceans**. There are four oceans—the Atlantic, Arctic, Indian, and Pacific.

- Look at the globe above. What color is used on the globe to show oceans?

- Globes also show the large bodies of land called **continents**. The seven continents are Africa, Antarctica, Asia, Australia, Europe, North America, and South America. Find North America and South America on the globe above. Which oceans do you see bordering these continents?

Social Studies Handbook

The Hemispheres

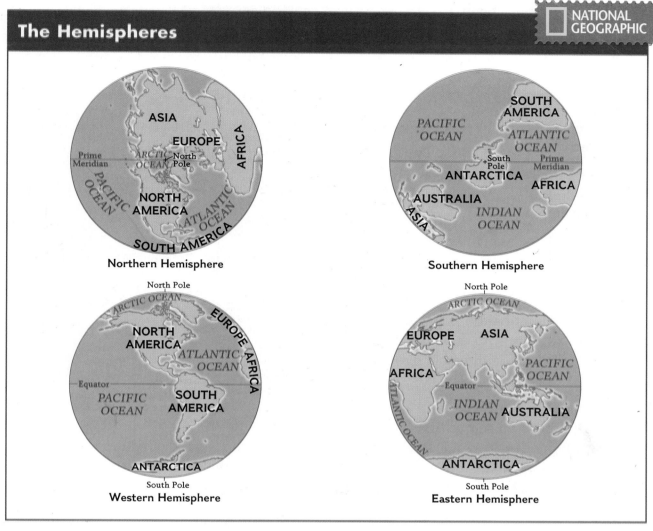

Northern Hemisphere

Southern Hemisphere

Western Hemisphere

Eastern Hemisphere

What are the four hemispheres?

- Look again at the globe on the previous page. You can see only half of the globe or sphere at one time. A word for half a sphere is **hemisphere**. The word "hemi" means half. Geographers divide Earth into four different hemispheres.

- Earth is divided into the Northern Hemisphere and Southern Hemisphere by the **equator**. The equator is an imaginary line that lies halfway between the North Pole and the South Pole. Look at the maps of the hemispheres above. Which continents are located on the equator? On which continent is the South Pole?

- Earth can also be divided into two other hemispheres. What are the names of these hemispheres?

Using Maps

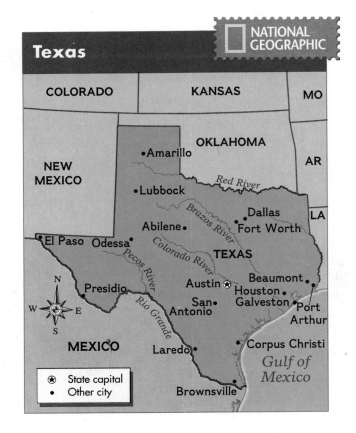

Texas

VOCABULARY

cardinal directions	relative location
compass rose	map key
intermediate directions	map symbol
	scale
	locator

What are cardinal directions?

- Directions describe the way you face or move to get somewhere. North, east, south, and west are the main directions, or **cardinal directions**.

- If you face the North Pole, you are facing north. When you face north, south is directly behind you. West is to your left. What direction will be to your right?

How do you use a compass rose?

- A **compass rose** is a small drawing on a map that can help you find directions.

- The cardinal directions are written as N, E, S, and W. Find the compass rose on the map above. In which direction is Odessa from Amarillo?

What are intermediate directions?

- Notice the spikes between the cardinal directions on the compass rose. These show the **intermediate directions**, or in-between directions.

- The intermediate directions are northeast, southeast, southwest, and northwest. The direction northwest is often written as NW. What letters are used for the other intermediate directions?

- Intermediate directions help us describe **relative location**. When we use relative location we describe one place in relation to another. For example, you can say that Austin is northeast of San Antonio.

Why do maps have titles?

- When using a map, first look at the map title. The title names the area the map shows. It may also tell you the kind of information shown on the map. Look at the maps below. What is the title of each?

Why do maps include symbols?

- A **map symbol** is a drawing that stands for real things.

- Many maps use blue to stand for water. What do dots sometimes stand for?

How can you find out what map symbols stand for?

- A **map key** gives the meaning of each symbol used on the map.

- When you look at a map, you should always study the map key. Look at the maps on this page. What symbol marks points of interest on the map of San Antonio?

- Draw your own map of a place where you live. Put in the streets. Use symbols to show where you live, your school, stores, a friend's house, and a park or playground. Finally, don't forget to insert a compass rose.

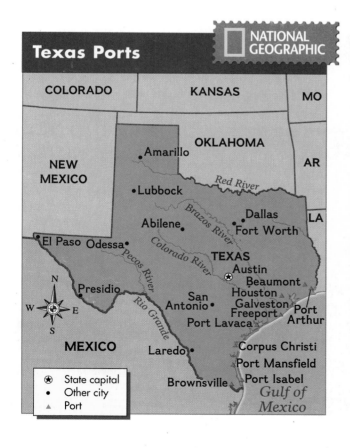

Texas Ports

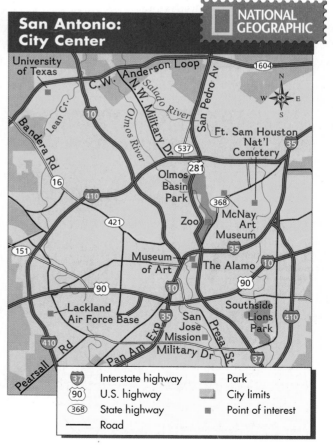

San Antonio: City Center

What is a map scale?

- How can you figure out the real distance between places? Most maps include a **scale**. The scale shows the relationship between distances on a map and real distances.

- The scales in this book are drawn with two lines. The top line shows distance in miles. What unit of measurement does the bottom line use?

How do you use a map scale?

- You can make a scale strip like the one on this page. Place the edge of a strip of paper under the scale lines on the map below. Mark the distances in miles.

- Use your scale strip to measure the distance between the Visitor Center and Cutoff Ridge. Place the edge of the strip under the two points. Line the zero up under the Visitor Center. What is the distance to Cutoff Ridge in miles?

What do locators show?

- A **locator** is a small map set onto the main map. It shows where the area of the main map is located. Where on the map below is the locator?

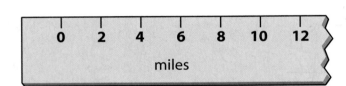

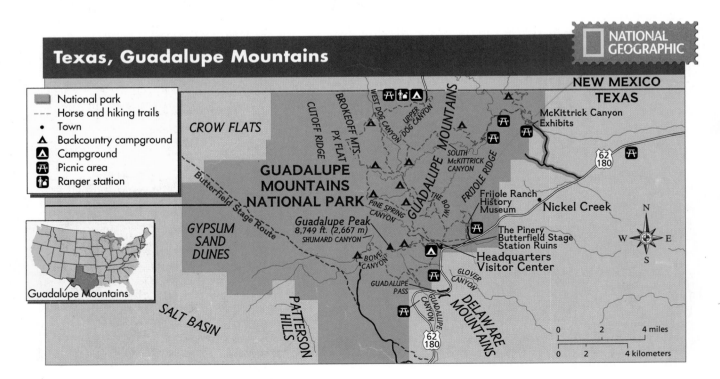

Texas, Guadalupe Mountains

NATIONAL GEOGRAPHIC

Different Kinds of Maps

VOCABULARY

political map	transportation map
physical map	
landform map	historical map

What is a political map?

- A **political map** shows information such as cities, capital cities, states, and countries. What symbol is used to show state capitals on the map below? What city is the capital of our state? What is the symbol for our nation's capital?

- Political maps use lines to show borders. The states or countries are also shown in different colors.

- Use the map on this page to answer these questions. Are states bigger in the west or the east? Which states border Canada? Which states border Mexico?

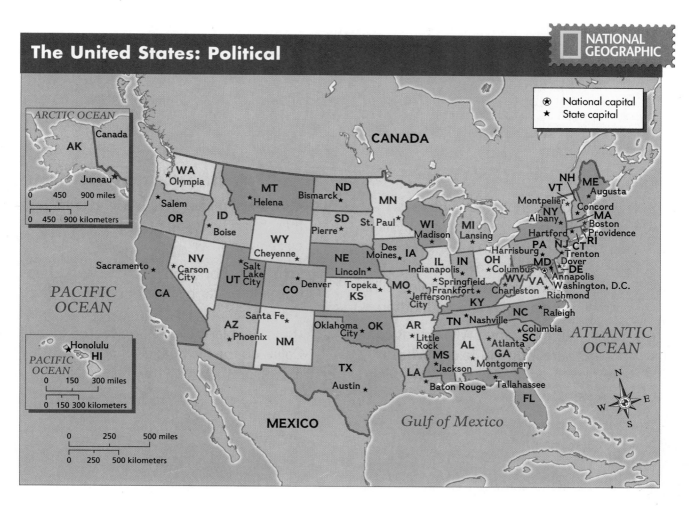

The United States: Political

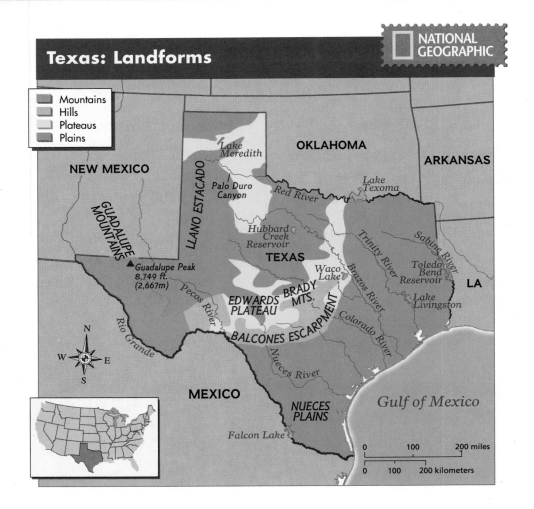

Texas: Landforms

NATIONAL GEOGRAPHIC

Legend:
- Mountains
- Hills
- Plateaus
- Plains

What are physical maps?

- There are different kinds of **physical maps** in this book. One kind of physical map shows landforms, or the shapes that make up Earth's surface. These maps are called **landform maps**. Mountains, hills, and plains are all examples of landforms.

- Look at the map above. What kinds of landforms are found in Texas? What mountains are found in the western part of our state?

What is a transportation map?

- A **transportation map** is a kind of map that shows how you can travel from one place to another.

- Some transportation maps show roads for traveling by car, by bike, or on foot. Other transportation maps may show bus, train, ship, or airplane routes. Look at the map of Dallas on the next page. What kinds of routes are shown on the map of Dallas?

What is a historical map?

- A **historical map** is a map that shows information about past events and where they occurred. What information do you think you would find on the historical map below?

- Historical maps often show dates in the title or on the map. What historical dates does the map below show?

- The map key tells you what the symbols stand for on the map. What is the symbol for a battle? In what order did the battles happen?

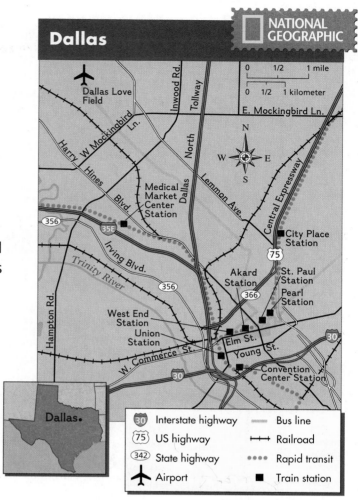

Dallas

NATIONAL GEOGRAPHIC

Dallas Love Field

Inwood Rd.
North Tollway
E. Mockingbird Ln.
W. Mockingbird Ln.
Harry Hines Blvd.
Lemmon Ave.
Central Expressway
Medical Market Center Station
City Place Station
Irving Blvd.
Trinity River
Akard Station
St. Paul Station
Pearl Station
Hampton Rd.
West End Station
Union Station
Elm St.
Young St.
W. Commerce St.
Convention Center Station

Dallas.

30 Interstate highway		Bus line
75 US highway		Railroad
342 State highway		Rapid transit
✈ Airport		■ Train station

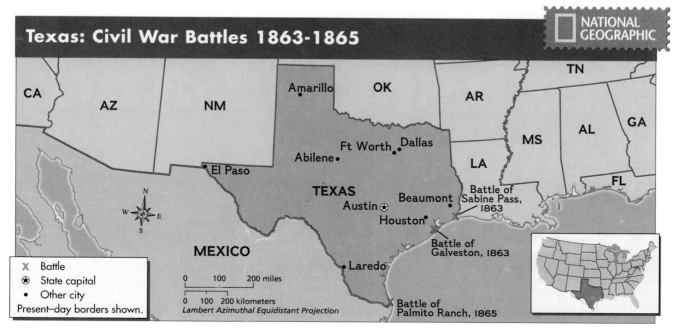

Texas: Civil War Battles 1863-1865

NATIONAL GEOGRAPHIC

CA
AZ
NM
Amarillo
OK
AR
TN
AL
GA
Ft Worth Dallas
Abilene
MS
El Paso
TEXAS
Austin ⊛
Beaumont
LA
FL
Battle of Sabine Pass, 1863
Houston
Battle of Galveston, 1863
MEXICO
Laredo
Battle of Palmito Ranch, 1865

X Battle
⊛ State capital
• Other city
Present–day borders shown.

0 100 200 miles
0 100 200 kilometers
Lambert Azimuthal Equidistant Projection

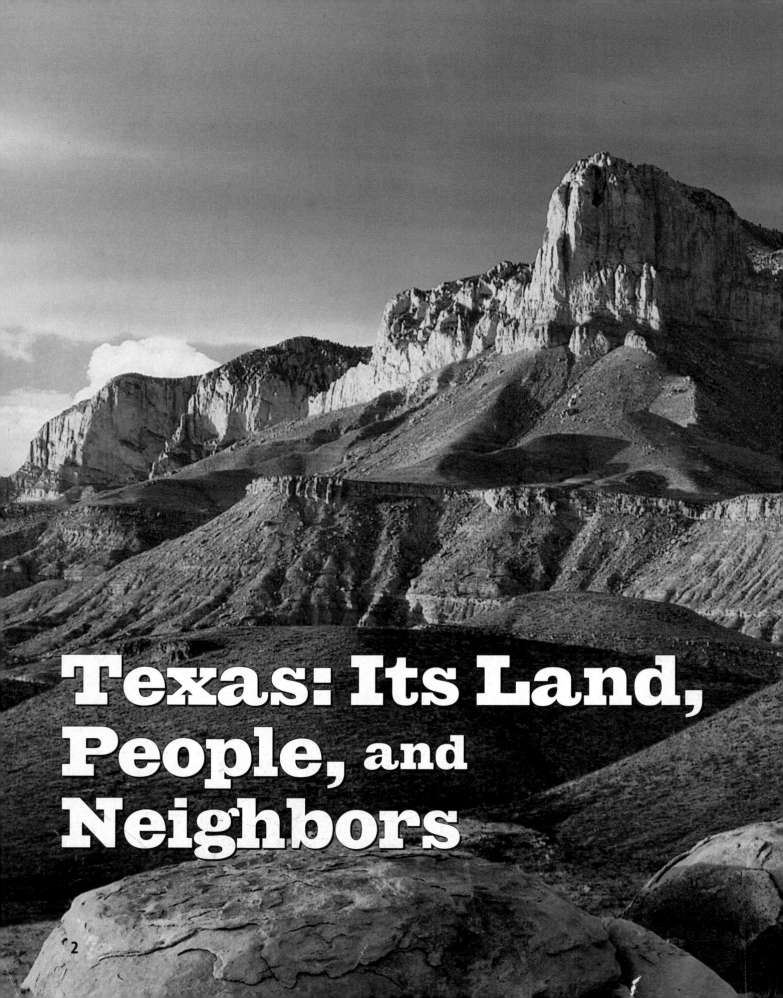

Texas: Its Land, People, and Neighbors

Sam Houston called Texas "the finest country . . . upon the globe." He had many good reasons to praise Texas. Visitors from all over the world come to see the many spectacular sites found in our state. They include **El Capitan** in the Guadalupe Mountains National Park. At 8,085 feet, it is one of the highest peaks in our state. In this Introduction, you will learn about these and other places and people that make Texas special.

The Western Hemisphere

Texas is part of the **Western Hemisphere**, which stretches from the North Pole to the South Pole. If you traveled through the Western Hemisphere, you would learn much about its **geography** (jee AHG ruh fee). Geography is the study of Earth and the way that people live on it and use it.

On your trip, you would see many different **landforms**. Landforms are the shapes that make up Earth's surface. A hill is one kind of landform. A **plain** is another. A plain is a large area of nearly flat land.

Your trip begins at the North Pole. Your first stop is the **tundra**, a huge plain that is frozen for most of the year.

South of the tundra, are the **Rocky Mountains**. They stretch from **Canada** to **Mexico**.

Heading farther south, you pass through **Central America**. Next you cross the **Panama Canal**, which links the Atlantic and Pacific Oceans. A **canal** is a waterway dug across land.

You are now in South America. In Brazil, you come to the **Amazon Rain Forest**, home to more than 50,000 kinds of plants.

Your trip ends at the South Pole in Antarctica. This continent is covered mostly by a huge sheet of ice.

READING CHECK What does the study of geography include?

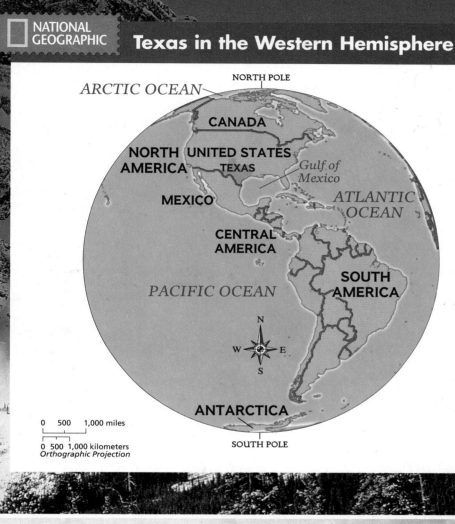

NATIONAL GEOGRAPHIC

Texas in the Western Hemisphere

Map Skill

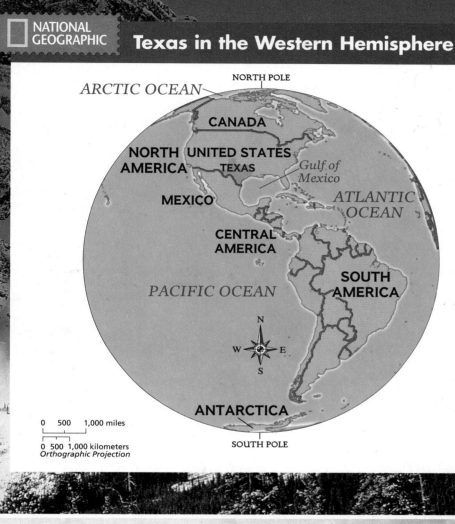

ARCTIC OCEAN — NORTH POLE

CANADA

NORTH AMERICA — UNITED STATES — TEXAS

Gulf of Mexico

MEXICO

ATLANTIC OCEAN

CENTRAL AMERICA

PACIFIC OCEAN

SOUTH AMERICA

N
W · E
S

ANTARCTICA

SOUTH POLE

0 500 1,000 miles

0 500 1,000 kilometers
Orthographic Projection

1. Which continents are in the Western Hemisphere?

2. What body of water is located between Canada and the North Pole?

3. What continent is farthest south in the Western Hemisphere?

The United States

The geography of the United States is full of variety. You have learned that the Rocky Mountains stretch through the western part of our country. In the middle, you find the low, flat **Interior Plains**. They are made up of the **Great Plains** and the **Central Plains**. Stretching for hundreds of miles, they are perfect for growing crops such as corn and wheat. Cattle and other animals graze on these plains.

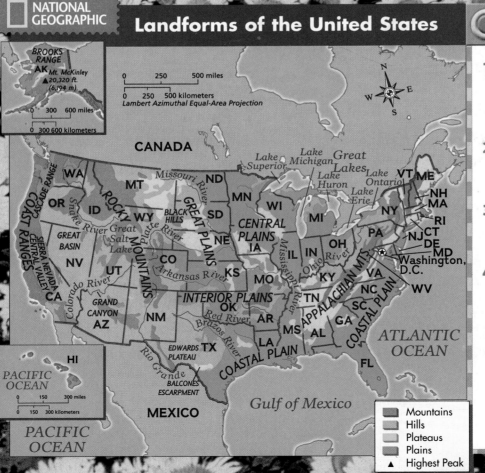

NATIONAL GEOGRAPHIC

Landforms of the United States

○ Map Skill

Mountains
Hills
Plateaus
Plains
▲ Highest Peak

1. What types of landforms does the Brazos River flow through?

2. Name a mountain range found in the United States.

3. Name three states located on the coastal plain.

4. How do the landforms found in our state make Texas different from most other states?

Another kind of plain is located near a **coast**. A coast is the land along an ocean. Along the Atlantic Ocean and Gulf Coast, you'll find the **Coastal Plain**. It is filled with sandy beaches and rocky shores.

Our country also has long, flowing rivers. One of the largest is the **Mississippi**. The **source**, or starting point, of the Mississippi is a tiny body of water in Minnesota called Lake Itasca. The Mississippi river is so long it takes a drop of water 60 days—two whole months—to travel from the river's source to its **mouth**, in Louisiana. The mouth is the place where a river empties into the ocean or another large body of water. The Mississippi grows wider as it flows. Why? It is fed by smaller rivers called **tributaries**.

Water is also found in swamps and marshes, such as the **Florida Everglades**. These are **wetlands**, places where the ground is very wet. Wetlands help control floods by soaking up extra water. They also provide a home for many plants and animals, such as the alligator.

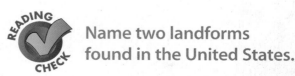

READING CHECK Name two landforms found in the United States.

Our State's Geography

Texas is the second-largest state in the United States. Only Alaska is larger.

Our state's geography has many different types of landforms. Suppose you flew in an airplane across Texas. On such a trip you would see many of our state's **natural features**. A natural feature is any part of Earth's surface formed by nature.

Your plane ride begins near the **Gulf of Mexico**. Heading west, you pass over the flat land of the Coastal Plain. Soon you reach the **Balcones Escarpment** (bal KOH nus e SKAHRP munt). An escarpment is a steep cliff. The Balcones Escarpment cuts across part of Texas from north to south.

You are now entering "Hill Country," which is part of a **plateau**. A plateau is a high, flat area that rises steeply above the surrounding land. As you continue northwest, you see the **Panhandle**. This is the most northern part of our state.

Farther west, the **Guadalupe** (gwahd ul OOP ay) **Mountains** appear. You fly over **Guadalupe Peak**, the highest mountain in our state. Between the mountains are **basins**—low, bowl-shaped landforms surrounded by higher land. Farther west, is our state's longest river, the **Rio Grande** (REE oh GRAHN dee). It forms part of the border between the United States and Mexico. *Rio Grande* means "big river" in Spanish. Part of the Rio Grande flows through **canyons**. A canyon is a deep valley with steep sides.

READING CHECK Where is the Panhandle located?

Texas: Landforms

NATIONAL GEOGRAPHIC

NM
Amarillo
OK
AR
Wichita Falls
Red River
Texarkana
Lubbock
Fort Worth
Dallas
Sabine River
GUADALUPE MOUNTAINS
Odessa
Colorado River
Abilene
Brazos River
Trinity River
LA
El Paso
Pecos River
TEXAS
BLUE MTS.
★Austin
Beaumont
Presidio
Houston
Port Arthur
San Antonio
Galveston
Nueces River
BALCONES ESCARPMENT
MEXICO
Laredo
Corpus Christi
Rio Grande
Brownsville
Gulf of Mexico

0 100 200 miles
0 100 200 kilometers

Mountains
Hills
Plateaus
Plains
★ State capital
• Other city

Map Skill

1. **Which states share a border with Texas? Which country shares a border?**

2. **Name two rivers that form part of Texas's borders.**

9

Our State's Climate

Every place has a pattern of weather over many years. This is its **climate** (KLI mit). Climate has two parts. The first is **temperature** (TEM pur uh chur). Temperature measures how hot or cold the air is. The second part of climate is **precipitation** (prih sihp ih TAY shun). Precipitation is moisture that falls in the form of rain, snow, sleet, or hail.

Different parts of our state have very different climates. One reason is elevation. The higher a place is above sea level, the colder its climate. The mountain

NATIONAL GEOGRAPHIC

Texas: Average January Temperatures

Degrees Fahrenheit	Degrees Celsius
over 60°	over 16°
51 to 60°	11 to 16°
41 to 50°	5 to 10°
30 to 40°	-1 to 4°

Albers Equal-Area projection

◯ Map Skill

1. Which has warmer temperatures in January, Lubbock or Galveston?

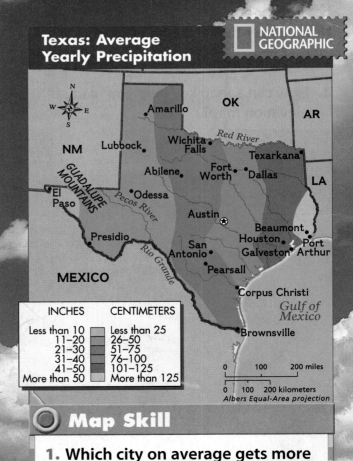

Texas: Average Yearly Precipitation

NATIONAL GEOGRAPHIC

INCHES	CENTIMETERS
Less than 10	Less than 25
11–20	26–50
21–30	51–75
31–40	76–100
41–50	101–125
More than 50	More than 125

Albers Equal-Area projection

◯ Map Skill

1. Which city on average gets more rain, Fort Worth or Texarkana?

areas of western Texas are cooler than the flatter areas in the east.

How far or near a place is to the equator also affects climate. The equator is one of the hottest places on Earth. The closer you are to it, the warmer the temperature. So cities in southern Texas, which are closer to the equator, are usually warmer. Cities in northern Texas tend to be cooler.

Large bodies of water also affect climate. Water heats up and cools off more slowly than air. This means the Gulf of Mexico stays chilly in the summer and warm during the winter.

Sometimes the climate can be dangerous. A **tornado** is a swirling funnel of wind that usually occurs over plains. It moves very quickly and with great force.

READING CHECK

Why is the climate of eastern Texas different from western Texas?

Our State's Resources

Environment (en VI run munt) is the surroundings in which we live. Our environment shapes us, but we also shape it. We cut down trees for lumber, construct canals, and build cities, among other things.

Environment includes the **natural resources** (REE sor sez) of a place. A natural resource is something found in nature that people can use.

Our state is rich in natural resources. Some are **renewable** (rih NOO uh bul). Renewable means that we can renew, or replace something. Rain, for example, replaces water drawn from our rivers. Trees can be replanted.

How an Aquifer Works

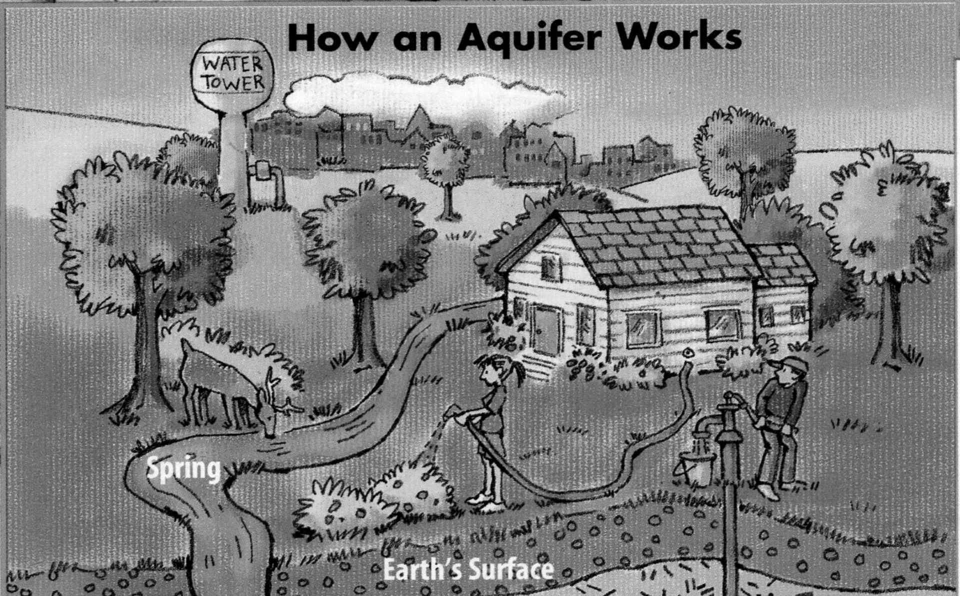

WATER TOWER

Spring

Earth's Surface

Limestone

Underground River

Bedrock

Diagram Skill

1. What layers does the pump go through before it reaches the underground water?

2. How is water being used in the diagram?

Other resources are **nonrenewable**. This means there is a limited supply. When we have used them up, they will be gone forever. **Minerals** are nonrenewable resources. A mineral is a natural substance found in the earth that does not come from plants or animals. Workers in Texas dig up minerals such as sulfur and uranium.

Fuels that power cars, buses, and airplanes are also nonrenewable resources. Oil, or **petroleum** (pih TROH lee um), is a thick, black liquid used to make gasoline. It is so plentiful in our state that many cities were built near oil fields.

Beneath some of our state's soil is a layer of limestone. It is a soft rock that absorbs rain like a sponge. This layer is called an **aquifer** (AHK wih fer). The Edwards Aquifer and the Ogallala (OH guhl lah lah)

Aquifer supply drinking water to millions of people.

Many of our resources will not last forever. They must be used wisely. Practicing **conservation** (kahn sur VAY shun) can help. Conservation is the careful use of natural resources. If we cut down trees, for example, we must make sure to plant new ones.

Another way to conserve resources is to **recycle** (ree SI kul). To recycle something is to use it again instead of throwing it out. It is also important to prevent **pollution** (puh LOO shun). Pollution is anything that dirties the air, soil, or water.

READING CHECK What is the difference between renewable and nonrenewable resources?

Writing an Outline

You have just learned about our state's resources. It might seem difficult at first to organize all the information you have read. Writing an **outline** helps you group facts and see how they are related. An outline is a plan that presents ideas about a subject in an organized way. It can help you better understand what you read.

VOCABULARY

outline

LEARN THE SKILL

Use the following steps when you create an outline, such as the one below.

1. **Identify the topic.**
   The topic is "Our State's Resources."

2. **Identify two main ideas.**
   Two main ideas are "Renewable Resources" and "Nonrenewable Resources."

3. **Include supporting details and facts.**
   Look back at pages 14–15. There are several details and facts that support the main ideas. For example, "Rain replaces river water," is a detail that supports "Renewable Resources." Supporting details and facts should be included in an outline.

4. **Organize the information.**
   When you create an outline, start with Roman numerals to show the sequence of the main ideas. Then under each of your main ideas, group the facts that support it. Place a capital letter beside each fact.

OUR STATE'S RESOURCES

I. Renewable Resources
   A. can be restored or replaced
   B. rain replaces water from rivers
   C. new trees can be planted

II. Nonrenewable Resources
   A. a limited supply
   B. minerals such as uranium
   C. fuels such as oil

TRY THE SKILL

Read the following article.

Fuels are an important natural resource. They are found deep beneath Earth's surface. They are drilled or dug out of the ground.

Fuels were formed from fossils. Fossils are the remains of animals or plants that lived long ago. Over time, they turned into coal, oil, and other fuels. Because they were formed from fossils, they are known as fossil fuels.

Now, create an outline organizing the information found in the article. Include a topic and supporting facts for each of the main ideas. Then use your outline to answer the following questions.

1. What is the topic of the article?

2. What are the main ideas?

3. What facts are related to fossils?

4. How can writing outlines help you better understand what you read?

EXTEND THE SKILL

An outline can also help you write a report. Read the following outline. Identify the topic and main ideas. Write a short report based on the outline. Then answer the questions below.

- How can an outline help you write a report?

- How can an outline help you compare and contrast information that you read?

RECYCLING

I. Why It Is Important
   A. helps conserve our resources
   B. helps prevent pollution

II. Ways to Recycle
   A. re-use paper
   B. collect cans and bottles instead of throwing them away

Our State's People

Over 20 million people live in our state. Some Texans live in **rural** areas. Rural means living in the countryside. Others live in **urban** areas. An urban area is a city and the communities that surround it. **Houston**, for example, is one of the busiest urban areas in the United States.

Every Texan has a special **heritage** (HER ih tihj). Heritage is the history a group of people share. People with a common heritage form an **ethnic group**.

Some Texans can trace their roots in our state deep into the past. They are Native Americans, who are also called American Indians. Their **ancestors** (AN ses turz) were the first people to live on this continent. Beginning with your parents and grandparents, your ancestors are all those in your family who were born before you.

For thousands of years, Native Americans were the only people living on the land that is now the United States. Starting in the 1600s, immigrants began to arrive. An immigrant is a person from another place who comes to a new land to live.

Immigrants looked to our country as a land of freedom. Here they could practice their religions. They could express their views freely. These rights are ours as Texans and as Americans.

Most immigrants came to Texas to find a better life. However, in the 1800s, thousands of African Americans were brought to Texas against their will in **slavery**.

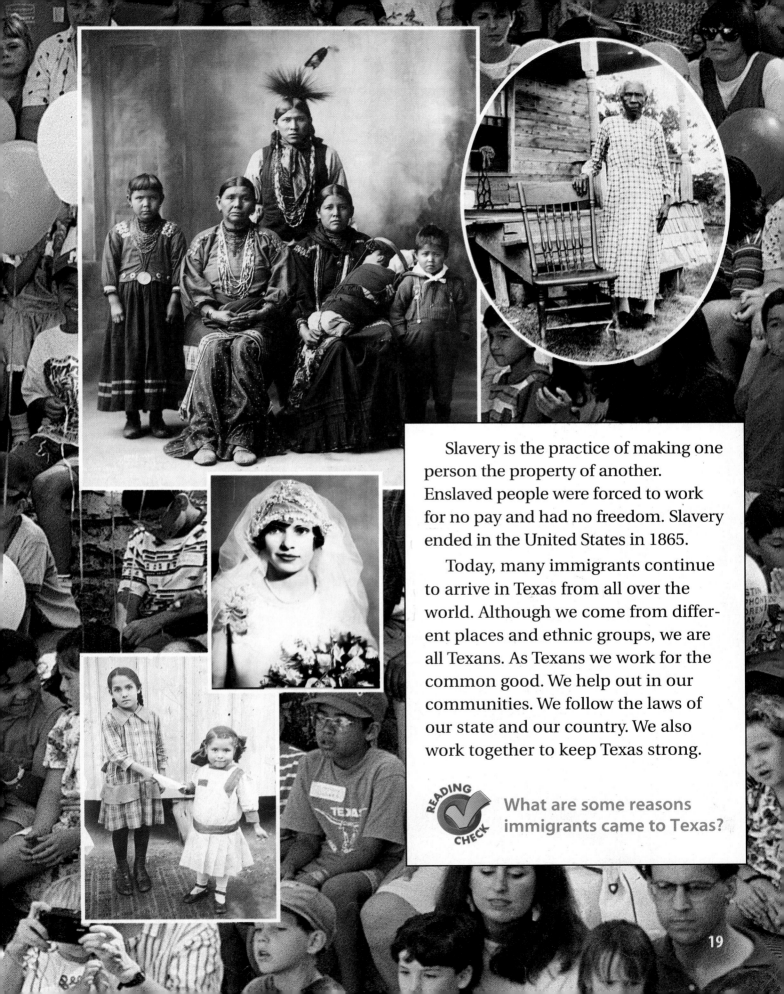

Slavery is the practice of making one person the property of another. Enslaved people were forced to work for no pay and had no freedom. Slavery ended in the United States in 1865.

Today, many immigrants continue to arrive in Texas from all over the world. Although we come from different places and ethnic groups, we are all Texans. As Texans we work for the common good. We help out in our communities. We follow the laws of our state and our country. We also work together to keep Texas strong.

READING CHECK What are some reasons immigrants came to Texas?

19

Our State's Cultures and Customs

"Honor the Texas Flag. I pledge allegiance to thee, Texas, one and indivisible."

Every Texan is proud to say these words. The Texas Pledge is something that each person in our state shares. But Texans are not all alike. We come from different groups that share different things.

One way to understand the different groups that live in Texas is to study their **cultures**. Culture is the way of life of a people. It includes many things people share. People observe holidays. They practice religions. These are parts of culture. So are music, clothing, even food.

Language is another important part of culture. For example, some of the city names in our state are

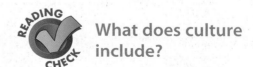

in Spanish, Mexico's main language. That's because Texas and Mexico were once part of Spain.

Customs are another important part of culture. A custom is the special way a group does something. Each culture has its own customs. When you sit down to eat, you may use a knife and fork. But some Texans will pick up chopsticks. Our state's different ethnic groups keep customs that may have started in other places.

Have you ever been to **San Antonio** during Fiesta, a ten-day, city-wide street fair? There you can see a parade of beautiful floats. You can hear all kinds of music, such as country, rock n' roll, and blues.

At Fiesta, you can also try many different foods, such as Mexican tortillas, Polish sausages, and Vietnamese egg rolls. These foods come from different cultures. But they are all served at Texan tables.

A variety of cultures helps make our state an exciting place. As Texans we respect the differences in each other's customs and history. We respect the freedoms of other people. Respect for others is part of the heritage of our state and our country.

READING CHECK What does culture include?

Regions of the United States

Geographers, or people who study geography, find it useful to divide our country into **regions** (REE junz). A region is an area with common features that set it apart from other areas.

The United States has six regions. They are the Southwest, Southeast, Northeast, Middle West, Mountain, and the West. Each is shaped by its environment, people, and history.

Each region has something special that sets it apart. The Southwest, for example, has the **Grand Canyon**, one of our country's most famous natural features.

Regions of the United States

Lambert Azimuthal Equal-Area Projection

Map Skill

1. How many states are part of the Southwest?

2. Which two regions have the most states?

The ways people earn a living can also make a region special. Fishing is an important part of the economy in the Southeast. Fishers there catch shrimp, crabs, and other shellfish.

The ways people use and change the land can shape a region. New-comers from all over the world came to live in the Northeast. They built many communities. Today, the North-east has many busy cities, such as Philadelphia, Boston, and New York.

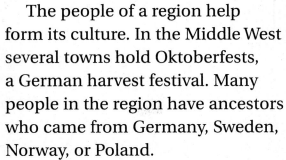

The people of a region help form its culture. In the Middle West several towns hold Oktoberfests, a German harvest festival. Many people in the region have ancestors who came from Germany, Sweden, Norway, or Poland.

The Mountain region is known for its tall slopes. Some are rugged and covered with heavy snow. Others have thick forests that provide a wealth of lumber.

Location can also shape a region. Some states in the West border the Pacific Ocean. Immigrants from China, Japan, the Philippines, and other countries along the Pacific live in the region. They built communities that reflect their cultures.

No region can meet all the needs of its people, so the regions of our country are **interdependent**. That means that people in one region depend on those in other regions to help meet their wants and needs.

Interdependence works because the regions stay connected. **Transportation** plays a big part in connecting the regions. Transportation means moving goods or people from one place to another.

READING CHECK

What are the six regions of the United States?

Problem Solving

Every day you face problems. Problem solving is a process you can use to find solutions. It can help you figure out how to open a stuck window, find a lost book, or solve a disagreement with a friend.

LEARN THE SKILL

Follow these steps to solve a problem.

1. **Identify the problem.**
   Here is an example. Marc is a fourth-grader who is concerned about the election for class president at his school. Last year, only a few students voted. He decides to make sure this year's election is different. So, he first identifies the problem: more students need to be encouraged to vote.

2. **Gather information.**
   Marc polls a group of students who did not vote in the last election. He asks them why they decided not to participate. Most say they did not know enough about the candidates to pick one.

3. **Identify the options.**
   Marc thinks of a couple of ways to solve the problem. Maybe the candidates could hand out flyers that explain what they would do as president. Or they could hold a debate.

4. **List the possible consequences.**
   Each option has a **consequence**, or result. Flyers might not give enough information. A debate would give the students a chance to see and hear the candidates and learn more about them.

5. **Choose a solution. Check with your parents, teacher, or other adult.**
   Marc decides to hold a debate. He asks his parents what they think about his solution. They agree with him. Marc asks the two candidates running for office if they would participate. Both agree. Marc then checks with the school principal to arrange a time and place.

6. **Evaluate the solution.**
   Most of Marc's class attends the debate. A week later, there is a high turnout at the election. Based on this final result, Marc **evaluates**, or judges the value of, his solution. Holding a debate was the best solution to the problem.

TRY THE SKILL

The Music Club at Elmwood Elementary School has a problem. It does not have enough money for all club members to attend a national elementary school music parade.

Marcy suggests waiting until next year, when the club will have more money. Jamal suggests sending three students and their parents on behalf of the entire club. Li suggests holding a bake sale to raise money so all members can participate and some parents can accompany the group.

Follow the steps on the previous page, to help the music club solve its problem.

1. How would you identify the problem?

2. What information would help solve the problem?

3. What are the possible options and consequences?

4. Will the school and parents approve of the solutions reached?

EXTEND THE SKILL

People across our country use problem-solving skills every day. Paul is a farmer in the Middle West. The geography and climate of his region allows him to grow wheat. However, he cannot grow oranges. Paul would like to use and enjoy both crops. Bob, a farmer in the Southeast can grow oranges, but not wheat. Think of a solution to Paul and Bob's problem. Then answer the questions below.

- How can Paul and Bob solve their problem?

- When might you need problem-solving skills in your daily life?

The Coastal Plain

Texas can be divided into regions also. They are the Coastal Plain, the North Central Plains, the Great Plains, and the Mountains and Basins regions.

The Coastal Plain is the largest region in our state. Here you find many different kinds of plant life, or **vegetation**. Geographers use these different kinds of vegetation to divide the Coastal Plain into five areas. The Coastal Plain begins at the Gulf of Mexico.

On the mainland you find beaches then **lowlands**. Lowlands have an elevation just above sea level. In part of the lowlands is the **Piney Woods**, known for its pine trees. To the west, the land rises slightly and the trees are replaced by **prairie**. Prairies are flat or rolling land covered with tall grass.

The Coastal Plain has many natural resources. The coast area, such as **Corpus Christi Bay**, has plenty of fish. The forests of the region provide wood.

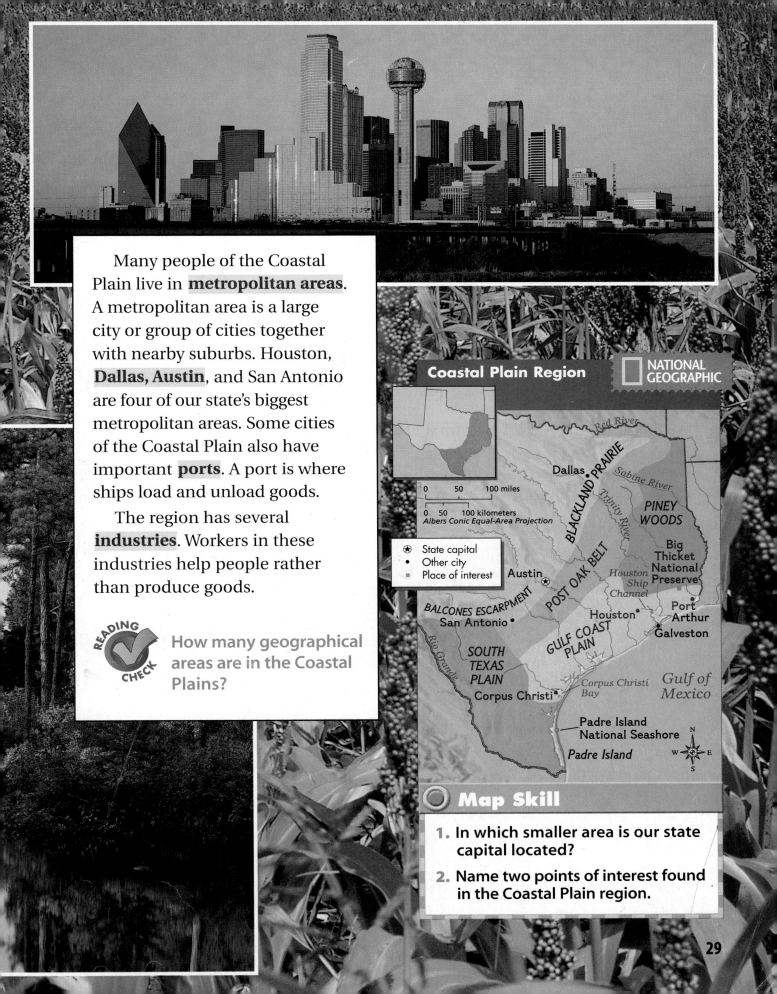

Many people of the Coastal Plain live in **metropolitan areas**. A metropolitan area is a large city or group of cities together with nearby suburbs. Houston, **Dallas, Austin**, and San Antonio are four of our state's biggest metropolitan areas. Some cities of the Coastal Plain also have important **ports**. A port is where ships load and unload goods.

The region has several **industries**. Workers in these industries help people rather than produce goods.

READING CHECK How many geographical areas are in the Coastal Plains?

Coastal Plain Region

NATIONAL GEOGRAPHIC

0   50   100 miles
0   50   100 kilometers
Albers Conic Equal-Area Projection

⊛ State capital
• Other city
▪ Place of interest

Red River
Dallas
BLACKLAND PRAIRIE
Sabine River
Trinity River
PINEY WOODS
POST OAK BELT
Big Thicket National Preserve
Austin
Houston Ship Channel
BALCONES ESCARPMENT
San Antonio
Houston
Port Arthur
Galveston
GULF COAST PLAIN
Rio Grande
SOUTH TEXAS PLAIN
Corpus Christi Bay
Gulf of Mexico
Corpus Christi
Padre Island National Seashore
Padre Island

N W E S

Map Skill

1. In which smaller area is our state capital located?

2. Name two points of interest found in the Coastal Plain region.

The North Central Plains

The land of the North Central Plains has a higher elevation than the Coastal Plain. Geographers divide the North Central Plains into three smaller areas. Find these areas on the map.

Mesas are a special landform found in this region. The word *mesa* means "table" in Spanish. **Buttes**, (BYOOTS) are another type of landform here. A butte is like a mesa, but smaller. It is a narrow hill with a flat top.

Grasslands make the region good for raising animals. There are many **ranches** in the North Central Plains. A ranch is a large area of land used to raise cattle, sheep, or horses.

The climate of the North Central Plains changes greatly from season to season. In the winter, snow and sudden blasts of cold air called *northers* are common. In the summer, temperatures can climb to more than 100°F.

North Central Plains Region

0   50   100 miles

0   50   100 kilometers
Albers Equal-Area Projection

W.T. Waggoner Ranch
Vernon•
Wichita Falls•

ROLLING PLAINS   Texas Cowboy Reunion
• Millsap
Stamford•
•Abilene

CROSS TIMBERS

Fort Worth•

GRAND PRAIRIE

• City
■ Place of interest

Much of the North Central Plains is rural. But the region is home to other businesses besides farming and ranching. Companies here make computers, soft drinks, and aircraft. Many people who do these jobs live in the cities of **Wichita Falls**, **Abilene**, and Fort Worth. Fort Worth's neighbor is Dallas, located on the Coastal Plain. Together Dallas and Fort Worth, along with their surrounding suburbs, form a huge metropolitan area called the **Metroplex**.

READING CHECK

Name two landforms of the North Central Plains.

Map Skill

1. **Which cities lie within the Rolling Plains?**

2. **Which area do you think might have had forests at one time?**

The Great Plains

Geographers divide the Great Plains of Texas into three areas. Find these areas on the map. The High Plains lie within the Texas Panhandle.

The Great Plains region is a high plateau. There is little rainfall here, so farmers use **irrigation** to grow crops. Irrigation is the practice of using pipes or ditches to bring water to fields.

The **Edwards Plateau** is marked with hills and deep valleys. This area is Texas Hill Country. Much of the wool produced in the United States comes from sheep that graze on the Edwards Plateau.

The **Permian** (PUR mee un) **Basin** is a major oil-producing area. It is located where the Edwards Plateau and the High Plains meet. The cities of **Midland** and **Odessa** are also found there.

The two largest cities in the Great Plains region are Amarillo and **Lubbock**. Amarillo is a center for the

cattle industry. In Lubbock there are factories that process cotton into different products. Cotton seeds are used to make cooking oil, soap, rope, paper, fertilizer, fuel, and plastics.

Summers are hot and dry in the Great Plains. Winters can be very cold and snowstorms are common in the Panhandle. The Great Plains can also be windy. People have built windmills to make use of the wind's power.

Name four products that come from the Great Plains region.

NATIONAL GEOGRAPHIC

Great Plains Region

Canadian River
Amarillo
CAP ROCK ESCARPMENT
HIGH PLAINS
Lubbock
Brazos R.
Tahoka
OGALLALA AQUIFER
Midland
Colorado River
Odessa
PERMIAN BASIN
Pecos River
San Angelo
LLANO BASIN
EDWARDS PLATEAU
L.B. Johnson National Historical Park
Rio Grande

- City
- Place of interest

0   50   100 miles
0   50   100 kilometers
Albers Conic Equal-Area Projection

Map Skill

1. What area does the Pecos River run through?

2. What acquifer is located in this region?

33

The Mountains and Basins

The Mountains and Basins region is in the western corner of Texas. Mountains in this region are part of the Rocky Mountain chain. They include the Guadalupe Mountains, the **Chisos Mountains**, and the **Davis Mountains**. Find them on the map on the next page.

The bowl-shaped basins between the Guadalupe Mountains are covered with **deserts**—dry land where little rain falls. The **Chihuahuan** (chi WAH wun) **Desert** is a flat, dry area that stretches into northern Mexico. You can find many plants and animals, such as the spade foot toad, that can survive in hot, dry climates.

The air over the desert is so dry that there are few clouds. Clouds hold heat. Without them, the temperature falls when the sun goes down.

This part of our state is far from the Gulf of Mexico's moist winds. Water comes mostly from **reservoirs**, because there are few natural lakes. A reservoir is a water storage area.

Over half a million people live in **El Paso**. This city is far from other large Texan cities you have read about. In fact, El Paso is so far west it is located in a different

time zone. A time zone is a region in which all the clocks are set to the same time. When it is seven o'clock in El Paso, it is eight o'clock in most of Texas!

El Paso is located where the borders of Texas, New Mexico, and Mexico meet. People from the United States and Mexico walk and drive across the border every day. Cross a bridge over the Rio Grande and you are in the Mexican city of **Ciudad Juarez** (see oo DAHD HWAHR ez). *Ciudad* means "city" in Spanish.

READING CHECK ✓

How does the dry climate affect life in the Mountains and Basins region?

Map Skill

1. What separates El Paso from Ciudad Juarez?

GUADALUPE MOUNTAINS

El Capitan

El Paso
Guadalupe Peak
Ciudad Juarez
Rio Grande

Guadalupe Mountains National Park

DAVIS MOUNTAINS   Fort Stockton

McDonald Observatory

CHIHUAHUAN DESERT

Alpine

Presidio
CHISOS MTS.

Big Bend National Park

- City
- Place of interest

0   50   100 miles
0   50   100 kilometers
Albers Conic Equal-Area Projection

Using Special Purpose Maps: Vegetation Maps

Vegetation maps are one kind of special purpose map. They show the plant life that grows in an area. Some of the vegetation maps in the area show forests, deserts, and even wetlands. Different kinds of vegetation grow in each of those areas. For example, in forests you find trees. In wetlands, you find tall marshy grasses. Other maps in the book serve a special purpose. They focus on specific kinds of information, such as rainfall or population.

> **VOCABULARY**
>
> vegetation map

LEARN THE SKILL

Study Map A on this page. Then follow the steps below to read vegetation maps.

1. Locate the title of the map.
The title of this map is United States: Vegetation. It shows the different kinds of plant types that are found throughout our state.

2. Locate the map key.
A vegetation map uses colors to show different kinds of plant areas. A map key can tell you the meaning of each color. On Map A, the color orange represents deserts.

Map A: United States: Vegetation

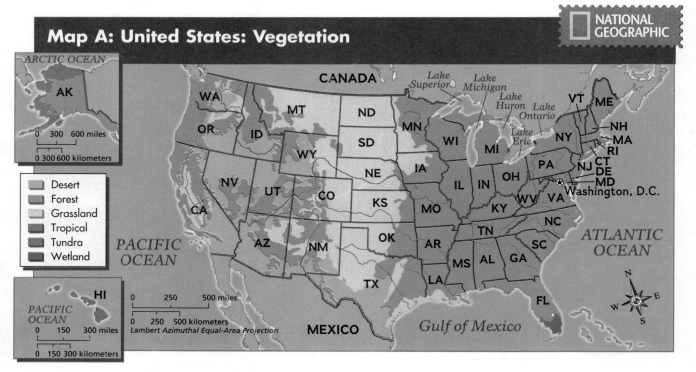

36

TRY THE SKILL

Now study Map B below. Use it to answer the following questions.

1. What is the title of the map?

2. Why is this a vegetation map?

3. What does the color dark green represent?

4. What kind of vegetation is shown on Map A but not Map B?

EXTEND THE SKILL

Vegetation maps can help you understand climate. Different plants grow in different climates. Desert plants need only a small amount of water to survive. Trees and grasses need a lot of rain to be healthy. Compare Map B to Map C. This is the same precipitation map of Texas that you have already used on page 12. Then answer the following questions.

- Where are the forests found in our state?

- Where are the deserts found in our state?

- Which area receives the highest amount of rain, East Texas or West Texas?

- How can reading vegetation maps help you understand plants and climate?

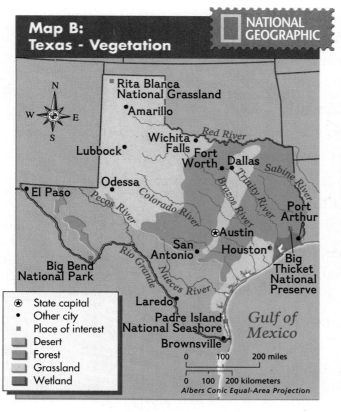

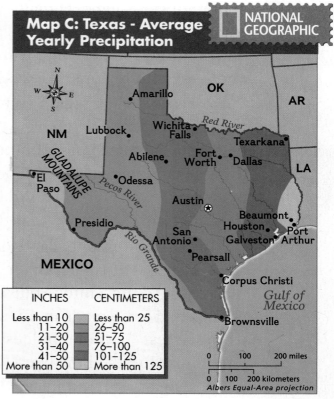

Texans One and All

In this Introduction, you have learned about our state's land, climate, and many resources. You have studied its people and cultures. You have also learned about the four regions of Texas.

No matter which region you live in, you can feel proud whenever you see the Lone Star flag flying. Another special thing Texans share is the bluebonnet, our state flower. Our state bird is the mockingbird. Our state tree is the pecan.

"Texas, Our Texas" became our state song in 1929. Thirty years later, when Alaska joined the United States, a change had to be made in our song. The word "largest" became "boldest." Can you think why? Find the word "boldest" in the song on the next page.

Texas, Our Texas

Words by Gladys Yoakum Wright and William J. Marsh   *Music by William J. Marsh*

Tex - as, our Tex - as! All hail the might - y State!
Tex - as, O Tex - as! Your free - born Sin - gle Star
Tex - as, dear Tex - as! From ty - rant grip now free;

Tex - as, our Tex - as! So won - der - ful, so great!
Sends out its ra - diance To na - tions near and far.
Shines forth in splen - dor Your star of Des - ti - ny!

Bold - est and grand - est, With - stand - ing ev - 'ry test; O
Em - blem of Free - dom! It sets our hearts a - glow, With
Moth - er of He - roes! We come, your chil - dren true, Pro -

Em - pire, wide and glo - rious, You stand su - preme - ly blest.
tho'ts of San Ja - cin - to And glo - rious A - la - mo.
claim - ing our al - le - giance, Our Faith, our Love for you.

Chorus (Repeat **ff**)

God bless you Tex - as! And keep you brave and

2nd time

strong, That you may grow in pow'r and worth Thru -

1.
out the a - ges long.

2.
out the a - ges long.

39

Introduction REVIEW

VOCABULARY REVIEW

Number a paper from 1 to 6. Beside each number write the term from the list below that best completes the sentence.

Western Hemisphere   **desert**

natural resource   **culture**

tundra   **time zone**

1. Something in the environment that people can use is a _____.
2. A _____ is a region where all the clocks are set to the same time.
3. An ethnic group has its own _____, or way of life.
4. An area where little rain falls is known as a dry land or _____.
5. A huge plain that is frozen for most of the year is called a _____.
6. North America and South America are two of the continents found in the _____.

TECHNOLOGY

For additional resources to help you learn more about the places you read about, visit **www.mhschool.com** and follow the links for Grade 4 Texas, Introduction.

SKILL REVIEW

7. **Geography Skill** Look at the map on this page. What landform in Texas has the lowest elevation?
8. **Geography Skill** Why might it be helpful to have an elevation map on a trip across Texas?
9. **Study Skill** How can writing outlines help you organize information?
10. **Thinking Skill** Why do you think it is important to know how to solve problems?
11. **Geography Skill** What does a vegetation map show?

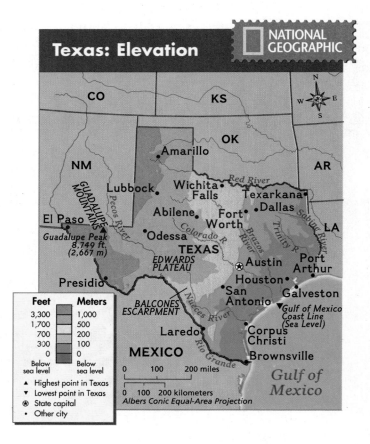

Texas: Elevation

Activities

- **Language Arts** Work together in teams to create a weather report for the local news. In the report, describe the weather for the past week. Also describe the overall climate for the current year.

- Next, make a poster about your local climate. Show the kind of clothing a person would wear during each of the four seasons in your area.

- Check your local newspaper or the Internet for articles on the weather and climate in your area. You might also find pictures to illustrate your poster. Consider using glitter, paints, and colored paper to make your poster special.

- **Plant Life** Make a map showing the plant life in your community. Are there parks and forests in your area? Or do you live near a desert? Perhaps you are in a wetlands area. Refer to Map B on page 37 for help.

WRITING ACTIVITIES

Writing to Inform Suppose you have a pen pal in another state. Your pen pal knows very little about Texas. Write a description of our state for him or her. Be sure to include information about the environment, the people, and the heritage of Texas.

Writing to Persuade Choose a region of our state and create your own travel brochure. Write a description that persuades tourists to visit. Mention any interesting sites or locations.

Writing to Express Describe a special celebration you have attended in our state. Include descriptions of any costumes people wore or any special food that was served. Also mention any activities held at the celebration. Include as many details as you can.

LITERATURE

The Flute Player

An Apache Folktale

Selection by MICHAEL LACAPA

This is an Apache folk tale about a girl and a boy who meet at a special hoop dance. This old tale, from centuries ago, shows the importance of the Apache relationship with nature.

The evening of the dance arrived and during the hoop dance, a young boy and a young girl became very, very interested in one another. People who saw them began talking. "Look! They don't even change partners. They dance only with one another."

It was true. The boy and the girl only danced with each other. Between the dances, the boy told the girl, "I play a flute." She told him, "Maybe someday, I will hear you play your flute, I will place a leaf in the river that runs through the canyon. When you see the leaf float past you, you will know that I like your song."

Early the next morning, the boy went to the canyon and played his flute. People working in the canyon in the cornfields said, "Listen, that sounds like the wind blowing through the trees." The girl listened to the flute player. She liked his song. She pulled a leaf from a tree, took it to the river and gently dropped it in. She watched it float away.

Write About It!

Write a paragraph that describes why you think nature is important to Native Americans. Then write why it is important to you.

Unit 1

Settling the Western Hemisphere

TAKE A LOOK

How has the Western Hemisphere changed?

The culture of Native Americans began to change when settlers arrived from Europe. Modern Native Americans still remember their heritage in celebrations.

Explore more about Native
Americans at our Web site
www.mhschool.com

THE Big IDEAS ABOUT...

People in the Western Hemisphere

For thousands of years, people have lived in North and South America. How did the first people arrive? Some historians believe that they walked over a land bridge from Asia to the Western Hemisphere 40,000 years ago. In this chapter, you will learn what Texas was like long ago.

LEARNING ABOUT THE PAST

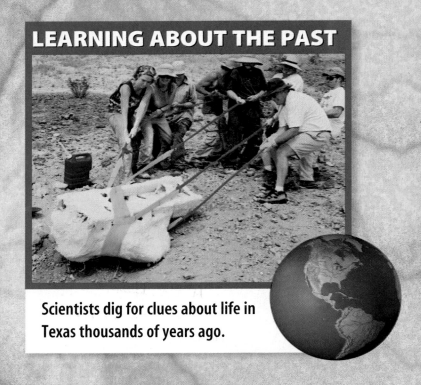

Scientists dig for clues about life in Texas thousands of years ago.

THE AZTEC PEOPLE

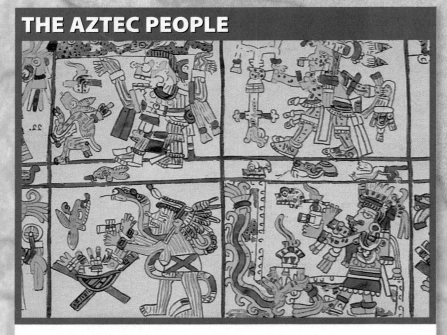

The Aztec had a rich culture filled with art and buildings that still exist today.

PEOPLE OF THE PLAINS

In the 1500s Native American groups made a home on the Coastal Plain and the Great Plains.

LIFE IN THE DESERT AND FOREST

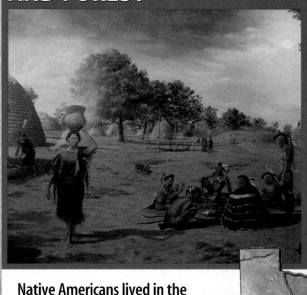

Native Americans lived in the deserts and forests of Texas.

Foldables

Make this Foldable to help organize what you learn about the first people to explore and settle Texas—the Native Americans.

1. Fold a sheet of paper into a shutter fold.
2. Fold the shutter fold in half like a hamburger.
3. Form four tabs by cutting along the fold lines in the middle of the two long tabs.
4. Label tabs with lesson titles.

People Come to the Americas

Why did people first come to North America and Texas?

VOCABULARY

Ice Age

glacier

hunters and gatherers

history

prehistory

archaeology

artifact

marsh

READING STRATEGY

Draw a main idea chart like this one. In each box, write something that we learn from artifacts.

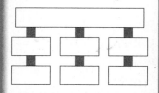

Lesson Outline

• The Ice Age

• Early Americans

• Early Texan Cultures

BUILD BACKGROUND

Native Americans have lived in Texas for hundreds of years. The word *native* means "one of the first people to live in a land." In this chapter, you will learn how the ancestors of Native Americans came to live in North America.

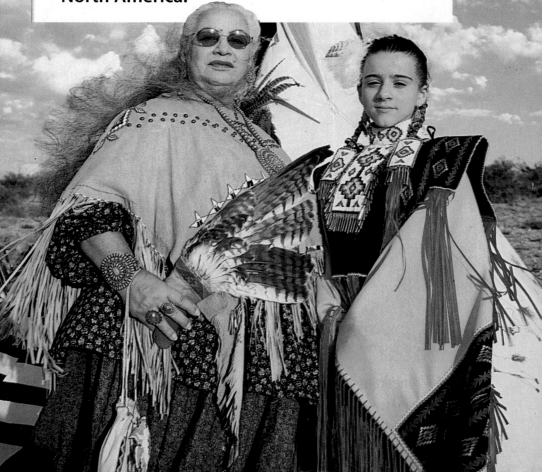

THE ICE AGE

The **Ice Age** was a time when the climate was so cold that **glaciers** (GLAY shurz), or huge sheets of ice, covered much of Earth's surface. Thousands of years ago, the glaciers moved south over the land. They flowed south of what is today called the Great Lakes.

Before the glaciers formed, large bodies of water separated North America from Northern Asia and Northern Europe. But during the Ice Age the level of the oceans dropped because so much water was frozen into glaciers. During this period a land bridge called **Beringia** (buh RIHN jee uh) connected Asia with North America. Some scientists believe that groups of people traveled across ice-covered land. They hunted animals and gathered shellfish for food. Look at the map on this page to learn which routes the first Americans might have taken.

Today the land bridge is gone. The **Bering Strait**, a body of water 56 miles across, separates North America from Asia. Almost all of the glaciers disappeared when the climate grew

These modern-day Lipan Apache are wearing traditional clothing.

warmer around 10,000 years ago. The glaciers covered all the land from Canada to Greenland to Northern Europe. Today the North Sea and North Atlantic Ocean again separate North America from Europe.

How did the Ice Age affect the geography of part of the Northern Hemisphere?

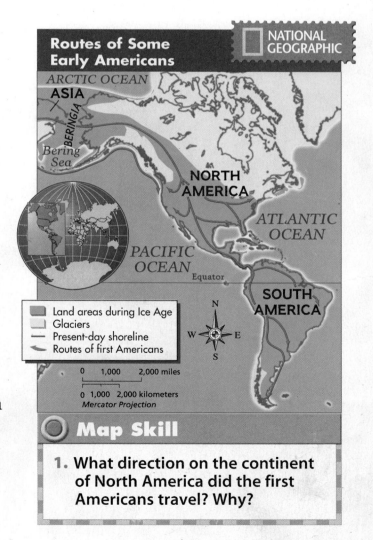

Routes of Some Early Americans

NATIONAL GEOGRAPHIC

ARCTIC OCEAN
ASIA
BERINGIA
Bering Sea
NORTH AMERICA
ATLANTIC OCEAN
PACIFIC OCEAN
Equator
SOUTH AMERICA

- ▇ Land areas during Ice Age
- ▢ Glaciers
- — Present-day shoreline
- ↙ Routes of first Americans

N
W — E
S

0   1,000   2,000 miles
0 1,000 2,000 kilometers
Mercator Projection

Map Skill

1. What direction on the continent of North America did the first Americans travel? Why?

49

EARLY AMERICANS

No one knows exactly when or how people first came to North America. Some scientists believe that small groups of people crossed Beringia from Asia about 40,000 years ago. Others may have sailed to North America along the edge of Beringia. Still others probably came from southern Asia by boat to South America. New information has caused some scientists to think that other groups sailed along the ice that flowed between Europe and North America.

Many Native Americans, however, believe they have always lived in North and South America.

Slowly, many different groups of **hunters and gatherers** spread out through North and South America. Hunters and gatherers are people who hunt and collect fruits and other foods to eat. Each group had its own culture.

Ancestors of Native Americans

Some scientists believe that people first reached Texas about 12,000 years ago. They think that small groups traveled into the area as they followed their sources of food.

The early hunters and gatherers left no written records. We use the word **history** to describe past events that are preserved in written records. The time before written records is known as **prehistory**. You will be able to understand the difference between these two words by remembering that *pre* means "before."

How do we know about prehistory? The study of prehistoric people who lived long ago is called **archaeology** (ahr kee OL uh jee). Archaeologists dig up the remains of ancient cities, villages, burial sites, and even garbage dumps. They find tools made by pre-historic people. They may find pieces of bones, pottery, or clothing. Objects made by people in the past are called **artifacts** (AR tuh faktz).

Archaeologists study artifacts to learn about how people lived in the past. Although prehistoric people lived a very long time ago, we are still learning about them today. At places

Seminole Canyon State Historical Park (far left) is home to some of the oldest cave paintings in the world (left).

Archaeologists work together to move an Alamosaurus bone to be studied.

like Seminole Canyon State Historical Park, we can see caves where they lived and drawings of the animals they hunted.

Alamosaurus

In 1997, scientists found part of a huge dinosaur in Big Bend National Park. They believe it is an *Alamosaurus*. In 2001, 10 of its neck bones were taken by helicopter to the Dallas Museum of Natural History. The largest one weighs about 1,000 pounds! "It's an opportunity to learn about this unusual animal," says Anthony Fiorillo, a museum scientist.

How have artifacts helped archaeologists learn about the past?

EARLY TEXAN CULTURES

About 2,100 years ago, some groups of early Texan hunters and gatherers began to stay in one place for longer periods of time. They began to grow crops and became the first Texan farmers. People in the central part of Mexico had already developed more advanced farming methods.

Soon people began to settle in villages and larger towns. Farming allowed them to have a regular food supply and even to grow more than they needed. As a result, some people could spend more time making clothing, tools, and pottery. They also had more time to spend on community activities and religious practices.

Over time, early Texans developed different cultures. Each one had its own language, beliefs, and ways of working and playing. Each culture also had its own type of clothing and shelter.

A group's culture developed as the group adapted to, or learned how to live in, its environment. Some groups also changed their environment. For example, farmers in the forest of the Coastal Plain made clearings in the forest in order to plant crops.

Groups who lived along the Gulf of Mexico were hunters as well as fishers. They lived on a **marsh**. A marsh is an area of low wetland that is covered mostly with tall grasses. Near the Gulf of Mexico the marshes are filled with salty seawater and are home to many birds, fish, and shellfish.

Changes in pottery or tools may show that other groups of people moved into an area. Bones of ancient people and animals give clues about what they might have looked like.

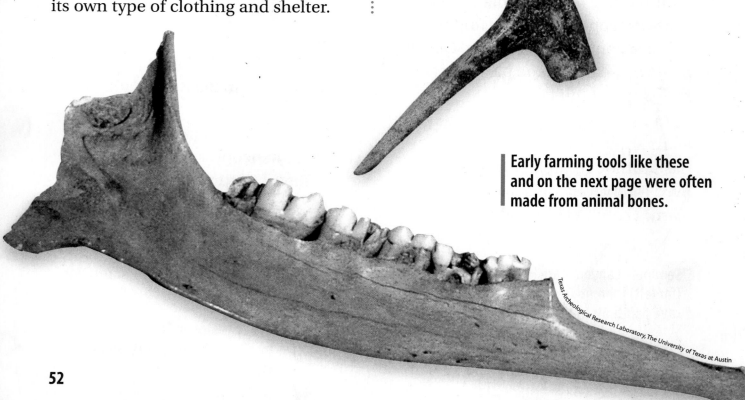

Early farming tools like these and on the next page were often made from animal bones.

Texas Archeological Research Laboratory, The University of Texas at Austin

Archaeology Today

The Pecos and Leon rivers are two places where archaeologists are working in Texas today. They have discovered clay figures of animals, pottery fragments, drills, tools and many kinds of arrows.

Archaeologists want to know if different groups of prehistoric people knew about each other. By comparing types of arrow points, they can guess whether different cultures met and shared their ideas about hunting.

 **Why did early Texans develop different cultures?**

PUTTING IT TOGETHER

To learn about early Texans, archaeologists carefully dig at the remains of mounds, villages, and burial sites. They search for clues such as art, artifacts, and bones.

At the same time people came to Texas, other groups lived in different parts of the Western Hemisphere. You will learn more about these groups and their cultures in the next lesson.

Review and Assess

1. Write one sentence for each of the vocabulary words:

   archaeology   **artifact**

   glacier   **Ice Age**

   marsh

2. How do archaeologists use artifacts to learn about the past?

3. **Identify** why prehistoric people came to North America and Texas.

4. How do archaeologists use artifacts to learn about the **culture** of a group of people from the past?

5. **Compare and contrast** the life of a hunter-gatherer and the life of a farmer.

Using the map on page 49, list some of the continents early Americans traveled through.

• •

Suppose you are an archaeologist. **Write** a description of an artifact in this lesson. What do you think it tells about the people who made it?

Working With Latitude and Longitude

Every place on Earth has an absolute, or exact, location. Imaginary lines that cross each other like a tic-tac-toe grid can help you describe the location of a particular place. They provide an "address" for the location.

This is different from the relative location of a place. If you say that San Antonio is near Austin, you are describing its location in relation, or in connection, to somewhere else. Relative location does not give an exact "address," like absolute location.

Pilots use this system of lines and "addresses" to keep track of where they are. Up among the clouds, a pilot must be sure of a plane's location at all times. Pilots also need an exact way to explain where they are going.

VOCABULARY

latitude
parallel
degrees
longitude
prime meridian
meridian
global grid

USING LATITUDE

Look at the map on this page and place your finger on the equator. This is the starting point for measuring **latitude** . Latitude is a measure of how far north or south a place is from the equator.

Lines of latitude are also called **parallels** because they are parallel lines. Parallel lines always remain the same distance apart and never cross each other.

Each line of latitude has a number. You can see that the equator is labeled 0°, meaning zero **degrees** . Degrees are used to measure distances and show locations on Earth's surface. The symbol ° stands for degrees.

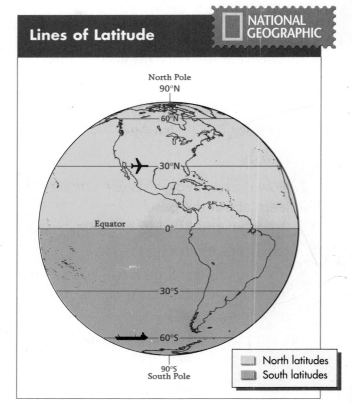

Lines of Latitude

NATIONAL GEOGRAPHIC

North Pole 90°N
60°N
30°N
Equator 0°
30°S
60°S
90°S South Pole

North latitudes
South latitudes

Now look at the lines of latitude north of the equator. Notice that these parallels are labeled N for "north." The North Pole has a latitude too, which is 90°N. The parallels south of the equator are labeled S for "south." The latitude of the South Pole is 90°S.

Look again at the map on the previous page. Find the ship that is sailing west. It is located at 60°S. Now find the airplane on the map. Along which parallel is it flying?

USING LONGITUDE

Look at the map on this page. It shows lines of **longitude** . Like parallels, these are imaginary lines on a map or globe. But instead of measuring distance north or south, they measure distance east or west of the **prime meridian** . *Prime* means "first." Lines of longitude are also called **meridians** . The prime meridian is the starting place for measuring lines of longitude. That's why the prime meridian is marked 0° on the map. Put your finger on the prime meridian. It runs through the western parts of Europe and Africa.

Look at the meridians to the west of the prime meridian. These lines are labeled W for "west." The lines to the east of the prime meridian are labeled E for "east." Longitude is measured up to 180° east of the prime meridian and up to 180° west of the prime meridian. Since 180°E and 180°W fall on the same line, this line is marked neither E nor W. This line runs through the Pacific Ocean.

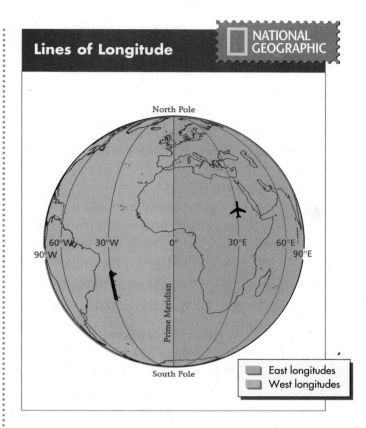

Lines of Longitude

Unlike lines of latitude, meridians are not parallel to one another. Look at the map on this page again. The meridians are far apart at the equator. They meet, however, at the North Pole and the South Pole.

Find the ship on the map. It is traveling along longitude 30°W. Now find the airplane on the same map. It is flying over the continent of Africa. Which line of longitude is the airplane traveling along? In which direction is it flying?

LEARN THE SKILL

The lines of latitude and the lines of longitude cross to form a grid. A grid is a set of crisscrossing lines. The grid on the map below is called a **global grid** because it covers the entire Earth.

1. **Locate the equator.**
   Remember that lines of latitude measure degrees north and south from the equator. Now find Canberra, Australia, and Bogotá, Colombia, on the map. Which of these two cities is closer to the equator? How can you tell?

2. **Locate the prime meridian.**
   Remember that lines of longitude measure degrees east and west from the prime meridian. Now find Ottawa, Canada, and Cairo, Egypt. Which city is east of the prime meridian and which city is west?

3. **Identify the degrees to find the "address."**
   Find Canberra again. It is located at about 30°S latitude. It is also located at 150°E. So we say that its location—or its "address"—is about 30°S, 150°E.

   When you locate a place on a map, always give latitude first and longitude second. You must also note north or south for the latitude, and east or west for the longitude. To describe a place that is not exactly at the point where two lines cross, use the closest lines.

Global Grid

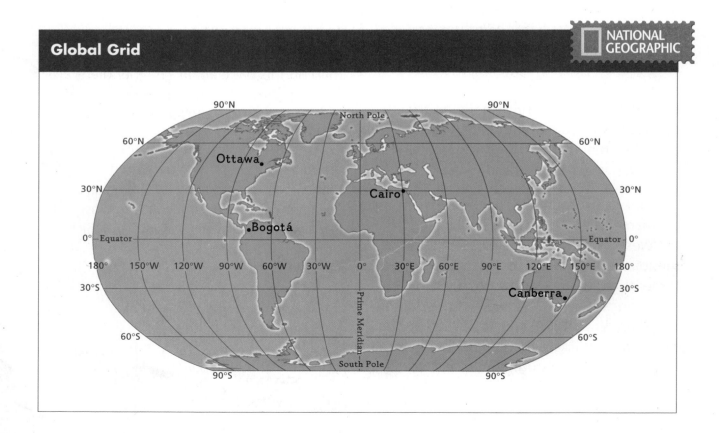

TRY THE SKILL

Use the map of Texas on this page to find two cities closest to the latitude and longitude "addresses" below. What is the name of each?

- 32°N, 98°W
- 36°N, 102°W

Describe the location of these two cities using latitude and longitude. You may use a ruler to help you find the closest lines.

- Houston
- San Antonio

Now answer the following questions.

1. How can the equator and prime meridian help you find lines of latitude and longitude?

2. Name two points of interest that are close to the same line of latitude.

3. What river runs between 104°W and about 101°W in Texas?

4. How can using latitude and longitude help you in your daily life?

EXTEND THE SKILL

Trace the map of Texas below. Place these cities on your map, using their latitude and longitude "addresses."

- Austin, 30°N, 98°W
- El Paso, 32°N, 106°W
- Brownsville, 26°N, 98°W

Now compare the map of Texas to the Global Grid on the previous page.

- How are the lines of latitude and the lines of longitude different?
- What types of people in our state would be likely to use latitude and longitude in their work?

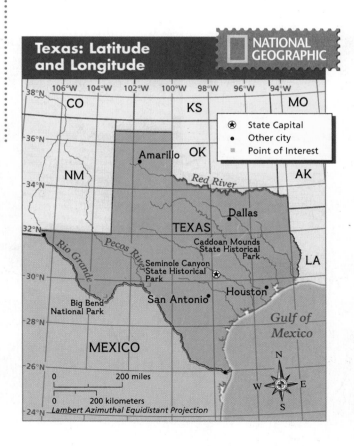

Texas: Latitude and Longitude

NATIONAL GEOGRAPHIC

State Capital
Other city
Point of Interest

Lesson 2

VOCABULARY

civilization
empire
religion
tribute

READING STRATEGY

Draw a word web like this one. List jobs that the Aztec did in Tenochtitlán.

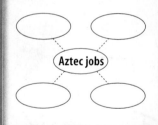

A Center of Civilization

What was life like for the Aztec people in Tenochtitlán?

Lesson Outline
• In Search of a Home
• The Aztec Empire
• Tribute

BUILD BACKGROUND

As Native Americans were living in what is today Texas, large **civilizations** were developing in other parts of the Western Hemisphere. A civilization is a culture that has developed systems of government, education, and religion. There were three major civilizations in the Americas during this time. They were the Maya, the Inca, and the Aztec.

IN SEARCH OF A HOME

The Aztec lived in an area of present-day Mexico that had many natural resources. They used these resources to build an **empire**. An empire is a large area containing different groups of people who are all ruled by a country or a single leader. Look at the map and locate where the three empires of the Western Hemisphere were located.

According to historians, sometime during the 1100s the Aztec left their homeland because the land had become too dry. For about 200 years they traveled south. As they moved, the Aztec met other groups of Native Americans. From these groups the Aztec learned how to farm.

The Aztec eventually reached **Lake Texcoco** (tay SKOH koh), Mexico. About 1325, on a small island in the lake, Aztec sources say they found the sign they were looking for. An eagle stood on a cactus, holding a snake in its mouth. The Aztec believed that this sign meant they had found a home.

Ruins of Tenochtitlán in Mexico City (left). Tenochtitlán means "place of the prickly pear cactus" (right).

The Aztec built a city on the island. They named their city **Tenochtitlán** (te noch tee TLAHN). Tenochtitlán became the Aztec capital.

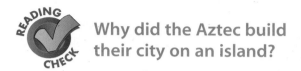

READING CHECK Why did the Aztec build their city on an island?

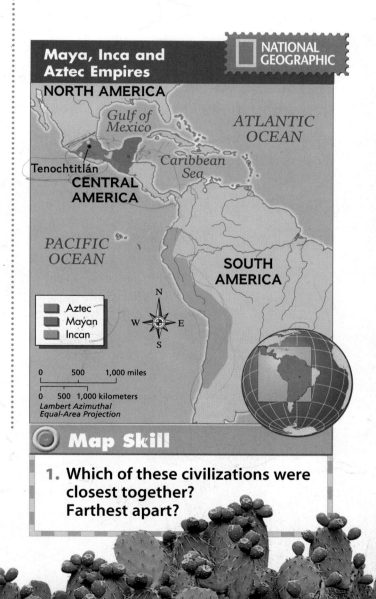

NATIONAL GEOGRAPHIC

Maya, Inca and Aztec Empires

NORTH AMERICA
Gulf of Mexico
ATLANTIC OCEAN
Tenochtitlán
CENTRAL AMERICA
Caribbean Sea
PACIFIC OCEAN
SOUTH AMERICA

Aztec
Mayan
Incan

N W E S

0   500   1,000 miles
0   500   1,000 kilometers
Lambert Azimuthal
Equal-Area Projection

Map Skill

1. **Which of these civilizations were closest together? Farthest apart?**

THE AZTEC EMPIRE

The environment around Lake Texcoco was ideal. The lake had water to drink and birds and fish to eat. Near the edge of the lake, farmers built gardens that seemed to float. They put thick poles into the water and filled the space between the poles with mud. Here they grew beans, corn, and squash.

The Aztec economy in Tenochtitlán was mostly based on farming and fishing. However, people also had jobs as potters, builders, and weavers. Busy outdoor markets were created. The diagram on the next page shows how Tenochtitlán may have looked.

The Aztec developed many skills. For example, they were expert builders.

Aztec mask

They built homes, schools, and temples. Both boys and girls went to school. An early visitor to Tenochtitlán wrote that most of the children there "know the names of all the birds, animals, trees and herbs . . . and what they are good for." Boys were trained from an early age to be soldiers.

The Aztec language, Nahuatl (NAH wah tul), was a spoken language. It was not written down the way we write today. The Aztec were able to write poetry and books by drawing pictures. About 200 Nahuatl poems still exist.

By the middle 1400s, Tenochtitlán was one of the largest cities in the world. Over 200,000 people lived there. Nearly as many people live in the city of Amarillo today.

Aztec Religion

Religion was very important to the Aztec. Religion is the way people worship. The Aztec worshiped many gods, although the most important was their sun god, Huitzilopochtli. They believed that soldiers who died in battle and people who were killed as offerings would join the sun as it moved across the sky. The Aztec hoped that by pleasing Huitzilopochtli they would have rich harvests and would win in battle.

Why was the environment around Lake Texcoco good for building a city?

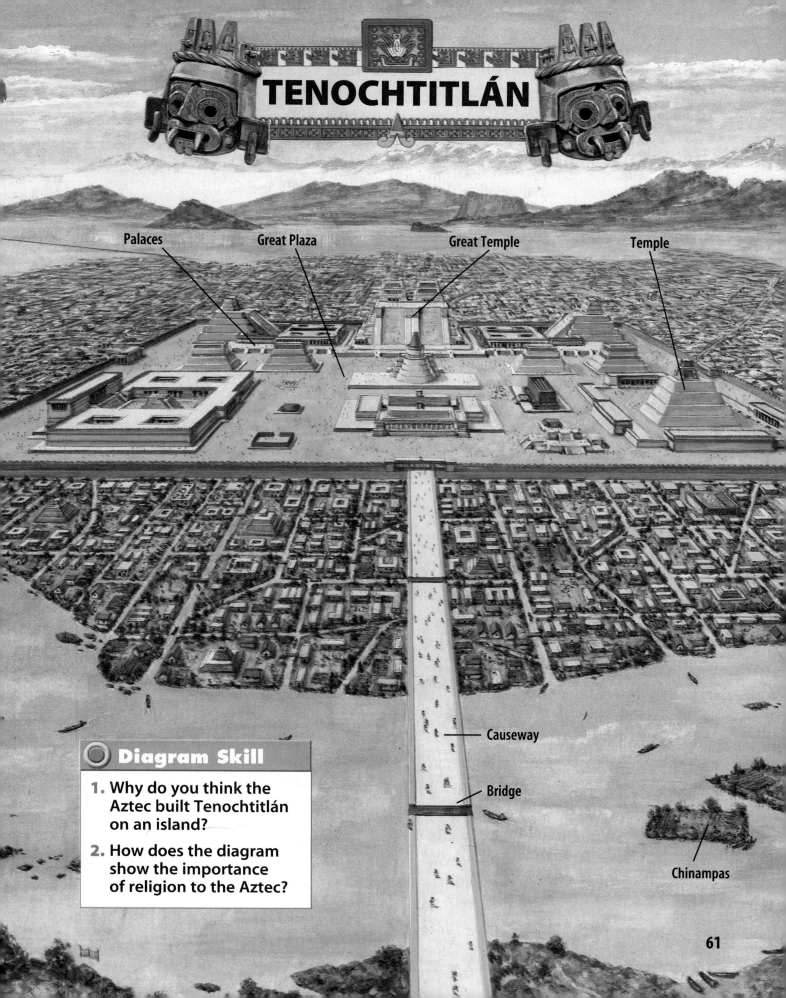

TENOCHTITLÁN

Palaces Great Plaza Great Temple Temple

Causeway

Bridge

Chinampas

◯ Diagram Skill

1. Why do you think the Aztec built Tenochtitlán on an island?

2. How does the diagram show the importance of religion to the Aztec?

The Aztec used detailed pictures to describe **tributes** they received.

TRIBUTE

Wars were often started by the Aztec. One of the goals of war was to have nearby groups of people pay them **tribute**. A tribute was payment in the form of goods and services. Tribute could include food, clothing and valuable stones. This payment was one of the ways in which the Aztec empire strengthened its economy.

One form of tribute was cocoa beans. These were used to make a chocolate drink called xocolatl (sho co lat il). We get the word *chocolate* and the name *Mexico* from the Aztec.

In addition to valuable goods, Aztec soldiers often brought prisoners back to the city of Tenochtitlán. Men, women, and children were forced into slavery. Some had to work to build large buildings. Other people were killed and offered to the Aztec sun god.

A Growing Empire

Tenochtitlán grew larger and stronger. Through wars, the Aztec continued to gain land and enslave

Exploring ECONOMICS

Aztec Money

Suppose money grew on trees. In a way, for the Aztec, it did. They used cocoa beans, which come from cacao trees, much like we use coins and dollar bills. Anything from gold to food and clothing could be bought with these beans. For example, a small cloak, or coat, cost between 65 and 100 beans.

The beans were a source of both food and wealth. The Aztec believed that power and wisdom came to those who ate the beans.

Activity

Suppose you lived in Tenochtitlán. List some jobs people in your city might do. Next to the list, write down how many cocoa beans would be paid for one week of each type of work. Which jobs would earn the most? The least? Explain why.

people. More food was needed for the city's growing population.

Fewer people in the city wanted to farm when slaves and people in conquered cities could do this hard work. They sold crafts and services instead.

To get more fruit, beans, honey and cocoa, the Aztec started even more wars. They also made cities they had already conquered send more cotton cloth, dyes and gems to them. This made the people in the conquered cities want to rebel.

 **What was the Aztec empire like and how did it grow?**

PUTTING IT TOGETHER

The Aztec were just one of many groups living in the Western Hemisphere at this time. Tenochtitlán was the center of Aztec civilization. Parts of Aztec culture, such as the Nahuatl language, survive today.

In the next chapter you will learn how the Aztec empire ended.

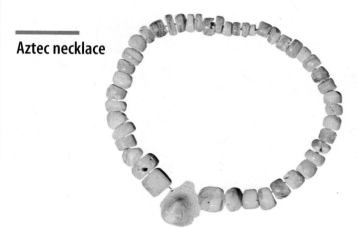

Aztec necklace

Review and Assess

1. Write one sentence for each of the vocabulary words:

   civilization   **empire**

   religion   **tribute**

2. How did the Aztec people choose the location of their city?

3. Describe what life was like in Tenochtitlán.

4. Suppose you were an Aztec farmer. Make a list of the crops you would grow and decide how many cocoa beans you will charge for amounts of each one.

5. Analyze how the environment affected the way the Aztecs lived.

Look back at the map on page 59. Then look at the Atlas map on page R14. Make a list of the present day countries that were once a part of the Inca empire.

Suppose you were an Aztec looking for a place to settle. **Write** a story, song or poem about your travels and arrival at Lake Texcoco, Mexico.

Native Americans of the Gulf Coast and the Plains

VOCABULARY

teepee
band
cradleboard

Find out!

How did Native Americans of the Gulf Coast and Plains live?

Lesson Outline

- The Karankawa
- The Comanche
- Comanche Culture

READING STRATEGY

Draw a diagram like the one here. List differences and similarities between Native Americans of the Gulf Coast and of the Plains.

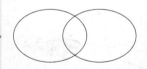

BUILD BACKGROUND

During the 1500s, the coastline along the Gulf of Mexico was home to the Karankawa (kah ran KAH wah) and the Coahuiltecan (kwah weel TE kan). They lived in the marshes of the Coastal Plain. Find these groups on the map on the next page.

THE KARANKAWA

Most of our information about Native Americans comes from the writings of Spaniards who came to Texas around 1530. However, most Europeans did not speak Native American languages. They probably did not understand everything they saw.

Fishing was the most important part of the Karankawa economy. Besides fish, the Karankawa ate clams, turtles, and underwater plants. They also hunted deer, bear, and alligators. Women gathered nuts, berries, and seeds for food.

The Karankawa moved their camp-site from place to place every few weeks. They traveled to wherever the fishing was best. They traveled in large canoes made from hollowed-out tree trunks. Because they moved often, the Karankawa needed houses that could be put up and taken down easily. These houses had frames made of willow poles and were covered with animal skins and woven mats.

By the time Texas became part of the United States in 1845, few Karankawa remained. Many had died from diseases brought unknowingly by early Europeans. Others had moved to Mexico or were killed in wars with other Native Americans or with new settlers from the United States.

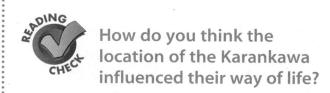

How do you think the location of the Karankawa influenced their way of life?

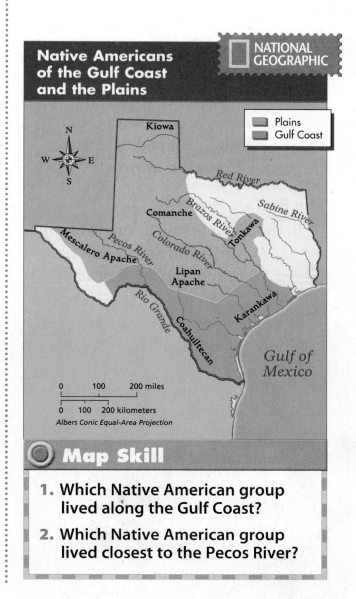

Native Americans of the Gulf Coast and the Plains

NATIONAL GEOGRAPHIC

Map Skill

1. **Which Native American group lived along the Gulf Coast?**

2. **Which Native American group lived closest to the Pecos River?**

THE COMANCHE

The grassy land to the north of the Gulf Coast was higher and drier than the land along the Gulf Coast. By the 1800s the Comanche were one of five groups of Native Americans living on the plains of western Texas. Look back at the map on page 65 to see these groups. They were all hunters.

Unlike the Karankawa, who had a traditional fishing economy, the Comanche economy was based on hunting buffalo. But like the Karankawa they moved their villages from place to place according to the seasons and food supply. The Comanche carried their homes, called **teepees**, with them. A teepee is a cone-shaped tent that can be put up and taken down quickly.

The Buffalo Hunt

In the 1500s Spanish sailors brought horses to North and South America. Before that time Native Americans hunted on foot. Horses allowed them to move about faster and farther. What might it have been like to hunt buffalo with the Comanche?

Suppose that you are a 10-year-old Comanche boy joining a buffalo hunt for the first time. Comanche hunting leaders have located a herd. They begin to surround it on horseback. As the huge, shaggy animals run by you the ground shakes. You know that the herd could harm you. Each buffalo is taller than an adult and weighs as much as ten people!

Buffalo were more than the main source of food for the Comanche. When a buffalo was killed, every part was used and nothing was wasted.

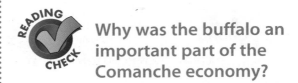

Why was the buffalo an important part of the Comanche economy?

Some Plains Native Americans lived and worked in villages that could be moved easily.

David R. Frazier Photo Library, Institute of Texan Cultures, San Antonio

How Some Native Americans Used the Buffalo

The Comanche, Lipan Apache, Mescalero Apache and other plains groups used every part of the buffalo to survive. Look at the chart to learn why the buffalo was so useful to many Native Americans.

Hide

Plains Indian Clothing

Plains Indian Teepee

Bone

Bone Needles

Horn

Plains Indian Headdress

Horn Spoon

Chart Skill

1. Why do you think the Comanche needed the buffalo to make needles?

2. Name two things that Plains Indians made from buffalo horns.

COMANCHE CULTURE

The Comanche were known as skilled riders and warriors. Each Comanche was part of a small family group called a **band**. Bands of Comanches first entered Texas in the 1600s from the Rocky Mountains. They were seeking open land, buffalo, and horses from the Spanish.

Comanche Children

Comanche women spent their days making clothing, cooking and doing other chores. Mothers had little time to look after their babies. To keep babies safe, they were laced into a wooden frame covered with deerskin soon after birth. These wooden frames were called **cradleboards**. Both girls and boys learned to swim at an early age. Since boys might be hunters someday,

they learned to ride a horse by age six. Comanche children were usually disciplined by an older sister. If there was no older sister, someone outside of the family corrected their behavior.

The Comanche Today

Today, there are 10,000 Comanche people in the United States. Many of them live in Texas. The Comanche are like other Americans. They are doctors, teachers, artists, and business leaders. But they have a special heritage. Every year, the Comanche hold a celebration in Walters, Oklahoma. During this time people wear clothing made from deerskin and colorful beads. They perform traditional dances. And they eat delicious food such as fried bread.

 **READING CHECK** Why did Comanche children learn to ride at a young age?

A Comanche warrior (left) was respected for his ability to hunt buffalo. A modern-day Comanche bolo tie slide (above) is made from beads.

PUTTING IT TOGETHER

The Karankawa and Comanche are two of the Native American groups who lived on the Gulf Coast and the plains of Texas. Archaeologists have studied artifacts and the writings of Spaniards to learn more about them.

In the next lesson you will read about other Native Americans who lived in our state. Later you will read why many of them had to leave Texas.

A Comanche woman with a baby in a traditional **cradleboard**.

Review and Assess

1. Write one sentence for each of the vocabulary words:

   band   **cradleboard**

   teepee

2. Which Native American people lived along the Gulf Coast?

3. How did the Karankawa and Comanche adapt to their environment?

4. What were some parts of Comanche **culture**?

5. What can you **conclude** about the Comanche from their uses for buffalo?

Use the map on page 65 to create a two-column chart that shows the name of each Native American group and the region in which each group lived.

· ·

Write a paragraph about how we can learn from the way Native Americans traditionally used natural resources. How can we use this knowledge to help us use natural resources more wisely in the future?

Native Americans of the Desert and the Forest

VOCABULARY

pueblo
adobe
trotline
crop rotation

How did the Native Americans adapt to their environment?

READING STRATEGY

Copy the diagram below. List differences and similarities between the Native Americans of the desert and of the forest.

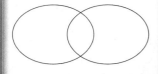

Lesson Outline

• The Jumano
• People of the Forest
• Caddo Culture

BUILD BACKGROUND

Different groups of Pueblo peoples lived in the dry areas of what is today the Southwest region of the United States. In Spanish **pueblo** means "village."

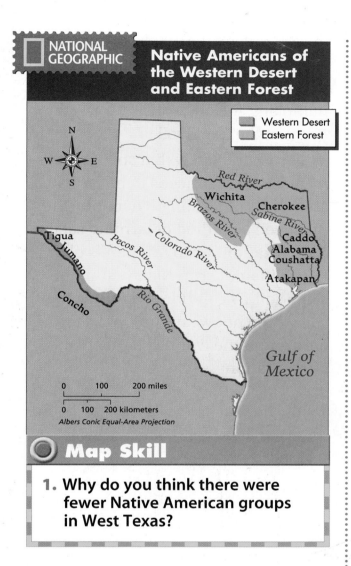

NATIONAL GEOGRAPHIC

Native Americans of the Western Desert and Eastern Forest

Western Desert
Eastern Forest

Red River
Wichita
Brazos River
Cherokee
Sabine River
Tigua
Jumano
Pecos River
Colorado River
Caddo
Alabama Coushatta
Atakapan
Concho
Rio Grande
Gulf of Mexico

0   100   200 miles
0   100   200 kilometers
Albers Conic Equal-Area Projection

◉ Map Skill

1. Why do you think there were fewer Native American groups in West Texas?

THE JUMANO

Historians do not know very much about the Jumano (hoo MAH noh) people. One group lived in the Mountains and Basins region of Texas. They were hunters and traders. Many other Jumano lived along the **Rio Grande**

The West Texas desert was home to some Native American groups.

from **El Paso** to the **Big Bend** . These people were mainly farmers.

Farming was not easy in the desert where the Jumano lived. The land was always dry. The Jumano adapted to their desert environment by using the water from creeks or streams to irrigate their land. Corn, squash, and beans were some of the crops that the Jumano grew. To add to their food supply, the Jumano also fished and hunted.

Jumano Culture

The Jumano built **adobe** houses. Adobe is brick made from mud or clay and straw that has been dried in the sun. Adobe walls helped to keep the inside of the houses warm in winter and cool in summer.

A Lost Culture

The Jumano villages along the Rio Grande disappeared hundreds of years ago. Some people think that the Jumano died from diseases brought by Europeans. Others believe the Spanish took the Jumano to Mexico as slaves. Many Jumano may have become part of the Kiowa and Apache cultures.

READING CHECK How did the Jumano adapt to life in the desert?

PEOPLE OF THE FOREST

The Native Americans of the forest lived in what is now eastern Texas. They made their homes in the Piney Woods. The Caddo were the first to live there. Other groups such as the Atakapan, the Wichita, the Cherokee, and the Alabama Coushatta (koo SHA tuh) moved there later. The Alabama Coushatta still live in eastern Texas today.

The Caddo

The Piney Woods had many natural resources. This area had plenty of rain to grow crops. The forests were full of animals and plants for food, and the waters were full of fish.

The Caddo used a **trotline** to catch fish. A trotline is a long, heavy fishing line that stretches across a stream. It has several baited hooks on it. It also has weights to keep it under water.

Making pottery, such as the bowl (right), was one activity in Caddo villages (below).

A trotline can catch more fish than a single baited hook.

Because the area was covered with forests, the Caddo had to cut down trees in order to farm. The community worked together to plant enough crops to feed hundreds of people. They grew pumpkins, melons, squash, corn and beans in the fertile soil.

The Caddo knew that soil is a natural resource that needs to be enriched after years of farming. Therefore, they practiced a method of farming called **crop rotation**. Crop rotation is planting a different crop each year in the same soil. The Caddo did this so the soil would not wear out. Today, farmers around the world still practice crop rotation.

The Minneapolis Institute of Arts

David R. Frazier Photo Library, Institute of Texan Cultures, San Antonio

Caddo houses could be built quickly because the entire community helped to build them.

Working Together

Several Caddo families could live in one house. Their houses looked like beehives or domes. They were 25 to 45 feet wide and could shelter 20 to 30 people.

The whole Caddo community pitched in to build a house whenever one was needed. Groups of men placed long poles in the ground. Then they tied the tops of the poles together. Others covered the frame with wood. Then grass gathered by women to cover the house was put on. Look at the steps to building a Caddo home on this page.

It was the responsibility of the families who were going to live in the new house to prepare a meal of corn and meat for the workers. With so many people helping, the job took less than a morning to do.

READING CHECK

How did the Caddo use their natural resources to provide for their needs?

CADDO CULTURE

Every Caddo group had its own leader, or chief. This leader, called a *caddi*, held a position of honor. This position was usually passed from fathers to their sons. But Caddo women sometimes became caddi. The caddi gave orders, made decisions, and supervised projects.

Religion was an important part of Caddo culture. One Caddo ceremony was a harvest celebration. Religious leaders would organize this celebration to show their thankfulness for the rich harvest. The leaders went for days without food, drink, or sleep. They also prayed that their people would have a good future.

The Caddo Today

By 1859 war and disease had reduced the Caddo to only a few hundred. Newcomers to Texas wanted to build on Caddo land and the Caddo were forced to move to what is today Oklahoma. About 2,000 of their descendants still live in the United States.

Caddo children live like other American children. They go to school, play sports, and watch TV. But they also learn traditional Caddo dances and songs. Elder Caddo teach them their language and traditions. For example, pottery is a traditional skill that Caddo women practiced. Today, some Caddo descendents are making pottery like their ancestors did. In this way, traditions are passed on through the generations. You can learn more about the Caddo people at Caddoan Mounds State Historical Park in Alto.

Caddo Tribal Heritage Museum

Modern-day Caddo celebrate their culture with ancient ceremonies.

A Sporting Tradition

Sports were part of life for Native Americans. Many games were used to train young men for war. Most Native Americans played a game of throwing darts. The Caddo held foot races to build strength and speed.

Not all games were used for training, some were just for fun. The Karankawa wrestled and the Caddo had a game like hockey. They also played guessing games by lining up their moccasins and hiding an object in one of them. The winner correctly guessed which shoe the object was in.

READING CHECK How are the Caddo today similar and different from their ancestors?

PUTTING IT TOGETHER

The Jumano and the Caddo were farmers and traders. Historians know little about the life of the Jumano or why they disappeared. Though the Caddo do not live in Texas today, their descendents celebrate their heritage in other parts of the United States.

Caddo Tribal Heritage Museum

Moccasins in traditional Caddo style.

Review and Assess

1. Write one sentence for each of the vocabulary words:

   adobe   **crop rotation**

   pueblo   **trotline**

2. Where did Native Americans of the forest culture live?

3. Identify ways Native Americans adapted to the desert and forest.

4. Describe how the Caddo were **governed** in their community.

5. **Compare** and **contrast** the people of the forest to the people of the mountains and deserts.

Use the map on page 71 to create a two-column chart that shows the name of each Native American group and the region in which each group lived.

• •

Suppose you could travel back in time to visit either the Jumano or the Caddo. Draw a picture of what your visit might be like.

Points of View

How Should Our Parkland Be Used?

Less than 3 percent of Texas's total land area is public land. National or state parks and wildlife areas make up most of this land. Texans want to take care of them. People disagree, however, about the best way to do this. Read the points of view below.

MARY KELLY
Executive Director, Texas Center For Policy Studies
Austin, Texas
Excerpt from an interview, 2001.

❝Parks have many different uses. One of them is to provide places where people can enjoy hiking, fishing, and swimming. Another use is to provide wilderness areas where we leave nature alone. Both uses are important. We should look for private property owners who want to sell land to the state that can be used for parks.❞

PETE GALLEGO
Democratic State Representative
Texas House of Representatives,
Alpine, Texas
Excerpt from an interview, 2001.

❝Where I live, tourism is really important. Visitors gas up their cars, eat at restaurants, and do many things that help the local economy. But we need to achieve a balance between preserving animals' homes and letting people visit their habitats. If you've never been to a wilderness area, you'll never understand why you should work hard to preserve it.❞

DAVID K. LANGFORD
Executive Vice President, Texas Wildlife Association
San Antonio, Texas
Excerpt from an interview, 2001.

  "All public lands should be open for people to use. You can build roads and provide access in a way that will work. It is up to us to manage parkland in ways that promote conservation. People need access to parks because it educates them about the outdoors and helps them appreciate the way things should be."

Thinking About the Points of View

1. Pete Gallego represents citizens in an area that includes two Texas national parks—the Guadalupe Mountains and Big Bend National Park. How do you think this influenced his point of view?

2. David Langford belongs to a group made up mostly of ranchers, hunters, and fishermen. How do you think this affected his point of view?

3. Mary Kelly leads a group that reports on the environment in Texas. Do you think this may have affected her opinion? How?

4. What other points of view might people have on this issue?

Building Citizenship

Courage
Some people would like to build homes and businesses on parkland. Discuss how conservation officials show courage by protecting natural habitats. How do you show courage?

Write About It!

Make a list of the different ideas people have expressed about how parklands should be used. Decide which ideas you think are most important and write a newspaper editorial expressing your point of view.

VOCABULARY REVIEW

Number a sheet of paper from 1 to 7. Beside each number write the word or term from the list below that matches the description.

adobe   archaeology

band   civilization

empire   pueblo

religion

1. brick made from clay and straw that has been dried in the sun
2. small family group to which some Native Americans belonged
3. Spanish word for "village"
4. the study of the way people lived in the past, including prehistoric times
5. a culture that has developed systems of government, education, and religion
6. the way people worship
7. a large area of different groups of peoples ruled by one country or leader

CHAPTER COMPREHENSION

8. How do we learn about the lives of people who lived a very long time ago?
9. Who were the Aztec?
10. What were some important aspects of Aztec culture?
11. Describe where the Karankawa lived and what their lives were like.
12. Why were horses so important to the Comanche?
13. How did the environment affect the types of homes built by the Jumano and Caddo cultures?

SKILL REVIEW

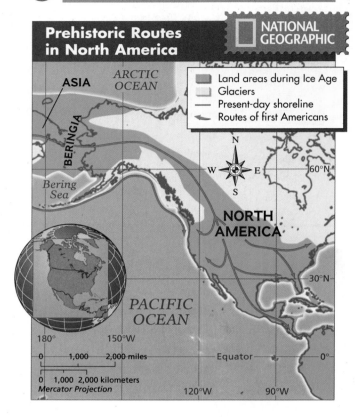

Prehistoric Routes in North America

NATIONAL GEOGRAPHIC

Land areas during Ice Age
Glaciers
Present-day shoreline
Routes of first Americans

14. **Geography Skill** At what latitude and longitude would Beringia have been?
15. **Geography Skill** Describe the path prehistoric people might have traveled using compass points.
16. **Geography Skill** What conditions affected the areas people could travel through?
17. **Study Skill** Write down the main idea of the chapter and list some supporting facts for it.
18. **Reading/Thinking Skill** How do you think prehistoric people decided which direction to travel in?

USING A TIME LINE

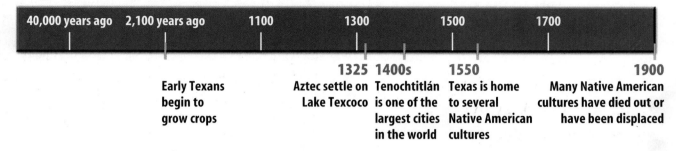

| 40,000 years ago | 2,100 years ago | 1100 | 1300 | 1500 | 1700 | |

1325
Aztec settle on
Lake Texcoco

1400s
Tenochtitlán
is one of the
largest cities
in the world

1550
Texas is home
to several
Native American
cultures

1900
Many Native American
cultures have died out or
have been displaced

**Early Texans
begin to
grow crops**

19. Did cities develop before or after people learned to grow crops?

20. Choose an event on the time line and explain why you might or might not have wanted to live in that time.

Activity

Writing About Culture The Jumano solved the problem of building homes in the desert by making adobe. Think of another problem they might have had and how they could have solved it.

Foldables

Use your *Foldable* to review what you have learned about the first people who came to the Americas and their descendents. As you look at the lesson titles on the tabs of your *Foldable*, mentally recall what you learned in each lesson; then review your notes under the tabs of your *Foldable* to check your memory and responses. Record any questions that you have on your *Foldable*, and discuss them with classmates or review the chapter to find answers.

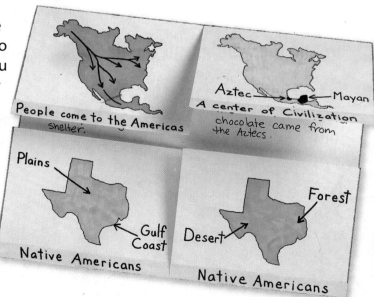

Chapter 2

THE Big IDEAS ABOUT...

Europeans Come to the Americas

In the late 1400s, people began to sail to the Western Hemisphere from Spain, France, and other parts of Europe. Their travels in the Americas would change the lives of the people living here and around the world. Read Chapter 2 to find out how contact between Native Americans and people from Europe changed life in Texas.

EUROPEANS BRING CHANGES

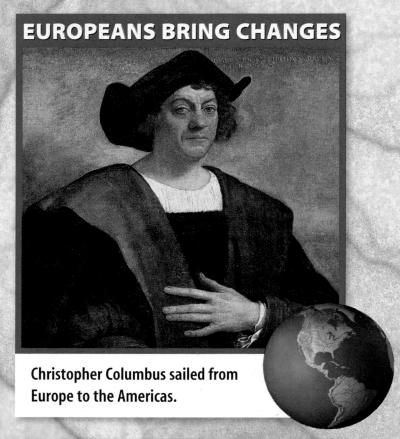

Christopher Columbus sailed from Europe to the Americas.

IN SEARCH OF GOLD

Spaniard Francisco Coronado and others hoped to find great wealth in the Southwest.

80

A MIX OF CULTURES

Newcomers from Spain brought their culture and traditions to the Americas.

THE ENGLISH IN THE AMERICAS

Newcomers also arrived from England. They came to other parts of North America to make a home.

Foldables

Make this Foldable study guide and use it to record what you learn about the Europeans who came to the Americas to explore and conquer.

1. Fold a sheet of 8 ½" x 11" paper in half like a hotdog, but make one side one inch longer than the other.

2. On the short side, cut three tabs equal distances apart. Label with lesson titles.

3. Sketch the Spanish and French Flags on the back.

Explorers and Conquerors

Find out! How did the arrival of Europeans affect Native Americans?

Lesson Outline
- The "New World"
- Europeans Bring Changes
- The End of an Empire

VOCABULARY

explore

colony

Columbian exchange

seeds of change

conquistador

conqueror

PEOPLE

Christopher Columbus

Hernando Cortés

Moctezuma II

Doña Marina

READING STRATEGY

Copy the chart. Write three facts about life in the Americas before and after Europeans arrived.

BEFORE	AFTER

BUILD BACKGROUND

In 1492 something happened that changed Native American cultures—and cultures everywhere—forever. People from other parts of the world sailed to the Americas. They were looking for land, riches, and adventure.

THE "NEW WORLD"

In August 1492 **Christopher Columbus**, an Italian sea captain, sailed from **Spain**. He commanded three ships—the Niña, the Pinta, and the Santa María. He was trying to find a route to the Indies in Asia.

Instead, he reached the **Bahama Islands**. Later, many Europeans said that Columbus had discovered a "New World." To the Native Americans already living there, North and South America were not "new" at all. Find Columbus's route on the map.

The Taino

On October 12, 1492, a sailor shouted *Tierra! Tierra!* ("Land! Land!"). Columbus was sure that he had reached the Indies. He called the people who lived there "Indians."

A replica of Columbus's ship the *Santa Maria* (left). This ship would have been guided with tools like this astrolabe (above).

The people Columbus met called themselves the Taino (TĪ noh). They were one of many Native American groups living on islands in the **Caribbean Sea**.

READING CHECK ✓ Why did Europeans call the Americas the "New World"?

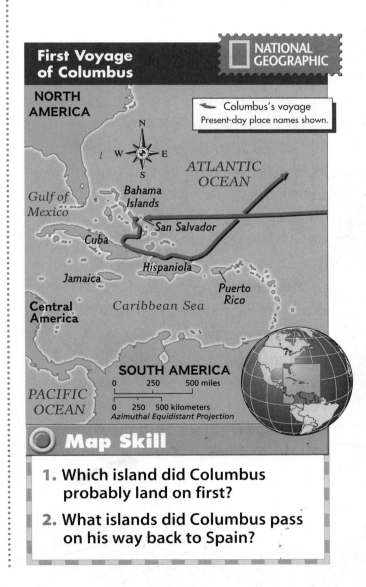

First Voyage of Columbus

NATIONAL GEOGRAPHIC

→ Columbus's voyage
Present-day place names shown.

NORTH AMERICA

ATLANTIC OCEAN

Gulf of Mexico

Bahama Islands

San Salvador

Cuba

Hispaniola

Jamaica

Puerto Rico

Central America

Caribbean Sea

SOUTH AMERICA

0   250   500 miles
0   250   500 kilometers
Azimuthal Equidistant Projection

PACIFIC OCEAN

Map Skill

1. **Which island did Columbus probably land on first?**

2. **What islands did Columbus pass on his way back to Spain?**

EUROPEANS BRING CHANGES

After reaching the Western Hemisphere, Columbus set out to **explore** the Caribbean islands. To explore is to travel to unfamiliar places in order to learn about them. Columbus and the Europeans who followed him were explorers. One of their goals was to set up **colonies** in this New World. A colony is a place that is ruled by another country.

The Columbian Exchange

Europeans brought crops to the Americas that were unknown there, such as wheat and sugarcane. They also brought horses and, unknowingly, diseases such as measles. These diseases killed many Native Americans.

Later, Columbus took gold, parrots, and various plants back to Spain. Crops from the Western Hemisphere such as corn, potatoes, and peanuts were brought to countries in Europe, Africa, and Asia over time. This movement of foods, animals, and diseases is part of what is called the **Columbian exchange**.

Of all the things included in the Columbian exchange, five were very important. They were potato, corn, sugar, horses, and disease. We call these five the **"seeds of change"** because they changed many lives around the world.

Doña Marina used her skills to help Cortés and Moctezuma II communicate with each other.

Hernando Cortés

One of the early explorers to follow Christopher Columbus to the Western Hemisphere was **Hernando Cortés** (cor TEZ). Cortés was a **conquistador** (kon KEES tah dawr) from Spain. In Spanish *conquistador* means **"conqueror,"** one who takes ownership by force. In the early 1500s, Cortés went to Mexico with more than 500 soldiers. He was determined to conquer lands, find gold, and spread the Roman Catholic religion.

Cortés and Moctezuma II Meet

In Chapter 1 you read about the rich Aztec empire in Mexico. In 1502 **Moctezuma** (mahk tuh ZOO muh) **II** became its ruler. Moctezuma II was a powerful leader. In 1519 he heard that newcomers had landed along the coast of Mexico. Moctezuma II sent gifts of gold and silver to the visitors. He hoped that Cortés would take the gifts and go home, but the conquistador wanted more gold. Nothing could stop him from trying to conquer Tenochtitlán, the capital of the Aztec empire.

Marching Toward Tenochtitlán

In one Mexican city, Cortés met an Indian woman. The Spanish called her **Doña Marina** (DOH nyah muh REE nuh). She helped Cortés communicate with Indian groups who were suffering under Moctezuma II. With her help Cortés learned about the sufferings of Indians under the rule of Moctezuma II. Many Indians joined Cortés. They wanted to attack Moctezuma and his city of Tenochtitlán.

In 1519 Moctezuma II welcomed Cortés to his grand city. Read how Cortés described Tenochtitlán to his king.

What changes did Europeans bring to the Americas?

Primary Source:

From Hernando Cortés: Second Letter to Charles V, 1520

The city has many public squares, in which are situated the markets and other places for buying and selling. There is one square . . . where are daily assembled more than sixty thousand souls, engaged in buying and selling; and where are found all kinds of **merchandise** *. . . for instance food, as well as jewels of gold and silver, lead, brass, copper, tin . . . There are . . . barbers' shops, where they wash and shave the head; and* **restaurateurs***, that* **furnish** *food and drink at a certain price.*

merchandise: goods
restaurateurs: people who own restaurants
furnish: to supply

FERDINAN·CORTESIVS

THE END OF AN EMPIRE

The Spaniards and their Indian followers took Moctezuma II prisoner. The Aztecs and the Spaniards were soon locked in battle. About 600 Spaniards and many more Aztecs were killed. Disease brought unknowingly by the Europeans killed thousands more over time. Though Moctezuma II was killed, Cortés was finally forced to leave Tenochtitlán. This was the biggest defeat the Europeans suffered in the Americas. To the Spanish, it became known as *la noche triste*, or "the sad night."

New Spain

In 1521 Cortés returned to Tenochtitlán with more soldiers. Again, many Indians joined him in battle against the Aztec. The Spaniards wore steel armor and headpieces. Each carried a shield and a sword. Using boats and cannons, the Spaniards conquered and burned Tenochtitlán. Cortés renamed the

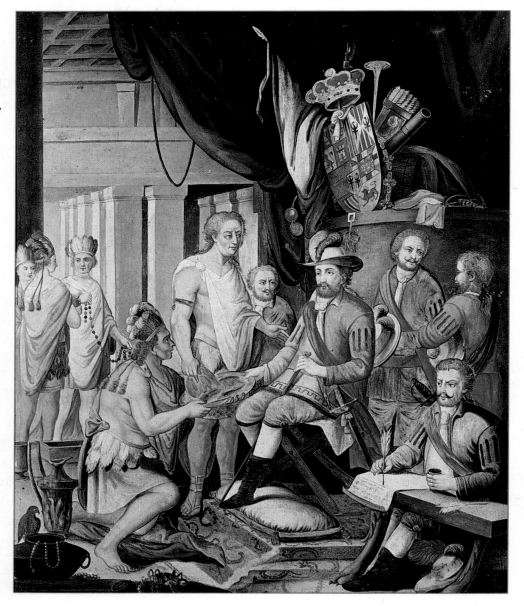

This painting shows a defeated Moctezuma II kneeling before Cortés.

empire Nueva España, or **New Spain**, after his homeland. New Spain included Mexico and the land of what is today Texas.

This event marked the joining of cultures, Native American and Spanish. Today you can visit the remains of Tenochtitlán in Mexico City.

 What lands were included in the colony of New Spain?

The Aztec weapons were not useful against Spanish armor and weapons.

PUTTING IT TOGETHER

Columbus and Cortés were among the first Europeans who came to explore, conquer, and bring settlers to the Americas. The linking of the Eastern and Western hemispheres would change the way of life for people all over the world. In the next lesson you will read about why more explorers came to the Americas.

Review and Assess

1. Write one sentence for each of the vocabulary words:

   colony   **conqueror**

   conquistador   **explore**

2. What was the Columbian exchange?

3. Analyze the effects of the arrival of Europeans on Native Americans.

4. Describe how Aztec and Spanish **cultures** were alike and different.

5. **Summarize** the reasons explorers traveled to the Western Hemisphere.

Activities

Use the scale of miles on the map on page 83 to create a scale strip. Then measure the distance from the Bahama islands to Hispaniola. About how many miles did Columbus sail?

Suppose you had an opportunity to interview Columbus and Cortés. **Write** a list of three questions you would ask each explorer. Then, working with a partner, take turns answering each other's questions the way Columbus and Cortés might answer.

Identifying Cause and Effect

In the last lesson, you read that explorers came from Europe to the Americas to gain land. The search for land was a cause . A cause is something that makes something else happen.

As a result of these travels, colonies were later set up. The colonies were an effect . An effect is what happens as a result of something else. Identifying cause and effect allows you to connect facts and events in a meaningful way. It helps explain why things happen.

VOCABULARY

cause

effect

LEARN THE SKILL

Read the passage below.

Fourth-grader Enrique just got a poor grade on his science test. However, he is doing well in math. His friend Natasha got a low score on the math quiz, but she understands science. So the two friends decide to help each other out. They meet one afternoon a week to study. As a result, Enrique's science grade goes up, and so does Natasha's math grade.

Follow these steps to identify cause and effect of an event and learn how they work together.

1. **Identify the cause of an event.**
   In the example above, Enrique and Natasha's low grades are the cause. It leads them to meet once a week to study.

2. **Identify the effect.**
   Their study meetings are the effect. They are what happens as a result of the low scores.

3. **Look to see if an effect becomes a cause.**
   Often, an effect causes something else in turn. Because Enrique and Natasha studied together, both of their grades went up. Looking at it this way, the study meetings are now the cause and the higher grades are the effect.

4. **Identify clue words.**
   Clue words can help you find causes and effects. Clue words that show causes include "because," "as a result of," and "since." Clue words that show effects include "so," "therefore," and "as a result."

TRY THE SKILL

Now read another passage.

Tina has trouble finding her way around because her family just moved into a new neighborhood. Therefore, she asks some of the young people on her block to help her map out the area. Several of them agree and the group gets together for a map-making party. As a result, Tina gets a map and makes some new friends.

1. What is the cause and what are the effects?

2. Which fact might be seen as both a cause and an effect?

3. What clue words are found in the passage?

4. How might identifying cause and effect help you in your daily life?

EXTEND THE SKILL

Identifying cause and effect can also help you to understand history. It can help you better understand events and facts from the past. In the last lesson, you read that conquistador Hernando Cortés came to the Americas and fought with Moctezuma II of the Aztec Empire. You may wish to look back at the lesson for help in answering the following questions.

- What caused Cortés to travel to Mexico?

- What were some of the effects of his expedition?

- How can identifying cause and effect help you understand history?

Europeans in the Southwest

Find Out!

Who were the first Europeans to explore the land now called Texas?

VOCABULARY

expedition

PEOPLE

Alonso Alvarez de Piñeda

Pánfilo de Narváez

Alvar Núñez Cabeza de Vaca

Estevanico

Francisco Vásquez de Coronado

Hernando de Soto

Luis de Moscoso de Alvarado

René Robert Cavelier, Sieur de la Salle

READING STRATEGY

Copy the chart. Write in three explorers in the order in which they explored Texas.

```
┌─────────────────┐
│                 │
└─────────────────┘
        ▼
┌─────────────────┐
│                 │
└─────────────────┘
        ▼
┌─────────────────┐
│                 │
└─────────────────┘
```

Lesson Outline

- Explorers in Texas
- A Walk Across Texas
- In Search of Gold
- More Early Explorers

BUILD BACKGROUND

"We Spaniards suffer from a disease of the heart which can only be cured by gold."

So wrote Hernando Cortés. After Cortés defeated the Aztec in 1521, stories of great wealth in the Western Hemisphere spread throughout Europe. Spain led Europe in the search for gold and land.

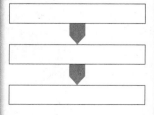

EXPLORERS IN TEXAS

In 1519, a Spanish explorer named **Alonso Alvarez de Piñeda** (ahl LAHN soh AHL vah rayz day pihn YAY dah) sailed along the coast of what is today Florida. He was the leader of an **expedition**, or a journey of exploration. Piñeda's expedition continued along the Gulf of Mexico from the west coast of Florida to Mexico. His crew drew maps of the coastline.

Narváez: Lost at Sea

Using Piñeda's maps, an expedition of 400 Spaniards led by **Pánfilo de Narváez** (PAHN fee loh day nahr VAH ays) reached the west coast of Florida in 1528. Narváez and most

Aztec masks of gold (left) were melted by the Spanish and made into coins. Narváez (right) used Piñeda's map (below) to reach Florida.

of his crew walked overland to find a place to build a colony. But several of them were killed by Native Americans defending their villages. Others died from hunger. The Spaniards decided to build boats and sail to Mexico. To make boats, the men cut trees for wood and used their clothing for sails. They melted metal buckles and spurs to make nails.

The men set sail in September 1528. As they neared the Texas coast, a storm wrecked the boats and many drowned. Narváez was never seen again. Few survivors reached land. Those survivors were met by the Karankawa.

READING CHECK
Why were Piñeda's maps important?

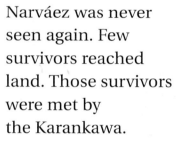

Cabeza de Vaca and Estevanico's Journey, 1534–1536

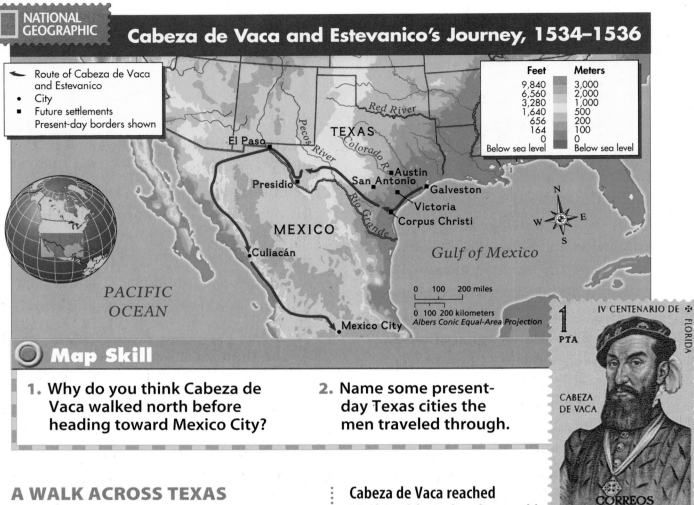

Route of Cabeza de Vaca and Estevanico
• City
■ Future settlements
Present-day borders shown

Feet	Meters
9,840	3,000
6,560	2,000
3,280	1,000
1,640	500
656	200
164	100
0	0
Below sea level	Below sea level

Red River
Pecos River
TEXAS
Colorado R.
El Paso
Presidio
Austin
San Antonio
Galveston
Victoria
Corpus Christi
Rio Grande
MEXICO
Culiacán
Gulf of Mexico
PACIFIC OCEAN

0   100   200 miles
0   100 200 kilometers
Albers Conic Equal-Area Projection

Mexico City

Map Skill

1. Why do you think Cabeza de Vaca walked north before heading toward Mexico City?

2. Name some present-day Texas cities the men traveled through.

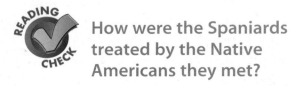

IV CENTENARIO DE ✶ FLORIDA
1 PTA
CABEZA DE VACA
CORREOS
ESPAÑA

A WALK ACROSS TEXAS

One of the men who survived the shipwreck was **Alvar Núñez Cabeza de Vaca** (NOON yayz kah BAY zah day VAH kah). Alonso del Castillo Maldonado and Andrés Dorantes also survived the shipwreck. So did a man named **Estevanico** (es tay vah NEE koh), who had been enslaved by Dorantes earlier.

The survivors were enslaved by the Karankawa. They did whatever they were told to do. After six difficult years, the four explorers escaped in 1534. They went west, looking for Mexico. Along the way, they met many groups of Native Americans who helped them. It took two years for the explorers to

Cabeza de Vaca reached Mexico with stories about gold.

walk the 3,000 miles to Mexico City. Trace their route on the map.

Cabeza de Vaca heard many stories from Native Americans about cities of gold. The Spaniards called them the Seven Cities of Cíbola (SEE buh luh). Spanish officials in Mexico asked Cabeza de Vaca to find those cities. However, Cabeza de Vaca was exhausted from exploring, so he returned to Spain.

READING CHECK

How were the Spaniards treated by the Native Americans they met?

92

BIOGRAPHY

Focus On: Courage

ESTEVANICO traveled the world at a time when most people stayed close to home. He was born in northern Africa. Slave traders brought him to Spain, then he came to Texas. Estevanico was brave in the face of hardships. He did not stop exploring.

In 1539, Estevanico and Fray Marcos de Niza (fray MAHR kos day NEE sah) set out to find the Seven Cities of Cíbola. Estevanico was the only member of the original four explorers to make the trip. Because of his language skills he often went ahead of Fray Marcos de Niza. At what is today the border of Arizona and New Mexico, he reached a Zuni village. Estevanico thought that this pueblo city was one of the seven cities of gold. Within days, however, he was dead. Historians think he never made it to Cíbola. Others think the Zuni may have killed him. We may never know for sure.

Link to Today Trace Estevanico's travels on the map on page 92. Write a paragraph about what it might be like to take that trip today.

THE LIFE OF ESTEVANICO	Around 1503: Estevanico is born in Morocco	1528: Estevanico is shipwrecked on the coast of Texas	1536: Estevanico arrives in Mexico City	1539: Estevanico dies
1500	**1510**	**1520**	**1530**	**1540**
LIFE AROUND THE WORLD	1502: Columbus begins his fourth voyage to the Americas	1512: Michelangelo finishes painting the Sistine Chapel ceiling	1534: Explorer Jacques Cartier claims what is now Canada for France	

IN SEARCH OF GOLD

Fray Marcos returned to Mexico with reports of gold. Spanish officials put together a mighty expedition to go to Cíbola. A Spanish conquistador, **Francisco Vásquez de Coronado** (VAHS kays de kohr oh NAHD oh), was put in charge of finding these cities. In 1540, Coronado led 300 Spaniards and 1,000 Mexican Indians north through Mexico into Texas. They took many horses, sheep, cattle, and pigs with them.

When they finally arrived at Cíbola they found buildings made of adobe, not gold. In a letter to Mexico, Coronado described these buildings.

Primary Source:

From **Coronado's Report to Viceroy Mendoza**
— *Sent from Cíbola, August 3, 1540.*

*. . . they are very good houses, with three and four and five stories, where there are . . . good rooms with **corridors**, and some . . . rooms underground and paved, which are made for winter, and . . . a sort of hot baths. The ladders, which they have for their houses, are all movable and **portable**, which are taken up and placed wherever they please. They are made of two pieces of wood . . . like ours.*

What did Coronado like about the houses?

corridor: a hallway or passageway
portable: easy to carry from place to place

Panhandle Plains Historical Museum

Coronado Is Disappointed

Using two Native American guides, the group continued through what is now New Mexico. When they returned to the Texas Panhandle the men were surprised by their first sight of buffalo. There were so many buffalo that the Spaniards compared them to fish in the sea. Coronado named this area *La Vega*, which means "fertile plain" in Spanish. This is how Vega, Texas, was named.

The explorers met with all kinds of Texas weather. In what is now West Texas, a hailstorm dented the men's helmets, broke all their pottery, and frightened their horses away.

Coronado's guides told stories of gold located to the north of Texas. But in 1542, after exploring 7,000 miles, Coronado and most of his group returned to Mexico without gold. They were very disappointed.

What were some of the things Coronado saw in and around present-day Texas?

Palo Duro Canyon has changed little since Coronado traveled through it. This mural of Coronado entering Palo Duro Canyon (left) is in the Panhandle-Plains Historical Museum.

MORE EARLY EXPLORERS

Before Coronado began exploring the Southwest, the Spanish explorer **Hernando de Soto** (er NAHN doh day SOH toh) led an expedition in the Southeast. But De Soto became ill and died in 1542. Before he died, he told **Luis de Moscoso de Alvarado** (loo EES day mohs KOHS oh day ahl vah RAH doh) to take his place as leader. Moscoso tried to lead his men to Mexico by traveling across what is now East Texas. But he gave up looking for an overland route, and left Texas for the Mississippi river. There the men built boats in which they sailed to the Gulf of Mexico and on to Mexico.

A French Colony

Spain was not the only country in search of gold and silver in the Americas. In 1682, a French explorer, **René Robert Cavelier, Sieur de la Salle** (re NAY roh BAIR cah vuhl YAY sihr de lah SAL), sailed down the Mississippi to the Gulf of Mexico. He claimed all of the surrounding land for France. He named it Louisiana in honor of his king, Louis XIV. Then he returned to France.

In July 1684 La Salle tried to return to Louisiana with more than 300 colonists. But instead he landed along the Texas coast, near what is now Victoria. There the French colonists built

HISTORY MYSTERY

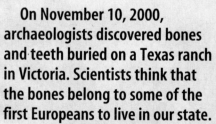

What happened to La Salle's colony at Fort St. Louis?

On November 10, 2000, archaeologists discovered bones and teeth buried on a Texas ranch in Victoria. Scientists think that the bones belong to some of the first Europeans to live in our state.

Since 1996, more than 60,000 artifacts have been found on the site of Fort St. Louis. These include eight iron cannons and pieces of pottery. As they study these artifacts, scientists may be able to tell what life was like in the colony. And by examining artifacts, archaeologists might even identify relatives of the colonists living today!

How might this discovery help us learn more about Texas history?

Fort St. Louis in 1685. The colonists experienced many hardships including bad weather, illnesses, and war with the Karankawa. By December 1688, the colonists had disappeared.

Who were some of the explorers who traveled across the land of Texas?

PUTTING IT TOGETHER

Spain lost interest in exploring the Southwest because Spanish explorers did not find gold. By the early 1700s several French settlements were built in Louisiana. Spanish officials became alarmed that France might claim Texas and build many more settlements. In the next lesson you will read about renewed Spanish interest in Texas.

The Granger Collection

René Robert Cavalier, Sieur de la Salle

Review and Assess

1. Write one sentence for the vocabulary word:

   expedition

2. Who was Estevanico?

3. Identify some of the first European explorers to Texas and what they did.

4. What did explorers hope to gain by finding gold and building colonies? How would this help the Spanish **economy**?

5. **Predict** what might have happened if Coronado had found gold in Cíbola.

Activities

Suppose you were a mapmaker for the explorers you read about in this lesson. Make a list of all the kinds of information you would need on a map so it could be followed by them.

• • • • • • • • • • • • • • • • • • •

Look at the political map of the world in the Atlas on page R4. Using the map, **write** a set of directions explorers could use to travel from Spain to Texas. Be sure to use cardinal and intermediate directions.

Reading Time Lines

To understand history, you need to know *when* things happened. You also need to know the *order* in which things happened. For example, did Narváez set off on his expedition to Florida before or after Piñeda created maps of the Gulf Coast area?

A **time line** can answer this question. A time line is a diagram that shows when events took place. It shows the amount of time that passed between events. A time line helps to give a sense of sequence, or order, to history.

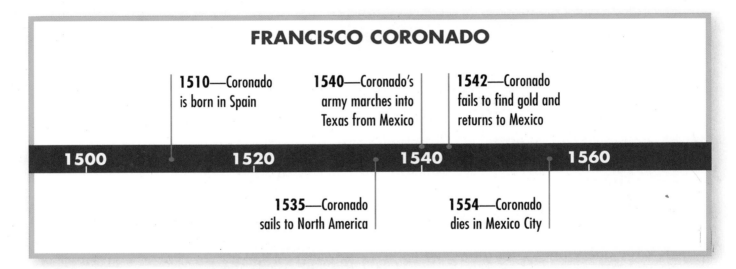

FRANCISCO CORONADO

1510—Coronado is born in Spain

1540—Coronado's army marches into Texas from Mexico

1542—Coronado fails to find gold and returns to Mexico

1500   1520   1540   1560

1535—Coronado sails to North America

1554—Coronado dies in Mexico City

LEARN THE SKILL

In the last lesson you read a biography about the explorer Estevanico. At the bottom of page 93, a time line shows important dates in his life. The time line above shows events in the life of conquistador Francisco Coronado.

1. **Identify the title of the time line.**
   The title of this time line is "Francisco Coronado." It charts events in his life: For example, Francisco Coronado was born in 1510.

2. **Note how much time each part represents.**
   Like most time lines, this one is divided into equal parts. Each part represents a certain number of years. On Coronado's time line, each part represents 20 years.

3. **Read from left to right.**
   The earliest event—Coronado's birth—is on the left side. The most recent event—Coronado's death—is on the right.

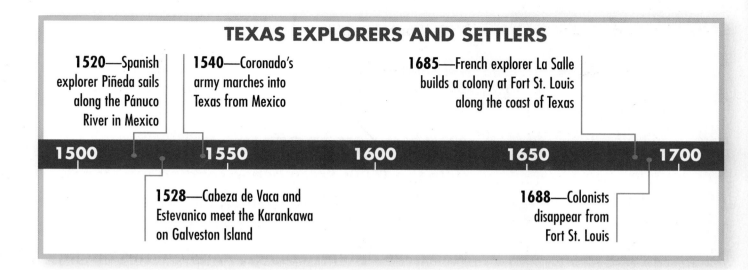

TEXAS EXPLORERS AND SETTLERS

1520—Spanish explorer Piñeda sails along the Pánuco River in Mexico

1540—Coronado's army marches into Texas from Mexico

1685—French explorer La Salle builds a colony at Fort St. Louis along the coast of Texas

1500   1550   1600   1650   1700

1528—Cabeza de Vaca and Estevanico meet the Karankawa on Galveston Island

1688—Colonists disappear from Fort St. Louis

TRY THE SKILL

As you can see, time lines can show events from a person's life. They can also be used for other kinds of topics. The time line above charts important events in the exploration of Texas.

1. What is the title of the time line?

2. How much time does each part represent?

3. Which event happened first?

4. Did French explorers or Spanish explorers reach the Southwest first?

5. Compare this time line to the one on the previous page. Which event appears on both?

6. In what other subjects would a time line be useful?

EXTEND THE SKILL

Time lines not only help you understand events from history. They can also help you examine events from your life. Suppose that you went to a new school in September, got an A in music class in December, joined the soccer team in October, and played a pilgrim in the Thanksgiving Play in November. Create a time line that shows these events in the order that they happened.

- How can a time line help you in your daily life?

Spanish Texas

What was it like to live under Spanish rule in New Spain?

Lesson Outline
• Building An Empire
• A Mix of Cultures
• Life at a Mission

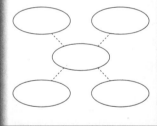
BUILD BACKGROUND

In the 1500s Spain began sending priests as **missionaries** to New Spain. A missionary is a person who teaches his or her religion to others who have different beliefs. Missionaries taught in settlements called **missions**. There, priests taught Native Americans the Roman Catholic religion.

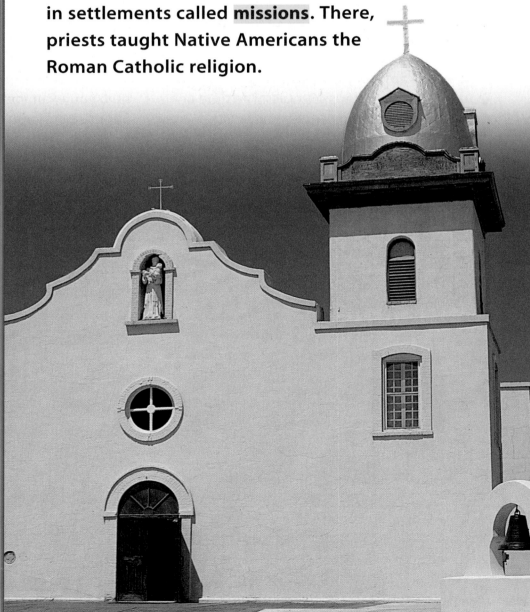

BUILDING AN EMPIRE

By the 1700s Spain renewed its interest in Texas. By mid-century many Spanish settlements and missions were built along the Rio Grande Valley. The first mission in Texas was **Ysleta** (ee SLAY tah) **Mission**, built in 1681 near present day El Paso. You can see a photograph of it on the opposite page.

Some Spaniards were given large amounts of land on which to build ranches, called ranchos. Cattle and horses were raised on ranchos. Other newcomers built and lived in towns called villas.

El Paso del Norte Ysleta (left) was built in 1681. An early painting of the Plaza and the church of El Paso (below).

To protect the missions from attacks by other Europeans and Native Americans, the Spanish also built **presidios** near the settlements. A presidio was a fort where soldiers lived.

Mexico City

The largest Spanish settlement in New Spain was Mexico City, built on the ruins of Tenochtitlán. To remind them of home, the Spaniards constructed the city to look like a city in Spain. They built Roman Catholic churches, a university, a post office, and a central plaza, or town square.

How did Spain build its empire along the Rio Grande Valley?

Mestizos can trace their families back to both Spanish settlers and native Mexican Indians.

A MIX OF CULTURES

As Spain's empire grew, Spanish and Mexican Indian cultures blended together to create a new culture. Spaniards saw foods such as *maize* (corn), beans, tomatoes, and potatoes for the first time. Mexican Indians were introduced to food brought from Europe—onions, wheat, and grapes. Large ranches were started for the Spaniards' horses and cattle.

Mexican Indians and Spaniards sometimes married. Their children were **mestizos**. Mestizos are people who are part Spanish and part Mexican Indian. In the early 1700s Mestizo and Spanish settlers came to what is today Texas. Many Africans were brought from Africa to work as slaves for Spanish families. Free Africans also arrived. The empire of New Spain was growing.

 What are some examples of how Spanish and Mexican cultures blended?

Exploring
TECHNOLOGY

Building with Adobe

Adobe is made of mud, straw, and water mixed together and then dried by the sun to make homes and other buildings. It is good for a desert climate because adobe holds heat in the winter and stays cool in the summer.

Native Americans built homes by patting adobe, waiting for it to dry, and then adding another layer. When the Spanish arrived they used wooden frames to shape the adobe into bricks. The bricks dried quickly and were easy to work with.

Activity

Why do you think the Spanish wanted to increase the speed at which buildings were made?

DATAGRAPHIC

The Spread of Missions

During the 1700s, missionary settlements grew throughout New Spain. Use the map and graph to answer the questions.

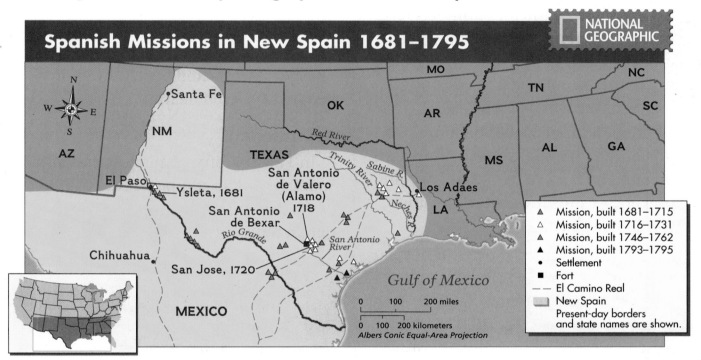

Spanish Missions in New Spain 1681–1795

NATIONAL GEOGRAPHIC

Legend:
- ▲ Mission, built 1681–1715
- △ Mission, built 1716–1731
- ▲ Mission, built 1746–1762
- ▲ Mission, built 1793–1795
- ● Settlement
- ■ Fort
- --- El Camino Real
- New Spain
- Present-day borders and state names are shown.

Scale: 0 100 200 miles
0 100 200 kilometers
Albers Conic Equal-Area Projection

Map labels: Santa Fe, NM, AZ, El Paso, Ysleta, 1681, San Antonio de Bexar, Chihuahua, San Jose, 1720, MEXICO, TEXAS, Red River, Trinity River, Sabine R., Neches R., San Antonio de Valero (Alamo) 1718, San Antonio River, Los Adaes, OK, AR, MO, TN, NC, SC, AL, GA, MS, LA, Gulf of Mexico, Rio Grande

QUESTIONS

1 Where were the most missions located in what is now Texas?

2 How many missions were built in Texas?

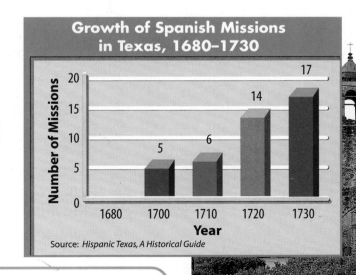

Growth of Spanish Missions in Texas, 1680–1730

Number of Missions (y-axis): 0, 5, 10, 15, 20

Years (x-axis): 1680, 1700, 1710, 1720, 1730

Values: 1700 = 5, 1710 = 6, 1720 = 14, 1730 = 17

Source: *Hispanic Texas, A Historical Guide*

To learn more, visit our Web site:
www.mhschool.com

LIFE AT A MISSION

Suppose you lived at a mission in 1700. Your day would revolve around community living with the Roman Catholic church at the center. Look at the diagram to see what a mission might have looked like.

You would get up at sunrise and be led in prayer by the missionaries. After breakfast you might help in the fields, growing corn, beans, or fruit. Or you might make tools, baskets, or pottery in one of the workshops.

At noon, there would be more prayers and a midday meal. Afterwards it would be back to work until evening prayers. At sunset you and the others would go to bed.

Native Americans at the Missions

Missions were built where Native Americans lived and worked. Missionaries forced Native Americans to live at the missions. Those who lived at the missions had to work very hard. Some even died because they were treated cruelly. Many disliked the missionaries' attempt to change their beliefs and their culture. However, some Native Americans felt safe at the missions. They were protected from unfriendly people who lived nearby.

San Antonio

In 1718 a group of missionaries and Spanish settlers stopped at the source of the San Antonio River. The area was rich in natural resources such as water

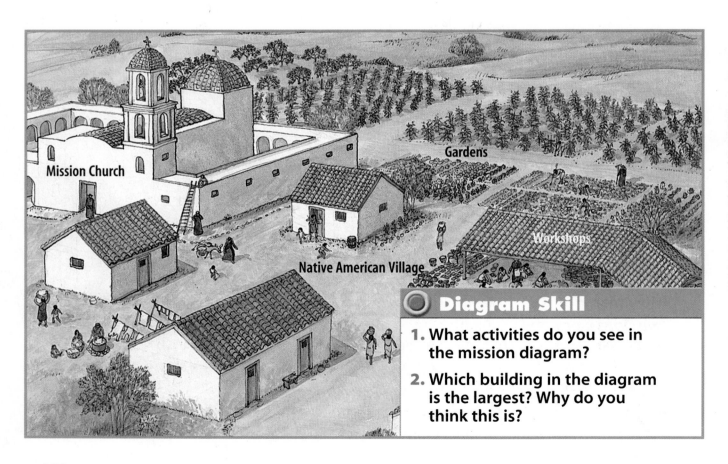

Mission Church

Gardens

Native American Village

Workshops

◯ Diagram Skill

1. What activities do you see in the mission diagram?

2. Which building in the diagram is the largest? Why do you think this is?

and building materials. The natural features of the land made it a good place for the mission of **San Antonio de Valero** (day vah LAIR oh). The mission's church later became known as the Alamo. A presidio, called **San Antonio de Béxar** (day BAY hahr), was built to protect the mission. **San Jose Mission** was built nearby in 1720. In 1731, a villa, San Fernando de Béxar, was founded between the two. Three other missions were later built in the area. A villa grew up around these missions and later became the city of **San Antonio**.

How did the lives of Native Americans change in New Spain?

San Antonio de Béxar helped protect the Alamo.

PUTTING IT TOGETHER

Between the late 1500s and early 1700s, Spain built a powerful empire in the Western Hemisphere. This empire expanded as new settlers arrived and missions were established. The Spanish brought a different language and the Roman Catholic religion. Spanish influence can be seen throughout Texas today.

Review and Assess

1. Write one sentence for each of the vocabulary words:

   mestizo   **mission**

   missionary   **presidio**

2. Name the first mission in Texas.

3. Describe what it was like to live under Spanish rule in New Spain.

4. Why was **geography** important to the Spanish when they chose the locations of each mission? How did the Spanish choose locations for their missions?

5. **Compare** and **contrast** the goals of the missionaries and the conquistadors.

Look back at the map on page 103. What geographic feature is near most of the missions?

• •

Suppose you are either a missionary or a Native American. **Write** a paragraph about life in the mission from that person's point of view.

What was life like for colonists in the Western Hemisphere?

Find Out!

VOCABULARY

pilgrim

PEOPLE

Pedro Alvares Cabral

Lesson Outline

- English Colonies in America
- Other Colonies

Colonization

READING STRATEGY

Draw a diagram like this one. Write similarities and differences between your life and the life of colonial children.

BUILD BACKGROUND

In the 1600s and 1700s many people came from Europe to build new lives in the Western Hemisphere. These men, women, and children came from countries such as Spain, Portugal, England, and France. Many came in search of a better life for their families. Others longed for religious freedom that they did not have in Europe. Some came in search of fortune.

ENGLISH COLONIES IN AMERICA

By 1733 newcomers from England had established thirteen colonies along the Atlantic. These colonies were the beginning of the United States. Find them on the map on this page.

On September 16, 1620, the **Pilgrims** set sail from England to North America on the *Mayflower*. A pilgrim is a person who travels to a place for religious reasons. In England the Pilgrims could not practice their own religion. In America they settled in a place called **Plymouth**. There they hoped to find the freedom to pray and live in their own way.

Life in an English Colony

Generally, people of all ages were expected to work hard all week. On Sundays, everyone attended church.

Children had many chores, but also had time for games.

Children had many chores. They had to gather firewood, berries, and wild plants. They also had to help with planting, harvesting, cooking, and cleaning.

Most colonial boys went to school to learn reading, writing, and math. Girls were usually taught at home.

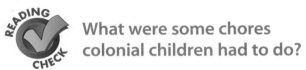

READING CHECK **What were some chores colonial children had to do?**

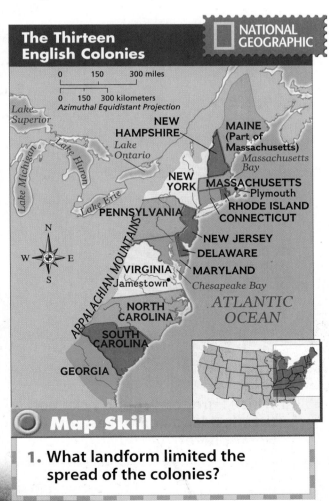

The Thirteen English Colonies

NATIONAL GEOGRAPHIC

0   150   300 miles
0   150   300 kilometers
Azimuthal Equidistant Projection

Lake Superior
Lake Michigan
Lake Huron
Lake Ontario
Lake Erie

NEW HAMPSHIRE
MAINE (Part of Massachusetts)
Massachusetts Bay
NEW YORK
MASSACHUSETTS
Plymouth
RHODE ISLAND
CONNECTICUT
PENNSYLVANIA
NEW JERSEY
DELAWARE
APPALACHIAN MOUNTAINS
VIRGINIA
Jamestown
MARYLAND
Chesapeake Bay
ATLANTIC OCEAN
NORTH CAROLINA
SOUTH CAROLINA
GEORGIA

Map Skill

1. **What landform limited the spread of the colonies?**

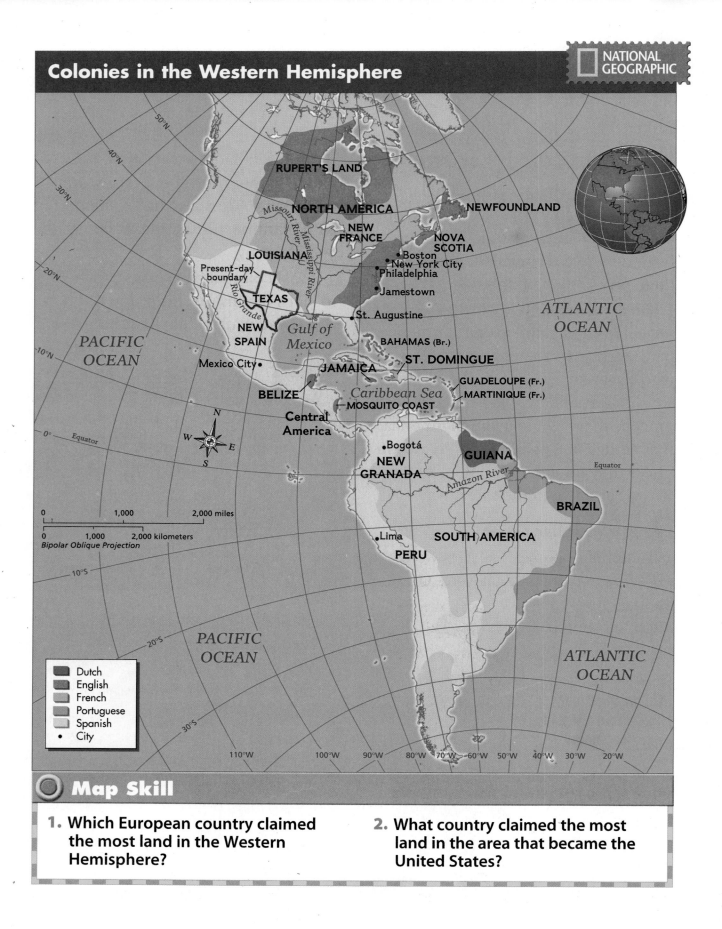

Colonies in the Western Hemisphere

NATIONAL GEOGRAPHIC

RUPERT'S LAND

NORTH AMERICA

NEWFOUNDLAND

NEW FRANCE

NOVA SCOTIA

LOUISIANA

Missouri River

Mississippi River

Boston
New York City
Philadelphia

Present-day boundary

Jamestown

TEXAS

Rio Grande

St. Augustine

ATLANTIC OCEAN

NEW SPAIN

Gulf of Mexico

BAHAMAS (Br.)

PACIFIC OCEAN

Mexico City

ST. DOMINGUE

JAMAICA

GUADELOUPE (Fr.)

BELIZE

Caribbean Sea

MARTINIQUE (Fr.)

MOSQUITO COAST

Central America

N
W   E
S

Equator

Bogotá

GUIANA

NEW GRANADA

Amazon River

Equator

BRAZIL

0   1,000   2,000 miles
0   1,000   2,000 kilometers
Bipolar Oblique Projection

Lima

SOUTH AMERICA

PERU

PACIFIC OCEAN

ATLANTIC OCEAN

Dutch
English
French
Portuguese
Spanish
• City

110°W   100°W   90°W   80°W   70°W   60°W   50°W   40°W   30°W   20°W

Map Skill

1. Which European country claimed the most land in the Western Hemisphere?

2. What country claimed the most land in the area that became the United States?

OTHER COLONIES

In 1500 **Pedro Alvares Cabral** (AHL vah rayz cah BRAHL) reached what is known today as **Brazil** in South America. **Portugal** claimed Brazil as a colony. It became a source of valuable natural resources for Portugal.

In 1608 French colonies were set up in Canada. The colonists were fur traders. Beaver fur hats were almost as valuable as gold to the French. Look at the map on the opposite page. Where else did France have colonies in the Western Hemisphere?

 **Why was beaver fur valuable to the French?**

PUTTING IT TOGETHER

Colonists from Europe came to the Americas in search of a better life. They also hoped to find wealth and the religious freedom they did not have in Europe.

Native Americans lived and worked on the land where colonies were built. Their lives were affected by the arrival of European colonists. Some helped the colonists learn to survive in a land new to them. However, many Native Americans were killed trying to defend their villages.

Review and Assess

1. Write one sentence with the vocabulary word:

   pilgrim

2. Who was Pedro Alvares Cabral?

3. Identify reasons why European colonists settled in the Western Hemisphere.

4. **Compare** and **contrast** the reasons Europeans came to Texas and the reasons Europeans came to Plymouth.

5. **Describe** life in the Plymouth Colony. When was it established?

Look at the political map on page R14. List the present day countries in South America that were once part of Spain. Refer to the map on page 108 for help.

. . . .

Suppose you were a ten year old who lived in one of the 13 English colonies. **Write** a journal entry describing what your life might have been like. Then draw a picture to go with your description.

VOCABULARY REVIEW

Number a sheet from 1 to 6. Beside each number write the word or term from the list below that correctly completes the sentence.

colony   conquistador

expedition   explore

mission   presidio

1. Piñeda led an ___ to the coast of what is now Florida.

2. Europeans set out to ___ the Americas and find places to build colonies.

3. Cortés was a ___ who used force to take land and gold.

4. The Spaniards thought the best place for a ___ was where Native Americans lived and worked.

5. A city or settlement in Mexico that was ruled by Spain was called a ___.

6. Spanish settlers depended on the nearby ___ to protect them.

CHAPTER COMPREHENSION

7. Who were Fray Marcos de Niza and Estevanico?

8. Why were European countries trying to establish colonies in North America?

9. Name the first mission built in Texas and the present-day city it was closest to.

10. What was life like for Native Americans living at the missions?

SKILL REVIEW

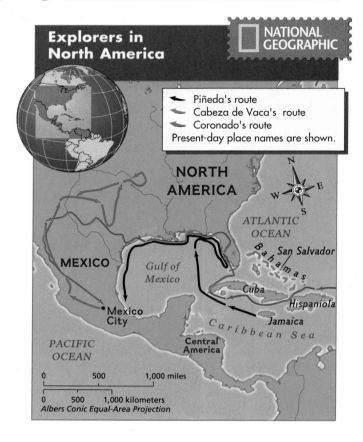

Explorers in North America

 NATIONAL GEOGRAPHIC

Piñeda's route
Cabeza de Vaca's route
Coronado's route
Present-day place names are shown.

NORTH AMERICA

ATLANTIC OCEAN

MEXICO

Gulf of Mexico

San Salvador

Bahamas

Mexico City

Cuba

Hispaniola

Jamaica

Caribbean Sea

PACIFIC OCEAN

Central America

0   500   1,000 miles

0   500   1,000 kilometers
Albers Conic Equal-Area Projection

11. **Reading/Thinking Skill** Look at the paths taken by each of the explorers. What caused them to take different routes?

12. **Study Skill** How much time passed between Cabeza de Vaca's and Estevanico's meeting with the Karankawa and Coronado's march into Texas?

13. **Study Skill** Why was Piñeda's expedition important to future explorers? Use a time line to show how expeditions increased or decreased after Piñeda.

USING A TIME LINE

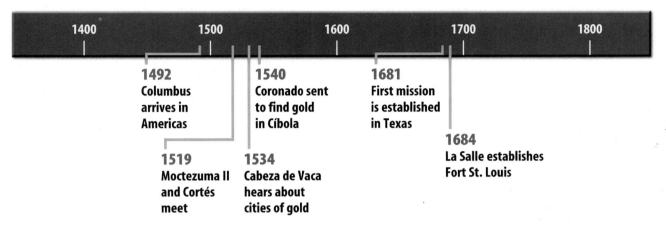

| 1400 | 1500 | 1600 | 1700 | 1800 |

1492 Columbus arrives in Americas

1519 Moctezuma II and Cortés meet

1540 Coronado sent to find gold in Cíbola

1534 Cabeza de Vaca hears about cities of gold

1681 First mission is established in Texas

1684 La Salle establishes Fort St. Louis

14. Between what two points on the time line would you place de Soto's expedition?

15. Describe the main focus of expeditions during the 1500s.

Activity

Writing About Culture Suppose you were an explorer on your way to North America. Write a description of what you hope to find based on the expeditions that you know about.

Describe the type of people you expect to meet on the way.

Foldables

Use your *Foldable* to review what you have learned about the first European explorers in Texas. As you look at the Spanish flag, mentally recall what you have learned about the Spanish as explorers, conquerors, and settlers; then review your notes under the tabs of your *Foldable* to check your responses. Repeat this activity while looking at the French flag. Record any questions that you have on your *Foldable*, and discuss them with classmates or review the chapter to find answers.

VOCABULARY REVIEW

Number a paper from 1 to 6. Beside each number write the word or term from the list below that completes the sentence.

band	colony
empire	expedition
mission	pueblo

1. The Spanish built a ___ in order to teach Native Americans about their religion.

2. The Aztec ___ was made up of many conquered lands ruled by Tenochtitlán.

3. ___ was the Spanish word used to describe Native American villages.

4. Members of the Comanche lived in small family groups called a ___.

5. Later explorers brought groups of settlers with them so they could start a ___.

6. An explorer might lead an ___ to search for gold and new lands.

TECHNOLOGY

For more resources to help learn about the people and places you studied in this unit, visit **www.mhschool.com** and follow the links for Grade 4 Texas, Unit 1.

SKILL REVIEW

7. **Reading/Thinking Skill** Describe the causes and effects of prehistoric people migrating.

8. **Reading/Thinking Skill** What caused Europeans to want to explore? What effect did this have on the Americas?

9. **Study Skill** Draw a time line of your own life. How is it similar and different from the time lines in this book?

10. **Geography Skill** Explain the difference between latitude and longitude.

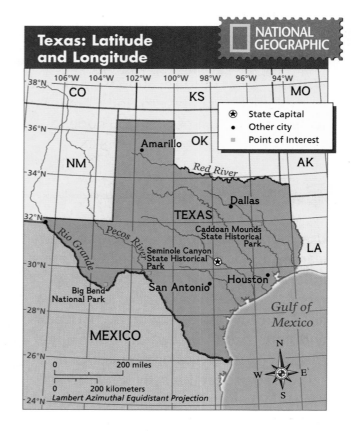

Texas: Latitude and Longitude

NATIONAL GEOGRAPHIC

State Capital
Other city
Point of Interest

Using two Native American guides, Spanish conquistador Francisco Vásquez de Coronado and his group continued through what is now New Mexico. When they returned to the Texas Panhandle, the men were surprised by their first sight of buffalo. There were so many buffalo that the Spaniards compared them to fish in the sea. Coronado named this area *La Vega*, which means "fertile plain" in Spanish. This is how Vega, Texas, was named.

The explorers met with all kinds of Texas weather. In what is now West Texas, a hailstorm dented the men's helmets, broke all their pottery, and frightened their horses away.

Coronado's guides told stories of gold located to the north of Texas.

But in 1542, after exploring 7,000 miles, Coronado and most of his group returned to Mexico without gold. They were very disappointed.

1 What area did Coronado and his men name *La Vega*?

   A New Mexico
   B West Texas
   C Mexico
   D the Texas Panhandle

2 According to the passage, Coronado and his men were disappointed because—

   A they met with many types of weather.
   B they did not find gold.
   C their horses ran away.
   D they traveled many miles.

WRITING ACTIVITIES TAKS Practice

⊕ **Writing to Inform** Suppose you were on the voyage with Columbus. Write a letter home telling about the land and people you have seen.

⊕ **Writing to Persuade** Suppose you lived in Tenochtitlán. Write an essay to try to persuade Cortés not to start a war.

⊕ **Writing to Express** Write about the life of a Caddo Native American.

Caddo pottery

113

LITERATURE

DEAF SMITH
SCOUT, SPY AND TEXAS HERO

SELECTION BY *Jo Harper*

ILLUSTRATED BY *Robert Barrett*

This is the story of Erastus "Deaf" Smith, who became a great hero in the fight for independence from Mexico. Erastus was known as "Deaf" because he was not able to hear. He joined the Texian volunteers as a scout and a spy. He helped Sam Houston win the Battle of San Jacinto. This battle marked the end of the Texas Revolution.

TIME TO FIGHT

. . . Deaf Smith was mad as a cornered rattler. General Cós had double-crossed him. Besides, he was embarrassed to be without a hat.

Deaf went back to General Stephen F. Austin. He said, "General Austin, I told you yesterday that I wouldn't take sides in this war. But, sir, I now **tender** you my services 'cause the Mexicans acted **rascally** with me!"

Stephen F. Austin was mighty proud to have Deaf Smith join the Texian volunteers. No one knew the Hill Country as well as Deaf did. No one could track as well. No one could speak Spanish as well. As it turned out, no one was more help to the Texians.

Deaf's family had hard times without him, but they made it out of San Antonio and to safety in Louisiana.

General Austin sent Deaf to serve under General Sam Houston. He didn't know Houston was already headed for San Antonio to help the men who were trapped in an old mission called the Alamo.

---

tender (ten′dər) to present for acceptance, to make a bid
rascally (ras′kə lē) to act dishonestly

115

TO THE ALAMO

Deaf Smith caught up with Houston at Gonzales, the town he had built. Right away they got news that the Alamo had fallen and all the soldiers in it were dead. Deaf Smith's first job was to find out if the dreadful news was true.

On his way to San Antonio, Deaf met a woman named Suzanna Dickenson. She had been at the Alamo. She told Deaf that the Alamo really had fallen. Colonel Travis, Davy Crockett, Jim Bowie, and all their brave soldiers were dead.

The Mexicans hadn't killed Mrs. Dickenson, her baby, or the servants because they weren't soldiers. Santa Anna even offered to send the baby to his family in Mexico City so she would be safe.

Mrs. Dickenson didn't want to let her baby go, so

Santa Anna gave her a horse and let her leave with the servants.

Deaf told Houston the terrible truth about the Alamo and that General Santa Anna and his huge Mexican army were marching to Gonzales.

The people of Gonzales panicked. They **skedaddled** out of town. Houston's volunteers weren't trained and weren't ready to stand and fight. They retreated.

Deaf Smith stayed behind. He had to destroy the beautiful town of Gonzales—the very town he had helped to build. If he didn't, it would give the enemy places to hide.

Deaf had **gumption**. He always did his job, hard or not. He burned Gonzales, the town that he loved.

---

skedaddled (ski da′dəl) to flee in a panic, run away

gumption (gump′ shən) common sense applied to the problems of life

Write About It!

Deaf Smith was a very important figure in Texas's fight for independence. **Describe** some of the characteristics that helped define Smith as a hero and leader of the Texas Revolution.

Unit 2

From Revolution to Statehood

TAKE A LOOK

How did the Revolution change life in Texas?

The fight for independence ended with Texas becoming an independent country. Today, many people visit the Alamo to learn about our state's history.

Explore more about
the Alamo at our Web site
www.mhschool.com

119

3

THE Big IDEAS ABOUT...

The Fight for Independence

Settlers soon became unhappy with Mexican rule in Texas. They wanted to be free from Mexico. Read on to find out the events that led to Texas's independence.

THE FATHER OF TEXAS

Stephen F. Austin brings the first three hundred settlers from the United States to Texas.

COLONISTS ARRIVE

Mexico agrees to let colonists from the United States move to Texas, hoping that they will help Texas grow strong.

REVOLUTION IN TEXAS

Most settlers become unhappy with Mexican rule in Texas and decide that Texas should become an independent republic.

THE BATTLE OF THE ALAMO

American and Tejano defenders of the Alamo are defeated by General Santa Anna and about 5,000 Mexican troops.

TEXAS IS FREE AT LAST

General Sam Houston defeats Santa Anna, who is captured after the Battle of San Jacinto.

NEW GOVERNMENTS

Colonies throughout the Western Hemisphere gain independence.

Foldables

Make this Foldable study guide and use it to record what you learn about the Texas Revolution, the Battle of the Alamo, and Texas independence.

1. Fold a sheet of paper into a shutter fold.
2. Sketch the Alamo on the front of the shutter fold.
3. Read and listen for main ideas and record them inside your Foldable.

Lesson

1

Moses Austin and Stephen F. Austin

Find! out!

Why is Stephen F. Austin known as the "Father of Texas"?

Lesson Outline
• The Louisiana Territory
• The Old Three Hundred
• San Felipe de Austin

BUILD BACKGROUND

In 1821 **Stephen F. Austin** started a colony on the coastal plain between the Colorado and Brazos Rivers. He described the area as the "most beautiful . . . for a town or settlement."

VOCABULARY

Louisiana Purchase
pioneer
The Old Three Hundred
frontier
Anglo-Americans
empresario
Tejano

PEOPLE

Stephen F. Austin
Thomas Jefferson
Moses Austin
Jane Long
Antonio Martínez
Don Martín de León
Patricia de la Garza de León

READING STRATEGY

Copy the chart. Starting with 1821, write three events that happened during the next two years.

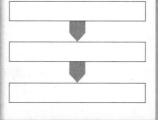

THE LOUISIANA TERRITORY

A very large area of land that stretched from the Mississippi west to the Rocky Mountains was called the **Louisiana Territory**. A territory is land owned by a country. A territory does not have the full rights of a state. In 1803 President **Thomas Jefferson** bought this area from France for the United States for $15 million. The land deal was called the **Louisiana Purchase**. It doubled the size of the United States.

By 1820 the eastern United States had become too crowded and costly for many Americans. Land was selling for about $1.25 an acre. However, land in the west was cheap and plentiful. In places such as Texas, land was selling for 12½ cents per acre. Many people decided to move west as **pioneers**. A pioneer is a person who is among the first of a group of people to settle in a new region.

People began heading west for many reasons. One reason was for adventure. Another reason was to find a new job. One of these pioneers was Stephen F. Austin. He was continuing a plan begun by his father, **Moses Austin**, to bring pioneers from the United States to Texas.

 What was the Louisiana Purchase?

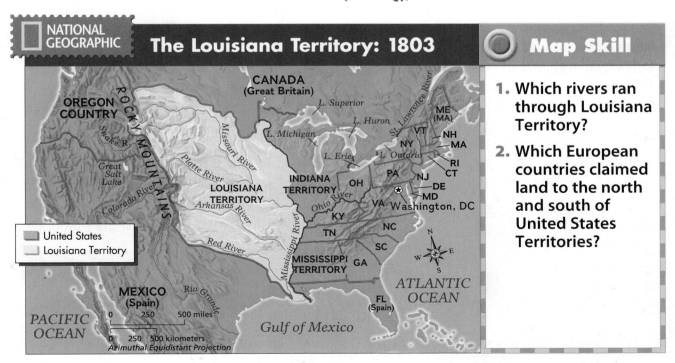

NATIONAL GEOGRAPHIC | **The Louisiana Territory: 1803** | **Map Skill**

1. Which rivers ran through Louisiana Territory?

2. Which European countries claimed land to the north and south of United States Territories?

THE OLD THREE HUNDRED

By 1825, nearly 300 families were living in Austin's Texas colony. These early colonists became known as **The Old Three Hundred**.

Among The Old Three Hundred was a brave woman named **Jane Long**. Long had traveled to Texas before with her husband in 1820. He led an expedition to try to free Texas from Spain. While he was away, Jane Long, who was expecting a child, spent a cold, lonely winter with her 12-year-old enslaved worker, Kian. She did not know that her husband had been killed. They defended themselves from unfriendly groups of Native Americans. At the abandoned fort where they lived, Long gave birth to a daughter. She was the first child born in Texas to parents from the United States. This is why Jane Long is often called the "Mother of Texas."

Moses Austin planned to bring pioneers to Texas (above). Jane Long and Kian defended themselves against Native American attacks (below).

In 1820 Moses Austin also traveled to Texas. He was a businessman from Missouri who wanted to settle the Texas **frontier**. *Frontier* is the word that United States settlers used to describe land beyond the edge of their settlement. Moses Austin rode to San Antonio to ask the Spanish governor for permission to bring settlers from the United States to Texas. Governor **Antonio Martínez** (mahr TEE nez) agreed.

Soon after returning home in 1821, Moses Austin died. His wife, Maria, wrote to their son Stephen: "He called me to his bedside and … begged me to tell you to take his place."

 Who were The Old Three Hundred?

BIOGRAPHY

Focus On: Responsibility

STEPHEN F. AUSTIN was just 27 years old when his father died. He was studying to become a lawyer. But as soon as he got his mother's letter, he dropped everything and went to San Antonio. There he got permission from Governor Martínez to take over his father's plan.

Austin did not think only of his own wants and needs. He felt a strong sense of responsibility for the welfare of others. He worked hard to earn money for his family and to help and protect the people he brought to Texas. As a result, he lived without many comforts. Sick from overwork, he died young at the age of 43.

Link to Today

What responsibilities do you have to people in your family, school, and community? Make a list of at least three.

THE LIFE OF STEPHEN F. AUSTIN	**1793** Stephen F. Austin is born in Austinville, Virginia	**1821** Stephen F. Austin's first colonists arrive in Texas	**1836** Stephen F. Austin dies in Columbia, Texas	**1839** The capital city is renamed in honor of Stephen F. Austin
1785	**1800**	**1815**	**1830**	**1845**
LIFE AROUND THE WORLD	**1801** Thomas Jefferson becomes President of the United States	**1804–1806** Lewis and Clark explore the Louisiana Territory	**1821** Spain sells eastern Florida to the United States for $5 million	**1827** The first photograph is taken

SAN FELIPE DE AUSTIN

Anglo-Americans began arriving in Texas from the United States by the end of 1821. An Anglo-American is a person with English or northern European ancestors.

In 1822 Austin returned to San Antonio. When he got there, he learned that Mexico had won its independence from Spain in 1821. Now Austin had to get new permission to settle his colony. After a year of delays, the new Mexican government approved Austin's plan, and he returned to his colony. When he arrived in 1823, Austin learned that some settlers had returned to the United States. He also discovered that some Karankawa and Tonkawa had

attacked settlements. The Native Americans were angry that the colonists were living on their hunting grounds.

In 1823 Austin chose a town on the Brazos River as his colony's capital. The Mexican governor of Texas named the town **San Felipe de Austin**.

Some members of The Old Three Hundred brought enslaved people with them to the colony. Settlers wanted these workers to help farm their land.

The Empresario System

The Mexican government had set up an **empresario** (em pre SAH ree oh) system in Mexico and in Texas by 1824. An empresario is someone who is given land by the government to sell to settlers. Stephen F. Austin was an empresario, for example.

Another empresario was **Don Martín de León** (dohn mahr TEEN day lee OHN). He and his wife, **Patricia de la Garza de León**, were two of many **Tejanos**, or Mexican people in Texas. De León brought 200 families from Mexico to settle in Texas. In 1824 Patricia de la Garza de León used her own money to help her husband found the town of **Victoria**.

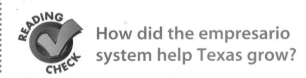

How did the empresario system help Texas grow?

Posters like this one encouraged people in the United States to settle in the Texas colonies.

PUTTING IT TOGETHER

After Mexico declared its independence from Spain in 1821, Texas was ruled by Mexico. Stephen F. Austin brought hundreds of Anglo-American families to Mexican Texas. Because of his important role in our state's history, Austin is often called the "Father of Texas."

Under the **empresario** system, the de Leóns were able to found the town of Victoria.

Review and Assess

1. Write one sentence for each of the vocabulary words:

   empresario   **frontier**

   pioneer   **Tejano**

2. What was the Louisiana Purchase? How did it change the United States?

3. Describe why Stephen F. Austin is called the "Father of Texas."

4. How did Stephen F. Austin show good **citizenship**?

5. Analyze the **effects** empresarios had on the settlement of Texas.

Look at the map on page 123. Then look at the political map of the United States on page R16. Make a list of all the present-day states that were once a part of the Louisiana Purchase.

• •

Suppose that you are Stephen F. Austin. **Write** a letter that would persuade other families to come to Mexican Texas. Then exchange your letter with a partner. Check for capitalization, punctuation, and spelling.

Colonists Come to Mexican Texas

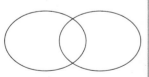

What was life like for colonists in Mexican Texas?

Lesson Outline
- A Difficult Journey
- How Colonists Lived

BUILD BACKGROUND

In the 1820s the Old Three Hundred and other colonists faced many challenges on their way to Texas. Here Texans re-enact the arrival of colonists.

A DIFFICULT JOURNEY

In the 1820s, traveling to Texas was not easy. Many Anglos came down the Mississippi on steamships or flatboats. While on board, people faced bad weather, poor drinking water, and spoiled food. Overland travelers faced problems such as broken wagon wheels, washed-out roads, and wild animals.

Once in Texas, there was little time to rest. After checking their land claim with the empresario, settlers went to work building their homes.

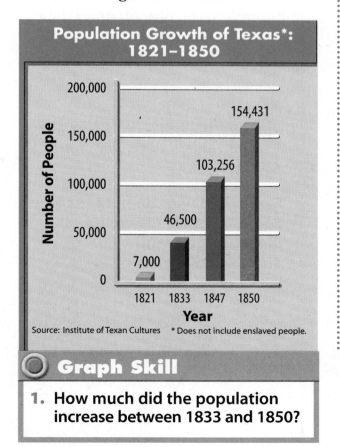

Population Growth of Texas*: 1821–1850

Number of People

- 1821: 7,000
- 1833: 46,500
- 1847: 103,256
- 1850: 154,431

Year

Source: Institute of Texan Cultures   * Does not include enslaved people.

Graph Skill

1. **How much did the population increase between 1833 and 1850?**

A Growing Colony

In the 1830s and 1840s settlers from all over the United States and Mexico, including immigrants from other countries, arrived. Europeans, including Danes, French, Germans, Irish, Italians, Eastern European Jews, Norwegians, and Swedes, came. Hundreds of free African Americans came and thousands of enslaved African Americans were brought to live in Texas. Each group brought its own culture.

Many Mexican leaders hoped the growing business and trade of Texas would help the economy of Mexico.

Settlers brought with them items such as this ceramic doll.

What were some of the problems that people faced on their way to Texas?

129

HOW COLONISTS LIVED

Many early colonists lived on the prairies of Texas. Homes on the prairie were sometimes simply dug out of the side of a hill. These homes were called **dugouts**. Dugouts provided shelter from the wind and dust. But they were dark and damp. Many people lived in dugouts only until they could build a house made of logs.

Farming in Texas

When the first settlers from the United States came to Texas, they practiced **subsistence farming**. This means they used all of the crops they grew for their own survival. On subsistence farms men, boys, and women plowed and planted and took care of livestock. Women and girls also cooked, tended vegetable gardens, sewed clothes, and made candles.

Later, many farmers began growing crops to sell. These are called **cash crops**. Sometimes farmers would **barter** their crops. To barter is to trade for goods and services without using money.

By the 1830s, Texas farmers were growing large amounts of cotton, sugarcane, and corn. Ranchers raised cattle for beef and hides. Towns formed because people needed places to sell their products. In towns, settlers could also buy goods they couldn't grow or make.

Texans Gather Together

Texans found time to gather and have fun. Men competed in hunting and log-rolling contests. Women met to sew quilts. Read how **Sallie Reynolds Matthews** remembered her childhood in West Texas.

Primary Source:

Excerpt from **Unknown Texas** *— by Jonathan Eisen and Harold Straughn, published in 1988.*

"Life was never [dull] to me even though there were no other little girls with which to play. I tagged along after my brothers . . . as they played. They would make traps and sometimes get a bird, which was always thrilling. They never put [the birds] in a cage, but would free them. . . ."

How might you compare the way Sallie Reynolds Matthews played to how you play today?

Music was a great source of fun in early Texas. Mexican, European, and African American music could be heard on ranches and farms.

 How did some Texans spend their free time?

PUTTING IT TOGETHER

Although the colonists had promised to be loyal to the country of Mexico, many saw themselves as Texans first. There were 46,500 settlers living in Texas by 1833. Most of them were from the United States. The leaders of the Mexican government began to wonder if these new Texans would remain loyal to Mexico.

Dugout homes provided shelter while settlers built houses above ground.

Review and Assess

1. Write one sentence for each of the vocabulary words:

   barter   **cash crop**

   dugout   **subsistence farming**

2. How did some colonists come to Texas?

3. Describe what life was like for colonists in Mexican Texas.

4. List some of the different **cultural groups** in Texas at this time.

5. Analyze why settlers had a need to build towns.

Suppose you were a colonist living in Mexican Texas. Some family members want to join you there. **Write** down what routes they might take from the United States to reach you. For help you may use the map on page R18.

. . . .

Write a paragraph comparing and contrasting what you do for fun with what early Texans did for fun. Then exchange your paragraphs with a partner. Check for spelling, capitalization, and punctuation.

Lesson 3

Revolution in Texas

Find Out! *Why were many Texans unhappy with their Mexican government?*

Lesson Outline
- Two Cultures Meet
- A New Mexican Law
- The Texas Revolution

VOCABULARY

bilingual
convention
delegate
tax
dictator
Texas Revolution

PEOPLE

Sam Houston

Antonio López de Santa Anna

William B. Travis

Martín Perfecto de Cós

READING STRATEGY

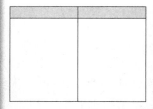

Copy the chart below. Fill in the two purposes of the Convention of 1832.

BUILD BACKGROUND

As the Texas colonies grew, the settlers did not always agree with the Mexican government. The settlers wanted to do things their own way and were unhappy with the government's rules. As a result, the settlers met with Austin to decide what to do.

132

You Are Here
1827 – 1835

The Huntington Library, Art Collections, and Botanical Gardens, San Marino, California

TWO CULTURES MEET

East Texas was hundreds of miles from Mexico City, the capital of Mexico. Settlers in Texas were mostly left to govern themselves. When Mexico began to take more control, some Texans began to resist.

Different Ways of Life

Some of the problems between the government of Mexico and settlers from the United States arose from differences between their cultures. In Texas all government papers were written in Spanish. Most United States settlers couldn't understand Spanish. Some people, such as Stephen F. Austin, were **bilingual**. This word describes people who are able to speak two languages.

Many new settlers also believed people should be able to choose their own religion. However, Mexican law only allowed the Roman Catholic religion.

READING CHECK What were some of the differences between Mexicans and Texans?

A map of colonies in Texas (above) shows Austin's colony and Spanish cities such as San Antonio (below).

The UT Institute of Texan Cultures at San Antonio

TEXAS FOREVER!!

The usurper of the South has failed in his efforts to enslave the freemen of Texas.
The wives and daughters of Texas will be saved from the brutality of Mexican soldiers.
Now is the time to emigrate to the Garden of America. A free passage, and all found, is offered at New Orleans to all applicants. Every settler receives a location of

EIGHT HUNDRED ACRES OF LAND.

Posters like the one above encouraged people to come to Texas.

A NEW MEXICAN LAW

Some Texans began to think about breaking away from Mexico. This worried Mexican leaders. As a result, Mexico passed a new law on April 6, 1830. The law stopped immigration to Texas from the United States. This meant that many families would be separated from their relatives in the United States. It also stopped slavery and put limits on trade between Texas and the United States. Many colonists became angry. The law would stop the growth of their businesses and towns.

Texans Take Action

The settlers decided to meet to discuss what could be done. In October 1832, Texans gathered for a **convention** in San Felipe de Austin. A convention is a formal meeting held for a special purpose. The goal of this convention was to find ways to improve relations between Texas and Mexico.

Delegates from sixteen areas of Texas went to the convention. A delegate is a person who is chosen to speak for a group. The delegates wanted immigration from the United States to continue. They also wanted Texas to become a state within Mexico. If Texas were a Mexican state, Texans would have more power to make law-making decisions.

Another convention was held in April 1833. One of the delegates was **Sam Houston**. After this convention Stephen F. Austin took the colonists' concerns to the Mexican government.

Houston was one **delegate** who went to the 1833 **convention**.

President Santa Anna of Mexico would not allow Texas to become a Mexican state.

Austin Goes to Mexico

Austin arrived in Mexico City on July 18, 1833. He wanted to meet with the president of Mexico, **Antonio López de Santa Anna**. But Santa Anna was away.

After waiting for Santa Anna for five months, Austin was discouraged. He wrote a letter to Tejano leaders in San Antonio. The letter asked the Tejanos to work with settlers from the United States to set up a state government for Texas.

Austin Meets Santa Anna

Santa Anna finally returned to Mexico City, where he met with Austin. Santa Anna would not let Texas become a Mexican state. But he did agree to allow immigration from the United States to continue. With this news, Stephen F. Austin headed back to Texas on December 10, 1833.

Austin's letter to Tejano leaders in San Antonio never arrived. It had fallen into Mexican hands. When Austin reached northern Mexico, he was arrested for disloyalty. He was put in jail for nearly a year. Austin finally returned home in 1835.

Anger and Conflict

Santa Anna sent troops to Texas. He also sent officials to collect **taxes**. A tax is money people must pay to a government for the services it provides. These actions angered Texans.

By 1835 many believed that Santa Anna was becoming a **dictator**. A dictator is a leader with complete control over the government. Texans, such as **William B. Travis**, wanted to break away from Mexico. Early in 1835, Travis led a group of about 20 men to confront Mexican soldiers at the town of **Anáhuac** (an NAH wok). Caught unprepared, the Mexicans gave up.

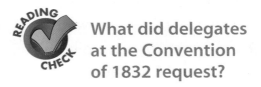

What did delegates at the Convention of 1832 request?

135

Lesson 4

The Battle of the Alamo

VOCABULARY

Battle of the Alamo

Texas Declaration of Independence

constitution

Goliad Massacre

PEOPLE

Jim Bowie

David Crockett

Juan Seguín

Gregorio Esparza

James Bonham

Suzanna Dickenson

Francisco Ruiz

David G. Burnet

Lorenzo de Zavala

James W. Fannin

READING STRATEGY

Copy the word web below. Fill in the names of four Alamo defenders.

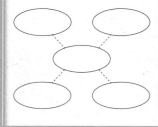

Find Out!

Why is the Alamo important to Texans and to United States history?

Lesson Outline

• Defending San Antonio

• The Alamo Is Taken

• After the Battle

BUILD BACKGROUND

"I am determined to [survive] as long as possible and die like a soldier who never forgets what is due to his own honor and that of his country." William B. Travis wrote these words on February 24, 1836. He and a group of Tejano and United States volunteers defended the Alamo against about 5,000 Mexican soldiers.

DEFENDING SAN ANTONIO

When the Texas Revolution began in 1835, San Antonio became a war zone. But for almost 120 years, the San Antonio de Valero mission had been a quiet place. Built by the Spanish in San Antonio in 1718, the mission is also called the Alamo. This name comes from the Spanish word for "cottonwood tree."

The Alamo is now the most famous battle site in our state's history. You can see a photograph of the Alamo on the opposite page.

Soldiers Prepare to Fight

After the Texas victory at San Antonio in December 1835, only about 100 Texan soldiers remained there.

In January 1836 word spread that Santa Anna's troops were marching northward from Mexico. Small groups of Texan soldiers began to move into San Antonio in case of a battle.

One soldier was **Jim Bowie**, who came with about 25 men. From Tennessee, **David Crockett** arrived with 12 volunteers. Twenty-five men from San Felipe de Austin joined William B. Travis. **Juan Seguín** (HWAHN say GEEN) and his company of Tejano men were among this group. One of Seguín's men, **Gregorio Esparza**,

brought his family into the Alamo. **James Bonham** also arrived, as did a group of men from Gonzales.

The Texans did not think Santa Anna would reach San Antonio until spring. They believed they had time to prepare for a fight.

READING CHECK Why did soldiers begin arriving in San Antonio in January 1836?

The Alamo (far left) was defended by Texans such as David Crockett (above) and Jim Bowie (right).

National Portrait Gallery, Smithsonian Institution, Washington, D.C. U.S.A. Detail

William B. Travis was among the Texans who were killed at the Alamo.

THE ALAMO IS TAKEN

The Mexican army, about 5,000 strong, marched north toward San Antonio. They were followed by 1,800 mules loaded with food and 200 oxcarts carrying supplies. They reached San Antonio on February 23.

Santa Anna ordered that a red flag be flown. It was a signal to the Texans to surrender or be killed upon defeat. William B. Travis and Jim Bowie answered this signal by firing a cannon from the Alamo. Bowie had brought 25 men with him to fight. They refused to surrender. Santa Anna then attacked. The **Battle of the Alamo** had begun.

The exact number of Alamo defenders is unknown, but they were clearly outnumbered. They sent Juan Seguín and several messengers for help, but no help came.

Santa Anna ordered his army to set up ladders against the Alamo and climb over the walls. When the battle was over on March 6, all of the Texan soldiers were dead. Historians believe that between 189 and 250 Texans, both Tejanos and new arrivals, died at the Alamo along with 600 to 800 Mexican soldiers.

READING CHECK

What advantage did the Mexican army have over the Texans at the Alamo?

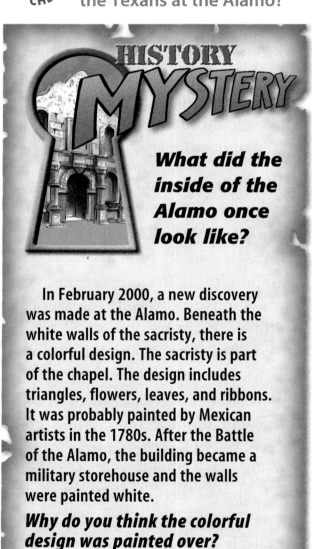

HISTORY MYSTERY

What did the inside of the Alamo once look like?

In February 2000, a new discovery was made at the Alamo. Beneath the white walls of the sacristy, there is a colorful design. The sacristy is part of the chapel. The design includes triangles, flowers, leaves, and ribbons. It was probably painted by Mexican artists in the 1780s. After the Battle of the Alamo, the building became a military storehouse and the walls were painted white.

Why do you think the colorful design was painted over?

The Alamo

The Alamo has been many things: a mission, a fort, a museum. When it was built in 1718, the mission San Antonio de Valero was much bigger than it is today. The diagram here shows what the Alamo looked like at the time of the battle in 1836.

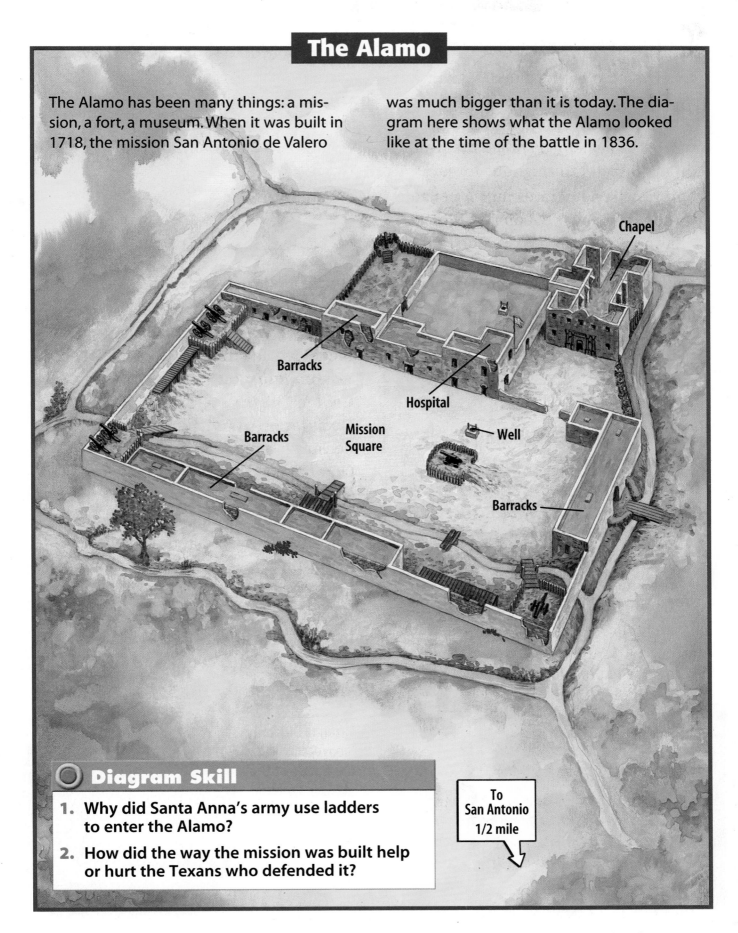

Chapel

Barracks

Hospital

Barracks

Mission Square

Well

Barracks

To San Antonio 1/2 mile

⦿ Diagram Skill

1. **Why did Santa Anna's army use ladders to enter the Alamo?**

2. **How did the way the mission was built help or hurt the Texans who defended it?**

AFTER THE BATTLE

When the battle ended, **Suzanna Dickenson** and her infant daughter, Angelina, were among the few survivors. They helped spread the word of the disaster throughout Texas.

Francisco Ruiz was mayor of San Antonio during the Alamo battle. Read how he described the reaction of the Mexican army after the battle was over.

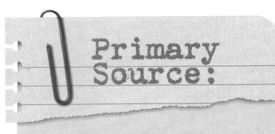

Primary Source:

Excerpt from **The Alamo Remembered: Tejano Accounts and Perspectives**
— *By Timothy M. Matovina, published in 1995.*

*"The **gallantry** of the few Texians who defended the Alamo was really wondered at by the Mexican army. Even the generals were **astonished** at their … resistance and how dearly victory had been bought."*

How does Ruiz describe the defenders of the Alamo?

gallantry: bravery
astonished: surprised

Declaring Independence

While the Battle of the Alamo was still being fought, Texas delegates met at a convention in the town of **Washington-on-the-Brazos**. There, George Childress wrote the **Texas Declaration of Independence** declaring separation from Mexico. On March 2, 1836, the delegates signed the declaration.

A **constitution** for an independent Texas was prepared at the convention. A constitution is a plan of government.

David G. Burnet and **Lorenzo de Zavala** (day zah VAH lah) were chosen to serve as president and vice president until Texans could vote for their own leaders.

Suzanna Dickenson (above) survived the **Battle of the Alamo**. Lorenzo de Zavala (right) became the first vice president of Texas.

The Goliad Massacre

After the Battle of the Alamo, Sam Houston took control of the Texas army. Meanwhile, about 300 Texans led by **James W. Fannin**, waited at Goliad. Fannin knew that Santa Anna's troops were headed there.

Just outside Goliad, there was a brief battle and Fannin gave up. He and his men were jailed at Presidio La Bahia. Santa Anna then commanded that all the Texans be killed.

This event became known as the **Goliad Massacre**. A massacre is the brutal killing of many people.

READING CHECK What was the purpose of the Texas Declaration of Independence?

PUTTING IT TOGETHER

Texans who fought in the Texas Revolution are remembered as heroes. Though they were defeated at the Alamo and Goliad, the struggle for Texans' independence continued. Santa Anna did not recognize the Texas Declaration of Independence.

James W. Fannin

Review and Assess

1. Write one sentence for each of the vocabulary words:

   Battle of the Alamo

   constitution

   Goliad Massacre

   Texas Declaration of Independence

2. Who was William B. Travis?
3. Analyze the importance of the Alamo in Texas history.
4. What were the **economic** reasons behind Santa Anna's actions?
5. What were some of the **causes** and **effects** of the Battle of the Alamo?

Activities

Suppose you were at the Alamo just before it was attacked. **Write** a message to other Texans asking for aid.

• •

Suppose you were a delegate at the convention in Washington-on-the-Brazos. The delegates have asked you to write the Texas Declaration of Independence. **Write** a paragraph declaring why you think Texas should be independent from Mexico.

Making Decisions

Making **decisions** is a skill that people use every day. Making a decision is the same as making a choice. Decisions may be simple, like deciding what clothes to wear, or more difficult, like deciding where to live. Whether simple or difficult, to make a good decision you have to know what your goal is.

> **VOCABULARY**
>
> decision

LEARN THE SKILL

Follow these steps to make a decision.

1. **Identify a goal.**

   Here is an example. Jimmy wants to join a school club. His goal is to learn a new skill. Students are starting a chess club and a poetry club. So, Jimmy must decide which club to join.

2. **Gather information.**

   Jimmy asks students from each group what activities they plan to hold. The chess club will practice twice a week during lunch hour. They will also attend competitions in different cities once a month. The poetry club meets after school. They promise to print a book of poems and hold readings at the local library.

3. **Identify the options.**

   If Jimmy joins the chess club he could learn more about the game, meet new people at competitions, and travel to other cities. If he joins the poetry club, he could have his poems printed and read them in front of audiences at the library.

4. **Predict the consequences of each option.**

   Each option has a consequence, or result. Playing chess is a skill Jimmy would like to learn. However, it would mean a lot of practice. Also, he is not sure if he can travel to all the competitions.

   Jimmy likes to write poetry and would enjoy seeing his poems in a book. But the club meets after school and he

might miss the bus home. Also, he is nervous about reading aloud in front of an audience.

5. **Make the decision that best helps you reach your goal. Check your decision with your parents, teacher, or other adult.**

Although Jimmy enjoys writing poetry, his goal is to learn a new skill. He wants to sign up for the chess club and attend as many competitions as he can. Jimmy checks with his parents before making a final decision.

TRY THE SKILL

Suppose you and your parents are planning a day trip somewhere in our state. Where would you and your parents go? You are mainly interested in learning more about Texas.

You live between two possible locations. The first is the Alamo Mission in San Antonio. Here you can tour the museum and explore the grounds. Your other choice is Big Thicket National Preserve in the Piney Woods. On this trip, you can canoe, hike, or watch wildlife such as hawks and alligators.

One thing to keep in mind is the weather. It has been raining lately and you might have to cancel a trip to the forest. But if it rains on your visit to the Alamo, you can go inside the museum.

Follow the steps on the previous page to make your decision. Then answer the questions below.

1. What is your goal?

2. What information would help you make a decision?

3. What are the possible options and their consequences?

4. What is the best choice and why?

5. Talk to your parents about your decision. How can decision-making skills help you in your daily life?

EXTEND THE SKILL

Understanding how to make decisions can also help you to understand history. People in the past needed to make decisions just as we do. The choices may have been different, but the process was the same. In the last lesson, you read about the Battle of the Alamo and the events that followed. Look back at the lesson to answer these questions.

- What decision did the delegates make at the convention in 1836?

- What consequences do you think resulted from their decision?

- How can understanding the decision-making process help you better understand history?

Independence at Last

Lesson Outline
- On the Road to Battle
- The Battle of San Jacinto

VOCABULARY

Runaway Scrape

Battle of San Jacinto

treaty

Treaty of Velasco

republic

PEOPLE

Sam Houston

Antonio López de Santa Anna

Erastus Deaf Smith

Hendrick Arnold

Henry Karnes

READING STRATEGY

Copy the chart below. Fill in the results of the Battle of San Jacinto.

BUILD BACKGROUND

On April 22, 1836, General **Sam Houston** prepared to fight for Texas's independence. He told his men, "Victory is certain! Trust in God and fear not! And remember the Alamo! Remember Goliad!" Houston's confidence helped lead the Texas army to victory over **Antonio López de Santa Anna.**

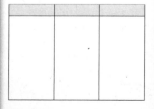

ON THE ROAD TO BATTLE

As the Mexican army made its way east from San Antonio, thousands of settlers panicked. People packed up what they could and fled their homes. Later, this flight would be known as the **Runaway Scrape**.

Houston Takes Control

General Houston learned from his scout, **Erastus Deaf Smith**, that Santa Anna and his troops were heading toward Gonzales. Houston ordered that Gonzales be burned, and that everyone there leave.

General Houston led 800 Texas soldiers to land along the Brazos River. For two weeks, he collected supplies and trained his army. An African American scout named **Hendrick Arnold** pretended to be a runaway slave. He could then get into Mexican camps and send information to Houston.

Houston headed south to the **San Jacinto River** to meet the Mexican army as it marched eastward. Find this river on the map.

The San Jacinto Memorial (left) was built to honor those who fought in the **Battle of San Jacinto**. At 570 feet tall, it overlooks the prairie where the battle was fought.

A Deadly Error

Santa Anna thought winning would be easy. He set up camp only one mile from the Texans' camp. He didn't tell his men to watch out for Texan soldiers.

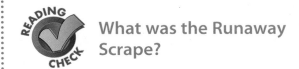

What was the Runaway Scrape?

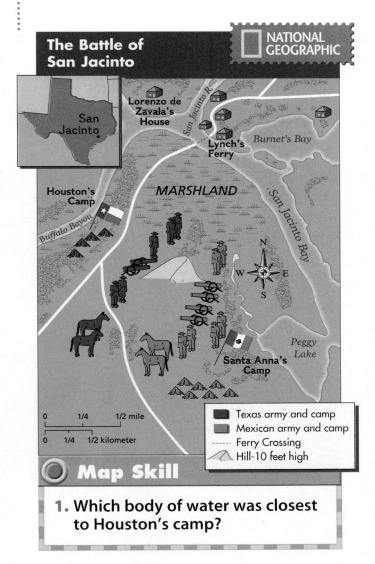

The Battle of San Jacinto

NATIONAL GEOGRAPHIC

Lorenzo de Zavala's House
San Jacinto R.
San Jacinto
Lynch's Ferry
Burnet's Bay
Houston's Camp
MARSHLAND
San Jacinto Bay
Buffalo Bayou
N W E S
Peggy Lake
Santa Anna's Camp

0   1/4   1/2 mile
0   1/4   1/2 kilometer

- Texas army and camp
- Mexican army and camp
- - - - Ferry Crossing
- Hill-10 feet high

Map Skill

1. Which body of water was closest to Houston's camp?

147

THE BATTLE OF SAN JACINTO

General Cós and about 540 more soldiers joined Santa Anna's men at dawn on April 21. Meanwhile, General Houston sent scouts Erastus Deaf Smith and **Henry Karnes** to destroy a bridge over nearby Simms Bayou. This bridge was the only link to the area. Now the Mexicans had no way to retreat from battle.

Remember the Alamo!

By afternoon the Texans were preparing for battle. Meanwhile, many of Santa Anna's soldiers were napping after their midday meal. General Houston led the Texas army out of the woods to attack. When they got close to the enemy, the Texan soldiers shouted "Remember the Alamo!" and "Remember Goliad!" as they opened fire. The Mexican army was completely taken by surprise.

The Texans chased Mexican troops into the bayou, where many drowned. When the battle was over, more than 600 Mexicans had died. Fewer than 10 Texans had fallen. After only 18 minutes, the **Battle of San Jacinto** was won.

El Presidente Is Taken

That night, Santa Anna dressed as a common soldier. He spent hours hiding in tall grass. Texan soldiers captured him the next day. But they

This painting of Santa Anna surrendering to Sam Houston hangs in the Texas capitol building in Austin.

The State Preservation Board

didn't know who he was. As they reached camp, some Mexican prisoners called out, "El Presidente!" Only then did the Texans realize that the man they had captured was Santa Anna. The Texan soldiers expected Santa Anna to be killed. But Houston refused. Instead, Houston decided to trade Santa Anna's freedom for Texas's independence.

Treaty of Velasco

Sam Houston's injuries required a doctor's attention. While the general was being cared for, President Burnet met with Santa Anna. They signed a **treaty** at the town of **Velasco** that ended the war. A treaty is a formal agreement between countries.

In the **Treaty of Velasco**, Santa Anna promised to remove Mexican troops from Texas. He agreed to trade prisoners of war. He also promised never to fight against Texas again. Both Burnet and Santa Anna agreed that the southern border of the newly independent Texas was at the Rio Grande.

Santa Anna also signed a secret treaty. In it he promised that the Mexican government would recognize Texas as an independent country.

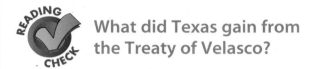 **What did Texas gain from the Treaty of Velasco?**

PUTTING IT TOGETHER

At the Battle of San Jacinto, Texans won independence from Mexico. In 1836 Texas became a **republic**. A republic is a form of government in which people choose leaders to represent them. As you will read, Mexicans and Texans would continue to disagree in the years to come.

Review and Assess

1. Write one sentence for each vocabulary word:

   Battle of San Jacinto   **republic**

   Runaway Scrape   **treaty**

   Treaty of Velasco

2. Who was Antonio López de Santa Anna?

3. Describe how Sam Houston was a good leader for Texas.

4. Explain how the **government** of Texas became a republic.

5. Identify the **causes** and **effects** of the Battle of San Jacinto.

How did geography affect the Texas victory at San Jacinto?

• •

Suppose you are Sam Houston. **Write** a journal entry about sparing Santa Anna's life.

Independence

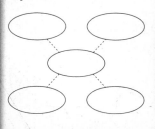
Find out!

Why did other European colonies want their independence?

Lesson Outline

• Liberty in the Western Hemisphere
• Independence for Mexico

VOCABULARY

American Revolution
Battle of Boyaca
Plan of Iguala

PEOPLE

George Washington
Miguel Hidalgo
José María Morelos
Augustín de Iturbide
Simón Bolívar

READING STRATEGY

Draw a word map like this one. Write the name of one key person from this lesson in each space.

BUILD BACKGROUND

Different European countries built colonies in the Western Hemisphere. Over time, these colonies desired to be free from European rule. In 1776 the thirteen British colonies were the first to declare independence. **George Washington** led the colonies' army against England in the **American Revolution**. These colonies became the United States of America.

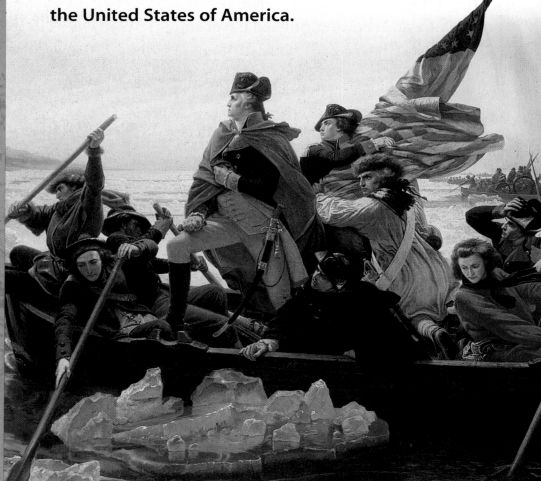

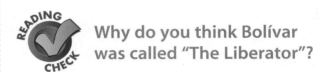
LIBERTY IN THE WESTERN HEMISPHERE

During the 1800s other colonies in the Western Hemisphere also began to fight against foreign rule.

Simón Bolívar

Simón Bolívar was born in 1783 in Caracas, **Venezuela**. Bolívar wanted to improve life in Venezuela. This meant freedom from Spain.

In 1810 Bolívar joined a rebel army that seized Caracas and declared independence from Spain. But the Spanish soon recaptured the city. Again, in 1813 Bolívar led the army against the Spanish. He succeeded. Venezuelans began to call him "The Liberator." The Spanish sent more troops. By 1815 Bolívar had to escape to Jamaica. While in Jamaica he asked both England and the United States for aid.

Bolívar then turned to the small Republic of Haiti for help. Haiti had gained its independence from France in 1804. The small republic gave Bolívar money and weapons.

In 1816 Bolívar returned to lead the fight in Venezuela. In 1819 he freed the territory of New Grenada at the **Battle of Boyaca**. The new state was named the **Republic of Colombia**. On December 17, 1819, Bolívar was named president. But the Spanish army still had control of Caracas. In June 1821, Bolívar and his army of 6,500 troops defeated the Spanish army in a major battle. Venezuela was now free.

READING CHECK Why do you think Bolívar was called "The Liberator"?

Simón Bolívar (right) led an army to free Venezuela from Spanish rule. Washington and his army cross the Delaware river (left) during the American Revolution.

Miguel Hidalgo's speech known as the "Cry of Dolores" began the Mexican fight for freedom from Spain.

INDEPENDENCE FOR MEXICO

Mexico had been under Spanish rule since 1521. But after a revolution that lasted 11 years, Mexico won independence from Spain in September 1821.

The Cry of Dolores

For 300 years, Spaniards ruled Mexico, as part of Nueva España or New Spain. Mexico was the richest of Spain's colonies. Its economy depended on silver mines and large farms. Nearly half of the money made in Mexico went to Spain. As a result, few Mexicans became rich. Most were poor.

In 1803 a priest named **Miguel Hidalgo** went to the church in **Dolores** in central Mexico. There he worked to help Native American and Mestizo farmers. He showed them how to grow olives and grapes and run small industries such as brick making. However, Spanish government workers soon destroyed the crops and did not allow industry. Mexico would have to buy these things from Spain.

Hidalgo soon realized that as long as Spain ruled Mexico, life for the poor would not improve. On September 16, 1810, Hidalgo gave a famous speech at his church. This speech became known as the "Cry of Dolores." It was the beginning of Mexico's war for independence.

In 1811 Hidalgo and his army of men, women, and children were defeated. Hidalgo was killed. **José María Morelos** (hoh SAY muh REE uh moh RAY lahs), a mestizo priest continued the struggle. Morelos was killed in 1815.

Agustín de Iturbide (a goos TEEN day ee TOOR bee day), a military officer, finally won independence for Mexico.

Iturbide had been chosen to lead the Spanish forces. But he switched sides, hoping to win power for himself.

In 1821, Iturbide wrote the **Plan of Iguala** (ee HWA lah). Under this plan Mexico would be ruled by a king and would remain a Roman Catholic country. It also promised equal rights for all Mexicans. On September 27, 1821, Iturbide and his army entered Mexico City, and Mexico became an independent country. However, on July 25, 1822, Iturbide seized power and made himself emperor.

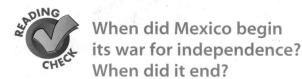 **When did Mexico begin its war for independence? When did it end?**

PUTTING IT TOGETHER

The desire for freedom from foreign rule spread throughout the Western Hemisphere. The thirteen British colonies became the United States of America. Mexico and the Republic of Colombia freed themselves from Spain by 1821. Now Mexico would have the freedom to make decisions about colonization in Texas.

Review and Assess

1. Write one sentence for each of the vocabulary words:

   American Revolution   Plan of Iguala

2. Who was Miguel Hidalgo?

3. Analyze reasons why European colonies in the Western Hemisphere wanted their Independence.

4. What was the **economic** reason for Spain to hold on to Mexico?

5. Why do you think the Republic of Haiti chose to help Bolívar?

Create a time line based on the information in this lesson. List major dates in the fight for independence.

. . . .

Suppose you were in Mexico in the 1800s. **Write** a speech that persuades people to understand why Mexico should be free from Spanish rule.

VOCABULARY REVIEW

Number a sheet of paper from 1 to 5. Beside each number write the word or term from the list below that matches the description.

bilingual   **constitution**

empresario   **subsistence farming**

treaty

1. growing crops to survive, not to sell
2. a plan of government
3. a formal agreement between countries
4. a person given land by a government to sell to settlers
5. people who are able to speak two languages

CHAPTER COMPREHENSION

6. Who were "The Old Three Hundred"?
7. Who were Don Martín de León and Patricia de la Garza de Léon?
8. Who was Augustín de Iturbide?
9. Where did early colonists in Texas live? What type of homes did they build?
10. What cash crops did farmers grow?
11. Why did Stephen F. Austin return to the United States in November 1835?
12. What was the Alamo called before the Texas Revolution? What does the name mean?
13. In addition to the Treaty of Velasco, Santa Anna signed a secret treaty. What did it say?

 ## SKILL REVIEW

14. **Reading/Thinking Skill** Suppose you and your friends are planning to spend an afternoon together. You can either ride your bikes to the town park, or you can visit a local fair in your neighborhood that has rides and games. Make a decision about what to do. What is your goal?
15. **Reading/Thinking Skill** How will you go about gathering information?
16. **Reading/Thinking Skill** What are your options?
17. **Reading/Thinking Skill** What decision will you make?
18. **Reading/Thinking Skill** Do you think you made a good decision? Why?

USING A TIME LINE

1800	1810	1820	1830	1840	1850

1803
Louisiana Purchase

1821
Mexico wins independence from Spain; Stephen F. Austin takes over Austin colony

1825
300 families living in Austin colony

1830
Mexico stops immigration to Texas from the United States

1836
Battles of the Alamo and San Jacinto; Texas becomes a republic

19. How many years after Mexico won independence from Spain did Texas win independence from Mexico?

20. What is important about the year 1830?

Activity

Learning About History A newspaper holds a lot of stories written by many people. As a class create a newspaper from the 1830s. Divide the class into groups of five or six. Each group chooses a role to play: settler, empresario, people of the Mexican government, Santa Anna, or others. Then write up an interesting account of an event from the chapter. Decide if your account will be a narrative, a comparison, or steps in a process. When each group is finished, assemble each of the stories in a class newspaper.

Foldables

Use your *Foldable* to review what you have learned about the Texas Revolution. As you look at the Alamo on the front of your *Foldable*, mentally recall the events that occurred before, during, and after the Battle of the Alamo. Review your notes on the inside and back of your *Foldable* to check your memory and responses. Record any questions that you have on your *Foldable*, and discuss them with classmates or review the chapter to find answers.

Chapter

4

THE Big IDEAS ABOUT...

The Journey to Statehood

You have read that after years of Mexican rule, Texas won its independence during the Texas Revolution. Yet, as you know, Texas is now part of the United States of America. Texas was an independent country for nearly nine years. In this chapter you will read about the many challenges Texas faced as a republic and about its early years as part of the United States.

TEXAS BECOMES A REPUBLIC

Texas becomes an independent nation with its own government.

THE LONE STAR STATE

After nine years as an independent republic, Texas becomes the 28th state of the United States of America.

AT WAR WITH MEXICO

Tensions between the United States and Mexico over the Texas border lead to war.

SETTLERS MOVE TO TEXAS

Pioneers come to Texas from other states and around the world to establish new settlements.

Foldables

Make this Foldable study guide and use it to record what you learn about Texas's journey to becoming a state.

1. Fold a sheet of large paper in half like a hamburger.
2. Fold this folded paper in half like a hamburger again.
3. This will result in four rectangles that are equal in size.
4. Draw the Lone Star Flag on the front of this folded book.

The Republic of Texas

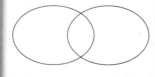

Who were the leaders of the Republic of Texas?

Lesson Outline

• New Challenges
• Presidents of Texas
• Houston's Second Term

VOCABULARY

Texas Rangers
congress
debt
term

PEOPLE

Sam Houston
Philip Bowles
Mirabeau B. Lamar

READING STRATEGY

Draw a diagram like this one. Write some of the differences and similarities between the first two presidents of Texas.

BUILD BACKGROUND

On March 2, 1836, at Washington-on-the-Brazos, after years of Spanish and then Mexican rule, Texas became a republic. Texas was now an independent country. It formed its own government. The government had the right to declare war, make laws, and raise money through taxes.

NEW CHALLENGES

Texas faced many challenges. It had very little money. Mexico also continued to try to recapture the land it had lost. Texas could not pay for a large army to defend itself. So, the leaders of the republic turned to the **Texas Rangers** for help.

The Texas Rangers were formed in 1835. They were farmers, ranchers, and townspeople who volunteered to defend the republic. Today the Texas Rangers are part of our state police force.

A Capital and a Flag

In the new republic, Texans voted for their own president and members of their own **congress**. Congress is the branch of government that makes laws.

The leaders of the new republic needed a capital city. In 1836, they chose the town of **Columbia** on the Brazos River. Later that year, the capital was moved to the larger city of Houston. Some Texans thought Houston was not close enough to the western part of Texas. So, in 1839 the capital was moved once again. The leaders chose Waterloo Village. They renamed it **Austin**.

The first leaders of the Republic of Texas also chose a flag. A lone star was chosen to represent the new republic. The Lone Star flag is still the flag of Texas today.

The capital at Columbia (left). Joanna Troutman made the first Lone Star flag in 1836 (top right). Sarah Dodson also made a flag for Texas (below).

What were some problems faced by the leaders of the new republic?

The Witte Museum

PRESIDENTS OF TEXAS

In 1836 **Sam Houston** became president of the Republic of Texas. In his first speech as president, he reminded Texans that independence was only the first step. They would continue to struggle in order to make Texas strong:

> "*A country situated like ours is* [surrounded] *with difficulties . . . Nothing but . . . patriotism, guided . . . by wisdom, can . . . surmount* [overcome] *the difficulties with which our . . . path is obstructed* [blocked]"

As president, Houston wanted to pay off the republic's large **debt**, or amount of money owed to others.

Texas had borrowed money to pay for military supplies during the revolution. The new government owed so much money that it did not even have money to buy paper for writing official letters!

Houston and Native Americans

Most Texans feared and disliked Native Americans because of the fighting between them. However, Houston admired Native Americans. He had lived with the Cherokee in Tennessee for three years. Houston thought it was wrong to force Native Americans off the land.

Sam Houston had signed a treaty with Cherokee Chief **Philip Bowles** during the revolution. Bowles agreed that the Cherokee would not attack settlers. In return Texas would give the Cherokee the right to live on land in East Texas. As president, Houston tried to turn this treaty into a law. The Texas congress refused.

Chief Bowles and President Houston tried to help the Cherokee.

Mirabeau B. Lamar

In 1838, **Mirabeau B. Lamar** (MIHR uh boh luh MAHR) became the second president of the republic. Lamar did not want Texas to join the United States. He thought Texans could build a strong nation on their own.

Lamar believed that education was the basis for a strong Texas. To do this he set aside land on which to build schools and colleges. Today Lamar is remembered as the "father of Texas education."

Lamar and Native Americans

To try to solve Texas's debt, president Lamar printed extra paper money. So much of it was printed, that the paper money soon became almost worthless. Lamar also bought ships for the Texas navy. Because of these purchases the republic's debt continued to grow.

Lamar wanted to take all the land in Texas away from Native Americans. To do this, the Texas army fought the Battle of Neches in 1839.

Chief Bowles and many other Cherokee were killed. Cherokee villages were burned. Then the Texas army drove the survivors across the Red River to what is today Oklahoma.

 READING CHECK Compare and contrast the beliefs of Houston and Lamar.

The Republic of Texas "redback" $50 note (below) was printed by Mirabeau B. Lamar (above).

HOUSTON'S SECOND TERM

In 1841, Sam Houston was chosen president of Texas for a second **term**. A term is a limited period of time. In Texas at this time, presidents served for three years. During his second term, Houston worked to reduce government debt and spending. He cut dozens of government jobs and lowered the pay of government officials. He even cut his own pay in half!

At the same time, Houston had to turn his attention toward Mexico. Santa Anna was threatening to start a war with Texas once again.

As you have read, Houston wanted to make Texas part of the United States. During his second term, Houston worked towards this goal. If Texas became part of the United States, it would be protected by the United States Army. If Texas remained independent, Mexico might try to take back some of Texas's land. Read what Houston wrote in a letter to a former President of the United States.

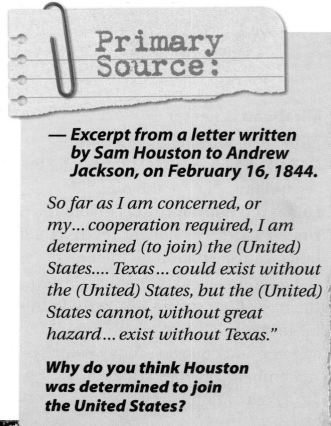

Primary Source:

— *Excerpt from a letter written by Sam Houston to Andrew Jackson, on February 16, 1844.*

So far as I am concerned, or my... cooperation required, I am determined (to join) the (United) States.... Texas... could exist without the (United) States, but the (United) States cannot, without great hazard... exist without Texas."

Why do you think Houston was determined to join the United States?

hazard: harm

Houston's home is now a museum in Huntsville.

Continued Service to Texas

Houston's second term as president ended in December 1844. Under the Texas Constitution he would not be allowed to run for president again. Houston moved to Huntsville and worked on plans to build a house. Still, he continued to support the fair treatment of Native Americans. In public, Houston greeted Native Americans when others would not.

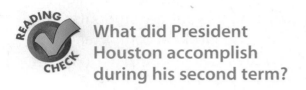

What did President Houston accomplish during his second term?

PUTTING IT TOGETHER

The Texas Republic lasted only nine years. During this time, a flag was chosen and land was set aside for schools. A capital city was chosen and named after Stephen F. Austin. Sam Houston became president again in 1841. He continued to work to make Texas part of the United States.

Star of the Republic Museum

Review and Assess

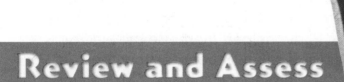

1. Write one sentence for each of the vocabulary words:

   congress   debt

   term

2. Who were the Texas Rangers?

3. Compare and contrast the first two presidents of the Republic of Texas.

4. Explain why Sam Houston might have wanted to pay off the republic's debts.

5. List some reasons the republic's debt continued to grow under President Lamar.

Activities

In 1844, Sam Houston wrote a letter explaining why Texas should be a part of the United States. Using the map on pages R16–R17, create a scale strip. Measure the distance Sam Houston's letter traveled from Austin to Andrew Jackson near Nashville in Tennessee.

• •

Suppose you had to design a new flag for Texas. First draw a picture of your flag. Then **write** a paragraph that explains what the colors, symbols, or drawings on your flag stand for. Tell why they represent Texas.

Being a Good Citizen
Saying Yes to Helping Others

Pablo Veliz mentors at Say Sí, an art program for kids in San Antonio. A mentor is a kind of teacher. Say Sí stands for "San Antonio Youth Yes!" In Spanish, *sí* means *yes*. On Saturdays about 45 young artists meet at the Say Sí art studio with 10 teenaged mentors. Pablo helps younger students draw, paint, and sculpt. They can also work on computer projects such as designing Web sites.

"I don't do their work for them," says Pablo. "They decide what to do. I help them do it." The students make all kinds of art projects. Desaray Elizondo has done everything from watercolors to woodcarving. One project she worked on was making furniture. When she and other Say Sí artists made wooden stools, Pablo helped them use the electric saw and other power tools safely. Students show their art projects at the Say Sí art gallery several times a year. When a new show opens, people from all over San Antonio come to see and buy the students' artworks. Sometimes everything sells out on opening night.

❝ I want to inspire others…❞

San Antonio

164

Some of the money goes to buy more art supplies for Say Sí. The artists keep the rest. Desaray sold her wooden stool.

"It was so exciting," she says. "I didn't care about the money. I was just so happy someone actually wanted to buy something of mine. Someday I would like to be a mentor like Pablo. I want to inspire others just as my mentors have inspired me." Pablo enjoys working with the students. "When I was their age," he says, "I really wish someone had encouraged me in my art work. I want to do that for them."

Be a Good Citizen

Making Connections

- **What are some ways people of different ages in your community help each other?**

- **How did people in the San Antonio community show their support for Say Sí and the arts?**

Talk About It!

- **How did older students mentor younger students at Say Sí?**

- **What are some advantages of having young people teach each other?**

Act On It!

In the Classroom

With your classmates, decide on a subject that you would like to learn more about. Ask your teacher for help in choosing a mentor. Invite your mentor to come and speak to your class.

In the Community

With your parents' or teacher's help, identify an after-school program in your community. What are some of the ways in which mentors could be helpful to kids in these programs? Write a letter describing your ideas to the leader of one program.

The Lone Star State

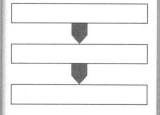

What events led to Texas becoming part of the United States?

VOCABULARY

Manifest Destiny
annexation
resolution
senator

PEOPLE

Anson Jones
James K. Polk
James Pinckney
Henderson

READING STRATEGY

Draw a chart like this one. List the sequence of events that led to Texas becoming part of the United States.

Lesson Outline

- Manifest Destiny
- Statehood or Independence?
- Senator Sam Houston

BUILD BACKGROUND

By 1840, the United States had accepted Texas as a country. However, Mexico did not.

In 1845, when Texas became the 28th state, a new United States flag was created. It had 28 stars.

MANIFEST DESTINY

A new idea called **Manifest Destiny** was sweeping through the United States by the 1840s. The idea was that the United States should move its borders west to the Pacific Ocean. It should also move its borders south to the Rio Grande. This meant that Texas would soon become part of the United States. This would require the **annexation** (an ek SAY shun) of Texas. Annexation means adding a territory to a country.

Look at the map below to see how the United States was growing in 1840. People in the United States knew Mexico was angry about losing Texas. Many feared war with Mexico.

Problems for Mexico

Although Mexico was free from Spanish rule in 1821, it faced new problems. Government leaders began fighting one another for power. As a result, Mexico could not build a strong government.

During the war with Texas, Mexico lost land, money, and supplies. The economy of Mexico was weak.

 **What is Manifest Destiny?**

NATIONAL GEOGRAPHIC
The United States: 1840

CANADA

Oregon Country

Unorganized Territory

Iowa Territory

Wisconsin Territory

MI

VT NH ME

NY MA

RI

PA CT NJ DE

IL IN OH

VA MD

MO KY

TN NC

AR SC

MS AL GA

LA

Florida Territory

MEXICO

THE REPUBLIC OF TEXAS

PACIFIC OCEAN

ATLANTIC OCEAN

Gulf of Mexico

Free state
Territory
Slave state

0   250   500 miles
0   250   500 kilometers
Albers Conic Equal-Area Projection

Map Skill

1. How many states were "free states"? List three.

2. What countries bordered the United States?

STATEHOOD OR INDEPENDENCE?

You have read that President Houston was for the annexation of Texas. Many Texans did not want Texas to join the United States. However, many other Texans did. Some who favored annexation had family in the United States. These Texans wanted to be a part of the same country. Others noted that the United States had a strong army and a strong money system. Texas had neither.

Some Texans, such as former President Lamar, wanted Texas to remain an independent nation. They believed that soon Texas could use its own resources to become rich. But if Texas joined the United States, they feared Texas would have to give up its land and its independence.

The Debate About Texas

The question of annexing Texas also became part of the debate about slavery in the United States. At that time, the United States Congress was equally divided between states that allowed slavery and those that did not. Texas allowed slavery. Adding Texas might upset the balance in the United States Congress between free states and slave states.

POLK AND DALLAS.

Anson Jones (left) of Texas and James K. Polk (above) of the United States both supported **annexation**.

The 28th State

In 1844 both the United States and Texas chose presidents that were for annexation. Texans chose **Anson Jones** as their president. In the United States, **James K. Polk**, a friend of Sam Houston, was chosen.

On March 1, 1845 the United States Congress passed a joint **resolution** [rez uh LOO shun], or decision. The resolution said that Texas could become a state. Texas would have to give up its forts and other military buildings. Texas would also have to raise money to pay its debt.

On July 4, 1845, President Jones and the Texas congress held a meeting in Austin. They had to decide about statehood. But before the delegates voted, Mexico tried to make a deal with Texas. Mexico did not want Texas to become a state. This would make the United States grow larger and stronger. In exchange for peace, Mexico would agree to accept the Republic of Texas. Mexico wanted Texas to remain independent and as a result—alone. Texans turned down the deal.

In October more than 4,000 Texans voted to become a state. Only 267 voted against it. Texans also voted to approve a state constitution.

On December 29, 1845, Texas became the 28th state of the United States. Anson Jones stepped down as the last president of the Republic of Texas on February 19, 1846. A governor would now lead Texas. **James Pinckney Henderson** was our state's first governor.

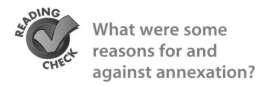

READING CHECK What were some reasons for and against annexation?

Exploring ECONOMICS

How Did Texas Get Out of Debt?

When Texas became a republic, its debt was $1.25 million. By 1845, Texas's debt had reached $9.95 million. In an agreement with the United States, Texas gave up a third of its land. In exchange, the United States gave Texas enough money to use for paying its debt.

Activity

Suppose you want a CD that costs $16. You have only $4, so you borrow the rest from your sister. If your weekly allowance is $1.50, how long will it take you to pay your debt?

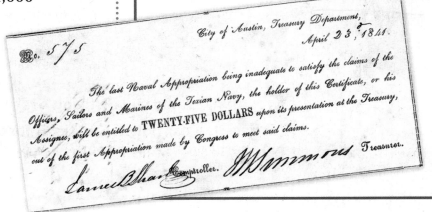

Six Flags Over Texas

Have you ever heard the phrase "Six flags over Texas"? It refers to the flags of the six nations that have ruled Texas since the first European exploration.

1519–1685; 1690–1821

Early Spanish explorers claimed the land of Texas for Spain. They left Texas in 1685 and returned a few years later.

1685–1690

La Salle, a French explorer, claimed Texas for France. Spain soon reclaimed the land.

1821–1836

After Mexico won its independence from Spain, the Mexican flag became the third to fly over Texas.

Star of the Republic Museum

1836–1845

Texas became an independent nation after the Texas Revolution. The Lone Star flag is still our state flag today.

1861–1865

Texas joined with the Confederate States of America during the Civil War. This was the first Confederate flag that flew over our state.

1845–1861; 1865–present

The American flag with 28 stars flew when Texas became the 28th state. Our 50-star flag flies throughout our country today.

Chart Skill

1. **If Texas did not become a state, what flag do you think would still be flying over Texas?**

2. **Which flag has flown over Texas for the longest continuous period?**

170

SENATOR SAM HOUSTON

Now that Texas was a state, it needed representatives in Washington, D.C. Sam Houston was chosen as a **senator**. A senator is a member of our nation's Congress. Sam Houston served as a senator from 1846 to 1859.

In Washington, D.C., Senator Houston continued to stand up for what he thought was right and helped the United States keep Texas secure in the coming years.

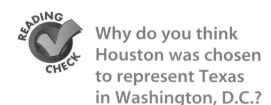 Why do you think Houston was chosen to represent Texas in Washington, D.C.?

PUTTING IT TOGETHER

Both Texas and the United States had to weigh many issues before deciding to unite. Among these issues were slavery and Manifest Destiny. Mexico was unhappy about annexation. The United States would soon find itself at war with its new southern neighbor.

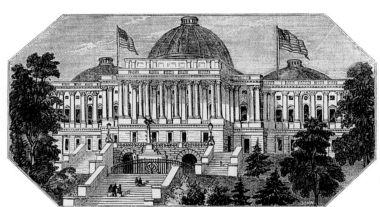

A painting of the Washington, D.C., Capitol as it looked in 1851.

Review and Assess

1. Write one sentence for each of the vocabulary words:

   annexation   resolution

2. What is Manifest Destiny?

3. Describe events leading to Texas joining the United States.

4. Analyze the reasons why Mexico didn't want Texas to join the United States.

5. Why did Texans want to join the United States?

Using the map on page 167, list the states that shared a border with Texas in 1840.

· ·

Suppose you lived in 1845. **Write** why you would or would not want Texas to be a state.

Reading Circle and Line Graphs

Suppose you wanted to know the population of our state and how it changed over time. It might be hard to draw a conclusion from a lot of different numbers. A **graph** can help you draw conclusions. Graphs are special diagrams that show information in a clear way. By presenting facts in a picture, they tell you a lot with only a few words.

<table>
<tr><td>VOCABULARY

graph
circle graph
line graph</td></tr>
</table>

LEARN THE SKILL

Look at the graph on this page as you follow the steps.

1. **Identify the type of graph.**
   The graph on this page is a **circle graph**. This kind of graph can show you how the parts of something make up or fit into the whole. Because each part looks like a slice of pie, a circle graph is sometimes called a pie graph.

   The graph on the next page is a **line graph**. It shows you how a piece of information changes over time. A line graph often shows an increase or decrease in number.

2. **Identify the graph's title.**
   The title of the circle graph on this page is "Texas Population 1850." That means this graph shows the population for different groups living in Texas in 1850.

3. **Study any labels on the graph.**
   Labels on the circle graph include "American and European" and

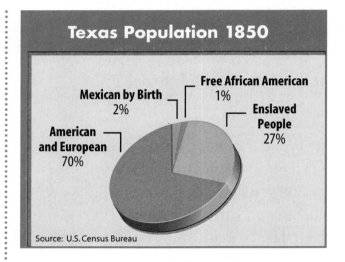

Texas Population 1850

Mexican by Birth 2%
Free African American 1%
American and European 70%
Enslaved People 27%

Source: U.S. Census Bureau

"Free African American." The graph's "slices" show different groups of people who lived in Texas in 1850.

4. **Compare facts and figures.**
   You can tell that the largest population group was "American and European" because this is the largest "slice" of the graph. The number 70 means that this group makes up seventy percent of the population. How does the circle graph help you to make a conclusion about the population of Texas in 1850?

TRY THE SKILL

Look at the graph on this page. Trace the line on the graph with your finger. Then study the labels. Use the graph to answer the following questions.

1. What kind of graph is it?

2. What time period does the graph show?

3. What does each dot stand for?

4. How does the population of Texas change?

5. How do graphs make it easier to understand history?

EXTEND THE SKILL

Suppose that the number of students in your school is 150 in the year 2004; 200 in the year 2005; 180 in the year 2006; and 220 in the year 2007. Make a line graph to show how the number of students changes over the four-year period. Use your graph to answer the following questions:

- What kind of graph is it?

- What does each dot stand for?

- How does the number of students change?

- How can circle and line graphs help you to **compare and contrast** information?

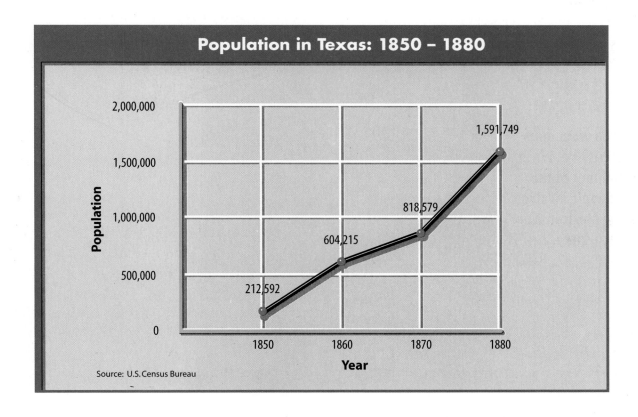

Population in Texas: 1850 – 1880

- 1850: 212,592
- 1860: 604,215
- 1870: 818,579
- 1880: 1,591,749

Source: U.S. Census Bureau

At War with Mexico

Why did the United States go to war with Mexico?

VOCABULARY

Mexican War

Treaty of Guadalupe Hidalgo

Compromise of 1850

PEOPLE

Zachary Taylor

Sarah Borginnis

Jane McNamus Cazneau

Winfield Scott

READING STRATEGY

Draw a word map like this one. Write the names of the key people involved in the Mexican War in each space.

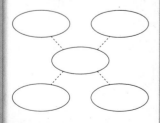

Lesson Outline

• Conflict Between the United States and Mexico

• War Breaks Out

• Treaty of Guadalupe Hidalgo

BUILD BACKGROUND

In the last lesson you read that the idea of Manifest Destiny was popular in the United States in the 1840s. When Texas joined the United States, Americans wanted our country to continue expanding as far as the Pacific Ocean. At the time, much of the land that is now south-western and western United States belonged to Mexico.

CONFLICT BETWEEN THE UNITED STATES AND MEXICO

Now that Texas was a state, Mexico believed the United States would try to take more of its lands. The Mexican government ordered its representative in Washington, D.C., to come home. Tension between the two countries was growing.

The United States said that Texas extended as far as the **Rio Grande**. Mexico disagreed. Mexico said that everything west of the **Nueces River** was still Mexican land. Look at the map to see where the countries placed their national boundaries.

President James K. Polk wanted to buy the land of what is today California and some southwest states from Mexico. He also wanted to talk about the southern border of Texas. In 1845 he sent a special representative to Mexico to discuss these matters.

The Mexican government refused to speak with Polk's representative. As a result, Polk decided to send about 3,500 United States soldiers to the Rio Grande. The soldiers were led by General **Zachary Taylor**.

United States soldiers follow Zachary Taylor into Mexico City.

Polk ordered Taylor and his men to camp at the Nueces River. From there, the troops moved across the river to the Rio Grande. This was a signal to Mexico that the United States would defend this area of Texas as its own.

READING CHECK **Why did Polk send a representative to Mexico?**

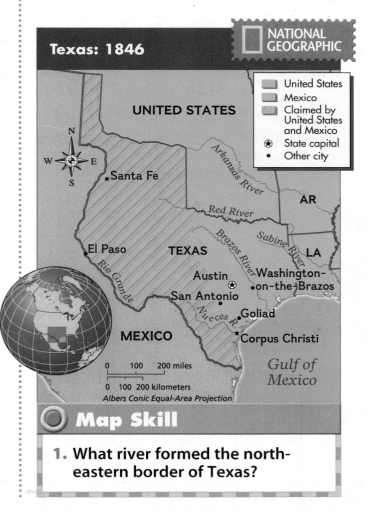

Texas: 1846

NATIONAL GEOGRAPHIC

- United States
- Mexico
- Claimed by United States and Mexico
- ⊛ State capital
- • Other city

UNITED STATES

Santa Fe

Arkansas River

AR

Red River

El Paso

TEXAS

Brazos River

Sabine River

LA

Rio Grande

Austin

Washington-on-the-Brazos

San Antonio

Nueces R.

Goliad

MEXICO

Corpus Christi

Gulf of Mexico

0 100 200 miles
0 100 200 kilometers
Albers Conic Equal-Area Projection

Map Skill

1. **What river formed the northeastern border of Texas?**

WAR BREAKS OUT

Mexico's response to the United States soldiers was to send its own soldiers to the Rio Grande. The two armies camped on opposite sides of the river. The United States soldiers played our national anthem, "The Star-Spangled Banner," on instruments such as fifes and drums. The Mexican soldiers played their own country's songs.

In May, the two armies began fighting. When Polk heard about the battles he said, "Mexico has . . . shed American blood on American soil." As a result, the United States declared war on Mexico on May 13, 1846.

Jane McManus Cazneau (above right), General Zachary Taylor (below left), and General Winfield Scott (below right), served during the Mexican War.

Texans in the War

Texans had a special interest in the **Mexican War**. More than 8,000 Texans signed up, including six groups of Texas Rangers. One Texan who served as an officer in the United States Army was former president Mirabeau B. Lamar. Also, James Pinckney Henderson took leave of his duties as governor and joined the soldiers. In addition to Texans, men from across the United States joined the war. Many women also served during the Mexican War. **Sarah Borginnis** traveled with General Taylor's army. She cooked, washed, loaded guns, and helped

carry wounded soldiers off the battlefield. Another woman who played an important part in the Mexican War was **Jane McManus Cazneau**. With the approval of President Polk, Cazneau went on a secret peace mission to Mexico City. During that mission, she became the only female to report from behind enemy lines.

Mexico City is Attacked

General Taylor's army crossed the Rio Grande into Mexico soon after the war began. President Santa Anna led the Mexican army. The United States soldiers were better equipped than the Mexican army. Early in 1847, the American army defeated the Mexicans at the Battle of Buena Vista (BWAY nuh VEE stuh). Soon after, the United States Army, led by General **Winfield Scott**, landed at Veracruz, Mexico. After heavy fighting, the army reached Mexico City.

Chapultepec (chuh PUL tuh pek) was a fort on a hill overlooking Mexico City. General Scott decided to attack it. On September 12, Scott's army attacked the fort. After a fierce battle, General Scott and his soldiers captured the fort. The United States flag was raised over Chapultepec and Santa Anna's army soon retreated.

Battle at Chapultepec

A white flag was raised over Mexico City the next day. The United States had won the Mexican War.

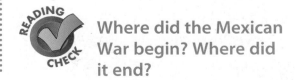

Where did the Mexican War begin? Where did it end?

TREATY OF GUADALUPE HIDALGO

The United States and Mexico signed the **Treaty of Guadalupe Hidalgo** (gwahd ul OOP ay hih DAHL goh) on February 2, 1848. Under this treaty, Mexico accepted the Rio Grande as the border between Texas and Mexico. Mexico also gave up all lands between Texas and the Pacific Ocean. These lands include what now makes up part or all of the states of California, Utah, Arizona, New Mexico, Wyoming, and Colorado. In return for this land, the United States paid Mexico $15 million. Mexicans living in those areas were promised American citizenship.

The Treaty of Guadalupe Hidalgo ended the dispute between the United States and Mexico over Texas. However, Texas still had one more border problem to settle.

Texans claimed all the land west to the Rio Grande. That land included about one-half of what is now New Mexico. The people in the city of Santa Fe, New Mexico, did not want to be part of Texas. They wanted to be a separate state or territory. Also, many people in the United States feared that Texans would bring slavery to this area.

Members of the United States Congress worked out a solution. As part of the **Compromise of 1850**, Texas accepted payment of $10 million to give the land up. A compromise is when two sides solve a disagreement by agreeing that each will give up something. Look at the map to see the borders of Texas today.

The Compromise of 1850 gave Texas the chance to pay off its debt. With the remaining money, our state was able to put money aside for the public school system.

READING CHECK What states did the United States gain as part of the Treaty of Guadalupe Hidalgo?

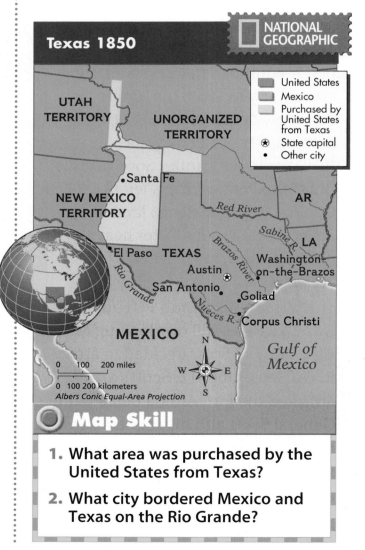

Texas 1850

NATIONAL GEOGRAPHIC

Legend:
- United States
- Mexico
- Purchased by United States from Texas
- ⊛ State capital
- • Other city

UTAH TERRITORY

UNORGANIZED TERRITORY

Santa Fe

NEW MEXICO TERRITORY

AR

Red River

Sabine R.

LA

El Paso   TEXAS   Brazos River

Rio Grande   Austin ⊛   Washington-on-the-Brazos

San Antonio   Goliad

Nueces R.   Corpus Christi

MEXICO

Gulf of Mexico

0   100   200 miles
0   100 200 kilometers
Albers Conic Equal-Area Projection

◉ Map Skill

1. **What area was purchased by the United States from Texas?**
2. **What city bordered Mexico and Texas on the Rio Grande?**

PUTTING IT TOGETHER

The Mexican War began in 1846 and ended in 1847. The Treaty of Guadalupe Hidalgo, signed in 1848, required that Mexico give up large areas of land to the United States. Thousands of settlers could now move to Texas and the new area of the United States.

Treaty of Guadalupe Hidalgo

Review and Assess

1. Write one sentence for each of the following words:

   Compromise of 1850

   Mexican War

2. What was the Treaty of Guadalupe Hidalgo?

3. Identify the main reasons that the United States went to war with Mexico.

4. When did the United States government declare war on Mexico? What event led to this?

5. Compare and contrast the Mexican War with the Texas Revolution.

Create a "Before and After" chart that shows the borders of the United States before and after the Mexican War. For help look at the maps on pages 175 and 178.

. . . .

Think about a time when you had a disagreement with someone. First **write** down what the disagreement was about. Then write a treaty that explains how you could have settled the disagreement peacefully.

Using Special Purpose Maps: Distribution Maps

In the Introduction, you learned about special purpose maps. Vegetation maps are one kind of special purpose map. **Distribution maps** are another. Distribution maps show how something is spread out over an area. Some of the things distribution maps can feature include language, climate, and products. The map on page 12 of the Introduction showing annual rainfall is an example of a distribution map.

<table>
<tr><td>VOCABULARY

distribution map</td></tr>
</table>

LEARN THE SKILL

Study Map A on this page. Then follow the steps below to read distribution maps.

1. **Identify the title of the map.**
   The title of this map is Texas Population, 1850. In the last lesson, you learned that the present borders of our state were formed in 1850. Map A shows how people were spread across Texas at that time.

2. **Locate symbols and a map key.**
   Dots appear on the map. The map key explains that each dot represents 1,000 people. They show exactly how people were distributed across our state in 1850.

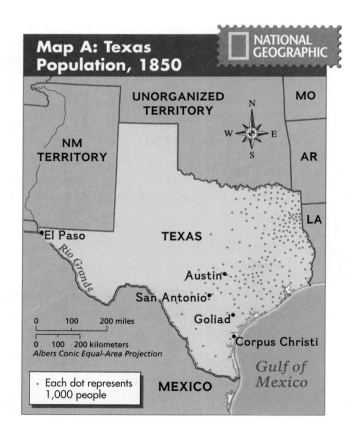

Map A: Texas Population, 1850

NATIONAL GEOGRAPHIC

UNORGANIZED TERRITORY

MO

NM TERRITORY

AR

LA

El Paso

TEXAS

Rio Grande

Austin

San Antonio

Goliad

Corpus Christi

0   100   200 miles
0 100 200 kilometers
Albers Conic Equal-Area Projection

Each dot represents 1,000 people

MEXICO

Gulf of Mexico

TRY THE SKILL

Map B shows how the population of our state is spread out today. Use both maps to answer the following questions.

1. Why is this a distribution map?

2. What symbol is found on the map? What does it represent?

3. Where was most of the population located in 1850?

4. Where is most of the population located today?

5. **Compare and contrast** Maps A and B.

6. How can distribution maps help you better understand history?

EXTEND THE SKILL

Draw a population distribution map for your school. First outline the classrooms in your school. Then use dots to show how many students are in each classroom. Use one dot for every five students. Then answer the following questions.

- How many students are in your school?

- How are they spread out across the different classrooms?

- What other kinds of subjects could you show on a distribution map for your area?

Map B: Population Distribution Today

NATIONAL GEOGRAPHIC

- ✪ State capital
- • Other city
- · Each dot represents 5,000 people

CO   KS

NM   OK   AR

• El Paso   • Dallas   LA

TEXAS

Austin ✪

San Antonio •   • Houston

N W E S

MEXICO   • Corpus Christi

Gulf of Mexico

0   100   200 miles
0   100   200 kilometers
Albers Conic Equal-Area Projection

181

Lesson 4

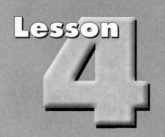

Settlers from Everywhere

VOCABULARY

political

PEOPLE

Henri Castro

Patricia de la Garza de León

READING STRATEGY

Draw a main idea map like this one. In each oval write something about the life of a pioneer.

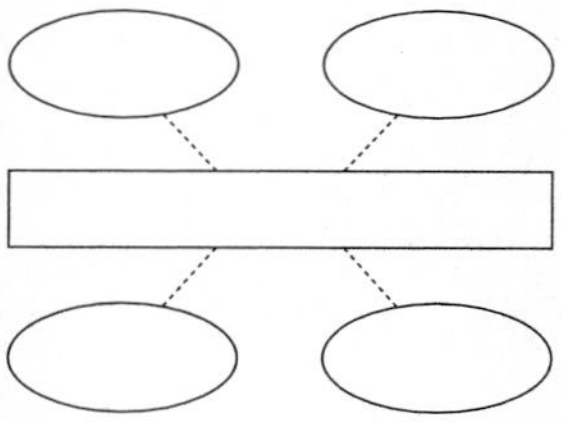

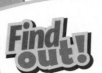

Find out! *What were some of the reasons that new settlers came to Texas?*

Lesson Outline

- Gone to Texas
- Settlers and Pioneer Life
- Life in Town

BUILD BACKGROUND

After the war with Mexico ended, many people in the United States began moving westward. In some states people left signs on their homes with the letters "GTT." These letters stood for "Gone to Texas." Many people continued to come to Texas after it became part of the United States. The new settlers came for land and better opportunities.

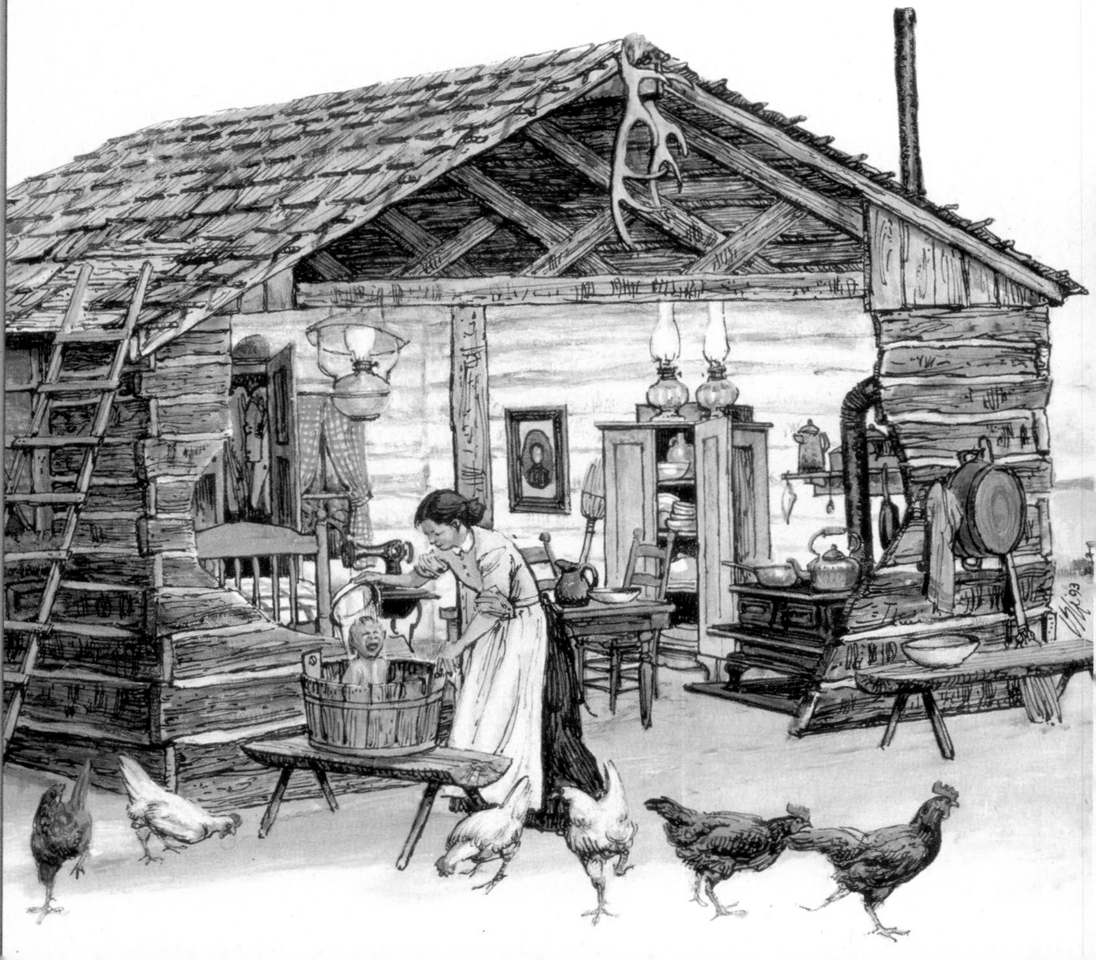

GONE TO TEXAS

By 1824, Texas was open for settlement to any who would come. In 1836, when Texas won its independence, more than 35,000 people lived here. By 1860, the number of Texans had grown to 600,000.

Many Roads to Texas

People came from all over the United States and from more than 26 countries. Most Mexicans and Anglo-American men and their families were given free land when they arrived in Texas. African Americans were not given land for free. Advertisements and letters written home by these pioneers helped spread the news. One Texan described what land meant to new settlers: "It is their own … with no rent or taxes to pay…. One feels free and one is free … certain that poverty [*being poor*] cannot threaten them."

Not all people came to Texas of their own free will. Thousands of enslaved people were brought to Texas by their owners.

From Around the World

The majority of pioneers came from other parts of the United States. They came from Louisiana, Mississippi, Arkansas, Tennessee, Georgia, Illinois, New York, and other states.

Others came from Europe. These pioneers left their homelands to find better jobs or to escape **political** or religious problems. *Political* means having to do with government.

How much did the population of Texas increase between 1836 and 1860?

HO! FOR TEXAS!

Cheap Homes, Good Investments, FOR IMMIGRANTS, COLONISTS and CAPITALISTS.

The UT Institute of Texan Cultures at San Antonio

You can see how settlers lived in the 1800s (left). Cartoon from *The Atlantic Monthly* (right) shows a "Gone to Texas" sign. Posters advertising land in Texas (above).

Many pioneers lived in log cabins like this one. Several family members slept in one room.

SETTLERS AND PIONEER LIFE

Settlers from Europe came from countries such as Poland, France, Germany, and from what is now the Czech and Slovak republics.

Czech and Slovak people settled in southeast Texas. The northeast was settled mostly by Norwegian, Irish, and Swedish immigrants. As many as one-third of new arrivals in Texas were enslaved African Americans.

A Frenchman named **Henri Castro** introduced many French immigrants to Texas. In September of 1844, he settled his first shipload of families in a town he named **Castroville**. On Christmas Eve in 1854, a small group of people from Poland arrived in an unsettled part of Texas. They celebrated the holiday under an oak tree, and named it **Panna Maria**.

The towns of **New Braunfels** and **Fredericksburg** were built by the Society for the Protection of German Immigrants in Texas. They brought thousands of people to central Texas.

The Life of a Pioneer

Building new homes and farms took hard work and courage. Pioneers found that life was filled with many dangers and challenges, such as rattlesnakes and drought.

Tejano settlers were often treated badly by new settlers. **Patricia de la Garza de León**, moved to Texas in the 1820s from Mexico. She supported Texas during the revolution. However, de León and her family were driven off their land by Texans angry with Mexico.

Life on the Farm

Most pioneers were farmers. They had come to Texas with few belongings. A farm family had to make or do almost everything to live on a farm.

Pioneers built their homes out of the natural resources they found nearby. Those who lived near wooded areas built log cabins. They also made the furniture for their homes, such as chairs, tables, and cabinets. They found a use for everything. To stuff mattresses they used corn husks. Corn cobs were burned for heat.

Most farmers grew cotton, corn, and potatoes. Usually they raised cattle, which provided milk and butter. Thomas Kosub came to Texas from Poland when he was 16 years old. In 1855, Kosub, his family, and 12 other families settled in San Antonio, Texas. Here, he recalls his first years in Texas.

READING CHECK What was the name of Henri Castro's first settlement?

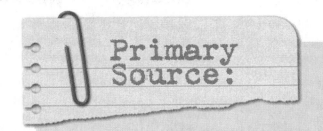

Primary Source:

***Excerpt from* The First Polish Colonies of America in Texas** — *Compiled by Rev. Edward J. Dworczyk, published in 1979.*

… Those with ready cash bought land immediately. Some rented small fields … Our main crop was corn…. There were no fences, so our cattle grazed far and wide.

In the latter part of 1856, we began building our church. We cut the thick live-oak trees for that purpose.… Without … the necessary **implements** *we lifted the heavy logs into wagons drawn by oxen and hauled them to the place of building.*

How did Thomas Kosub and the other settlers build their church?

implements: tools

DATAGRAPHIC

The Growth of Texas

Texas grew by about 7,000 people a year while it was a republic. When Texas became part of the United States, people continued to come to our state. These people brought their languages and traditions with them. Look at the chart and map below to answer the questions.

Immigrants in Texas: 1850–1860

NATIONAL GEOGRAPHIC

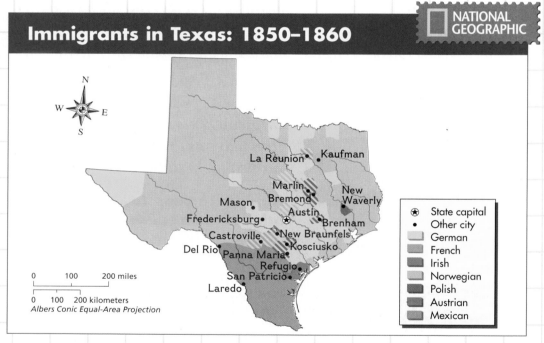

Map legend:
- ⊛ State capital
- • Other city
- German
- French
- Irish
- Norwegian
- Polish
- Austrian
- Mexican

Cities: La Réunion, Kaufman, Marlin, Bremond, New Waverly, Mason, Austin, Fredericksburg, Brenham, Castroville, New Braunfels, Del Rio, Kosciusko, Panna Maria, Refugio, San Patricio, Laredo

0 100 200 miles
0 100 200 kilometers
Albers Conic Equal-Area Projection

Words Borrowed from Other Languages

German		pretzel	strudel	sauerkraut
Polish		pierogi	polka	kielbasa
Mexican		taco	fiesta	tortilla
Norwegian		ski	iceberg	slalom
French		ballet	omelet	croissant

QUESTIONS

1. List three words that describe food.
2. What words do we get from the two largest immigrant groups in Texas?

To learn more, visit our Website: www.mhschool.com

LIFE IN TOWN

Sometimes farmers would go into town. Towns were crowded and had many businesses. Some shops in town belonged to brickmakers, wheelmakers, saddlemakers, and tailors. In town people could also find a doctor or lawyer.

 **What were some businesses found in towns?**

PUTTING IT TOGETHER

Between 1836 and 1860 many new settlers came to Texas. They built their homes, made their own clothes, and grew their own food. These settlers helped change the land and life of our state.

Star of the Republic Museum

German pioneers brought plates like this one (left), and customs such as music and dance to their new homes (right).

Review and Assess

1. Write one sentence for the vocabulary word:

   political

2. Who was Patricia de la Garza de León?

3. Analyze the reasons new settlers came to Texas.

4. Summarize life on a farm in the 1850s.

5. What countries in Europe did some settlers come from?

Activities

Look back at the Datagraphic map. Why do you think most people settled in East Texas? Make a list of some of the natural resources they found there and how they were used.

• •

Suppose you were a ten year old from a country in Europe. You moved to Texas only a few months ago. **Write** a letter informing your relatives in Europe what life is like in Texas.

Chapter 4 REVIEW

VOCABULARY REVIEW

Number a sheet of paper from 1 to 5. Beside each number write the word or term from the list below that matches the description.

annexation   congress

debt   political

resolution

1. adding a territory to a country
2. the branch of government that makes laws
3. having to do with government
4. the amount of money owed to others
5. a decision

CHAPTER COMPREHENSION

6. Why was the capital of Texas moved from Columbia to Houston?
7. List some features of the treaty between Cherokee Chief Philip Bowles and President Sam Houston.
8. At first, the United States and its citizens were uncertain about annexing Texas. Why?
9. Why did President Polk send a special representative to Mexico in 1845?
10. Name some women who served during the Mexican War. What were their roles?
11. Settlers moved to Texas from around the world. List some places they came from.
12. What did settlers build their homes with?

SKILL REVIEW

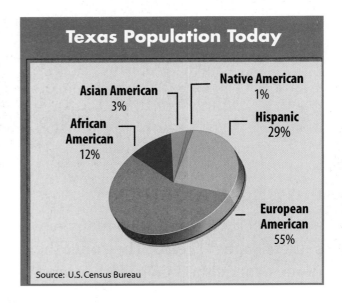

Texas Population Today

Asian American 3%
Native American 1%
African American 12%
Hispanic 29%
European American 55%

Source: U.S. Census Bureau

13. **Geography Skill** What do distribution maps show?
14. **Geography Skill** Name two things distribution maps can feature.
15. **Geography Skill** What type of symbols might be used in distribution maps?
16. **Study Skill** Describe how a circle graph and a line graph are different.
17. **Study Skill** Look at the circle graph above. Which group makes up the largest portion of the Texas population today? Which makes up the smallest?
18. **Study Skill** Compare this graph to the circle graph on page 172. How has the percentage of European Americans in the total population of Texas changed from 1850 to today?

USING A TIME LINE

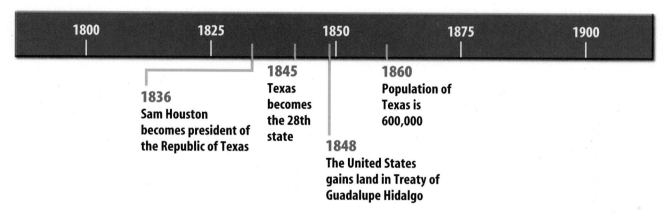

| 1800 | 1825 | 1850 | 1875 | 1900 |

1836
Sam Houston becomes president of the Republic of Texas

1845
Texas becomes the 28th state

1848
The United States gains land in Treaty of Guadalupe Hidalgo

1860
Population of Texas is 600,000

19. Did the population of Texas reach 600,000 before or after Texas became a state?

20. Describe the time period between 1836 and 1845.

Activity

Learning About Citizenship Suppose you and your community have just moved to Texas from another country. Life in Texas is difficult and not at all what you expected. But you decide to make it your home. One day, about 6 months after your arrival in Texas, the United States declares war on Mexico. In groups, decide if you would join the war and defend your new home. Then have one person from each group tell the class your group's decision and the reasons why or why not.

Foldables

Use your *Foldable* to review what you have learned about Texas's journey to statehood. As you look at the Lone Star Flag on the front of your *Foldable*, mentally recall the events that occurred before, during, and after Texas became a state. Review your notes on the inside of your *Foldable* to check your responses. Record any questions that you have on your *Foldable*, and discuss them with classmates or review the chapter to find answers.

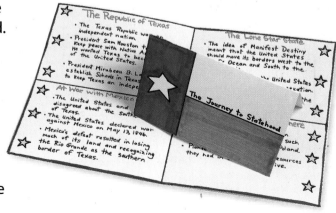

Unit 2 REVIEW

VOCABULARY REVIEW

Number a paper from 1 to 5. Beside each number write the word or term from the list below that completes the sentence.

convention   **delegate**

dictator   **frontier**

senator

1. The Texas ___ was settled by people from the United States.

2. In 1832 Texans gathered for a ___ to discuss a Mexican law limiting immigration to Texas.

3. A ___ is a person who is chosen to speak for a group.

4. Many Texans wanted to break away from Mexico because they believed Santa Anna was becoming a ___.

5. Sam Houston became a ___ of the United States Congress representing the state of Texas.

TECHNOLOGY
For more resources to help you learn more about the people and places you studied in this unit, visit **www.mhschool.com** and follow the links for Grade 4 Texas, Unit 2.

SKILL REVIEW

6. **Reading/Thinking Skill** Describe one decision you made today. What steps did you take to make it?

7. **Study Skill** What kind of graph would you use to show how the population of the United States changed between 1840 and 1860?

8. **Study Skill** How do graphs make some information easier to understand?

9. **Geography Skill** Why is the map below a distribution map?

10. **Geography Skill** Are more people found in the eastern or western parts of Texas?

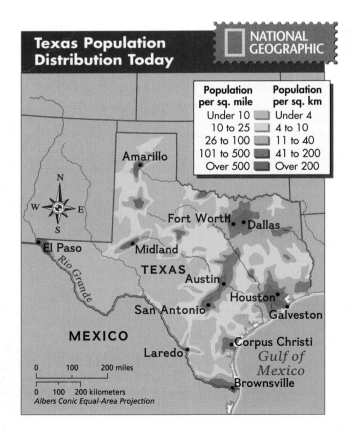

Texas Population Distribution Today

Stephen F. Austin was just 27 years old when his father died. He was studying to become a lawyer. But as soon as he got his mother's letter, he dropped everything and went to San Antonio. There he got permission from Governor Martínez to take over his father's plan.

Austin did not think only of his own wants and needs. He felt a strong sense of responsibility for the welfare of others. He worked hard to earn money for his family and to help and protect the people he brought to Texas. As a result, he lived without many comforts. Sick from overwork, he died young at the age of 43.

1 Stephen F. Austin's reason for deciding to go to San Antonio was to—

   A start a new life
   B study to become a lawyer
   C take over his father's plan
   D visit Governor Martínez

2 Which of these sentences is the best summary of the last paragraph of this article?

   A Stephen F. Austin felt a strong sense of responsibility toward others.
   B Stephen F. Austin earned money for his family.
   C Stephen F. Austin protected people.
   D Stephen F. Austin lived without many comforts.

WRITING ACTIVITIES *TAKS Practice*

- **Writing to Inform** Suppose you were one of "The Old Three Hundred." Write a letter home telling about life on the Texas frontier.

- **Writing to Persuade** Suppose you wanted to start a settlement in Mexican Texas in 1820. Write a letter to Governor Antonio Martinez explaining why he should let you become an empresario.

- **Writing to Express** Write about the life of a settler in the Republic of Texas.

Mary Crownover Rabb, one of the Old Three Hundred.

LITERATURE

Freedom's Gifts
A Juneteenth Story

Selection by Valerie Wesley
Illustrated by Sharon Wilson

Lillie and June ask Aunt Marshall to tell them the story of Juneteenth. This was the day enslaved African Americans in Texas first heard they were free.

"Tell us what it was like before freedom came?" June asked. June had heard the story before, but she loved to listen to Aunt Marshall tell it.

Aunt Marshall didn't say anything for a while. "June-teenth always sets me to rememberin'. Those times were ugly, filled with so much evil and meanness, I don't even want to think about them on a day as good as this one. We were born grown back then—at least we felt it," she said softly, and her eyes got the faraway look, the "rememberin'" look that usually told June she didn't want to be bothered. But Aunt Marshall was talking now. June stole a glance at Lillie, who listened, too.

A butterfly **swooped** down from a stalk of weed to a flower and then finally to a twig that lay in the grass. "She is freer than we were then." Aunt Marshall nodded toward the butterfly. "A bluebird. An ant that could crawl where it wanted. You had nothing but your mama's arms

---

swoop (swüp) to rush down suddenly

or your sister's to warm up to at night, and them that owned you could take your family away anytime they wanted. Like they did my big sister. My Sophie."

A look of sadness crossed Aunt Marshall's face, and June could see the sparkle of a tear in her eye. June knew that she was thinking of things it hurt her to remember. She was sorry that she had asked Aunt Marshall about those old times.

"But they couldn't take your thoughts, the way your mama sung softly to you, or the way your sister's arms felt against yours. I kept them close and tight within me."

"And then freedom came?" Lillie asked.

"Finally. Two and a half years after everybody else was free," June answered, remembering what she'd already learned about that first Juneteenth.

"What happened that day, Aunt Marshall?" Lillie asked, and June realized that Lillie had never heard Aunt Marshall's story.

"I was in the barn that day," Aunt Marshall said, "gathering some eggs. I heard all this laughing and shouting and carrying on, folks screaming out like they'd lost their minds. I was scared to come out, they was making so much **commotion**. But I was a little 'un, I didn't know what freedom meant. Everybody was looking for kin who'd been lost or sold or snatched. Mamas for their babies, husbands for their wives. Then Sophie found me, and I knew it must be true. That freedom *had* come. 'We're free, Marshall! Free. Free. Free!' Sophie told me. And then she laughed. I'll remember that laugh, so sweet and deep, until the day I die."

---

commotion (kə mō′shən) a noisy confusion; disorder

Write About It!

Juneteenth is a special day for all Texans because it represents freedom. Write a paragraph that describes what freedom means to you.

Challenge and Opportunity

TAKE A LOOK

How did life change after the Civil War?

Many Texan farmers began to raise cattle. New railroads made it easier to transport goods. Towns and cities grew all over Texas.

196

Explore more about cattle
trails at our Web site
www.mhschool.com

THE Big IDEAS ABOUT...

Civil War and Reconstruction

By the 1850s, many landowners used enslaved African American workers in Texas. Over time, the use of enslaved workers and other issues divided the people of the United States. Read on to find out how this division affected our country and changed life in Texas.

SLAVERY IN TEXAS

African American workers had their own culture and traditions but were not free.

A DIVIDED COUNTRY

Disagreements between Northern and Southern states led to Civil War.

FIGHTING TEXANS

The members of Hood's Brigade fought for the South during the Civil War. They were known for their skill and bravery.

REBUILDING A COUNTRY

After the war ended, Texas had to rebuild its economy, its land, and some cities. It also had to work to rejoin the United States.

SLAVERY IN BRAZIL

Plantations, slavery, and new independence are all things Brazil had in common with Texas during the 1800s.

Foldables

Make this Foldable study guide and use it to record what you learn about the Civil War and Reconstruction.

1. Fold a sheet of 8 ½" x 11" paper in half like a hamburger, but leave one side of the paper 1" longer than the other.

2. On the short side, make three cuts equal distance apart, forming four tabs.

3. Write the title of the chapter on the 1" tab. Label the other tabs with the titles of the four lessons in this chapter.

Slavery in Our State

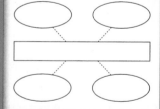

What was life like for enslaved African Americans in Texas?

Lesson Outline
• Plantation Life
• A Rich Culture
• Remaining Free

VOCABULARY

plantation

PEOPLE

William Goyens

READING STRATEGY

Copy the chart you see here. Write the main idea of this lesson in the center. Add supporting details as you read.

BUILD BACKGROUND

When Clara Anderson was six years old, she was brought to Texas as an enslaved worker. Later she described her life on a plantation. On the next page you can read how she described her life.

PLANTATION LIFE

A **plantation** is a large farm where crops such as cotton or sugarcane are grown. Each plantation was like a small town. Some of the enslaved people were blacksmiths, carpenters, and weavers, but most worked in the hot, dusty cotton fields. In Texas there were few plantations. Most farmers owned fewer than 10 slaves.

A popular saying in the 1850s was "Cotton is King." In the South, it was the most important cash crop.

Enslaved people worked from dawn to dusk filling burlap sacks with cotton. Even children worked in the fields. Some of the women did the housework, fixed meals, or cared for the owner's children. They were only free from work on Sundays and some holidays.

The few laws that protected enslaved workers were rarely enforced. They could be beaten or sold at any time. Families could also be broken up if the parents and children were sold to different owners.

Clara Anderson remembered,

The folks would give me a little to eat … there [were] some little children who lived nearby, and every day when they would come from school, they'd leave me some food. They'd hide this food in a tree stump, where I'd go and [get] it. Those children would bring me buttered bread, cakes, and other things.

Some enslaved people rebelled by stealing crops or destroying property. Others escaped to Mexico or to states without slavery.

What is a plantation?

Enslaved African Americans like Clara Anderson (left) worked on plantations like the Polley Plantation in the 1800s (right).

DATAGRAPHIC

Growth of Slavery and Cotton Production

In the 1850s, much of the Texas economy was based on cash crops. Study the graphs to see how the economy of Texas depended on enslaved African Americans.

Enslaved Population of Texas

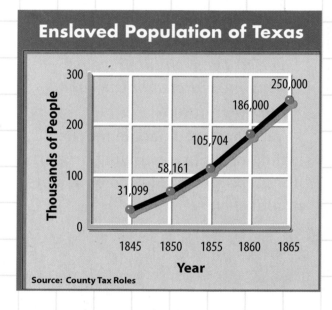

Thousands of People / Year

- 300
- 250,000
- 200
- 186,000
- 105,704
- 100
- 58,161
- 31,099
- 0

1845 1850 1855 1860 1865

Source: County Tax Roles

Cotton Production in Texas

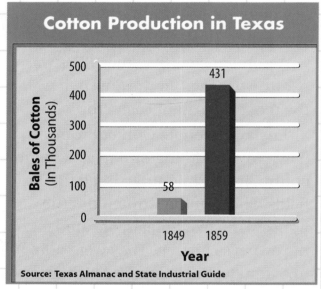

Bales of Cotton (In Thousands) / Year

- 500
- 431
- 400
- 300
- 200
- 100
- 58
- 0

1849 1859

Source: Texas Almanac and State Industrial Guide

QUESTIONS

1. How many more enslaved Texans were there in 1860 than in 1850?

2. Cotton production data was only collected every ten years by the government. Make a prediction about how much cotton might have been produced in the year 1855.

To learn more, visit our Web site:
www.mhschool.com

A RICH CULTURE

In spite of the harsh conditions, enslaved African Americans kept their rich culture alive. One important part of their culture was music. They often sang while they worked in the fields. Many songs were based on rhythms from traditional African songs.

Some songs helped to pass the time. Others were ways of communicating with each other. These songs described their hardships, hopes, and beliefs. Other songs called "spirituals" were religious. Some of these spirituals are still sung in African American churches today. The following words are from a spiritual. As you read the words, think about what they mean.

A Storytelling Tradition

Another important part of African American culture was the oral tradition of telling stories. Parents and grandparents told stories to children. Some enslaved Texans could read and write, but most were not allowed to learn. Telling stories was a way to remember the past.

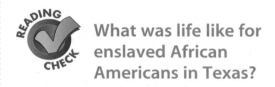

What was life like for enslaved African Americans in Texas?

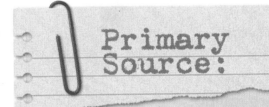

Primary Source:

"Help Me"

Oh, in times like these,
Oh, in times like these,
Yes, in times like these
I need the Lord to help me
when I'm burdened down.

In the music section of your library, look up the words to another spiritual. What is the song about?

BIOGRAPHY

Focus On: **Honesty**

WILLIAM GOYENS was a free African American who came to Texas when it still belonged to Mexico. His reputation for honesty helped him in both business and politics.

Goyens spoke three languages: English, Spanish, and Cherokee. This made him very important to the different governments of Texas. The Native Americans, Spaniards, and Americans all needed someone they trusted to help them talk to each other.

In Mexican Texas, Goyens negotiated treaties between the government and the Cherokee. During the Texas Revolution, he was an interpreter for Sam Houston. He continued to work with the Cherokee when Texas became a republic and later when it joined the United States. Each group valued his honesty in translating what they were saying.

Link to Today

Why would honesty be important for translators like Goyens? Write a paragraph about why it is important for people to trust a translator.

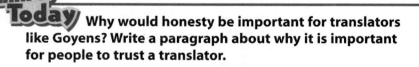

THE LIFE OF GOYENS	**1796** Goyens is born in Moore County, North Carolina	**1820** Goyens moves to Nacogdoches, Texas, to live	**1830** Translates for Government	**1832** Goyens marries Mary Sibley	**1836** Goyens acts as interpreter for Sam Houston	**1856** Goyens dies on June 20
	1775	1800	1825	1850		1875
LIFE AROUND THE WORLD	**1804** Napoleon becomes emperor of France	**1820** The Missouri Compromise is signed	**1830** Revolution in France	**1833** Slavery is abolished in the British Empire	**1849** California Gold Rush	

REMAINING FREE

Although some African Americans like Goyens were free, their lives continued to be difficult. Some white Texans treated them badly. In addition, in 1840 all free African Americans were ordered to leave their homes in Texas. A new law stated that they would need to get special permission from the Texas government if they wanted to stay.

Some left Texas, but others stayed in places where the law was not strictly enforced. By 1860 only about 355 free African Americans still lived in Texas.

How were free African Americans in Texas treated?

PUTTING IT TOGETHER

As plantations grew larger in Texas, slavery became more important. Landowners thought they would make more money by using enslaved workers. African American slaves worked hard. They also created a rich culture that is still part of life in Texas today.

The children of plantation owners were often cared for by enslaved workers.

Institute of Texan Cultures at San Antonio

Review and Assess

1. Write a sentence for the vocabulary word:

   plantation

2. What was Texas's most important cash crop?

3. Describe the life of enslaved African Americans in Texas.

4. What effect did the growth of cash crops have on slavery in Texas during the early 1800s?

5. What were two parts of African American culture in Texas? What **caused** them to become so important?

Activities

Using the physical map of Texas on page R20, describe which parts of Texas would be good for growing crops.

• •

Suppose you were William Goyens. **Write** a letter describing how life in Texas has changed for African Americans from the 1820s to the 1850s.

Summarizing

In the last lesson, you read about slavery and plantation life during the 1800s. Stories from history are usually filled with information. In order to understand what you read, it is helpful to summarize the information. In a **summary**, you briefly tell the most important information in your own words.

> **VOCABULARY**
>
> summary

LEARN THE SKILL

Read the paragraph below. Then follow the steps to create a summary.

Slavery became a central part of life in the South. In all of the Southern states, the hard labor of enslaved workers kept the plantations booming. Southern plantations grew crops like cotton, tobacco, sugar, and rice. By 1860, one quarter of all families in the South had enslaved African American workers.

1. Identify the topic.
As you read, look for the topic of a paragraph or section. In the paragraph above, the topic is underlined. It reads: "Slavery became a central part of life in the South."

2. Identify the most important information.
Look for facts that support the topic. Titles, headings, and key words can help you find important information. Important information in the paragraph above, also underlined, includes: "…enslaved workers kept the plantations booming" and "By 1860, one quarter of all families in the South had enslaved African American workers."

3. Organize the information.
Organize the most important information in a clear way. Only include facts that relate to the topic. The sentence "Southern plantations grew crops like cotton, tobacco, sugar, and rice" does not tell you enough about the topic. Therefore, it should not be included in a summary.

4. Write a summary in your own words.
Remember to keep your summary brief. A summary on the above paragraph would read:

"Slavery was an important part of life in the South. Plantations kept growing due to the work of enslaved African Americans. One fourth of all Southern families had enslaved workers by 1860."

TRY THE SKILL

Read the following paragraph about the history of cotton in Texas.

Cotton has long been an important cash crop in Texas. It was first grown by Spanish missionaries in the middle 1700s. Several thousand pounds were produced each year. _In the early 1800s, American colonists began to grow the crop._ Cotton was mainly grown in East Texas along the Brazos River. _By 1852, Texas was one of the top ten cotton-producing states._

Write a brief summary. Use your summary to answer the following questions.

1. What is the topic?

2. What is the most important information?

3. What facts are not useful to include in a summary on cotton growing?

4. How can writing a summary help you in your studies?

EXTEND THE SKILL

The summary below focuses on William Goyens. However, it contains information that does not relate to the topic. Rewrite it using only the most important information.

William Goyens was a free African American who worked with the different governments of Texas. He lived in Nacogdoches with his wife Mary. Goyens spoke three languages. Because of this skill, he was able to arrange treaties with the Cherokee. He also helped Sam Houston speak with the Cherokee. After the revolution, he bought some land that was later called "Goyens's Hill."

Use your summary to answer the following questions.

- What is the topic?

- What facts should not be included in a summary?

- How can writing a summary help you find the **main idea** when you read?

A Nation Divided

Find! out!

Why did Texas leave the United States?

Lesson Outline
- Two Sides of an Issue
- Texans Take Action
- Civil War

READING STRATEGY

Copy the chart you see here. Write the events that led Texas into the Civil War in the order that they happened.

BUILD BACKGROUND

"The planting states have a common interest … the protection of that interest is certain. United they will have … power for their own protection, and their exports [goods] will make … allies [friends] of all commercial and manufacturing powers."

These words were written by **Jefferson Davis**, a United States senator from Mississippi in November of 1860.

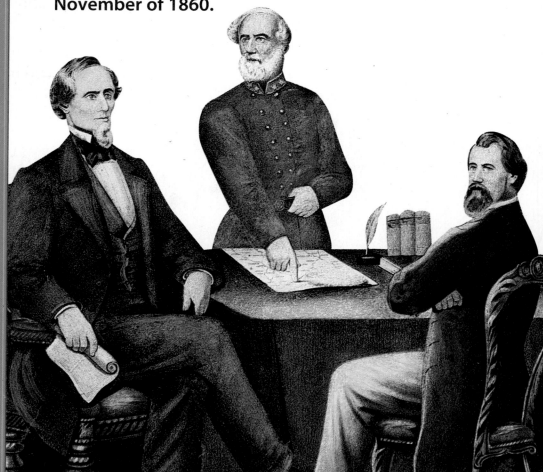

TWO SIDES OF AN ISSUE

In Texas and other parts of the South, more enslaved people were being used to work on the growing farms and plantations. By 1860 about one out of every four Texans was enslaved. In most Northern states, slavery was illegal. People there left their farms to go to cities and work in factories that produced goods. For example, cotton from the South was shipped to factories in the North to be made into cloth.

As you have read, many Southerners believed they needed to use enslaved people to make money from their crops. They also believed that the voters of each state should be able to decide about slavery and other issues. This view was called **states' rights**. It meant the states should be able to make their own laws about any issue that was not granted to Congress in the United States Constitution.

In the North, slavery was against the law in most states. Many Northerners believed slavery was wrong and should be ended everywhere in the United States. Some wanted **abolition**, or an end to slavery. Both white and free black abolitionists worked to end slavery.

Texas Divided

In order to keep the Texas economy growing, most white Texans thought slavery was necessary. Many slave owners claimed that they provided enslaved African Americans with proper food, clothing, and shelter. They argued that their workers were well cared for.

READING CHECK ✓ What is meant by the term "states' rights"?

Jefferson Davis (center, left) predicted the Southern states would unite around their shared belief in **states' rights** (right).

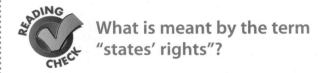

SOUTHERN
State Rights, Free Trade and Anti-Abolition
TRACT NO. 1.

TEXANS TAKE ACTION

Not all Texans believed in the practice of slavery. Some acted on their beliefs. **Melinda Rankin** came to Texas as a Christian missionary. She taught in **Huntsville** and wrote several articles and books about Texas.

She moved to **Brownsville** in 1852 and became the director of a girls' school there. Rankin spoke out against slavery in Texas. This made her very unpopular with other Texans. As a result, the president of her school fired her.

Some slave owners did change their minds about slavery. Jewish slave owners Joseph and Helena Landa from New Braunfels decided to free their slaves. Their decision made some Texans so angry that Joseph's life was in danger. He fled to Mexico.

Many Northerners thought slavery should be outlawed by the national government. They disagreed with many white Texans and other Southerners about the issues of states' rights and slavery.

As a result of these disagreements, Southerners began to talk about leaving the **Union**. The word *Union* describes the group of states that make up the United States. Not all Texans believed that our state should leave the Union. They had worked hard to become a state. They wanted to remain a part of the United States.

In 1861, **Abraham Lincoln** became President of the United States. Lincoln was not an abolitionist, but he believed no more slave states should be added to the Union. White Southerners thought Lincoln would use his position as President to end slavery everywhere.

University of Texas at Austin

Melinda Rankin (above)
and Abraham Lincoln (left)
both took part in the slavery debate.

A Decision Is Made

In 1860, Governor Sam Houston was asked to call a vote on whether Texas should **secede** from, or leave, the Union. Some Southern states had already voted to secede. Houston did not want to secede and refused. He hoped Texans would agree with him if they had more time to think about the issue. But most Texans did not change their minds. They wanted Houston to let them vote on the issue.

On January 28, 1861, delegates from all over Texas met to decide whether or not to secede. After four days of discussion, the Texas delegates voted to leave the Union. A few weeks later a statewide vote was held. A large majority of Texans agreed to secede.

Texas joined with ten other Southern states to form the Confederate States of America, or the **Confederacy**. The Confederacy chose Jefferson Davis of Mississippi as president of this new country. Look at the map below to find the states of the Confederacy.

READING CHECK What happened when Melinda Rankin spoke up against slavery?

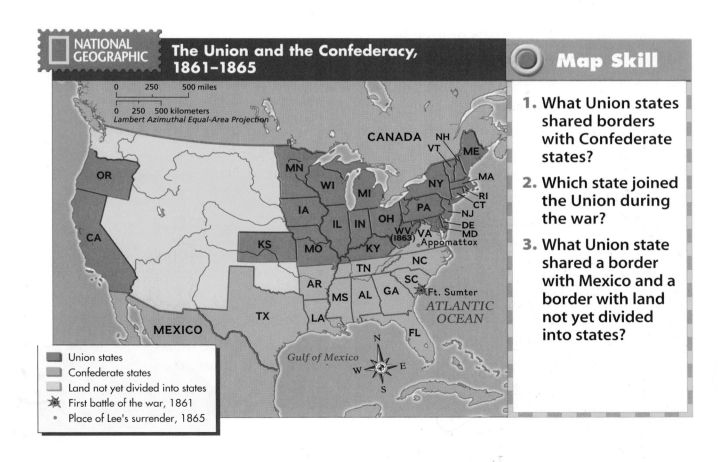

NATIONAL GEOGRAPHIC

The Union and the Confederacy, 1861–1865

0   250   500 miles
0   250   500 kilometers
Lambert Azimuthal Equal-Area Projection

CANADA

OR, CA, MN, WI, MI, IA, IL, IN, OH, KS, MO, NY, PA, NJ, WV (1863), VA, MD, DE, RI, CT, NH, VT, ME, MA

KY, TN, NC, SC, AR, MS, AL, GA, TX, LA, FL, KY, NC

Appomattox

Ft. Sumter

ATLANTIC OCEAN

MEXICO

Gulf of Mexico

N E S W

Union states
Confederate states
Land not yet divided into states
First battle of the war, 1861
Place of Lee's surrender, 1865

Map Skill

1. What Union states shared borders with Confederate states?

2. Which state joined the Union during the war?

3. What Union state shared a border with Mexico and a border with land not yet divided into states?

CIVIL WAR

As part of the Confederacy, Texas had to adjust to being part of a new country. State leaders created a new constitution. In many ways it was very similar to the state's existing constitution. However, a statement was added to strengthen the rights of white Texans to enslave workers. In addition, a part of the old constitution that allowed owners to free their enslaved workers was removed. The new constitution required all government officials to take an oath of loyalty to the Confederacy.

Houston Refuses an Oath

You have read that Governor Sam Houston did not want Texas to secede. However, he had no choice once Texans voted for secession.

When Houston was asked to take an oath of loyalty to the Confederacy, he refused. As a result, Houston could not remain governor of Texas. In 1861, **Edward Clark** replaced Houston as governor and took the oath of loyalty to the Confederacy.

Houston continued to think that Southerners were wrong to secede. Read the following speech given by Houston about what he thought would happen after secession.

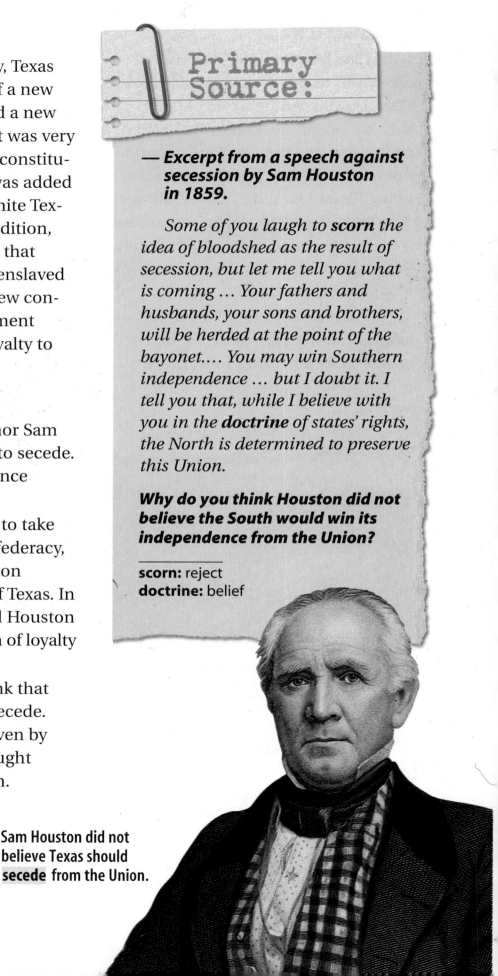

Primary Source:

— *Excerpt from a speech against secession by Sam Houston in 1859.*

*Some of you laugh to **scorn** the idea of bloodshed as the result of secession, but let me tell you what is coming … Your fathers and husbands, your sons and brothers, will be herded at the point of the bayonet.… You may win Southern independence … but I doubt it. I tell you that, while I believe with you in the **doctrine** of states' rights, the North is determined to preserve this Union.*

Why do you think Houston did not believe the South would win its independence from the Union?

scorn: reject
doctrine: belief

Sam Houston did not believe Texas should **secede** from the Union.

212

Shots Are Fired

On April 12, 1861, Confederate soldiers in South Carolina fired on Union troops at Fort Sumter. This marked the beginning of war with the United States. The **Civil War**, or the "War Between the States," would last over four years. It would be the bloodiest conflict in American history.

Why did Edward Clark replace Sam Houston as governor of Texas?

PUTTING IT TOGETHER

Texas seceded from the Union and joined with ten other states to form the Confederacy. The formation of the Confederacy led to the Civil War.

The Civil War began when soldiers at Fort Moultrie fired on Fort Sumter.

Review and Assess

1. Write one sentence for each of the vocabulary words:

   abolition   **Civil War**

   Confederacy   **secede**

   states' rights   **Union**

2. What was the Confederacy?

3. Analyze the reasons why Texas seceded from the United States.

4. Identify what role the **economy** of Texas played in the decision to secede.

5. Suppose you lived in Texas in 1860. How would you **decide** whether to vote for or against secession?

Activities

Using the map on page 211, describe how the size and borders of Texas might have been important to the Confederacy. Then make a chart listing Confederate states and Union states.

• •

Suppose you were Sam Houston. **Write** a letter to Texans reminding them of how hard they worked to become a state. Explain why you think Texas should not secede.

Lesson 3

War Between the States

Find out!

What role did Texas play in the Civil War?

Lesson Outline
- Texan Fighting Forces
- The War in Texas
- Slavery and the War's End

VOCABULARY

cavalry

Terry's Texas Rangers

Hood's Texas Brigade

blockade

Davis Guards

Emancipation Proclamation

PEOPLE

Benjamin Franklin Terry

John Bell Hood

Robert E. Lee

Rosanna Osterman

Ulysses S. Grant

READING STRATEGY

Copy the chart. Write in the main idea of this lesson. Then write in the supporting details.

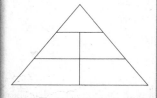

BUILD BACKGROUND

With the beginning of the war in 1861, white Texan men signed up to fight for the Confederate Army. Somewhere between 60,000 and 90,000 Texans fought for the Confederacy. Not all Texans chose to fight with the South. More than 2,000 men from Texas joined the Union Army instead. Some of these men were former slaves, free blacks, and abolitionists.

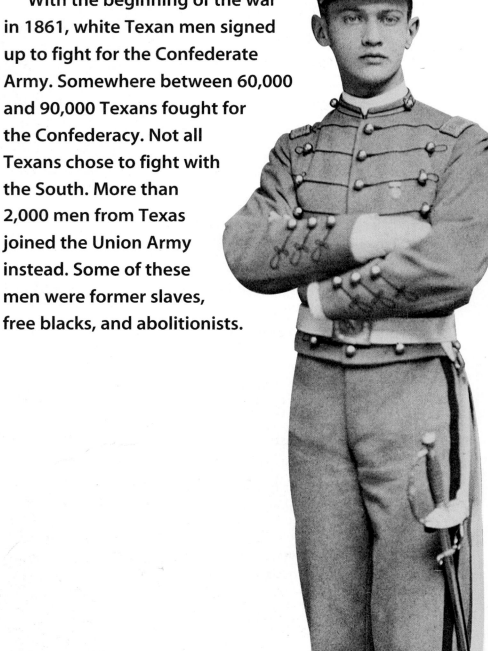

TEXAN FIGHTING FORCES

Although Texas sent many men to fight against the Union, most of the battles took place in the East. However, Texan soldiers became known for their skill and bravery across the South.

Terry's Texas Rangers

Texan **Benjamin Franklin Terry** was first assigned to Virginia, where he fought in the First Battle of Bull Run. When the Confederate leaders saw how many men were killed, they sent Terry back to Texas to recruit more men for a **cavalry** force. A cavalry is a group of soldiers who fight on horseback.

Colonel Terry asked for volunteers who could provide their own supplies, including a horse, saddle, and bridle, guns, knives, and blankets. Over 1,000 Texans joined Terry. They became the Eighth Texas Cavalry unit, but everyone called them **Terry's Texas Rangers**. They were known as one of the hardest fighting cavalry units in the war, fighting in major battles such as Shiloh, Perryville, and Chickamauga. Even though Benjamin Franklin Terry was later killed while leading a charge, his men fought together for the rest of the war.

Hood's Brigade

Another important Texas fighting group was **Hood's Texas Brigade**. They were led by General **John Bell Hood** and served under General **Robert E. Lee**. Hood's brigade fought on the front lines of several major battles. Because of this, they suffered many casualties.

READING CHECK ✓ Who was Benjamin Franklin Terry?

Soldiers such as members of Hood's Brigade (right), which fought under this flag (below), and this young Confederate soldier (left) fought during the Civil War.

Lesson
5
The Western Hemisphere

The End of Slavery in Brazil

Find! out!

What events led to Brazil's independence?

VOCABULARY

export
brazilwood
monarchy

PEOPLE

Dom João
Dom Pedro I
Dom Pedro II

READING STRATEGY

Draw a diagram like this. Write some differences and similarities between Texas and Brazil in the 1800s.

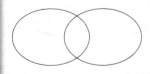

Lesson Outline

• Brazil
• The Rulers of Brazil

BUILD BACKGROUND

During the 1800s most of the Western Hemisphere went through great changes. In South America, **Brazil** transformed from a colony to a republic. In this lesson you will read about Brazil and its similarities and differences with Texas during this time.

BRAZIL

By the 1800s Brazil had been a Portuguese colony for over three hundred years. It had a population of more than three million people. About two-thirds were enslaved workers. They or their ancestors were brought by force to Brazil from Africa.

Portugal's colony of Brazil was rich in natural resources. These resources were **exported** to other countries to keep the economy of Portugal and Brazil strong. An export is something that is sold or traded to another country. The colony of Brazil exported goods such as **brazilwood** to Europe. Brazil got its name from this tree. Brazilwood trees were used to make a popular red dye. People in Europe used this dye to color cotton and wool for clothing. It was so valuable that pirates often attacked ships carrying brazilwood.

Enslaved people were used to keep the economy growing. They were forced to work in the gold and diamond mines, and on cattle ranches and plantations. Most plantations in Brazil, like those in Texas, were huge. The few towns and cities in Brazil served the plantations. Townspeople packed and shipped the coffee, sugar, cotton, and tobacco that the plantations produced.

 What is Brazil named after?

Enslaved Africans (above left) were brought to Brazil to harvest coffee beans (above) and rubber (below) on plantations. Today coffee and rubber are part of Brazil's economy.

229

THE RULERS OF BRAZIL

Dom João was the King of Portugal in 1807. In Portuguese *Dom* means "sir" and *João* means "John." When war broke out in Europe he fled with his family to the Portuguese colony of Brazil. He liked Brazil so much that he decided to live there. In 1821 Dom João put his son in charge of Brazil. Dom João then returned to Portugal.

Brazilians wanted to become independent from Portugal. In 1822 **Dom Pedro I** agreed and declared Brazil's independence. However, he made Brazil a **monarchy** and declared himself king. A monarchy is a country ruled by a king or queen.

Dom Pedro I soon became unpopular in Brazil. He wanted to end slavery there. But since the economy of the country depended mostly on enslaved labor, many Brazilian business owners grew angry. Fearing a rebellion, Dom Pedro I turned the monarchy over to his son in 1831.

Under **Dom Pedro II**, Brazil began to modernize. Telegraph lines improved communications. Railroads were built. Also, many new schools opened.

Like his father, Dom Pedro II also wanted to end slavery. In 1871 he passed a law that freed children born to people in slavery. Then, in 1885 he passed another law that freed all enslaved people over the age of 60. Finally, in 1888, the Brazilian government freed all remaining people in slavery.

Dom Pedro II (above) is being crowned King of Brazil. He helped bring railroads (below) to Brazil.

The Republic of Brazil

After slavery had been abolished, plantation owners became very angry. They had no workers, and Dom Pedro II did not give them any money to keep their businesses running. In 1889, along with the Brazilian army, the plantation owners rebelled against Dom Pedro II. Dom Pedro II was forced to flee to Europe. He no longer ruled Brazil. Brazil became a republic with leaders chosen by the people.

 **Why did the army and landowners rebel against Dom Pedro II?**

PUTTING IT TOGETHER

Many more connections between Texas and Brazil in the 1800s can be made. Plantations, slavery, and new independence are all things they had in common. Today, communications and trade are two things that link Texas and Brazil across the Western Hemisphere.

Rio de Janeiro, Brazil

Review and Assess

1. Write one sentence for each of the vocabulary words.

   brazilwood   export

   monarchy

2. Who was Dom João?

3. Analyze the events that led to Brazil becoming a republic.

4. During the 1800s, how did Brazil and Portugal keep their **economy** strong? Give examples.

5. **Compare** and **contrast** Brazil and the Republic of Texas during the 1800s.

Create a time line listing important events on Brazil's road to independence.

• •

Make a list of the ways in which Dom Pedro II modernized Brazil.

Chapter 5 REVIEW

VOCABULARY REVIEW

Number a sheet of paper from 1 to 5. Beside each number write the word or term from the list below that matches the description.

amendment **cavalry**

plantation **sharecropper**

states' rights

1. a group of soldiers who fight on horseback
2. a person who grows crops on some- one else's land, then gives part of that crop to the owner as payment for use of the land
3. a large farm where cash crops such as cotton or corn were grown
4. an addition to the United States Constitution
5. belief that the people of each state have the right to decide laws for themselves

CHAPTER COMPREHENSION

6. What effect did the growth of cash crops have on the growth of slavery?
7. Describe what life was like for enslaved African Americans in Texas.
8. What were some reasons Texas decided to secede and join the Confederacy?
9. What important announcement did Lincoln make in the Emancipation Proclamation?
10. Why was the Battle of Palmito Ranch in Texas important?
11. What role did the Freedmen's Bureau play in Reconstruction?

SKILL REVIEW

Battle of Galveston 1863

12. **Geography Skill** What is a map scale?
13. **Geography Skill** Is the map above a small-scale map or a large-scale map?
14. **Geography Skill** Would you use the map above or on page 220 to find the Battle of Palmito Ranch?
15. **Geography Skill** What is the distance between Fort Scurry and Fort Point?
16. **Study Skill** Write a summary about the life of William Goyens.
17. **Study Skill** Summarize the role Texas and its citizens played in the Civil War.
18. **Study Skill** Write a summary of the events of Reconstruction in Texas.

USING A TIME LINE

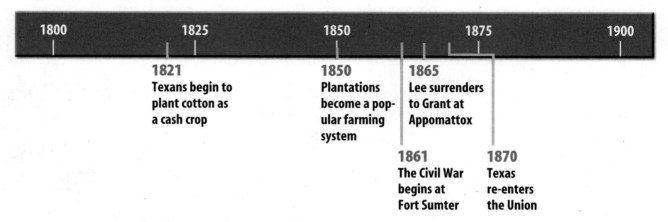

| 1800 | 1825 | 1850 | 1875 | 1900 |

1821
Texans begin to
plant cotton as
a cash crop

1850
Plantations
become a pop-
ular farming
system

1865
Lee surrenders
to Grant at
Appomattox

1861
The Civil War
begins at
Fort Sumter

1870
Texas
re-enters
the Union

19. Between what two points on the time line would you show Texas seceding from the Union?

20. Name and describe the time period between the surrender at Appomattox and 1870.

Activity

Learning About Culture Storytelling and music were important parts of the culture of enslaved African Americans. Ask a member of your family about events in your family's past. Write a story or song that tells about this event.

Foldables

Use your *Foldable* flowchart to review what you have learned about the Civil War and Reconstruction in Texas. As you look at the titles on the front of your *Foldable*, mentally recall the events that occurred in Texas before, during, and after the Civil War. Review your notes under the tabs of your *Foldable* to check your responses. Record any questions that you have on your *Foldable*, and discuss them with classmates or review the chapter to find answers.

Slavery in our State

A Nation Divided

War Between the States

Reconstruction

CIVIL WAR AND RECONSTRUCTION

6 THE Big IDEAS ABOUT...

New Growth, New Challenges

In the late 1800s, life in Texas continued to change. Cattle ranching became a booming industry in our state. Cowboys and cattle trails were a way of life for many Texans. Over time, these were replaced by railroads to carry freight across Texas. Even Native Americans were affected by these changes. They were forced to leave Texas for land set aside for them in Oklahoma.

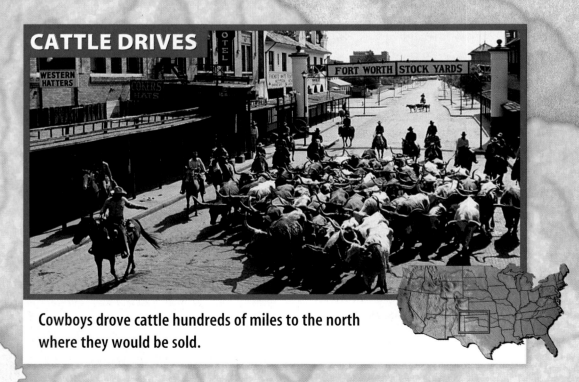

CATTLE DRIVES

Cowboys drove cattle hundreds of miles to the north where they would be sold.

RAILROADS

Railroads made transportation easier. They helped many cities and businesses in Texas grow.

CONFLICTS ON THE PLAINS

Conflicts between Texans and Native Americans over land increased. As a result, the Native Americans were forced to leave Texas.

Foldables

Make this Foldable study guide and use it to record what you learn about the Texas frontier after the Civil War.

1. Fold an 11" x 17" sheet of paper in half like a hot dog. Make one side 1" longer than the other.
2. Fold into thirds.
3. On the short side, cut along the fold lines forming three tabs.
4. Write the title of the chapter on the 1" tab. Write the titles of the three chapter lessons on the front of the other three tabs.

Cowboys and Cattle Trails

Find! out!

In what ways were cowboys a part of the Texas economy?

Lesson Outline
- Life on the Plains
- The Cattle Drive
- A Way of Life Ends

VOCABULARY

longhorn
brand
cattle drive
stampede
barbed wire

PEOPLE

Lizzie Johnson Williams
Joseph Glidden

READING STRATEGY

Make a chart like this one. Write three things about cowboy culture before and after the introduction of barbed wire.

Before	After

BUILD BACKGROUND

After the Civil War, Texas farmers could no longer rely on enslaved workers. African Americans would now be paid for their work. That meant the cost of farming would rise. In the 1860s people across the United States were hungry for beef. As a result, many Texas farmers began to raise cattle.

The Roland P. Murdock Collection, Wichita Art Museum

LIFE ON THE PLAINS

Longhorn cattle first came to Texas in the 1500s when people from Spain and Mexico settled here. The cattle were called longhorns because their horns could measure up to six feet apart!

Over the next 300 years, many new settlers in Texas became ranchers. Some lived along the Rio Grande and the **Nueces** and **San Antonio** Rivers. A few of their cattle escaped and ran wild. The number of cattle in Texas increased. By 1865, people began to call Texas the "cattle kingdom."

Cowboy Clothing

Cowboys wore clothing that helped them do their job. The shape of the broad-brimmed cowboy hat kept the rain and wind out of their faces. Chaps, which were worn over pants, were made of leather. They were used to prevent high brush from scratching the cowboys' legs.

There were about 38,000 cowboys working in the United States between 1870 and 1885. Many of them were Tejanos. Others came from different parts of the United States. Historians estimate that one in four cowboys were African American. Some women worked as cowgirls, too. They were successful in riding, roping, and herding.

Ranchers hired "line riders" to patrol the edges of the ranch. This protected the cattle from thieves and wild animals. Since there were no fences to keep cattle from wandering, cowboys went on roundups. At a roundup, cowboys rode on the Texas plains and gathered the grazing cattle. A **brand** marked each animal. This brand identified which ranch owned the cattle.

READING CHECK What were some things that helped a cowboy do his or her job?

Herding cattle along trails (left) required experienced cowboys such as Bill Pickett (right).

Western History Collections, University of Oklahoma Libraries

Cattle Trails in the 1800s

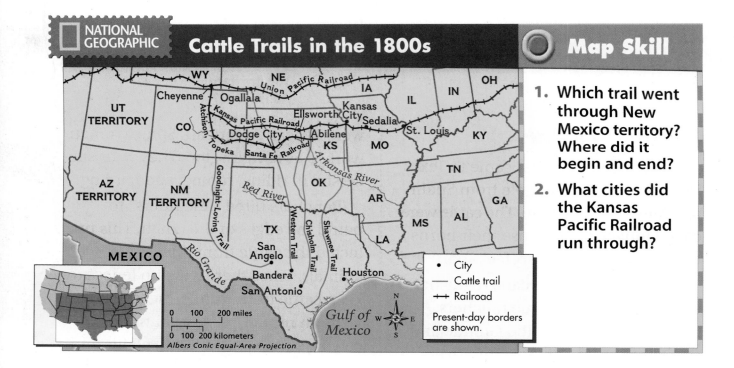

1. Which trail went through New Mexico territory? Where did it begin and end?

2. What cities did the Kansas Pacific Railroad run through?

City
Cattle trail
Railroad
Present-day borders are shown.

Gulf of Mexico

0   100   200 miles
0   100 200 kilometers
Albers Conic Equal-Area Projection

THE CATTLE DRIVE

Ranchers depended on cowboys to lead their livestock along cattle trails from Texas to northern states. This trip was called a **cattle drive**. Look at the map on this page to see the different cattle trails. Livestock were taken to states such as Wyoming, Nebraska, and Kansas. There they were sold and then sent by train to markets in the Northeast.

Ranchers could get more money for their livestock by sending their cattle north. Cattle there sold for $40. In Texas they sold for only $4.

Between 1866 and 1890, about ten million cattle were driven from the Texas plains to markets in Kansas and Missouri. That's about half the population of Texas today! At that time, the cattle industry was the biggest business in the West.

The Chisholm Trail

One of the most famous cattle trails was the **Chisholm** (CHIHZ um) **Trail**. It stretched about 800 miles from San Antonio, Texas, to Abilene, Kansas. Since cattle can walk only about ten miles a day, the drive could last three months or more.

One of the few women to drive her own herd of cattle was **Lizzie Johnson Williams**. She bought her longhorn cattle with money she earned as a teacher and writer. Soon her ranch in Driftwood, near Austin, grew so large that she was called the "Cattle Queen of Texas." Williams traveled in a horse-drawn buggy. She rose early each morning to count the cattle in her herd.

Cowboys weren't the only people on the cattle trails. There was also a trail boss and a cook.

Hazards on the Cattle Drive

Cattle drives were difficult and dangerous. To drive longhorns, two cowboys led the herd and at least two would follow behind. Several cowboys would ride on each side of the herd. They traveled across the plains and through rivers during dust storms, snowstorms, and rain.

Loud thunderstorms caused many **stampedes**. A stampede is a herd of frightened animals running wild. To stop a stampede, cowboys had to circle the cattle on horseback. It sometimes took several hours to bring the herd under control.

READING CHECK What was the purpose of the cattle drive?

Lizzie Johnson Williams (left) drove her own longhorn cattle (above right) on the trails.

Institute of Texan Cultures at San Antonio

Primary Source:

Cowboys: Memories of the Early Days

— *Excerpt from Mrs. Jack Miles in Texas*

— *edited by Jim Lanning and Judy Lanning*

On one occasion we gathered eleven hundred cattle. . . . One wild cow . . . tried to run over me and get back into the herd . . . I ran that old heifer for thirty minutes. . . . All at once she made a break . . . I slapped my spurs into [my horse] Grand Pap and wheeled around to head her off when my saddle turned under his belly and I fell . . . Jack and the boys came running to me. . . . They fixed my saddle and I went on duty again. . . .

What were the dangers this woman faced on a roundup?

THE OLD CHISHOLM TRAIL

Verse

1. Come a-long boys, and lis-ten to my tale.

I'll tell you of my trou-bles on the old Chis-holm trail.

Refrain

Come a ti yi yip-py, yip-py ay, yip-py ay,

Come a ti yi yip-py, yip-py ay.

2. I woke one mornin' on the old Chisholm trail,
A rope in my hand and a cow by the tail. *Refrain*

3. I started up the trail on October twenty-third,
Started up the trail with the old cow herd. *Refrain*

4. On a ten dollar horse and a forty dollar saddle,
I'm gonna punch those Texas cattle. *Refrain*

5. It's bacon and beans 'most ev'ry day ,
I'd as soon be a-eatin' prairie hay *Refrain*

6. It's cloudy in the west and it looks like rain,
And I left my old slicker in the wagon again. *Refrain*

7. I'm gonna see the boss, gonna get my money,
Goin' back home to see my honey *Refrain*

A WAY OF LIFE ENDS

The cattle driving years didn't last long—about 25 years. In 1873 **Joseph Glidden** began producing **barbed wire**. The sharp points on a twisted wire was inexpensive and easy to put up. The barbed wire fence put an end to both cattle grazing free and driving cattle across the wide plains.

READING CHECK

How did barbed wire change cowboy culture?

PUTTING IT TOGETHER

After the Civil War, Texas became the "cattle kingdom." Cowboys earned a living by caring for cattle and taking them to market. Fences made of barbed wire made it hard to drive cattle. However, railroads were built to carry cattle north. Ranching is still big business in Texas today.

Barbed wire brought an end to cattle drives.

CHAMPION BARB WIRE!

(Pat. Nov. 4th, 1879.)

and the **Least Dangerous** Barb Wire known. "A rod for every pound." sample to 119,121,125,127

Infringes no patents. **Galvanised** after being made, it is **Indestructible.** Is the most visible and eff..tive.

HAZARD MANUFACTURING CO., No. 87 Liberty Street, New York. Send for circular and

Kansas State Historical Society

Review and Assess

1. Write one sentence using each of the vocabulary words or terms:

   barbed wire   **brand**

   cattle drive   **longhorn**

   stampede

2. What did Joseph Glidden invent?

3. Analyze how cowboys contributed to the Texas economy.

4. Describe the cowboy way of life.

5. What was the **cause** and **effect** of driving cattle to northern states?

Activities

Suppose you need to give directions to a cowboy using the Goodnight-Loving Trail. Locate the Goodnight-Loving Trail on the map on page 238. **Write** directions from San Angelo to the end of the Western Trail.

Suppose you are a cowboy guarding a herd. **Write** the words to a short song describing your job.

Being a Good Citizen
Kids Helping Kids in Court

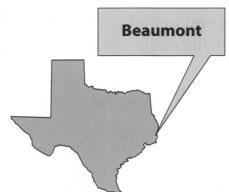

Beaumont

Every Tuesday night, Kennette Ruben stands before a judge in a courtroom. She's not in trouble, but she is helping young people who are. For five years, Kennette has served on the Teen Court in Beaumont. It is a real court run entirely by volunteers. All of the court members are teenagers except for the judge. Some act as lawyers. Others sit on a six-person jury that decides how these teens will be punished. The punishment is usually community service. "The person might work in a library shelving books, at a school picking up trash, or fixing food at a soup kitchen," says Kennette. Every person sent to this court is in trouble for the first time. Many got in trouble for fighting in school or not acting properly in the classroom.

Before serving as a Teen Court defense lawyer, Kennette and the other volunteers were trained. "I learned how a real court works and how lawyers act. I gained listening and speaking skills so I could help kids. I explain to the teens on trial what will happen in the courtroom and how they should act. I tell the jury what punishment I think they should have. Then it's up to the jury to decide."

Working in Teen Court has been an eye opener for Kennette. "It gave me more respect for the law. I learned so much about why we have laws in our community."

"I learned…why we have laws…"

Be a Good Citizen

Making Connections

- Think about the rules in your school that everyone must follow. Why is it important to obey these rules?

- What are some ways that people in your community work to prevent children from getting into trouble?

Talk About it!

- Why do you think teenagers might be embarrassed to be judged by other teens?

- What might a jury in Kennette's court consider when it decides how to punish someone?

Act On It!

In the Classroom

As a class, identify an example of a student breaking a rule. Then write a short list of possible punishments. You may vote to decide on a punishment, or ask your teacher to be the judge.

In the Community

What are some ways young people could help each other stay out of trouble in your city or town? Make a chart listing possible problems and solutions to those problems. Give your chart to your school principal or local police department.

Making Generalizations

Suppose that in your area the heaviest rainfalls occur in March, April, and May. What do these months have in common? They are the months of spring. Knowing this, you might state, *"In my community, spring is the rainiest season."*

The above statement is a generalization. It ties together different examples to show how they share a similar idea or feature. A generalization can help you see what different facts, items, or events have in common. It can also help you make sense of new information about a topic.

LEARN THE SKILL

Follow these steps to make a generalization about cattle trails in the 1800s.

1. **Identify the topic.**
   To make a generalization you must first identify the topic. In this case, the topic is *cattle trails*.

2. **Gather examples.**
   Next, gather examples about your topic. In Lesson 1, you read that cattle trails began in Texas. From there, they stretched into Kansas, Nebraska, Wyoming, and Colorado.

3. **Identify similarities in the examples.**
   What do these states have in common? They are all located in the western part of the country.

4. **Make a statement or generalization.**
   Make a statement showing how the examples share a similar idea or feature. *"Ranching was a big industry in the West"* is a generalization about the topic. You might be able to make more than one generalization from the same information.

TRY THE SKILL

In the last lesson, you also read about cowboys. They wore broad-brimmed hats to keep the rain off their faces. Leather chaps were worn to protect their legs against brush. They also wore bandanas to protect their faces against the dusty wind. Use these examples to answer the following questions.

1. What is a generalization?

2. What generalization can you make about the articles of clothing listed above?

3. What steps did you take to make your generalization?

4. Why is it important to have several examples to make a generalization?

EXTEND THE SKILL

Understanding how to make a generalization can also help you to understand history. It helps you see how different facts and events from the past are related. As you have read, barbed wire and railroads came to Texas in the late 1800s. At this same time, more settlers moved into our state. They built farms, ranches, and homes on land once part of the open range. Use these examples to answer the questions below.

• What generalization can you make about barbed wire, railroads, and new settlers?

• How does making a generalization help you understand history?

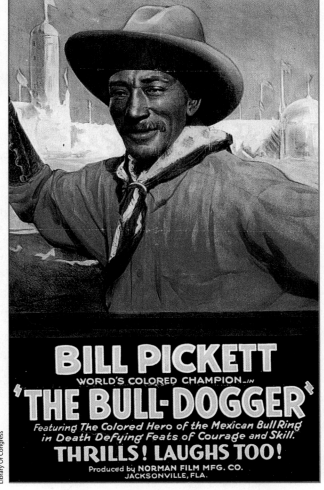

245

Changes in Texas

Find! out!

How did the spread of railroads change Texas?

Lesson Outline
- New Ways to Govern
- Extending the Railroad
- Farmers Face Challenges

VOCABULARY

Grange

reform

Texas Railroad Commission

PEOPLE

Norris Wright Cuney

Sarah Horton Cockrell

James Hogg

BUILD BACKGROUND

As more railroads were built in the late 1800s, Texas began to grow rapidly. Wherever track was laid, towns and cities grew there, too. Since it was now faster and easier to transport goods, industry grew. New cities in West Texas attracted people from all over the United States.

READING STRATEGY

Draw the chart below. List three facts about Texas before and after the spread of railroads.

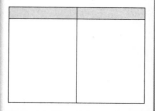

246

You Are Here
1869 – 1900

NEW WAYS TO GOVERN

In 1875 a convention was held to change the Texas Constitution. Texas leaders believed that the old constitution of 1869 gave too much power to just a few officials.

A new constitution was adopted in 1876. It cut state expenses and lessened the power of the governor and other officials. It also guaranteed that people would not be denied the right to vote because of their race.

African Americans in Government

Although guaranteed the right to vote, African Americans were denied other rights. Still, between 1870 and 1900, 43 African Americans were elected to the Texas state legislature.

A businessman named **Norris Wright Cuney** worked hard to fight against the separation between blacks and whites. For 20 years, Cuney was a delegate at every Republican National Convention.

African Americans still faced challenges in Texas even though they made gains in government and business. As you have read, during Reconstruction Southern states passed laws called "Black Codes." In some states, for example, African Americans were

DAVID ABNER. J. L. GERMAN. W. B. WRIGHT. E. L. DOHONEY. J. E. HAYNES. WM. REYNOLDS. B. B. DAVIS. W. D. S. COOK. A. T. McKINNEY. J. S. MILLS. WM. E. BRADY

Texas State Library & Archives Commission

Railroads (left) helped Texas to grow. Some African American delegates (above), worked for changes in government.

not allowed to own land or to vote. In 1868, the passage of the Fourteenth Amendment in the United States Constitution gave African Americans the rights of all citizens.

In the 1890s new laws forced the separation of blacks and whites in public places, such as trains. The areas reserved for blacks were not as good as those for whites.

READING CHECK

How were African Americans' rights limited in the late 1800s?

247

EXTENDING THE RAILROAD

After Reconstruction, the government of Texas wanted more railroads to be built. The state offered land to railroad companies for each mile of track they laid. To pay for the cost of building the track, the railroad companies sold the land to settlers.

Only about 500 miles of railroad lines had been built in Texas before the Civil War. By 1900, about 10,000 miles of track had been laid. Look at the map on this page to see how railroads grew between 1870 and 1900.

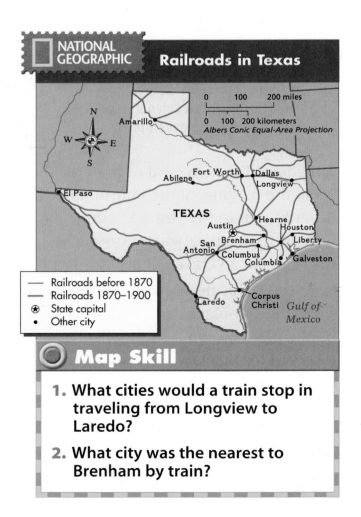

NATIONAL GEOGRAPHIC
Railroads in Texas

0   100   200 miles
0   100   200 kilometers
Albers Conic Equal-Area Projection

Amarillo

Fort Worth   Dallas
Abilene   Longview
El Paso

TEXAS

Hearne
Austin   Houston
Brenham   Liberty
San
Antonio Columbus   Galveston
         Columbia
Laredo   Corpus
         Christi   Gulf of
                   Mexico

— Railroads before 1870
— Railroads 1870–1900
⊛ State capital
• Other city

Map Skill

1. **What cities would a train stop in traveling from Longview to Laredo?**

2. **What city was the nearest to Brenham by train?**

Exploring TECHNOLOGY

How Trains Have Changed

The first trains in Texas had steam engines. Workers shoveled wood or coal into the train's firebox, a kind of oven. Heat from the firebox caused the water in a nearby tank to boil and become steam. Pressure from the steam pushed special metal rods called pistons. The pistons moved gears, which turned the wheels of the train.

Today, most trains run on electricity or diesel fuel instead. They cause less pollution.

Activity

Use your school library, the Internet, or another source to look up steam engine trains. Then draw a diagram of a steam engine. Explain what each part is and what it does.

Immigrant Labor

With so much track to lay, Texans looked to immigrants for help. Chinese immigrants built many of the railroads in Texas and across the United States. In 1869, a small group of Chinese men and one woman arrived in Houston. They cleared the land and laid down track for the Houston and Texas Central Railway.

In the 1880s more Chinese people arrived to build rail lines all the way west to El Paso. The Chinese workers were often given the most difficult and dangerous work. After the railroads were finished, many Chinese people stayed in Texas. Many started their own businesses including restaurants and grocery stores. These new businesses provided services to booming Texas cities.

The Growth of Cities

Cities grew in Texas mainly because of the railroads. By the 1870s railroad tracks had reached Dallas, Fort Worth, Austin, and San Antonio. Railroad travelers could reach Laredo and El Paso by 1881. Houston became an important railway and steamboat stop. Within two years, El Paso's population and economic resources doubled.

Trains brought new people and new businesses to Texas. A businesswoman named **Sarah Horton Cockrell** helped Dallas grow during this period. In 1872 she built a bridge across the Trinity River and charged money to those

The first Chinese woman to arrive in Texas (bottom left). Sarah Horton Cockrell (right) helped to develop the city of Dallas (above).

who crossed it. She also built two large hotels and ran several other businesses. When Cockrell died in 1892, she owned about one-quarter of the city's downtown area.

Railroads between Texas and other states made it easier for families to stay in touch. When a new stop was created on a railroad line Texans celebrated.

What were the economic results of the growth of railroads in Texas?

249

FARMERS FACE CHALLENGES

In order to feed a growing population, Texas farmers grew more crops than ever. But prices dropped because there was such a large food supply. Farmers watched the price of cotton drop from 31 cents to 7 cents per pound over three years.

While prices fell, farmers' costs were rising. This was a result of railroads charging farmers more than large businesses to transport goods.

The Grange

Most banks would not lend money to farmers. Bankers worried that farmers would not be able to repay loans. Many farmers were caught in a trap.

Farmers throughout the country united to solve these problems. They formed an organization called the **Grange**. The first local Grange in Texas was created in 1873. Over 40,000 farmers had joined by 1876.

By joining the Grange, farmers were able to buy less-expensive supplies. The Grange gave members a chance to share information about farming and ranching. These changes, or **reforms**, intended to make things better.

Governor James Hogg

Many Texans thought railroad fees were unfair. One was **James Hogg**. Hogg had worked to create the **Texas Railroad Commission** in 1891. The next year, he became governor of Texas. The railroad commission forced one railway line that had stopped sending trains to small towns to start up again. It also stopped train companies from charging more for short trips than for long ones. Governor Hogg, a Democrat, became very popular among rural Texans.

READING CHECK For what purpose was the Grange created?

Grange Poster

PUTTING IT TOGETHER

Railroads helped towns and cities to grow. But growing numbers of people moving to West Texas created problems for Native Americans. New Texans built their homes on lands where Native Americans lived and hunted. This created problems for both groups. In the next lesson you will learn how Native Americans responded to these problems.

Grange posters (far left) and Governor James Hogg (left) called attention to the unfair treatment of farmers.

Review and Assess

1. Write one sentence using each of the following words:

   Grange   **reform**

   Texas Railroad Commission

2. Who was James Hogg?

3. Describe how railroads changed our state.

4. How were African Americans **governed** in Texas in the late 1800s?

5. **Make a generalization** about how railroads caused cities to grow.

Look at the map on page 248. Which region of Texas had the most railroads before 1870? Which had the least? Write a paragraph explaining why you think these regions were like this.

Suppose you lived in West Texas in 1885. **Write** a journal entry about the first train coming to your town in 1880. Be sure to include where the train came from and what it carried.

Frontier Wars

What led to conflict between settlers and Native Americans?

Lesson Outline
- Medicine Lodge Creek
- The Red River Campaign
- The Conflict Continues

Find out!

VOCABULARY

Treaty of Medicine Lodge Creek

reservation

PEOPLE

Satanta

William Tecumseh Sherman

Quanah Parker

Cynthia Ann Parker

Ranald S. MacKenzie

Henry O. Flipper

READING STRATEGY

Copy the chart. Write how Native Americans lived before and after the Treaty of Medicine Lodge Creek.

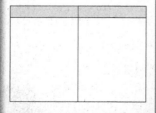

BUILD BACKGROUND

"... when I go up to the river I see camps of soldiers.... These soldiers cut down my timber [forest], they kill my buffalo; when I see that, my heart feels like bursting." Kiowa Chief **Satanta** wrote these sad words in 1867.

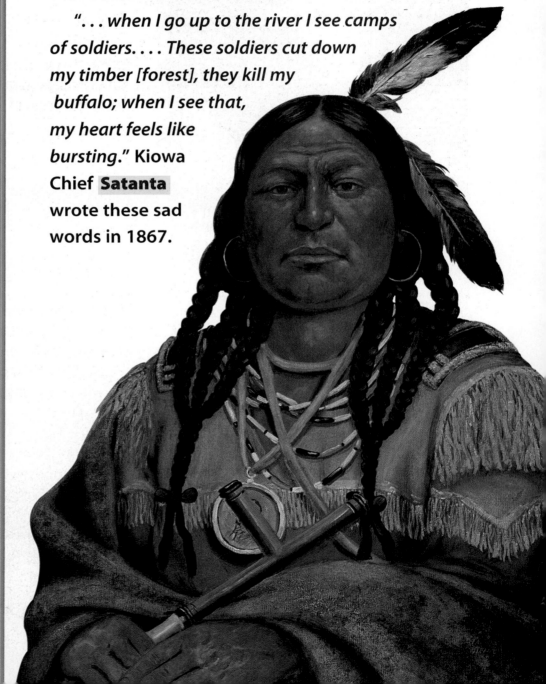

252

MEDICINE LODGE CREEK

In 1866 the United States government sent soldiers to Texas. They were ordered to stop Native Americans from raiding settlers' farms and ranches. Government representatives also met with Comanche, Kiowa, Cheyenne, Apache, and Arapaho chiefs in Kansas. There, at Medicine Lodge Creek, the representatives and some of the chiefs signed the **Treaty of Medicine Lodge Creek** in 1867.

This treaty stated that Native Americans would move to Indian Territory, in what is now Oklahoma. There they would live on **reservations**. A reservation is land set aside by the government. Some Native Americans refused to leave their land and did not sign the treaty.

Both the United States and Native Americans broke the Treaty of Medicine Lodge Creek. The United States government decided to send General **William Tecumseh Sherman** to Texas.

While Sherman was in Texas, a wagon train carrying settlers was attacked by Native Americans. Seven settlers were killed. Satanta and two other chiefs were arrested and sentenced to death. In exchange for promises of peace though, Satanta was set free. Sherman, however, decided to force the Native Americans of Texas onto reservations.

READING CHECK What was the Treaty of Medicine Lodge Creek?

Chief Satanta (left) and other Native Americans signed the **Treaty of Medicine Lodge Creek** (below).

BIOGRAPHY

Focus On: **Leadership**

QUANAH PARKER was a leader who brought together two cultures. His father was a Comanche chief. His mother was a white settler, **Cynthia Ann Parker**, who had been captured as a child and raised by the Comanche.

When Quanah Parker first became a chief, he fought hard against the white settlers. He wanted to protect the Comanche way of life. But when he saw he could not win, he agreed to move his people to a reservation.

In order to survive, Parker urged his people to live like the settlers. He had schools built, and he helped people learn to farm and raise cattle. Parker became a successful rancher.

Link to Today Think of someone you know who is a leader. List at least three ways this person has improved life in your school or community.

THE LIFE OF QUANAH PARKER	Around 1845 Quanah Parker is born	1867 Quanah Parker refuses to sign the Treaty of Medicine Lodge Creek	1875 Quanah Parker leads the Comanche to a reservation in Oklahoma	1884 The town of Quanah, Texas, is named after Chief Quanah Parker	1911 Quanah Parker dies
	1840	1860	1880	1900	1920
LIFE AROUND THE WORLD		1869 The Suez Canal is opened in Egypt	1883 Thomas Edison invents the lightbulb	1914 World War I begins	1920 Gandhi begins non-violent protest against British in India

Unlike Native Americans, buffalo hunters wanted only the hides of animals they killed.

THE RED RIVER CAMPAIGN

Quanah Parker and other chiefs led raids against buffalo hunters. As a result, the Texas Rangers joined 3,000 soldiers from the United States in 1874. They wanted to force Native Americans to move to reservations. Most Native Americans surrendered. But a few groups decided to camp along the Red River and prepare for war.

Losing the Buffalo

As you have read, the Native Americans of the plains needed buffalo to survive. They used almost every part of the animal. However, buffalo hunters wanted only the hides. Hides sold for up to three dollars each. By killing hundreds of buffalo in a day, hunters could get rich. One hunter described his work: "The biggest killing I ever made was 106 buffalo before breakfast."

In 1878, buffalo hunters killed about 100,000 buffalo in Texas in two months. Hunters were killing so many buffalo that Native Americans worried about how they would survive without them.

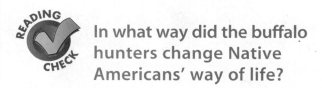

In what way did the buffalo hunters change Native Americans' way of life?

255

THE CONFLICT CONTINUES

A group of Comanche, Kiowa, and Cheyenne were living in villages at the bottom of Palo Duro Canyon. This canyon is located along the Red River in northwest Texas. On September 28, 1874, army scouts found the villages.

Five hundred soldiers climbed down about 1,000 feet into the canyon to attack the camps. They were led by Colonel **Ranald S. MacKenzie**.

During the short battle, three Native Americans and one soldier were killed. MacKenzie's men destroyed the Native Americans' food supply and killed more than 1,000 of their horses. Then the soldiers burned the villages.

Many Native Americans escaped but they could not live long without food, shelter, or horses. By November most moved to reservations. Finally in June 1875, Quanah Parker, too, led his people to a reservation.

At the time, some Kickapoo and Apache remained along the Mexican border. But by 1880 they had been forced out of Texas and into Mexico.

The Buffalo Soldiers

Two special army units were sent to states such as Texas to fight Native Americans. The Ninth and Tenth Cavalries were made up of only African American soldiers. These soldiers fought so well that they became known throughout the state. Native Americans called them "Buffalo Soldiers" after the animal they held sacred.

Buffalo Soldiers were African American cavalry units stationed in Texas.

Museum of New Mexico

The Buffalo Soldiers guarded the border between Mexico and Texas. They fought against cattle thieves, and protected wagon trains and stagecoaches. They also built new roads and telegraph lines.

Henry O. Flipper

Henry O. Flipper was the only African American army officer. He joined the Tenth Cavalry in Texas as a lieutenant. Flipper served four years in West Texas. He brought Quanah Parker's group to a reservation from Palo Duro Canyon.

Who were the Buffalo Soldiers?

Public Affairs Office, Department of Army

Henry O. Flipper

PUTTING IT TOGETHER

Many Native Americans were either killed during the Red River campaign or died afterward from disease or hunger. Those who survived were very bitter. They were no longer able to live on the open plains. Their days of hunting buffalo were over. Life was hard on reservations.

Today's Texans include members of more than 300 Native American groups. They live and work across our state and in three reservations in Texas.

Review and Assess

1. Write one sentence using each of the following vocabulary terms or words:

   reservation

   Treaty of Medicine Lodge Creek

2. Who was Chief Satanta?

3. Analyze the causes and effects of the conflicts between Native Americans and settlers in Texas.

4. What did **government** representatives do in 1867?

5. What **conclusions** can you make about Native Americans losing the buffalo?

Activities

How did the geography of Palo Duro Canyon aid Colonel Ranald S. MacKenzie and his men?

• •

Suppose you were one of the chiefs who did not sign the Treaty of Medicine Lodge Creek. **Write** a paragraph explaining your decision.

VOCABULARY REVIEW

Number a sheet of paper from 1 to 5. Beside each number write the word or term from the list below that matches the description.

Grange   **longhorn**

reform   **reservation**

stampede

1. one of a breed of cattle having very long horns

2. herd of cattle running wild

3. an association formed in the late 1800s to make life better for farmers by sharing information

4. a change designed to make things better

5. land set aside by the United States government for a purpose, such as for Native Americans to live on

CHAPTER COMPREHENSION

6. Identify two difficulties cowboys faced in herding cattle.

7. Name some of the effects the expansion of the railroads had on life in Texas.

8. What was the Treaty of Medicine Lodge Creek?

9. Describe the work done by the Buffalo Soldiers.

 ## SKILL REVIEW

Museum of New Mexico

10. **Reading/Thinking Skill** What is a generalization?

11. **Reading/Thinking Skill** Look back at Lesson 2. What generalization can you make about Norris Wright Cuney, Sarah Horton Cockrell, and James Hogg?

12. **Reading/Thinking Skill** In Lesson 3 you read about Native Americans, buffalo hunters, and buffalo soldiers. What generalization can you make about buffalos and history?

13. **Reading/Thinking Skill** How can generalizations help you understand history?

USING A TIME LINE

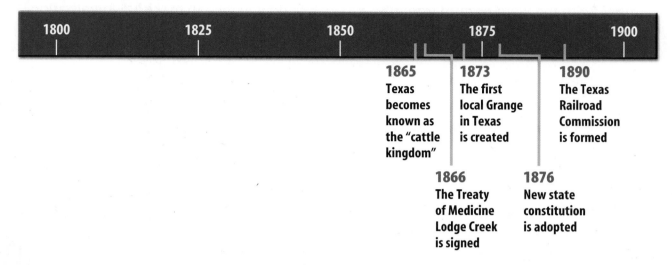

| 1800 | 1825 | 1850 | 1875 | 1900 |

1865
Texas becomes known as the "cattle kingdom"

1866
The Treaty of Medicine Lodge Creek is signed

1873
The first local Grange in Texas is created

1876
New state constitution is adopted

1890
The Texas Railroad Commission is formed

14. What were some of the reasons cattle drives ended? Indicate when this happened on the time line.

15. On the time line above indicate between which two years 43 African Americans were elected to the Texas state legislature?

Activity

Learning About Culture Suppose you were living in a Texas railroad town in the 1880s. What are some businesses you might want to start? Write or draw an advertisement for your business.

Foldables

Use your *Foldable* to review what you have learned about cattle trails, railroads, and frontier wars. As you look at the drawing of the longhorn cow, mentally recall what you learned in each lesson. Review your notes under the tabs to check your memory and responses. Record any questions that you have on your *Foldable*, and discuss them with classmates or review the chapter.

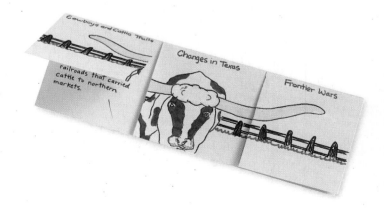

Unit 3 REVIEW

VOCABULARY REVIEW

Number a paper from 1 to 5. Beside each number write the word or term from the list below that completes the sentence.

amendment   reform

reservation   stampede

states' rights

1. ____ is the belief that the people of each state have the right to decide laws for themselves.

2. A(n) ____ is added to the United States Constitution when a change needs to be made.

3. Cowboys might spend several hours bringing a cattle ____ back under control.

4. The Grange was an association of farmers who worked for ____.

5. By 1900, most Native Americans had been forced to move to a(n) ____.

TECHNOLOGY

For more resources to help you learn more about people and places you studied in this unit, visit **www.mhschool.com** and follow the links for Grade 4 Texas, Unit 3.

SKILL REVIEW

6. **Reading/Thinking Skill** What steps do you take to make a generalization?

7. **Study Skill** Write a summary of the changes in Texas during Reconstruction.

8. **Study Skill** Summarize the effect of railroads on farming and ranching in Texas.

9. **Geography Skill** What does a map scale tell you about the map?

10. **Geography Skill** Why is it useful to have maps drawn at different scales?

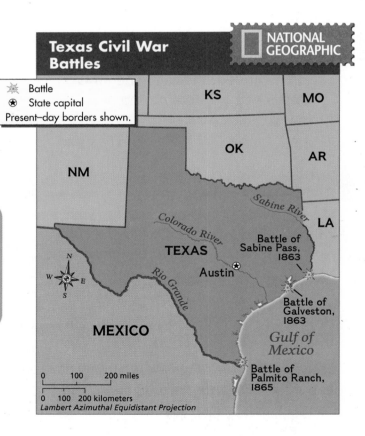

Texas Civil War Battles — NATIONAL GEOGRAPHIC

Test Power

The Texas Constitution of 1876 guaranteed that people would not be denied the right to vote because of their race. Between 1870 and 1900, 43 African Americans were elected to the Texas state legislature.

African Americans still faced challenges in Texas even though they made gains in government and business. Texas and other Southern states passed laws called "Black Codes." In some states, for example, African Americans were not allowed to own land.

1   Based on the information in the article which generalization can you make?

   A   African Americans' rights were limited in the 1880s.
   B   The Texas Constitution passed laws called "Black Codes."
   C   African Americans had no power in the 1800s.
   D   Many African Americans worked as sheriffs.

2   The author probably wrote this article to—

   A   give an opinion
   B   tell about famous people
   C   solve a problem
   D   tell readers about real events

WRITING ACTIVITIES *TAKS Practice*

● **Writing to Inform** Write a letter to someone who lives in Europe explaining the events of the Civil War and its effect on the United States.

● **Writing to Persuade** Suppose you were a farmer in Texas who wanted to start a local Grange. Write a letter to persuade other farmers to join.

● **Writing to Express** Describe the life of cowboys in Texas. Include as much detail as you can about their work, dress, and culture.

LITERATURE

THE SPINDLETOP GUSHER

Selection by Carmen Bredeson
Illustration by Linda Pierce

January 10, 1901 was the day oil was found on Spindletop in Beaumont, Texas. Patillo Higgins drilled his first well on Spindletop in 1893.

On the hill, Curt and Al Hamill and Peck Byrd finished putting a new bit on their drill. As they lowered the sharpened bit into the 1,020-foot… hole, a strange hissing noise filled the air. Suddenly, a thick **plume** of mud shot up from the bowels of the earth, and with it came 4 tons of drilling pipe. The men ran for their lives, dodging the huge chunks of metal that rained down around their heads.

---

plume (plüm) a long, moving column of a substance such as smoke or gas

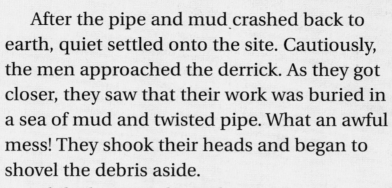

After the pipe and mud crashed back to earth, quiet settled onto the site. Cautiously, the men approached the derrick. As they got closer, they saw that their work was buried in a sea of mud and twisted pipe. What an awful mess! They shook their heads and began to shovel the debris aside.

While they were knee-deep in mud, the earth began to shake and an explosion ripped through the air. With a huge deafening roar, greenish black oil spurted from the ground. The **geyser** of oil climbed higher and higher, until it reached 100 feet…above the top of the wooden derrick.

The curious in [Beaumont] soon crowded onto rooftops and strained to get a glimpse of the plume of oil. Hundreds more wanted a closer look. They saddled their horses and hitched up their buggies for the 4-mile… ride to the site. Before long, the area around Spindletop was jammed with onlookers. They came to see history being made.

geyser (gī zer) An underground spring that shoots hot water or steam into the air

Write About It!

The Hamill brothers and the men who worked on Spindletop were very brave. Research and write about another day in Texas history when people showed their courage.

The 20th Century

TAKE A LOOK

How did Texas change in the twentieth century?

At the beginning of the twentieth century oil was discovered in Texas. This discovery and inventions from across the nation changed life in Texas.

Explore more about oil
at our Web site
www.mhschool.com

THE Big IDEAS ABOUT...

A Time of Change

Texas went through good times and hard times during the twentieth century. The discovery of oil brought wealth and jobs. New inventions such as the automobile and the telephone made it easier to travel and to communicate. Two world wars brought Texans together, but many died fighting. Read on to learn how the century affected Americans everywhere.

SPINDLETOP GUSHER!

The first oil gusher in Texas was struck near Beaumont.

WORLD WAR I

In 1918, the United States entered World War I on the side of the Allied Powers.

WORLD WAR II

Houstonians and Americans everywhere celebrated the end of World War II in 1945.

CIVIL AND EQUAL RIGHTS

In 1964, the Civil Rights Act was passed. It gave equal rights to Americans regardless of religion, sex, or race.

Foldables

Make this Foldable study guide and use it to record what you learn about the changes that occurred in Texas during the first half of the twentieth century.

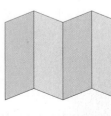

1. Fold an 11" x 17" sheet of paper in half like a hamburger.
2. Fold the hamburger in half like a hot dog, forming four long rectangles.
3. Refold to form an accordion.
4. On one side, write the titles of the four lessons at the top of the four columns.

Oil at Spindletop

How did oil change the way of life in our state?

VOCABULARY

kerosene
gusher
boom town
entrepreneur
refinery
crude oil
petrochemical

PEOPLE

Pattillo Higgins
Anthony Lucas

READING STRATEGY

Copy the word map below. Fill in four products that are created from oil.

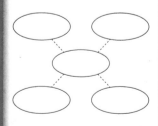

Lesson Outline
- A Valuable Resource
- It's a Gusher!
- A New Economy

BUILD BACKGROUND

In the early 1900s, the economy of southeast Texas was based on subsistence farming and the lumber business. But all that was about to change. **Pattillo Higgins** was sure that there was oil near **Beaumont**.

A VALUABLE RESOURCE

In the Introduction you read that petroleum, or oil, is more valuable than gold. The Karankawa used it to waterproof their bowls. Spanish explorers used petroleum to stop leaks in their boats. Later, pioneers used it to grease tools and wagon wheels.

In the 1850s, settlers began heating petroleum to produce **kerosene**. Kerosene could be burned as fuel in a lamp to provide light.

Oil in a Cow Pasture

Producing kerosene made oil more valuable than ever. People began digging into the ground in hopes of finding more. They wanted to "strike oil" to sell it.

In the late 1800s, Pattillo Higgins was one of these people. This real estate developer lived in Beaumont. Higgins liked to picnic in a cow pasture on a nearby hill called **Spindletop**. There he noticed gas bubbles escaping from a stream. Higgins wondered if there might be oil underground.

Higgins told a group of land owners and businessmen about Spindletop. They agreed to form an oil company. The company paid for tools that would drill into Spindletop in search of oil.

Rock and Mud

All through the 1890s, Higgins tried drilling into Spindletop. But the tools couldn't dig very deep into the earth. He hit nothing but rock and mud. Years passed and no oil was discovered. By 1899 there was no more money left to drill into Spindletop.

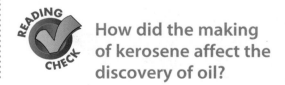

READING CHECK How did the making of kerosene affect the discovery of oil?

Texans reenact the discovery of oil at Spindletop (left) which made developer Pattillo Higgins (top) wealthy.

269

IT'S A GUSHER!

Pattillo Higgins refused to give up. He brought **Anthony Lucas**, a mining expert, to Beaumont. He agreed to hire a crew that would continue to search for oil at Spindletop.

In October 1900, Lucas's crew started drilling a well. On January 10, 1901, as the crew was working, mud suddenly exploded from the well! Then a cloud of gas hissed out. Next there was silence. But it did not last for long. A rumbling noise began to build. At last a fountain of oil, or **gusher**, burst into the air.

Boomers and Boom Towns

News of the Lucas gusher quickly spread. Beaumont became a **boom town**—a community that grows rapidly. Thousands of people streamed into Beaumont. These boomers were hoping to grow rich. Within a few months the population of Beaumont rose from 10,000 to 50,000. However, the increase in population brought many problems.

Finding a place to sleep in Beaumont became difficult. Many set up tents. Some slept in shifts if they could find a bed. Others slept in the street.

Before long the water became unfit to drink. Some Beaumonters became **entrepreneurs** (ahn truh pruh NUR) and sold clean water on the street. An entrepreneur takes risks by selling products they think people will want to buy. At one point the price of water was one dollar per gallon. That would be like paying $20 today!

Mining expert Anthony Lucas (above) struck oil while working for Pattillo Higgins. Thomas Hart Benton (left) depicted a **boom town** in this painting.

After Spindletop, boomers rushed to build their own oil rigs. By 1903 Boiler Avenue (right) in Spindletop was crowded with oil derricks.

Texas Energy Museum

Oil Changes Business

Before Spindletop, coal was the major source of fuel in the United States. The average oil well only produced about 1,200 barrels of oil a year. Spindletop changed that. In just one year Spindletop produced 3.59 million barrels of oil. By 1903 it produced 17.4 million barrels.

As a result of Spindletop, more than 500 new companies formed and began doing business in Beaumont. The oil boom not only changed business in Texas, but in the United States and around the world as well.

This new fuel powered ships, trains, and factories. Oil was shipped to Germany, England, and Mexico. Read the following to find out how supply and demand affected the price of oil.

Compare and contrast the ways in which oil was used before and after 1900.

Exploring ECONOMICS

Supply and Demand

Before Spindletop, there was not much oil available in the United States, although demand was high. *Demand* is the willingness of people to buy something and the ability to pay for it. The price of oil in early 1900 was one dollar per barrel. Soon after Spindletop the *supply* of oil increased. Supply is the willingness and ability to sell something in the market. With so much oil being produced the price of oil quickly dropped to 25 cents and then down to 3 cents per barrel.

Activity

There are 42 gallons in one barrel of oil. Look up the price of a gallon of oil in a newspaper. Now figure out how much one barrel of oil costs today.

The Power of Plastic

Plastics are all around us. They are used to make everyday appliances found in your home, and also rockets that fly into space! Each year more than 100 million tons are produced. But where do plastics come from?

People make plastics from petrochemicals. Plastics can be molded into many different shapes when heated. Thin layers of plastic coat electrical wires. Thick layers may strengthen the floor of a building.

Plastics are used to make sneakers, umbrellas, and bicycle helmets. Even shampoo and sunglasses! Plastics can help save lives, too. Life jackets, artificial hearts, and safety glasses are all made from plastics. Why do you think our country produces more plastic than steel, aluminum, and copper combined?

A NEW ECONOMY

The oil boom created many new kinds of businesses. In Beaumont, **Port Arthur**, and Sabine Pass, oil **refineries** (ri FĪ nuh rees) were built. A refinery is a factory where oil is refined or separated into parts to be used. The oil that is transported to refineries is called **crude oil**. Crude oil is the petroleum that lies near the surface of the earth. **Petrochemicals** are produced from the separated parts of crude oil. The diagram on the next page shows you how crude oil is refined.

 What are some products made from petrochemicals?

PUTTING IT TOGETHER

The discovery of petroleum changed Texas and the world forever. Boom towns appeared overnight. Oil has brought jobs, people, and wealth to our state. Today Texas produces over 1 million barrels of oil a day. Each year, our state provides about one-third of the total supply in the United States. Petrochemical products have changed the way we live. In the next lesson you will read about how other businesses in our state have grown and changed.

Refining Crude Oil

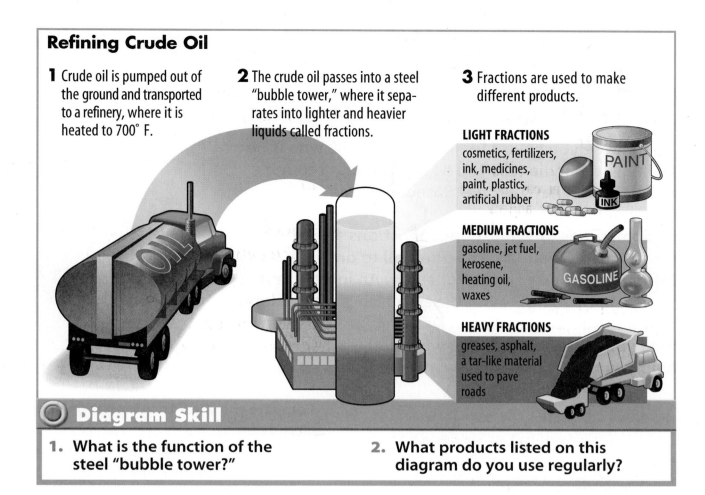

1 Crude oil is pumped out of the ground and transported to a refinery, where it is heated to 700° F.

2 The crude oil passes into a steel "bubble tower," where it separates into lighter and heavier liquids called fractions.

3 Fractions are used to make different products.

LIGHT FRACTIONS
cosmetics, fertilizers, ink, medicines, paint, plastics, artificial rubber

MEDIUM FRACTIONS
gasoline, jet fuel, kerosene, heating oil, waxes

HEAVY FRACTIONS
greases, asphalt, a tar-like material used to pave roads

Diagram Skill

1. What is the function of the steel "bubble tower?"

2. What products listed on this diagram do you use regularly?

Review and Assess

1. Use the following vocabulary words in a sentence:

boom town   **entrepreneur**

gusher   **petrochemical**

refinery

2. What is a refinery?

3. Analyze how the discovery of oil changed the way of life in our state.

4. How did the creation of a boom town cause Beaumont to change?

5. Make a **generalization** about how the oil boom helped the economy of Texas.

Activities

Make a chart showing three events that must happen in order for products to be made from crude oil.

. . . .

 Suppose you were a newspaper reporter present at Spindletop on January 10, 1901. **Write** an article describing the events of the Spindletop gusher.

Drawing Inferences

Suppose you have a friend named Eddie who is not feeling well. Eddie tells you he has sniffles, a cough, and a fever. What's wrong? Based on Eddie's clues, you figure out he has a cold.

Sometimes meanings or connections are not always made clear. It can be helpful to draw **inferences** when you read or study. An inference is something you figure out based on clues and information that you already know. Drawing inferences can help you better understand what you read. It can also help you make sense of new information.

VOCABULARY

inference

LEARN THE SKILL

Follow the steps below to draw an inference.

1. **Identify clues.**
   Suppose a family has just moved into the house next door to yours. When you go over to introduce yourself, you find them unpacking their things. In one box, they have a baseball bat, balls, and a glove. In another box, they have packed in-line skates and tennis rackets. The family tells you they plan to put up a basketball hoop in their yard. They ask if you would like to play sometime.

2. **Compare the clues to information you already have.**
   You know that bats, balls, gloves, skates, rackets, and hoops are all sports equipment. You also know that people often own items based on their interests.

3. **Draw an inference.**
   You figure out that your new neighbors enjoy playing sports. To draw this inference, you put the clues together with the information you already had. Drawing inferences is like "reading between the lines."

TRY THE SKILL

In the last lesson, you also read about the oil industry. Read the following passage. Then answer the questions below.

Oil has long been considered "black gold" in our state. Texas produces over 1 million barrels of it a day. Texan refineries break it down into gasoline, heating oil, and other valuable parts. Petrochemicals made from petroleum are used to make paint, plastics, and many other products.

1. What inference can you draw about oil and our state?

2. What clues did you use?

3. What information did you already have that helped you draw the inference?

4. How can drawing inferences help you better understand what you read?

EXTEND THE SKILL

Knowing how to draw inferences can also help you understand history. It helps connect facts and events from the past. Read the following passage about the discovery of oil in Texas. Then draw an inference and answer the questions below.

Pattillo Higgins searched for oil for nearly 10 years. His tools could not dig very deep. By 1899 he had run out of money. Several of his supporters believed it was hopeless, but Higgins kept up the search. In 1901 he finally struck oil.

- What inference can you make about Pattillio Higgins and oil?

- How can drawing inferences help you better understand history?

The "Great War" and the 1920s

Find out! *How did the 1920s affect Texans?*

Lesson Outline
• World War I
• Texans Join the War Effort
• Communications

VOCABULARY

World War I
Allied Powers
Central Powers
Roaring Twenties
invention
communication

PEOPLE

Marjorie Stinson
Katherine Stinson
Gail Borden, Jr.
Scott Joplin
Josephine Lucchese

READING STRATEGY

Draw the chart below. List three facts about life in Texas before and after the invention of the car.

Before	After

BUILD BACKGROUND

"I will build a motor car for the great multitude [most everyone]."

Henry Ford spoke these words in 1907. Ford made some of the first cars driven on the roads of Texas.

WORLD WAR I

The years leading up to the 1920s were years of growth in the United States. Between 1900 and 1914, electricity came to our towns and cities. Indoor plumbing was introduced. The first cars came to Texas. Times were good for many Texans.

Then in Europe in 1914, a nobleman named Archduke Francis Ferdinand, was killed. Ferdinand was a nobleman in line to rule the European empire of **Austria-Hungary**. His death started what became known as **World War I**, or the Great War. For the first time ever, countries around the world would fight a war against one another.

America Enters the War

At first most Americans wanted to stay out of World War I. But when ships carrying United States passengers were attacked, Americans became angry. Finally, the United States joined the war on the side of the **Allied Powers** on April 6, 1917. The Allied Powers included Great Britain, France, Russia and Italy. The "Allies" fought the **Central Powers**. The Central Powers included Germany, Austria-Hungary, Bulgaria, and Turkey.

READING CHECK What made World War I different from earlier wars?

Texans (left) were urged to fight in **World War I**. Throughout the nation posters (below) called for volunteers.

IF YOU WANT TO FIGHT! JOIN THE MARINES

277

TEXANS JOIN THE WAR EFFORT

Texans entered the war as soldiers, sailors, marines, and nurses. Women were not allowed to fight. But along with hundreds of other women, **Marjorie Stinson** and **Katherine Stinson** did their part. These two sisters helped train United States and Canadian military pilots at their flying school. Today you can visit the Stinson Air Center in San Antonio.

Texans helped to build military equipment and participated in food rations that helped feed soldiers. They produced oil for ships and planes. People also raised money for the war effort.

World War I also led to conflicts in Texas. Some German Americans were treated as possible enemies. It was also against the law to teach the German language in schools.

In 1918, World War I ended when the Allied Powers defeated the Central Powers. Americans everywhere were happy the war was over. Businesses were growing. More people than ever had jobs. Because it was such a successful time for many Americans, the 1920s became known as the **Roaring Twenties**.

Katherine Stinson (above) trained military pilots. Parades and ceremonies were held for returning soldiers (left).

New Inventions

Inventions created between 1900 and 1930 changed American culture. An invention is a newly created product. The invention that may have changed Texans' lives most was the automobile.

Automobiles were being made and driven in America since the early 1900s. During the Roaring Twenties, cars became popular very quickly. In 1917 there were just 200,000 cars in Texas. The number of cars in our state jumped to more than a million by 1926!

Cars made Texans' lives easier. People could travel more quickly. Farmers could drive their crops to the market. And since cars are fueled by gasoline, they kept our oil industry growing.

Inventions of the early 1900s included electric appliances (top right) and Gail Borden's evaporated milk (below).

Some inventions, like the vacuum cleaner, made household chores easier. The first pop-up toaster was made in 1919. New products like frozen foods and the refrigerator made it easier to cook meals.

In 1853, **Gail Borden, Jr.**, invented a new way to produce milk. By removing some of the water from milk, Borden could store and transport it more safely. During the Civil War, Borden's milk fed thousands of soldiers. After the war, Borden opened factories in and around Borden, Texas.

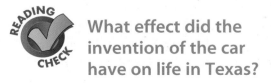 **What effect did the invention of the car have on life in Texas?**

COMMUNICATIONS

Inventions such as the radio and telephone helped Texans to stay in touch with each other and the rest of the world. There were only 500 radios in Americans' homes in 1920. By 1924, there were more than 2 million! In March 1920 the Dallas radio station WRR broadcast its first program. Now Texans could listen to the news, weather reports, and even bedtime stories on the radio. They could also hear music by Texan musicians **Scott Joplin** or **Josephine Lucchese**.

At the same time, other forms of entertainment were becoming popular across the country. Millions of Americans went to the movies each week. Every city had its "picture palaces," where people cheered at silent movies or laughed at comedians like Charlie Chaplin. Wesley Tilley was a successful silent filmmaker in Texas. His company started by showing movies at night outside of the Alamo. In 1927, the first full-length "talking" movie, *The Jazz Singer*, was shown starring Al Jolson.

Texans went to performances by musicians like Josephine Lucchese (right) and Scott Joplin (center). They also enjoyed movies (left).

The UT Institute of Texan Cultures at San Antonio

Radio and movies marked the growth of the **communications** industry. Businesses in communications are involved in the exchange of information between people.

What are some of the businesses that make up the communications industry?

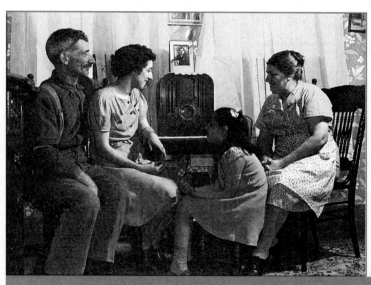

PUTTING IT TOGETHER

Americans felt both excitement and sadness during the first 30 years of the 1900s. World War I was especially deadly because airplanes carried new weapons. Other new inventions changed the way Texans lived, worked, and played. More jobs were created by growing businesses, such as the automobile industry. The Roaring Twenties was a successful time for most Texans, though some groups still struggled. In the next lesson you will learn why these good times would not last.

A family enjoys a radio program.

Review and Assess

1. Write one sentence for each of the vocabulary words or terms.

   Allied Powers   **Central Powers**

   communication   **invention**

   Roaring Twenties   **World War I**

2. Why did the United States enter World War I?

3. Analyze how life in Texas was affected by the 1920s.

4. In what ways did Texans show good **citizenship** during World War I?

5. **Draw a conclusion** about the growth of the automobile industry.

Make a list of four ways that Texans helped World War I soldiers. Then illustrate each item on your list.

• •

Working in small groups, decide on an idea for a new radio show. Then **write** a short song or jingle, introducing your show.

The Great Depression and World War II

How did the Depression and WW II affect Texans?

VOCABULARY

Great Depression
stock
New Deal
World War II
Axis Powers
Allies

PEOPLE

Franklin D.
  Roosevelt
Audie Murphy
Dwight D.
  Eisenhower
Oveta Culp Hobby
Cleto Rodriguez

READING STRATEGY

Draw the diagram below. Write the main idea and programs behind the New Deal.

Lesson Outline
• The Great Depression
• Roosevelt and World War II
• Texas During the War

BUILD BACKGROUND

Woody Guthrie lived in the Panhandle during the **Great Depression**. He said ". . . *when the dust kept whistling down the line blacker and more of it, there was plenty of everything sick . . . and worried.*"

YEARS OF DUST

RESETTLEMENT ADMINISTRATION
Rescues Victims
Restores Land to Proper Use

THE GREAT DEPRESSION

In the 1920s many Americans bought **stocks**. Stocks are shares, or parts, of ownership in a company. People hoped to earn money as businesses grew and stock prices went up. In October 1929 prices began to fall. As a result, many stockholders grew worried.

On October 29, 1929, these worried stockholders hurried to sell their stocks. The stock market "crashed" as prices fell to rock bottom.

Texans and Americans everywhere suffered after the stock market crashed. Those who had taken loans from banks often did not have the money to pay the banks back. As a result, many banks went out of business. If this happened, people who had money there, lost it. Since people could not afford to buy things, companies needed fewer workers. Many people lost their jobs. The Great Depression of the 1930s had begun.

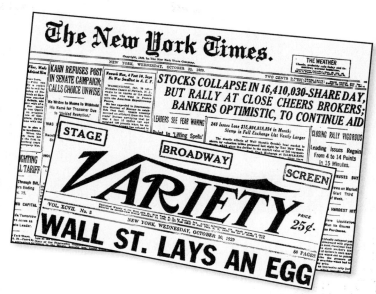

READING CHECK What led to the Great Depression of the 1930s?

A Ben Shahn poster (far left) shows how farmers were affected by severe drought. It made land too dry and dusty to farm. Newspapers reported on the stock market crash (above). Many who lost their jobs counted on soup lines (left) for food.

The UT Institute of Texan Cultures at San Antonio

283

President Franklin D. Roosevelt (below) created work programs, like the WPA. Texan artists in the WPA designed this post office mural (left) in Rockdale, Texas.

ROOSEVELT AND WORLD WAR II

Texas was hit very hard by the Great Depression. Between 1929 and 1933 more than 65,000 people lost their jobs. Farmers could not afford to keep their farms going. Many people in rural areas moved to cities to find jobs. But jobs were scarce in urban areas, too.

A new President was chosen in 1932. **Franklin D. Roosevelt**, or FDR as he was called, promised to help Americans through the hard times.

FDR Library

Roosevelt created programs he called the **New Deal**. New Deal programs put people to work improving their communities, some to help farmers, and others to help banks.

One New Deal program was the Works Progress Administration, or WPA. This program put artists, musicians, writers, and teachers to work throughout our state and country.

The Civilian Conservation Corps, or CCC, was made up of young men who built schools, parks, and bridges. They built landmarks such as the San Jacinto Monument at Buffalo Bayou near Houston, and the River Walk in San Antonio.

After Americans spent years struggling through the Great Depression, **World War II** began in 1939. The **Axis Powers**, led by Germany, Italy, and Japan, fought against the **Allies**. The Allies were led by Great Britain, France, and later the Soviet Union.

For nearly three years, the United States tried to stay out of the war. But on December 7, 1941, Japanese planes bombed the United States naval base at Pearl Harbor, Hawaii. The United States Congress declared war on Japan the next day. Germany and Italy, in turn, declared war on the United States.

Houston Public Library

Some Famous Texans

More than 750,000 men and women from our state served in the armed forces in World War II. General **Dwight D. Eisenhower** from Denison commanded Allied troops in Europe. Lieutenant **Audie Murphy** from Hunt County was the most decorated soldier during the war. Colonel **Oveta Culp Hobby** from **Killeen** was commander of the Women's Army Corps.

Thousands of African Americans from Texas served in the war. However, most were separated from white troops and were not allowed to fight in battles. Native Americans and Mexican Americans from Texas also served in World War II. Fourteen Texans received the Medal of Honor, including Mexican American Staff Sergeant **Cleto Rodriguez** of San Antonio.

READING CHECK What made the United States join World War II?

Brave Texans include Oveta Culp Hobby (top), Audie Murphy (far left), and Cleto Rodriguez (left).

SAVE FREEDOM OF SPEECH

BUY WAR BONDS

TEXAS DURING THE WAR

Texans worked hard to support the war effort. Communities across our state collected old tires for their rubber and scrap metal for military supplies. Texas provided much of the oil the military needed for fuel. Many Texans purchased war bonds to help pay the costs of the war. A bond is a piece of paper from a government that represents a loan. Women took over many jobs that men did before they left to fight. Many women worked in factories making weapons and equipment to help fight the war.

About 500 African American nurses trained for service during the war. They often worked under fire close to enemy lines. With people working at jobs that supported the war effort, World War II helped end the Great Depression.

In addition to army training camps, the government built 21 prisoner of war camps in Texas. These camps held 45,000 Japanese, German, and Italian soldiers by the end of the war.

In Kenedy, Crystal City, and Seagoville the government also set up "relocation" camps. Many Americans were afraid that Japanese Americans might be disloyal to the United States.

Posters encouraged people to buy bonds (above). Texan women trained as nurses (below) and took over many other jobs.

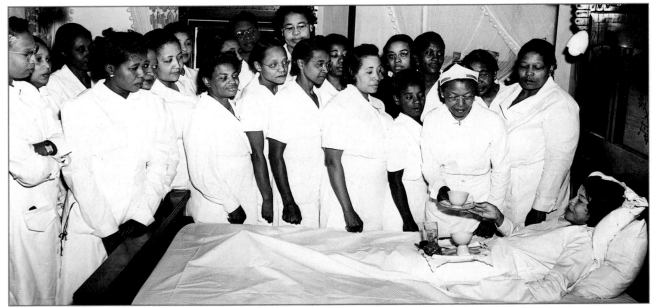

National Archives

Japanese families were sent to relocation camps in Texas.

As a result, more than 5,000 Japanese Americans were confined to these camps until the war ended. Most of these people were taken from their homes in California. Many lost their homes and businesses.

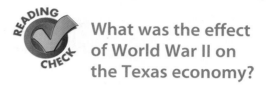
What was the effect of World War II on the Texas economy?

PUTTING IT TOGETHER

The Great Depression ended the Roaring Twenties. New Deal programs helped provide jobs. Texas and many other states did not recover from the Depression until World War II.

Germany and Japan surrendered to the United States and the Allies in 1945. Finally, Texans, like other Americans, were able to look forward to the future.

Review and Assess

1. Write one sentence for each of the vocabulary words:

   Allies   **Axis Powers**

   Great Depression   **New Deal**

   stock   **World War II**

2. Who was Franklin D. Roosevelt?

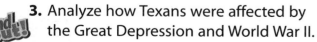

3. Analyze how Texans were affected by the Great Depression and World War II.

4. How did New Deal programs affect the **culture** of Texas?

5. **Draw a conclusion** about how World War II helped end the Great Depression.

Activities

Make a chart showing three different jobs Texans did through the Civilian Conservation Corps.

• •

 Suppose your great grandfather was a soldier during World War II. **Write** five questions to ask him about his experience.

4

Civil and Equal Rights

In what ways have Texans fought for civil and equal rights?

Lesson Outline
- Women's Rights
- Segregation
- The Civil Rights Movement
- Equality for All

VOCABULARY

suffrage

discrimination

segregation

civil rights

PEOPLE

Christia Adair

Miriam A. Ferguson

Juanita Craft

Martin Luther King, Jr.

Lyndon B. Johnson

Lady Bird Johnson

Jovita Idar

Henry Cisneros

Henry B. González

Mario Gallegos, Jr.

READING STRATEGY

Draw the diagram. List three events in the order they happened.

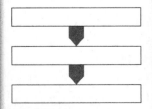

BUILD BACKGROUND

Christia Adair was an African American who fought for a woman's right to vote. She was turned away from voting in 1918.

We dressed up and went to vote, and when we got there, well, we couldn't vote. . . . that just hurt our hearts real bad . . .

Texas State Library & Archives Commission

Miriam A. Ferguson

WOMEN'S RIGHTS

The struggle for **suffrage** (SUF rihj), or the right to vote, lasted for many years. Finally, in 1920, two years after the war, the Nineteenth Amendment to the United States Constitution gave women the right to vote.

After winning the right to vote, some women ran for public office. The first woman governor of our state was **Miriam A. Ferguson**, a Democrat. "Ma" Ferguson was chosen in 1924. Some believed that she was chosen to stand in for her husband, former Governor James Ferguson. He was removed from office in 1917 for breaking the law.

In the last lesson you read about Colonel Oveta Culp Hobby. Hobby was also the second female Presidential cabinet member in history. Read how Hobby learned to value equality as a child growing up in Killeen.

READING CHECK What was the goal of the suffrage movement?

Primary Source:

excerpt from **Texas Women Who Dared to be First**
—*by Jean Flynn, 1999*

"*My father taught me I could turn the world around just as well as my brothers . . . my mother and father didn't* **categorize** *what was for a girl and what was for a boy to do.*"

What do you think Hobby meant by "turn the world around"?

categorize: to sort by group

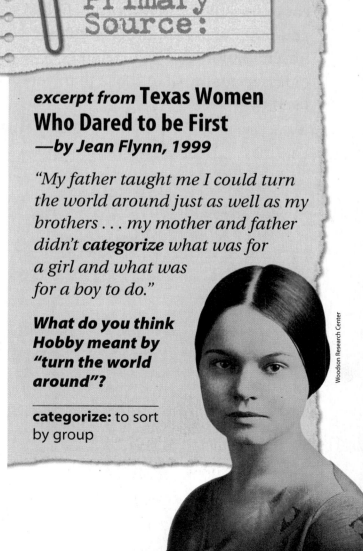

Woodson Research Center

SEGREGATION

As you read earlier, women are not the only group who are **discriminated** against. Discrimination is the unfair difference in the treatment of people. Others, including Native Americans, African Americans, and Mexican Americans, have also struggled for equal rights in the United States.

Until the 1960s, African Americans were **segregated** (seg rih GAY ted) from other groups. Segregation is the practice of keeping blacks and whites separate. Blacks were not allowed to go to the same schools as whites, or join the same clubs, or even eat in the same restaurants. Schools and other areas that were used by African Americans were usually of lesser quality than those that were used by whites.

Houston Public Library

Christia Adair worked hard in the 1950s and 1960s to open public places to African Americans. She also worked to have signs for "whites only" taken down at the Houston airport. Christia Adair had a park named after her in Harris County, Texas.

Juanita Craft of **Round Rock** and Dallas also fought for **civil rights** in Texas. Civil rights are the rights of all people to be treated equally under the law. In 1944 Craft was the first African American woman to vote in Dallas County. For fifty years, Craft worked toward equality for African Americans in schools and other public places. When she was 73, Craft, a Democrat, was elected to the Dallas City Council. There she worked toward equality for Hispanic and Native Americans.

Library of Congress

Christia Adair (above) and Juanita Craft (left) were two women who worked for **civil rights** in Texas.

THE CIVIL RIGHTS MOVEMENT

Leaders such as **Martin Luther King, Jr.**, of Georgia, led marches for civil rights. In 1963, the largest civil rights march took place in Washington, D.C. About 250,000 people were there.

In 1964 President **Lyndon B. Johnson** signed the Civil Rights Act into law. Johnson and his wife, **Lady Bird Johnson**, lived in Johnson City. Lady Bird Johnson campaigned throughout the south for civil rights.

The Civil Rights Act made it illegal for businesses to treat people differently because of their race, sex, or religion. The next year, the United States Congress passed the Voting Rights Act. This law outlawed practices—like special taxes—that were used to keep African Americans from voting.

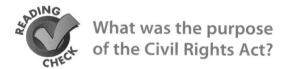 **What was the purpose of the Civil Rights Act?**

Some civil rights marches, such as this one in 1963 in Washington, D.C., were led by Martin Luther King, Jr. (left). President Johnson (above) signed the Civil Rights Act in 1964.

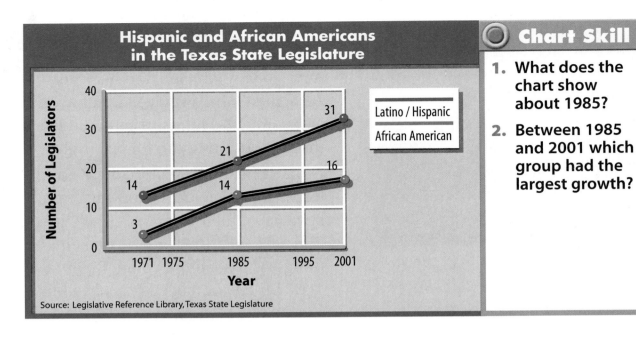

Hispanic and African Americans in the Texas State Legislature

Number of Legislators (y-axis: 0, 10, 20, 30, 40)

Year (x-axis: 1971, 1975, 1985, 1995, 2001)

Latino / Hispanic: 14, 21, 31
African American: 3, 14, 16

Legend:
- Latino / Hispanic
- African American

Source: Legislative Reference Library, Texas State Legislature

Chart Skill

1. What does the chart show about 1985?

2. Between 1985 and 2001 which group had the largest growth?

EQUALITY FOR ALL

In the early 1900s **Jovita Idar** of Laredo formed the League of Mexican Women to fight discrimination. She worked to provide free education for Mexican children. As a reporter for *La Cronica* and *El Progreso*, she spoke out against violence toward Mexican Americans. **Henry B. González**, a Democrat, became the first Mexican American Texas state senator in 1957.

As mayor of San Antonio from 1981 to 1989, Democrat **Henry Cisneros** urged Hispanic and white residents to work together to solve problems. Later, Cisneros worked against segregation in public housing.

The UT Institute of Texan Cultures at San Antonio

Jovita Idar (left) fought to improve conditions for Mexican Americans. Henry Cisneros (above) worked to end **segregation**. Today Texas Senator Mario Gallegos, Jr., (right) continues to work for equal rights.

Today Mexican Americans such as Democratic State Senator **Mario Gallegos, Jr.**, of Houston continue to work for equal rights in jobs and education.

Native Americans also fought for equal rights. In the 1870s they were forced to move to reservations. Native Americans were finally given the rights of other citizens when the Indian Citizenship Act was passed in 1924.

What Texas groups have fought against discrimination?

PUTTING IT TOGETHER

American women gained the right to vote more than 80 years ago. However, it was not until 1965 that all Americans could freely vote. Even though gains have been made for many groups of Americans, more still needs to be done in the fight for equality.

State Senator Mario Gallegos, Jr.

Review and Assess

1. Write one sentence for each of the following vocabulary words or terms.

   civil rights   **discrimination**

   segregation   **suffrage**

2. Who was Martin Luther King, Jr.?

3. Compare and contrast the ways that Texans have worked toward civil and equal rights.

4. In what ways did Texan Juanita Craft show good **citizenship**?

5. **Draw a conclusion** about how the efforts of early suffragists change women's lives.

Activities

Make a chart listing three people from this lesson. Next to each name list the person's accomplishments.

. . . .

Suppose you wanted to lead a civil rights group. **Write** a paragraph describing why you would be a good leader.

VOCABULARY REVIEW

Number a sheet of paper from 1 to 5. Beside each number write the word or term from the list below that matches the description.

communication   discrimination

entrepreneur   New Deal

segregation

1. an exchange of information between people
2. a person who owns and runs a business or businesses
3. an unfair difference in the way people are treated
4. programs set up by President Franklin D. Roosevelt during the Great Depression
5. the separation of two groups of people

CHAPTER COMPREHENSION

6. What caused the Great Depression of the 1930s?
7. Name at least three products that are made from crude oil.
8. What was the importance of Spindletop to the Texas economy?
9. What year did women win the right to vote? What is the right to vote called?
10. With which countries did the United States fight World War I? World War II?
11. What was the main idea behind the Civil Rights Act of 1964?
12. Suppose you were living in Texas in 1941. Write a diary entry telling a friend what you did to help the war effort.

SKILL REVIEW

13. **Reading/Thinking Skill** What is an inference?
14. **Reading/Thinking Skill** What steps should you follow to draw an inference?
15. **Reading/Thinking Skill** How can drawing inferences help you better understand history?
16. **Reading/Thinking Skill** Read the section under "New Inventions" on page 279. What inference can you make about the gasoline engine?
17. **Reading/Thinking Skill** What inference can you make about the effect the automobile industry has had on the oil industry?
18. **Reading/Thinking Skill** Name some occasions in school when you might need to draw inferences?

USING A TIME LINE

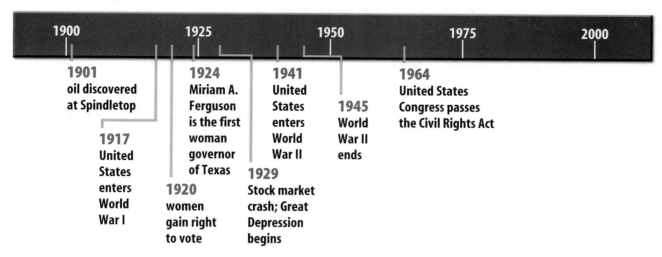

| 1900 | 1925 | 1950 | 1975 | 2000 |

1901
oil discovered
at Spindletop

1917
United
States
enters
World
War I

1920
women
gain right
to vote

1924
Miriam A.
Ferguson
is the first
woman
governor
of Texas

1929
Stock market
crash; Great
Depression
begins

1941
United
States
enters
World
War II

1945
World
War II
ends

1964
United States
Congress passes
the Civil Rights Act

19. How many years passed between women gaining the right to vote and the passing of the Civil Rights Act?

20. Choose the event from the time line that had the biggest effect on the economy of Texas. Then write a paragraph explaining the effects this event had.

Writing About Government Working with a small group, make a chart listing at least four ways that the United States government helped Texans during the years 1900 to 1964. Then illustrate your chart.

Foldables

Use your *Foldable* to review changes that took place in Texas during the first half of the twentieth century. As you look at your field of oil wells, mentally recall events before, during and after World Wars I and II. Review your notes under the lesson titles on the back of your *Foldable* to check your memory and responses. Record any questions that you have on your *Foldable*, and discuss them with classmates or review the chapter to find answers.

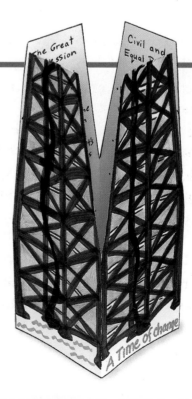

Economic Growth

The many goods and services provided by Texans make up our state's economy. People across the country and around the world use products that come from Texas. In this chapter, you will learn more about the Texas economy and how our local industries help it to grow.

DOING BUSINESS

Every Texan is a part of our economy. Some start businesses, while others buy the goods and services they sell.

IMPORTANT TEXAS INDUSTRIES

The Texas triangle is home to industries such as manufacturing, food processing, and high-technology.

FARMS AND RANCHES FOR THE FUTURE

Farmers and ranchers use modern technology to raise crops and livestock.

Foldables

Make this Foldable study guide and use it to record what you learn about the economic growth of Texas.

1. Fold a sheet of paper like a hamburger, but make one side 1" longer than the other.

2. Make two cuts on the short side, dividing it into three equal sections.

3. Write the title of the chapter on the 1" tab, and the three lesson titles on the three cut tabs.

Our Free-Enterprise Economy

Find Out!

How does the free-enterprise economy work in Texas?

VOCABULARY

free-enterprise system
profit
investor
assembly line
consumer

READING STRATEGY

Copy the chart you see here. Write a sequence of events for this lesson as you read.

Lesson Outline

- Getting Started
- Producers and Consumers
- Succeeding in Business

BUILD BACKGROUND

In the United States, our economy is based on a **free-enterprise system**. Under this system anyone can own and run a business. The owners decide what to make or sell. Each of us decides what to buy based on what we want or need and how much we are willing to pay. Under this system, everyone makes his or her own economic decisions.

Asian American students in Houston (right) started a business (left) to learn about the **free-enterprise system** .

GETTING STARTED

Most Saturdays, students from high schools near **Houston** attend a special school to study Chinese culture. In the fall of 2000, the students at the school decided to learn about the free-enterprise system by starting a business called Millennium Enterprise.

Choosing a Product

The students wanted to make and sell products that were unusual, attractive, and interesting to people in their community. Student Duke Hwang (hwayng) suggested making large paper animals. "I thought the animals would be a special gift for friends and family. I knew there was nothing like it in a store," said Hwang. The group decided to make paper owls, cats, chickens, and swans.

The students became entrepreneurs. As you have read, entrepreneurs are people who risk using their money to create products they think people will buy. If a business is successful, an entrepreneur makes a **profit**. Profit is money a business earns after it pays for supplies, tools, salaries, and other costs. It is a return for hard work—and for taking a risk.

Choosing Managers

Every business needs leaders, called managers. They create a plan for the business, assign tasks, and check to see that everyone does their job properly. James Chen was one of the company managers.

The students asked Wenie Chen, a teacher, and Peter Hwang, a business owner, to be their advisors. They knew good advice would help their business to succeed.

How did the students choose a product to make and sell?

Students created an **assembly line** (left) to make animals (below) from folded pieces of paper.

PRODUCERS AND CONSUMERS

The students soon learned that it takes hard work to make a business succeed. Starting a business also costs money. Most businesses need to borrow money to get started. Often businesses borrow money from **investors**. An investor is someone who puts money into a business and expects to get some of the profit in return. The investors in Millenium Enterprise were the students, a few of their family members, and some people in the community.

With the money from their investors, the students bought the materials and tools to make their products. The students also found out they could get recycled paper to use at no cost. "This helped keep costs down, which pleased our investors," said James Chen.

Making the Product

Each paper animal consists of almost 250 triangles. One student might take four hours to make one animal. So the students thought of a better way. They formed an **assembly line** to make the work go faster. On an assembly line the work of making a product is divided into many different steps. Cars, for example, are manufactured on assembly lines. Some students cut the paper into pieces. Others folded it into small triangles. Others glued the triangles together to make different animals. Still others prepared gift boxes.

Competition and Customers

Once they made the products, the students had to let **consumers** know about them. Consumers are people who buy a product or use a service.

Amy Lin was in charge of advertising. She and other students made posters to put up at the Chinese center. One student used his computer to create a Web site about their products. Students also showed product samples to teachers and classmates at their high schools.

The students also set up a booth at a trade fair in a local shopping mall. Many shoppers came to look at their products. "People who bought them told their friends and this brought in more buyers," said Lin.

Making Choices

In the free-enterprise system, consumers have many choices. At a shoe store Texans can choose from many different brands of tennis shoes. Grocery store shelves hold dozens of

different kinds of soap or cereal. Each business wants shoppers to choose its product.

Because producers are competing against each other for consumers, each tries to make the best product it can. Producers also try to set a price for their product that will be close to prices set by other businesses selling the same product.

READING CHECK **How does competition help the consumer?**

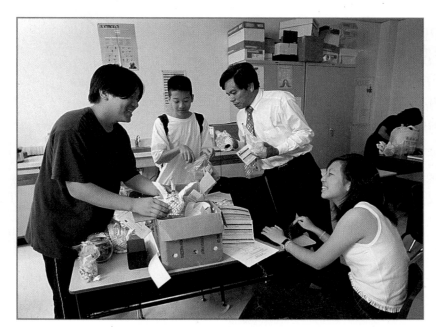

A proud student (above) shows off an owl she helped to make. Millennium Enterprise students worked together to package an animal for shipment to a customer (left).

Some entrepreneurs who succeed in business want to share what they have learned with others. On page 304, you will read about an entrepreneur who is using her knowledge and experience to give something back to her community.

Another way entrepreneurs help the community is by creating jobs. Businesses in some industries need many employees, but others need only one or two. Most businesses in the United States have fewer than 500 employees. You will learn more about small businesses from the datagraphic on the next page.

SUCCEEDING IN BUSINESS

"When we were deciding how much to charge for our paper animals," said Lin, "we tried to guess how much people our age would be willing to pay for a gift item like this. We knew that if our price was too high, consumers would choose something else instead."

In the first year, investors in Millennium Enterprises made a profit of 38 cents for each dollar they invested. The students sold over $2,000 worth of goods and earned a profit of more than $120. They even won an award for most creative new product from an organization that teaches students about business.

 READING CHECK How did the students decide on a price for their product?

The paper animals were packed carefully (below). **Consumers** learned about the products through advertising (above).

DATAGRAPHIC

Small Businesses in Texas

A company that has fewer than 500 employees is called a small business. In 2000, 99 out of every 100 companies across our country were small businesses. Use the charts on this page to learn more about small businesses in Texas.

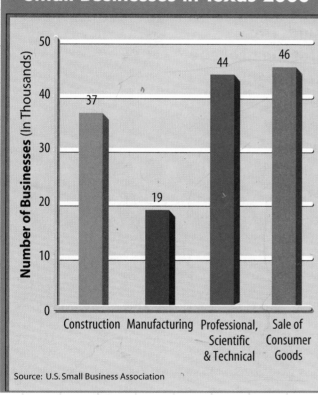

Small Businesses in Texas 2000

Number of Businesses (In Thousands)

- Construction: 37
- Manufacturing: 19
- Professional, Scientific & Technical: 44
- Sale of Consumer Goods: 46

Source: U.S. Small Business Association

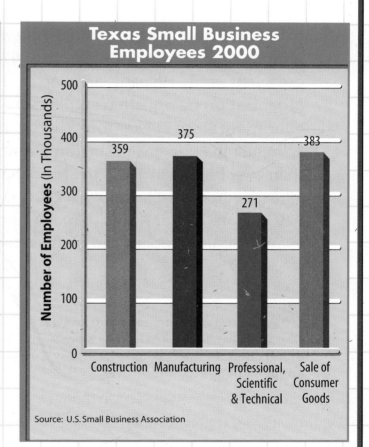

Texas Small Business Employees 2000

Number of Employees (In Thousands)

- Construction: 359
- Manufacturing: 375
- Professional, Scientific & Technical: 271
- Sale of Consumer Goods: 383

Source: U.S. Small Business Association

QUESTIONS

1. In what industry were the largest number of small businesses?

2. What industry employed the fewest people in small businesses?

3. What conclusion can you draw based on the two charts?

To learn more, visit our Web site:
www.mhschool.com

BIOGRAPHY

Focus On: Leadership

Sara Martínez Tucker is a special business leader. Tucker went to the University of Texas at Austin. When she graduated, she got a job with a major telephone company. Tucker worked hard. She became the first Hispanic woman executive at the company.

But Tucker did not stop there. She wanted to help other people reach their goals. In 1997, she became president of the Hispanic Scholarship Fund. This organization helps Latino students pay for their college education. Since Tucker took charge, the Hispanic Scholarship Fund has raised more money than ever before. In 1997, the fund gave away $3.5 million in scholarships; in 2000, it gave $20 million. Tucker wants to make sure that every Hispanic student can go to college.

Link to Today Interview someone you know who went to college. Then write a paragraph about how a college education might be helpful to you.

Hispanic Scholarship Fund

THE LIFE OF SARA MARTINEZ TUCKER	1955 Sara Martínez Tucker is born in Laredo	1979 Tucker gets a masters degree from the University of Texas at Austin	1990 Tucker is promoted to executive at a phone company	1997 Tucker becomes president and CEO of the Hispanic Scholarship Fund
1950	**1965**	**1980**	**1995**	**2010**
LIFE AROUND THE WORLD	1950-53 The Korean War is fought	1969 Neil Armstrong is the first person to walk on the moon	1991 The cold war ends	2008 China is scheduled to host the Olympic Games

PUTTING IT TOGETHER

There are many ways of participating in the free-enterprise system. The students who formed Millennium Enterprises did so by starting a business. These same students and their family members also invested in the business to earn a profit. Finally their customers took part in the free-enterprise system by buying the paper animals.

Pineapple

Review and Assess

1. Write one sentence for the vocabulary words:

   assembly line   **consumer**

   investor   **profit**

2. What is the free-enterprise system?

3. Describe some of the ways you participate in the free-enterprise system in Texas.

4. In the free-enterprise system, producers and consumers make decisions. Make a graphic organizer showing the decisions the students at Millennium Enterprise made to create a successful business.

5. How did the students **solve the problem** of making more paper animals in less time?

Write a paragraph describing a business that you would like to run. Think about what type of goods or services you would produce and how you would let consumers know about your product.

• •

Make an Entrepreneur Chart. On one side make a list of the risks of starting your own business. On the other side list the rewards of owning your own business.

Modern Industries in Texas

VOCABULARY

technology
manufacturing
food processing
high-tech industry
service industry
tourist

PEOPLE

Mae Jemison

READING STRATEGY

Copy the chart you see here. Write the main idea of this lesson in the center. Add supporting details as you read.

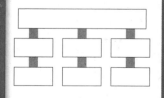

What kinds of businesses are growing in Texas today?

Lesson Outline
• Modern Industries
• Space Technology
• At Your Service
• Industry and Environment

BUILD BACKGROUND

Many industries in Texas made goods by mass production during World War II. This means making a lot of one item, all exactly the same. However, one important industry didn't develop until after World War II. Today, the **technology** industry is a growing part of our economy. Technology is the use of scientific ideas, special skills, and tools to meet people's needs.

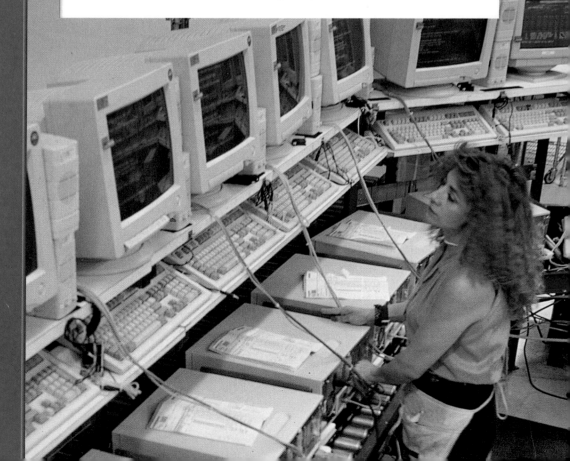

MODERN INDUSTRIES

Only ten countries in the world have economies larger than our state! The Texas economy is made up of many different businesses. Some are large companies that have offices around the world. Others may only have a few people working at them.

Texan Oil

You have already read about the beginnings of the oil industry in Texas. Today, more than 150,000 Texans are employed in all of the energy-producing industries, such as oil, gas, and coal. Texas is the top oil producer in the United States. It also has the advantage of having the eighth largest port in the world. The **Houston Ship Channel** is a 50-mile-long waterway between Houston and the Gulf of Mexico. Ships carrying petrochemicals leave Houston and travel to more than 200 countries around the world.

An Industry Leader

Manufacturing and **food processing** are two more Texas industries. Manufacturing is the making of goods by machinery. Texas manufactures many products such as lumber, electronics, and chemicals.

Food processing includes any business that uses raw food to create products to be sold. These factories may produce canned soup, refined sugar, packaged rice, or even potato chips.

One of the most important food processes involves cottonseeds. The seeds are processed to remove the cottonseed oil for use in cooking oil, mayonnaise, and margarine. The crushed seeds are fed to livestock.

READING CHECK ✓ **What kinds of industries are included in our state?**

The **technology** industry (left) and the **food processing** industry (above) are important parts of the Texas economy. Many products (right) are made in our state.

Smoky Hill Salsa Verde
Mesquite Roasted Jalapeños
MEDIUM
Austin Spice Company
Refrigerate After Opening
Net Wt. 12 oz. (360g)

307

SPACE TECHNOLOGY

"Houston, Tranquility base here, the Eagle *has landed."*

"Rocket Tranquility, we copy you on the ground . . . We're breathing again."

The entire world watched and listened when Buzz Aldrin and Neil Armstrong first landed on the moon. They almost ran out of fuel and had to give up the mission. When Aldrin spoke the words above, the relieved response came from Mission Control in a suburb of Houston named **Clear Lake**.

Today, it is called the **Johnson Space Center** and employs more than 3,000 people. Astronauts train at the special school there. The center also plans and supervises programs such as the Hubble Telescope, International Space Station, and missions to Mars.

Thinking Smaller

Not all technology is the size of a spaceship. Advanced electronics use computer chips so small that 25 of them fit into one inch.

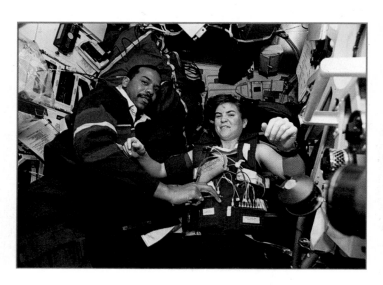

Texas is the home to training facilities for astronauts (top) and companies that make tiny processing chips (below).

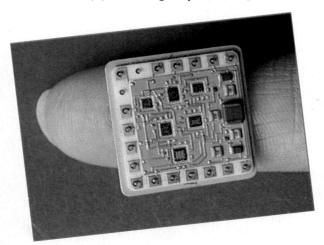

Since the 1950s, Texas has been home to many electronics companies. Calculators, cash registers, CD players and VCRs contain electronics designed in Texas.

If your home or school has a computer in it, there's a good chance a company headquartered in cities such as Houston or Austin made it. Texas also exports computers to countries such as Australia, Spain, and India.

These companies make up the **high-tech industry**. They develop goods based on an advanced knowledge of science and math. The "tech" in *high tech* is technology. Only California has more high-tech jobs and exports than Texas.

READING CHECK Name some items that contain electronics made in Texas.

BIOGRAPHY

Focus On: Courage

When Mae Jemison was born in 1956, there were few women or minorities in the sciences. It took courage for her to decide to study chemical engineering and go to medical school.

After working as a doctor for several years, she decided to do something that required even more courage. She applied to join the space program. As an astronaut, she trained to work aboard the space shuttle.

In September of 1992, she became the first African American woman to go into space. While in orbit, she conducted more than 44 experiments.

Today, she is an entrepreneur and has her own company in Houston that explores ways to use advanced technology in under-developed countries. She also teaches college classes.

Link to Today

Using your school library or the Internet, find out what other former astronauts have gone on to do. Explain how their current work requires courage, even if it isn't as dangerous as going into space.

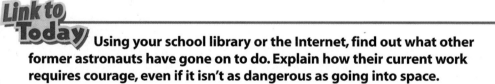

THE LIFE OF MAE JEMISON:	1956 born in Decatur, Alabama	1983 works as a doctor in the Peace Corps	1992 becomes the first African American woman in space aboard the *Endeavor* space shuttle	1993 starts her own company called The Jemison Group
1955	**1965**	**1975**	**1985**	**1995**
LIFE AROUND THE WORLD	1969 astronauts walk on the moon	1981 first space shuttle flight is made by *Columbia*	1986 space shuttle *Challenger* explodes a few seconds after take-off	1989 first night time launch of a space shuttle

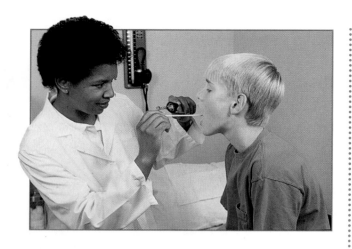

AT YOUR SERVICE

Many people continue to move to the major cities of our state from rural areas and from other parts of the United States. Businesses need offices and factories to do their work. The people who work for these businesses need homes. Both of these needs are met by the construction industry in Texas. People in the construction industry probably built the house you live in and the school you attend.

The **service industry** is made up of people whose job is to help others. Doctors, teachers, salespeople, and firefighters are all in the service industry. So are people working in stores, restaurants, and the government.

The service industry is the largest industry in Texas and employs 2.8 million people. By 2000, the industry was also responsible for creating two out of every five new jobs.

Some service workers help **tourists**, or visitors, who come to Texas. The tourism industry helps visitors to learn about our state and enjoy the time they spend in Texas.

Doctors (above) are part of the service industry. Tourists at the San Antonio Riverwalk (below) support our economy.

In 1999, people from all over the world took 178 million trips to places in our state. Jobs in the tourism industry include making travel arrangements, running hotels, working at airports, and leading tours of historical areas.

Economic Areas

Many businesses are located in Texas because of our state's resources. Some businesses need to be near natural resources such as oil, forests, or ports on the Gulf of Mexico. Other resources are found in our cities.

More than 82 percent of Texans live in urban areas. As of 2000, Dallas is Texas's largest city with more than two million people in it. Houston and San Antonio are the second and third largest cities in Texas. Both Dallas and Houston are among the top ten largest cities in the United States.

Look at the map on this page and locate the three largest cities in our state. You will see that they form a triangle. More than 80 percent of the Texan population lives within 200 miles of the center of this "Texas triangle." This area is also the home of many Texas schools and colleges. For example, more than 44,000 students attend Texas A&M University, located in the middle of the triangle.

The population of these cities makes it easy for industries to hire the workers they need. They are also centers for schools, universities and hospitals. Highways and public transportation between the cities make it easy for people to travel. This triangle forms an economic region of resources that can help businesses to succeed.

READING CHECK What types of work do people in the service industry do? How do you know?

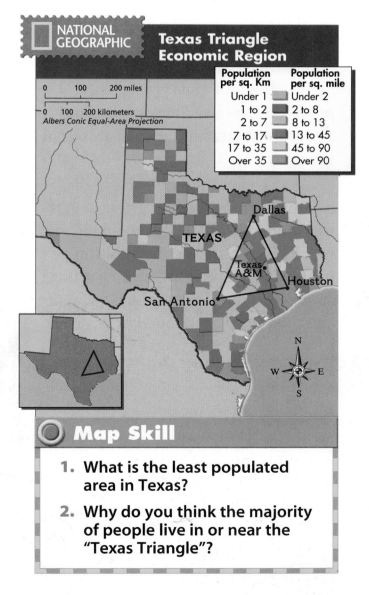

NATIONAL GEOGRAPHIC

Texas Triangle Economic Region

Population per sq. Km	Population per sq. mile
Under 1	Under 2
1 to 2	2 to 8
2 to 7	8 to 13
7 to 17	13 to 45
17 to 35	45 to 90
Over 35	Over 90

0   100   200 miles
0   100   200 kilometers
Albers Conic Equal-Area Projection

Dallas
TEXAS
Texas A&M
Houston
San Antonio

Map Skill

1. What is the least populated area in Texas?

2. Why do you think the majority of people live in or near the "Texas Triangle"?

311

INDUSTRY AND ENVIRONMENT

Texas industries supply the country and the world with many important goods. These industries also provide jobs and income for our state. However, the rapid growth of these industries can also affect our environment.

Factories, trucks, ships, and cars can all cause pollution. Ships traveling to Texas ports can leak oil or chemicals. Petrochemical products are dangerous if they are not handled carefully, and toxic chemicals are used to manufacture electronics. Even homes and hospitals create waste materials that can damage the land and water unless they are disposed of correctly.

Texans want their state to have a healthy environment. To preserve it, the state and individual cities regulate how waste materials and chemicals can be treated. They spend money to learn about what damages the environment and how it can be stopped or reversed.

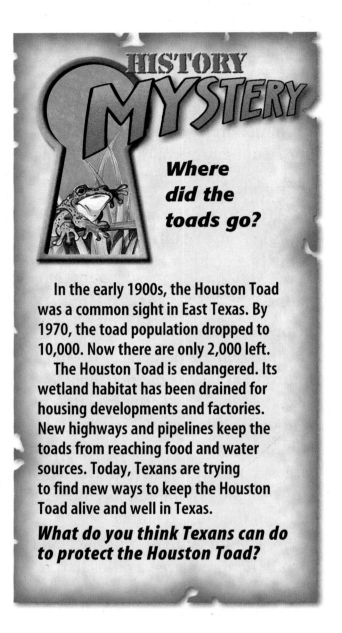

HISTORY MYSTERY

Where did the toads go?

In the early 1900s, the Houston Toad was a common sight in East Texas. By 1970, the toad population dropped to 10,000. Now there are only 2,000 left.

The Houston Toad is endangered. Its wetland habitat has been drained for housing developments and factories. New highways and pipelines keep the toads from reaching food and water sources. Today, Texans are trying to find new ways to keep the Houston Toad alive and well in Texas.

What do you think Texans can do to protect the Houston Toad?

Economy and Environment

The Texas Natural Resource Conservation Commission is a government agency that protects our environment. It does this by deciding how money should be spent to clean up the environment.

Dangerous materials (left) that are not disposed of properly by industries must be cleaned up to protect our environment and wildlife (right).

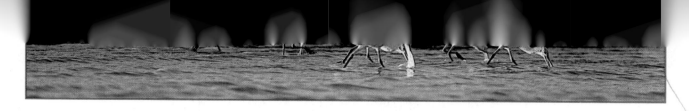

The commission also promotes conservation efforts, monitors dangerous waste materials, and recommends legislation.

We know that our land and people are the key to our strong economy. Preserving our state's environment is an important part of keeping the Texas economy in balance.

 READING CHECK What are some ways the environment in Texas can be harmed?

PUTTING IT TOGETHER

Texas is the home of many industries today. Some, such as food processing and manufacturing, developed from earlier industries in farming and making military supplies. Other industries serve people in towns and cities, or even visitors to our state. One of the newest and biggest industries in our state is technology. In the next lesson, you will learn how technology is helping some of the oldest industries in Texas to advance.

Review and Assess

1. Write one sentence for each vocabulary word.

   food processing   **high-tech industry**

   manufacturing   **service industry**

   technology   **tourist**

2. Who is Mae Jemison?

3. **Find! Out!** Choose one industry in Texas today and describe the businesses, people, and the products that make it up.

4. What are some ways the **government** of Texas protects our environment?

5. Make a **generalization** about the reasons Texas cities are home to many kinds of businesses.

Choose an industry you read about in this lesson. Using your textbook, school library, or the Internet, find out how many jobs this industry had over the last twenty years. Make a graph or chart of your information.

• •

Write a letter to a business you would like to see move to Texas. Explain why Texas is a good place to do business and what resources might be helpful to the business. Then exchange your letter with a partner. Check for spelling, punctuation, and capitalization.

Reference Sources

If you wanted to learn more about astronauts, you could do research using **reference sources**. These are books and other sources that contain facts about many different subjects. They can be found in a special part of the library called the reference section.

LEARN THE SKILL

The steps below show ways to use reference sources.

1. **Use a dictionary.**
   You might want to know the exact meaning of the word *astronaut*. To find out, you would look in a **dictionary**. A dictionary gives the meanings of words. It shows how to pronounce and spell each word.

2. **Use guide words.**
   The words in a dictionary are arranged in alphabetical order. To find your word quickly, you can refer to **guide words**. These appear at the top of each page of the dictionary. They tell you the first and last words defined on that page.

3. **Use an encyclopedia or a CD-ROM.**
   Another useful reference tool is an **encyclopedia**. This book or set of books gives information about people, places, things, and events. Like a dictionary, topics in an encyclopedia are

arranged in alphabetical order. Suppose you want to learn more about space shuttles. You would look in the encyclopedia volume, or book, with the letter *S* on the spine.

A newer kind of reference source is the **CD-ROM**. A CD-ROM is a compact disc that you "read" with the aid of a computer. Like an encyclopedia, a CD-ROM contains facts about many subjects. It may also include sounds, music, and even short movies! The **Internet** is another new kind of reference source. It is a computer network. If you use a computer that has an Internet connection, you can "visit" sources of information such as schools or government offices.

TRY THE SKILL

Look at the sample dictionary page below. Use it to answer the following questions.

1. What is the last word to be defined on the page?

2. Would the word *star* appear on the page? How about the word *spaceship*?

3. Which volume of the encyclopedia would you use to learn more about Buzz Aldrin?

4. Some encyclopedias have guide words instead of letters. Suppose you had a volume covering everything from *Mars* to *Space*. Would it contain an article about *rockets*? What about *sun*?

EXTEND THE SKILL

Use reference sources in your school or local library to write a paragraph on the Hubble Space Telescope. Include the meaning of the word *telescope* and information on how telescopes work. Use your paragraph to answer the following questions.

- Which reference source did you use to find the meaning of the word *telescope*?

- Which reference source did you use to research how telescopes work?

- When are reference sources useful to students?

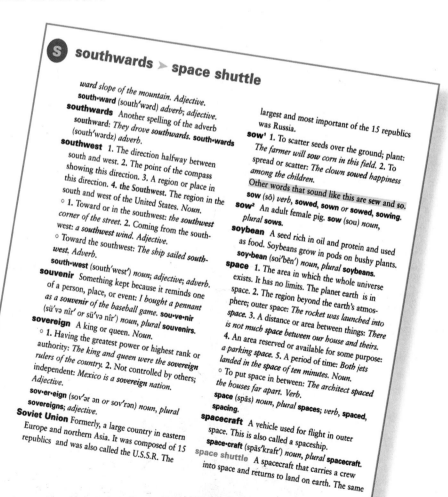

S southwards ➤ space shuttle

ward slope of the mountain. *Adjective.*
south·ward (south′wərd) *adverb; adjective.*
southwards Another spelling of the adverb southward: *They drove southwards.* **south·wards** (south′wərdz) *adverb.*
southwest 1. The direction halfway between south and west. 2. The point of the compass showing this direction. 3. A region or place in this direction. 4. **the Southwest.** The region in the south and west of the United States. *Noun.*
∘ 1. Toward or in the southwest: *the southwest corner of the street.* 2. Coming from the southwest: *a southwest wind. Adjective.*
∘ Toward the southwest: *The ship sailed southwest. Adverb.*
south·west (south′west′) *noun; adjective; adverb.*
souvenir Something kept because it reminds one of a person, place, or event: *I bought a pennant as a souvenir of the baseball game.* **sou·ve·nir** (sü′və nîr′ or sü′və nîr′) *noun, plural* **souvenirs.**
sovereign A king or queen. *Noun.*
∘ 1. Having the greatest power or highest rank or authority: *The king and queen were the sovereign rulers of the country.* 2. Not controlled by others; independent: *Mexico is a sovereign nation. Adjective.*
sov·er·eign (sov′ər ən or sov′rən) *noun, plural* **sovereigns;** *adjective.*
Soviet Union Formerly, a large country in eastern Europe and northern Asia. It was composed of 15 republics and was also called the U.S.S.R. The

largest and most important of the 15 republics was Russia.
sow¹ 1. To scatter seeds over the ground; plant: *The farmer will sow corn in this field.* 2. To spread or scatter: *The clown sowed happiness among the children.*
Other words that sound like this are sew and so. **sow** (sō) *verb,* **sowed, sown** or **sowed, sowing.**
sow² An adult female pig. **sow** (sou) *noun, plural* **sows.**
soybean A seed rich in oil and protein and used as food. Soybeans grow in pods on bushy plants. **soy·bean** (soi′bēn′) *noun, plural* **soybeans.**
space 1. The area in which the whole universe exists. It has no limits. The planet earth is in space. 2. The region beyond the earth's atmosphere; outer space: *The rocket was launched into space.* 3. A distance or area between things: *There is not much space between our house and theirs.* 4. An area reserved or available for some purpose: *a parking space.* 5. A period of time: *Both jets landed in the space of ten minutes. Noun.*
∘ To put space in between: *The architect spaced the houses far apart. Verb.*
space (spās) *noun, plural* **spaces;** *verb,* **spaced, spacing.**
spacecraft A vehicle used for flight in outer space. This is also called a spaceship.
space·craft (spās′kraft′) *noun, plural* **spacecraft.**
space shuttle A spacecraft that carries a crew into space and returns to land on earth. The same

Farming and Ranching

Find out!

VOCABULARY

agriculture
irrigation
agribusiness
specialize

PEOPLE

Richard King

READING STRATEGY

Copy the diagram you see here. As you read, use it to show how farming and ranching have changed over time.

Before	After

Lesson Outline
- Technology on the Farm
- Agribusiness
- Training for Tomorrow

BUILD BACKGROUND

In earlier chapters, you learned that the first European settlers farmed only enough to provide for their food. Later, plantations grew to be like small towns. They had all of the skills, labor and supplies needed to support the plantation's crops and animals. After the Civil War, sharecroppers worked many farms while other Texans raised cattle to make money. As more people moved to the cities during the 1900s, farming and ranching would have to adapt again.

Modern farms in Texas use equipment to harvest crops (far left) and to irrigate fields (left).

TECHNOLOGY ON THE FARM

In 1940, just before World War II, there were 418,000 farms in Texas. By 1997 there were only 194,000 farms and fewer than half of them were run full-time. Many Texans had left their farms to work in the cities. Those who remained in farming after World War II began to use new technologies and business practices to change the **agriculture** industry. Agriculture is the business of growing crops and raising animals.

One way Texas farms adapted was through technology. Factories could produce large quantities of the tools needed to farm the land. This made tools cheaper to buy and easy to replace. New machines were built to plant and harvest crops.

Farmers used more technology to bring water to areas that were once too dry. Supplying water to dry areas using pipes or ditches is called **irrigation**.

Irrigation makes it easier for farmers to grow crops in all parts of Texas. For example, cotton was once only grown in the middle and eastern areas of Texas. Today, much of our cotton is grown on the High Plains and in the Rio Grande Valley because these areas are irrigated.

Today, farmers also use computers and scientific research in their work. Computers provide detailed weather information, control irrigation systems, and track the profits farmers make from growing crops. Farmers use scientific research to help plants resist diseases and pests. All of these things make it possible to farm larger sections of the land with fewer people than in the past.

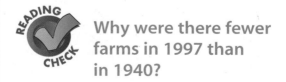

READING CHECK Why were there fewer farms in 1997 than in 1940?

AGRIBUSINESS

Agribusiness is another way farming in Texas has changed. An agribusiness is a farm or ranch which is combined with other businesses, such as food processing.

The smallest type of agribusiness might be a family farm that ships prepared food to customers. Another agribusiness might combine crop growing and food processing.

Some agribusinesses are successful because they **specialize** in only one kind of farming. To specialize means to work on a particular product. A specialized agribusiness might produce cattle feed or fertilizer to sell to other farmers. Many of these specialized

Computers and satellites provide detailed weather forecasts to farmers and ranchers.

agribusinesses work together to do all of the work that was once done on one farm or ranch.

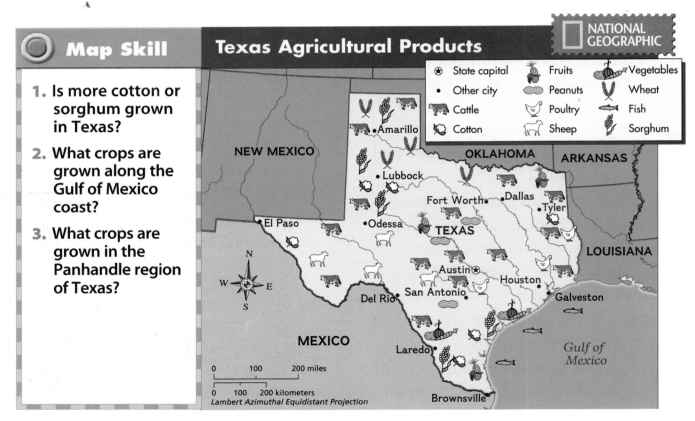

Map Skill

1. Is more cotton or sorghum grown in Texas?

2. What crops are grown along the Gulf of Mexico coast?

3. What crops are grown in the Panhandle region of Texas?

Texas Agricultural Products

NATIONAL GEOGRAPHIC

⊛ State capital	🍍 Fruits	🧅 Vegetables
• Other city	🥜 Peanuts	Wheat
🐄 Cattle	🐓 Poultry	🐟 Fish
Cotton	🐑 Sheep	Sorghum

NEW MEXICO

OKLAHOMA

ARKANSAS

Amarillo

Lubbock

TEXAS

El Paso · · Odessa

Fort Worth · Dallas

Tyler

LOUISIANA

Austin ⊛

Houston

Del Rio · San Antonio

Galveston

MEXICO

Laredo

Gulf of Mexico

0   100   200 miles

0   100   200 kilometers
Lambert Azimuthal Equidistant Projection

Brownsville

Helicopters are used on the King Ranch to round up cattle. Many farmers keep track of their cattle with special ear tags (below).

Ranches Today

Modern ranches are surrounded by miles of fences and use highly developed equipment to manage herds of cattle. The **King Ranch** in South Texas is one of the largest working ranches in the United States. It began when **Richard King** purchased a land grant of 15,500 acres in 1853.

Today the ranch has expanded to 825,000 acres and is surrounded by more than 2,000 miles of fencing. It is so large that the ranchers use helicopters, in addition to horses, to move around the ranch.

Cattle on King Ranch are branded, but they are also given electronic tags so the ranchers can track each animal's feeding schedules, health records, and other information. Instead of being rounded up for a cattle drive, the cattle are herded into corrals and onto trailer trucks for shipping. King Ranch has also expanded its ranching worldwide. There are ranches in several parts of the United States as well as in Brazil and Australia.

Like many modern farms and ranches, King Ranch also has several agribusinesses of its own. In addition to raising cattle, the ranch also focuses on raising horses, farming, and tourism. Other ranchers in our state earn their living from animals other than cattle. Goats, horses, sheep, and even ostriches are all raised on Texas ranches.

READING CHECK **What is an agribusiness?**

VOCABULARY REVIEW

Number a sheet of paper from 1 to 5. Beside each number write the word or term from the list below that matches the description.

agribusiness **irrigation**

manufacturing **profit**

technology

1. the use of special skills, scientific ideas, and tools to meet people's needs

2. money a business earns after it pays for supplies, tools, salaries, and other costs

3. the making of goods by machinery

4. a large farm or ranch which is combined with other businesses

5. the use of ditches or pipes to bring water to dry areas

CHAPTER COMPREHENSION

6. Describe how the free-enterprise system works.

7. List two ways you or your family participates in our state's economy.

8. Make a chart of some Texas industries and the types of jobs they create.

9. Explain what an agribusiness is and give one example.

10. What are some ways that young people in Texas learn about farming?

11. How has **technology** changed the way farms and ranches in Texas operate?

12. **Compare and contrast** farming in Texas before and after World War II.

SKILL REVIEW

13. **Study Skill** What is a reference source?

14. **Study Skill** Name two kinds of reference sources.

15. **Study Skill** Suppose the guide words on a dictionary page are *agriculture* and *astronaut*. Would the word *astronomy* be found on the same page?

16. **Study Skill** Which reference would you use to listen to music or watch short movies?

17. **Study Skill** How can reference sources help you write a report?

USING A GRAPH

18. What type of jobs has Texas created more of?

19. In what year did Texas have nearly 3 million service industry jobs?

20. How do you think this graph will have changed by the year 2021?

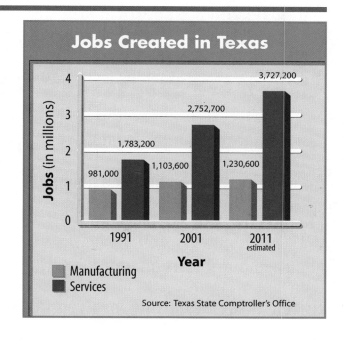

Jobs Created in Texas

Jobs (in millions)

- 1991: Manufacturing 981,000; Services 1,783,200
- 2001: Manufacturing 1,103,600; Services 2,752,700
- 2011 estimated: Manufacturing 1,230,600; Services 3,727,200

Year

■ Manufacturing
■ Services

Source: Texas State Comptroller's Office

Activity

Learning About Business Suppose that you are an entrepreneur. Choose a business you would like to start. Using your textbook, school library, or the Internet, learn more about the industry your business would be part of. Prepare a report describing your business, the industry it belongs to, and why Texas would be a good place for it to grow.

Foldables

Use your *Foldable* to review what you have learned about the economic growth of Texas during the twentieth century. As you look at the titles of the three lessons on the front of your *Foldable*, mentally recall the cause and effect of each area of economic growth. Review your notes under the tabs of your *Foldable* to check your memory and responses. Record any questions that you have on your *Foldable*, and discuss them with classmates or review the chapter to find answers.

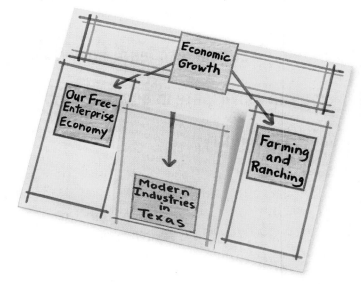

Government and You

You can make changes in your community. You can help the people of our state. You can learn more about your rights as an American citizen. How? By getting involved with government. In this chapter, you will read about our local, state, and national governments. You will learn about how they work and the services they provide. You will also learn how you can participate in government and our country.

IN YOUR TOWN

Voting is one way people participate in government. Here voters celebrate their candidate's election.

IN OUR STATE

This seal is on the floor of the Capitol Building, the seat of our state's government.

IN OUR COUNTRY

The United States Capitol Building in Washington, D.C., houses one branch of our national government.

IN OUR HEMISPHERE

This map of the Western Hemisphere shows the United States and other countries that are part of the Western Hemisphere.

Foldables

Make this Foldable study guide and use it to record what you learn about the government of Texas.

1. Fold a sheet of paper like a hot dog, but make one side 1" longer than the other.

2. Make two cuts on the short side, dividing it into three equal sections.

3. Write the title of the chapter on the 1" tab, and the three lesson titles on the front of the cut tabs.

Our Local Government

Find Out! *What services does your local government provide?*

Lesson Outline
• Citizens and Government
• How Local Government Works

VOCABULARY

citizen
elect
jury
municipal government
mayor
city council
city manager
special district
county

READING STRATEGY

Make a word web like this one. Write in one fact about each type of local government.

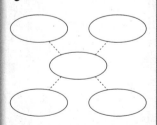

BUILD BACKGROUND

Why is it important to have a government in your town or city? Local government is needed to make decisions. Community leaders, such as Mayor Leo Montalvo of McAllen, a Democrat, decide on matters about schools, parks, and the police. They can even make decisions about constructing new buildings and putting up playgrounds. In this lesson, you will read about the ways in which our city, county, and other local governments affect our lives.

Mayor Leo Montalvo

326

CITIZENS AND GOVERNMENT

Texans are proud to be **citizens** of the United States. A citizen is a person who is born in a country or who has earned the right to become a member of that country.

In our country, citizens **elect** their government leaders. To elect is to choose by voting. Leaders carry out the wishes of the people who elected them.

United States citizens have special rights, such as voting, but also responsibilities. Citizens must take care of their community and keep it safe and clean. People over the age of 18 should be available to serve on a **jury**. A jury is a group of citizens chosen to hear the facts of a case and make a decision. Citizens must also pay taxes. Local governments use tax money to provide services for their areas.

Government Services

The town or city where you live has a **municipal government**. Municipal, or city, governments provide services such as building and repairing sidewalks and street lights. Many municipal governments decide where new homes and businesses should be built. They also run libraries and local police departments. If there is a fire, the municipal fire department puts it out. Helping people is what government is all about.

READING CHECK How are government leaders chosen?

Town **mayors** (left), police officers (top right), and libraries (below) are all parts of local government.

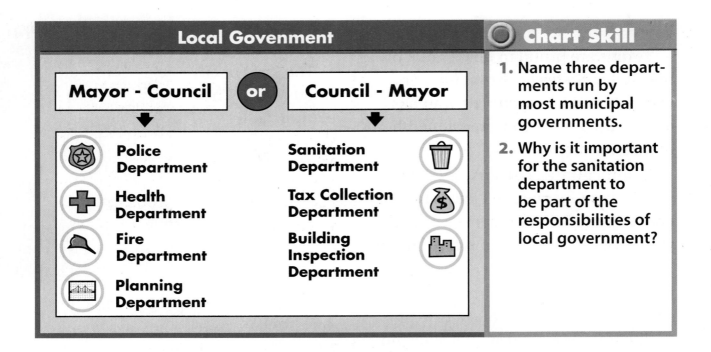

Local Government

| Mayor - Council | or | Council - Mayor |

Police Department

Health Department

Fire Department

Planning Department

Sanitation Department

Tax Collection Department

Building Inspection Department

Chart Skill

1. Name three departments run by most municipal governments.

2. Why is it important for the sanitation department to be part of the responsibilities of local government?

HOW LOCAL GOVERNMENT WORKS

Municipal governments are usually run by a **mayor** and a **city council**. The mayor is the head of the municipal government. The city council is a group of people that makes laws and helps run a city or town. Traditionally, city councils in Texas have five to nine members. Voters in a community elect both the mayor and the city council members. The chart on this page shows the departments in most municipal governments in Texas.

Mayors and city council members usually do not work for the government full-time. They often have other jobs. In cities such as Dallas and San Antonio, the mayor and city council hire a full-time **city manager** to run the city's daily business.

Special Districts

A **special district** is another kind of local government found in our state. It is an area formed for a special purpose. For example, one kind of special district might oversee public road safety. Another might be responsible for garbage removal.

A school district is run by a group of elected officials called school board members or trustees. They decide how to spend the district's money, help plan what students learn, and make other decisions about schools.

County Government

County government is a third kind of local government. A county is one of the sections into which a state is divided. There are 254 counties in Texas—more than in any other state!

County governments in Texas repair county roads and run the local courthouse and jail. Counties may also operate some hospitals, museums, and airports.

READING CHECK What do city managers do?

PUTTING IT TOGETHER

Local government, elected by voters in a community, provides many services to its citizens. Government leaders also make decisions that affect our health, safety, and education. Local governments often work with our state government to solve problems. You will learn about the state government of Texas in the next lesson.

Repairing roads is one service the local government provides to its **citizens**.

Review and Assess

1. Write one sentence using each of the following vocabulary words:

   citizen   **county**

   elect   **jury**

   mayor

2. What is a special district?

3. Describe three services provided by local government.

4. What are the responsibilities of **citizens** in a community?

5. **Compare** and **contrast** the roles of municipal governments and special districts.

Activities

Look at the county map in the Atlas on page R22. Find the county you live in and make a list of all the counties that surround it.

• •

Write to the mayor of your town or city to find out more about what he or she does.

Reading and Thinking Skills

Recognizing Point of View

Suppose you and your friends are talking about pets. Steve says German shepherds make the best pets because they are loyal and easy to train. Felicia believes Siamese cats are better because they are playful and easy to care for.

Each of your friends has a different **point of view**. A point of view is the way a person looks at something. People often look at the same subject from different points of view. Being able to recognize a person's point of view helps you make up your own mind about a subject.

VOCABULARY

point of view
fact
opinion
editorial

LEARN THE SKILL

Read the passage below. Then follow the steps to recognize a person's point of view.

Hector Diaz has the hardest job in our community. As our sheriff, he is in charge of our county's law-enforcement department. Sheriff Diaz has important responsibilities. He fights crime and makes sure citizens obey the law. I believe his hard work keeps us safe.

1. **Identify the subject.**
   In the previous passage the subject is Sheriff Hector Diaz and how well he performs his duties.

2. **Identify statements of fact and opinion.**
   To identify point of view you need to know if the person is expressing **facts** or **opinions**. A fact is a statement that can be proven. Facts can be looked up in reference sources, such as dictionaries and encyclopedias. In the passage above, *"he is in charge of our county's law-enforcement department"* is a statement of fact.

   An opinion expresses a person's belief. It cannot be proven. *"Hector Diaz has the hardest job in our community"* is an opinion. Opinions are one way a person expresses a point of view.

3. **Identify clue words or phrases.**
   Clue words or phrases like *"I feel,"* *"I think,"* and *"I believe"* can tell you how a person feels about a subject.

330

An example is, *"I believe his hard work keeps us safe."* How a person feels about a subject is also part of his or her point of view.

4. **State the point of view expressed.** Carefully examine the person's opinions and feelings on the subject. Then in your own words, state the person's point of view. *"The writer thinks Sheriff Hector Diaz works hard and is good at his job"* is a statement about the previous passage.

TRY THE SKILL

Read the following exchange from a debate. Then answer the questions below.

Ahmad: Skateboarding is a fun way for kids to get exercise. Doctors report that skateboarding strengthens muscles and improves balance. Most skateboarders behave responsibly. I think we do not need to create laws to keep them safe.

Julia: Skateboarding is a dangerous sport. If kids skateboard in the street, it can back up traffic and cause accidents. Over a thousand skateboards were sold in our community last year. I believe we should create laws to limit their use.

1. What is the subject?

2. What is Ahmad's point of view?

3. What is Julia's point of view?

4. What clue words or phrases did you use?

5. After reading both sides, what is your point of view on the subject?

EXTEND THE SKILL

Newspapers print **editorials**, which give an editor's point of view on a subject. Unlike a news article, it mainly states an opinion rather than facts. Read the following editorial on a small town election. Then answer the questions below.

WHO'LL MAKE THE BETTER MAYOR?
By Sam Ginsberg

I believe Adrienne Kim has been the best mayor we have ever had. She understands the concerns of our citizens better than Mike Powell, the candidate running against her. Mayor Kim has served our city for the past four years. She has built new parks, opened a hospital, and started a clean-up campaign.

Mike Powell has had a lot of success in the business world. He has earned millions with his footwear company. However, he has not worked in government before. I think Powell should serve on the city council for a few years to gain experience. Then, he can run for mayor in the next election. For all these reasons, I urge you to re-elect Mayor Adrienne Kim.

- What is the subject?

- What facts are included in the editorial?

- What is the editor's point of view?

- Why is it important to recognize a person's point of view?

Lesson 2

VOCABULARY

budget
branch
checks and
 balances
executive branch
legislative branch
bill
veto
judicial branch

PEOPLE

Mario Gallegos, Jr.
Ann Richards
Barbara Jordan

READING STRATEGY

Make a chart like
this one. In each
column, write in
the function of
each branch of
government.

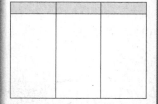

Our State's Government

Find! out! *What are the jobs of each branch of our state government?*

Lesson Outline

• Working for You
• Branches of Government
• Learning About Government

BUILD BACKGROUND

"I saw my parents get involved
in their community. They tried to
help the people around them,"
says **Mario Gallegos, Jr.**
"That inspired me to follow
in their footsteps. " Today
Gallegos is a Texas state
senator. Every day
members of our state
government make
important decisions.

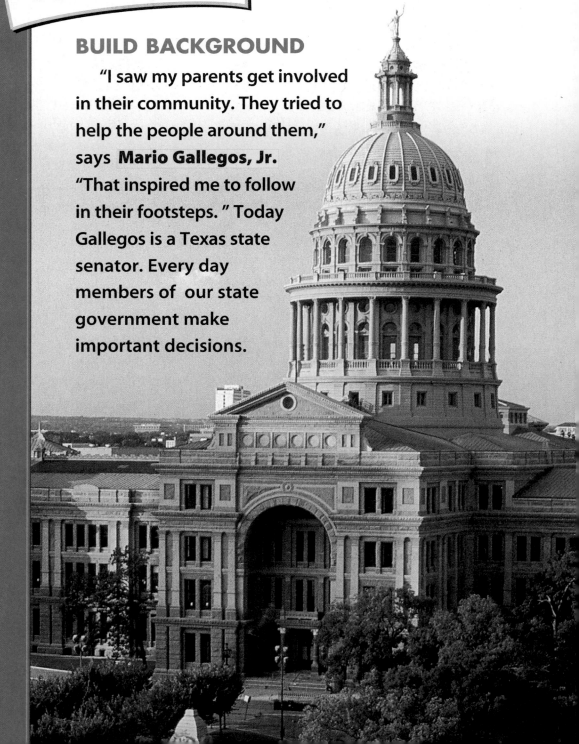

WORKING FOR YOU

Our state government is located in **Austin**, the capital of Texas. Austin lies along the Colorado River in central Texas. Many state government offices are housed there.

The Capitol Building is found near the center of Austin. It was built in the 1880s and modeled after the United States Capitol in Washington, D.C. Did you know that the Texas Capitol is seven feet taller?

Government Services

Our state government provides services for the people of Texas. For example, the government helps pay for education. State workers take care of state parks and highways. Our state government also works to protect the health, safety, and jobs of its citizens. Texans pay taxes to provide for all of these services and others.

To decide how much to spend on services, the state government makes

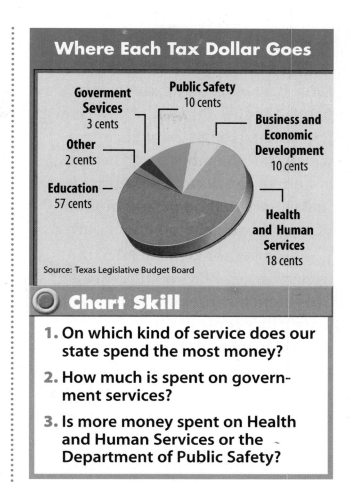

Where Each Tax Dollar Goes

Goverment Sevices 3 cents
Public Safety 10 cents
Other 2 cents
Business and Economic Development 10 cents
Education — 57 cents
Health and Human Services 18 cents

Source: Texas Legislative Budget Board

Chart Skill

1. **On which kind of service does our state spend the most money?**

2. **How much is spent on government services?**

3. **Is more money spent on Health and Human Services or the Department of Public Safety?**

a plan for using taxes. This plan is called a **budget**. The circle graph above shows how the Texas government spends our tax money.

 READING CHECK How does the state government decide how to spend money from taxes?

The Texas Capitol Building (left) is located in Austin (below), along with many other state government offices.

BRANCHES OF GOVERNMENT

The Texas Constitution sets up the three **branches** of our state government. A branch is a part of government. Each branch of government keeps watch over the other two. This is a system of **checks and balances**. It makes sure that no person or group of people can gain too much power.

The governor is the head of the **executive** (eg ZEK yoo tihv) **branch**. This branch carries out the laws of the state. The people of our state elect the governor. He or she then serves for a term of four years. The governor helps set goals for our state. He or she also chooses people to run state departments, such as the Department of Public Safety.

Democrat **Ann Richards** has written, "[g]overnment touches every part of our lives." She served as governor of our state from 1991 to 1995.

Read a quote from the speech she gave at her inauguration in 1991.

The legislative branch writes and passes laws in our state.

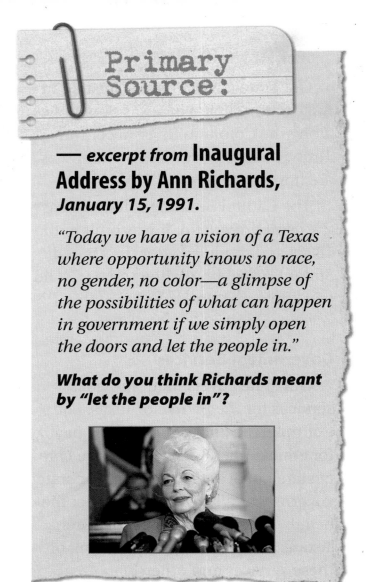

— *excerpt from* **Inaugural Address by Ann Richards,** *January 15, 1991.*

"Today we have a vision of a Texas where opportunity knows no race, no gender, no color—a glimpse of the possibilities of what can happen in government if we simply open the doors and let the people in."

What do you think Richards meant by "let the people in"?

An inauguration is the ceremony of putting a person into an elected office.

The governor's office is located in Austin. So is the Capitol Building, which houses the **legislative** (LEJ is lay tihv) **branch**. This branch writes the laws of our state.

The legislative branch has two parts—the Senate and the House of Representatives. The 31 senators and 150 representatives are elected by Texas voters. State senators serve four-year terms and representatives serve two-year terms.

Senators and representatives work and vote on **bills**. Bills are proposals for laws. How does a bill become a law? It goes through a step-by-step process.

Let's follow the history of one bill. In 1977, a bill came before the Texas legislature proposing that chili be made the state dish. Ben Z. Grant and Ron Bird were two Democratic members of the House of Representatives. They wrote the bill. Some representatives argued that shrimp gumbo should be the state dish. Others wanted to vote for barbecue. After some debate, chili won the House vote. In the Senate, the bill passed without any problems.

The bill then went to former Democratic Governor Dolph Briscoe. If he had disagreed with the bill, he could have decided to **veto**, or reject it. Instead, he signed it. Chili became the state dish of Texas. Follow the steps in the chart on this page to see how a bill becomes law.

The **judicial** (joo DISH uhl) **branch** of state government interprets, or explains, our state's laws. This branch is made up of judges who work in courts.

The highest courts in Texas are the Court of Criminal Appeals and the Supreme Court. Voters in Texas elect nine judges to each of these courts. They each serve six-year terms.

What is the system of checks and balances?

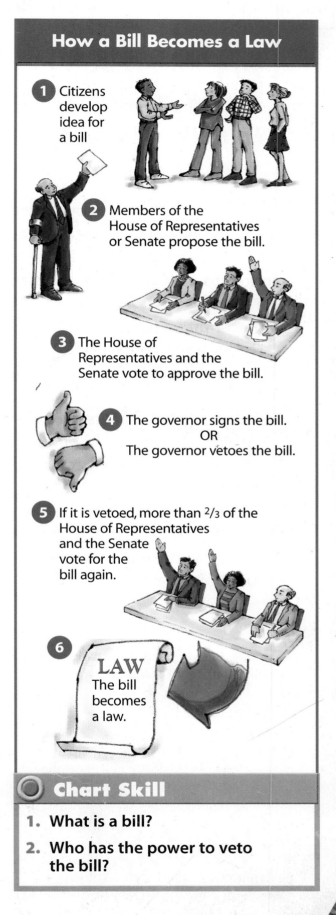

How a Bill Becomes a Law

1. Citizens develop idea for a bill

2. Members of the House of Representatives or Senate propose the bill.

3. The House of Representatives and the Senate vote to approve the bill.

4. The governor signs the bill.
OR
The governor vetoes the bill.

5. If it is vetoed, more than 2/3 of the House of Representatives and the Senate vote for the bill again.

6. LAW The bill becomes a law.

Chart Skill

1. What is a bill?

2. Who has the power to veto the bill?

BIOGRAPHY

Focus On: Honesty

Barbara Jordan was born in Houston. In 1966, Jordan became the first African American woman to win a seat in the Texas Senate. Jordan, a Democrat, worked to pass civil rights legislation. She went on to serve as a United States Representative from 1973 to 1979.

Throughout her career, Jordan received many honors and awards. In 1994, she was awarded the Presidential Medal of Freedom.

Barbara Jordan valued honesty. She has said, "[Behaving correctly] means being honest, telling the truth, and doing what you said you were going to do. Listen to the small still voice within you and you will probably do the right thing."

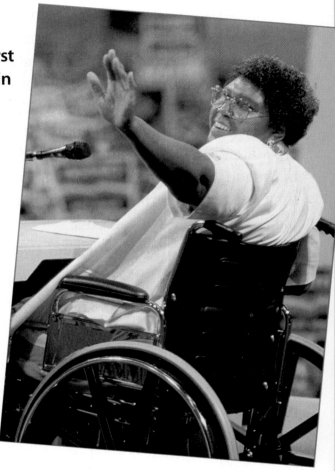

Link to Today Research another woman who served in government. What qualities, such as honesty, did she possess?

THE LIFE OF BARBARA JORDAN	1936 born in Houston	1966 is elected state senator	1967 sworn into the Texas Senate	1973 becomes a United States representative	1994 receives Presidential Medal of Freedom	1996 Barbara Jordan dies in Austin
	1920	1940	1960	1980		2000
LIFE AROUND THE WORLD			1964 Congress passes the Civil Rights Act	1973 Tiger Woods is born		1999 United States Women's Soccer Team wins World Cup

LEARNING ABOUT GOVERNMENT

Lone Star Boys' State and Bluebonnet Girls' State programs help students learn more about our state government. Every year thousands of high school juniors gather in Austin for one week to take part in the program. The experience teaches them about state government. These high school students also learn about our state leaders and how they work. The first step to getting involved in our government is to become informed.

Students in Texas learn about the government in a mock legislative session.

What are some ways you can learn more about our state government?

PUTTING IT TOGETHER

Our state government cannot work without the involvement of its citizens. You can participate by reading your local newspaper, learning about issues in Texas, and writing to your representatives. Learning about government now will help you become an educated voter in the future.

Review and Assess

1. Write one sentence using each of the following vocabulary words:

   bill   **budget**

   veto

2. How does a bill become a law in our state?

3. Describe the duties of each branch of our state's government.

4. Name some of the ways citizens participate in **government**.

5. What was Barbara Jordan's **point of view** on being honest?

Suppose you and your friends collected money to support projects in your community. Create a circle graph like the one on page 333, to show how the money would be divided and used.

• •

Ask your teacher to help you identify your state representative. Then **write** a letter or E-mail to him or her about an issue that concerns you.

Being a Good Citizen
Kids Caring for the Environment

One day in 1997, Kate Klinkerman watched her father dump used motor oil on the ground around their barn. "The crude oil seeps into the water below the ground and pollutes the water," says Kate. "Many people in our county have wells. They might drink this water." Most residents of Victoria County disposed of crude oil this way. Kate and two friends decided to find a better way.

Victoria County

Kate and her friends Barbara Brown and Lacy Jones began planning an oil recycling program. The owners of a local recycling plant explained how oil is recycled. The plant agreed to take used oil and recycle it. The girls then contacted the Texas Natural Resource Conservation Commission. Texas officials gave them two 450-gallon tanks, or containers for holding used oil. Local oil and chemical companies bought three more tanks. County officials agreed to let them put the tanks at grocery stores, recycling centers, and an elementary school. "To let people know about the program," says Barbara, "we gave talks at schools, business groups, and 4-H clubs. We called our project 'Don't Be Crude.' We showed how oil dumping hurts the Earth. We gave out T-shirts, bumper stickers, and containers that say 'Don't Be Crude' for collecting the recycled oil."

News about the program spread quickly. Stories in local newspapers, on television, and radio helped. Today people in Victoria County bring over 2,000 gallons of oil to collection centers each month. "Don't think," says Barbara, "that just because you're a kid you can't do anything. Many people get involved when they get the chance. It's so amazing how much just a few kids can do. We helped people to help themselves."

❝Don't think that just because you're a kid you can't do anything.❞

Be a Good Citizen

Making Connections

- **What are some ways that people in your community work to protect the environment?**

- **Does your community have a recycling program? What kinds of materials are recycled in this program?**

Talk About It!

- **Why did the three friends need the help and support of state and local government officials to make their program successful?**

- **Where would you look to find information on recycling? What might you say if you were giving a talk about caring for the environment?**

Act On It!

In the Classroom

Recycling is just one way we can help the environment. Working in small groups, decide on a way that you could make a difference to the environment you live in. Then write an outline showing the steps it would take to put a plan into action.

In the Community

Check newspapers or the Internet to identify an environmental issue in your area. Write a letter to the editor of your local newspaper explaining what could be done to solve the problem.

Our Nation's Government

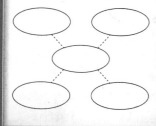
Find! out! *What are the rights and responsibilities of American citizens?*

VOCABULARY

democratic republic

candidate

political party

United States Congress

United States Supreme Court

PEOPLE

George W. Bush

READING STRATEGY

Make a word web like this one. In each circle, write one fact about the United States Constitution.

Lesson Outline

• The United States Government

• The Three Branches

BUILD BACKGROUND

In the United States, we live by a plan of government. The United States Constitution is that plan. Our country's first leaders wrote it more than 200 years ago. This plan states that our nation is run by a set of rights and laws. The leaders of our national government create, explain, and carry out these laws. In this lesson, you will learn more about our country's government and the laws that protect us all.

UNITED STATES GOVERNMENT

"I pledge allegiance to the flag of the United States of America, and to the Republic for which it stands, one Nation under God, indivisible, with liberty, and justice for all."

When you say the Pledge of Allegiance, you are making a promise. You are promising to be loyal to the United States and to support our country's government.

The Constitution

Running a government is not easy. After declaring our country independent in 1776, our first leaders decided they needed to create a plan. In 1787 they wrote the Constitution. This document sets up and explains our national government.

The Constitution made our country a **democratic republic**. Democracy means the power to rule comes from the people. In our democratic republic, citizens elect leaders to run the country and make decisions for them.

In an election, **candidates** are the people who run for office. Usually candidates are members of a **political party**. A political party is a group of citizens who share many of the same ideas about government.

The White House (left) is home to our nation's president. Young children become citizens of the United States.

The Democratic and Republican parties are the largest political parties in the United States.

Government Services

Like our local and state governments, the United States government provides services. One of these is defense. Our government runs our armed forces. It also pays for ships, planes, and weapons to defend our country, and others.

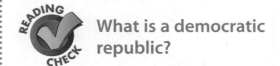

READING CHECK What is a democratic republic?

THE THREE BRANCHES

Our national government is located in **Washington, D.C.** Like our state government, our country's government has three branches. Find these branches on the chart on the following page.

The President is the head of the executive branch of government. This person is elected every four years. The President makes sure the laws of our

---

The **Supreme Court** (above) is the head of the judicial branch. Our 43rd president, George W. Bush (below), is from Texas.

country are carried out. The President also meets with leaders of other countries, and is Commander in Chief of our military forces. The President chooses people to head national departments for such areas as transportation and defense.

The legislative branch of our national government is called the **United States Congress**. Congress writes and passes laws for the entire country. Congress has two parts, the House of Representatives and the Senate.

Voters of every state elect two senators. The number of representatives elected depends on how many people live in the state. Texas, which has a large population, elects 30 people to the United States House of Representatives. Senators serve for six years and representatives serve for two years.

The courts make up the judicial branch. This is the third branch of our national government. The **United States Supreme Court** is the highest court in our country.

The President selects the nine justices, or judges, who sit on the Supreme Court. Each judge serves for life. The justices hear cases that come from the lower courts. They also decide whether laws passed by Congress agree with the Constitution.

Rights and Responsibilities

Congress, the President, and the Supreme Court work to protect the rights of American citizens.

With rights come responsibilities. Citizens must pay taxes and obey our country's laws. At election time, it's important that we vote.

Texas Leaders

Many Texan men and women have played important roles in our country's government. In the past 50 years, our state has sent one Democrat—Lyndon B. Johnson—and three Republicans—Dwight D. Eisenhower, George Bush, and our current President, **George W. Bush**—to the White House.

Some Texans who have served in Congress include Senator Kay Bailey Hutchinson, Senator Phil Gramm, former Senator John Tower, and former Representative Sam Rayburn. Others have headed important government departments, such as Alberto Gonzales, the White House Chief Counsel.

READING CHECK Which branch does the President head?

National Government: Three Branches

EXECUTIVE	LEGISLATIVE	JUDICIAL
President	**Congress** (100 Senators, 435 Representatives)	**Supreme Court** (9 Judges)
• Carries out laws • Meets with leaders of other countries • Leads military	• Makes laws for our country • Decides how much money to spend	• Makes sure our laws follow the Constitution

Chart Skill

1. What are the President's duties?

2. How many senators and representatives does Congress have?

3. Who are the highest officials of the judicial branch of our government?

343

BIOGRAPHY

Focus On: Loyalty

George Walker Bush became our country's President in 2001. Bush's father, who is also named George Bush, was President from 1989 through 1992. As President of the United States, George Walker Bush supports low taxes, a strong military, and better schools.

George Walker Bush is loyal to the people of Texas. Before becoming President, he was the Republican governor of our state. He also worked in the Texas oil business and owned the Texas Rangers baseball team. Although President Bush lives in Washington, D.C., he often spends time at his 1,600-acre ranch in Crawford, Texas.

Link to Today

Interview a parent, grandparent, teacher, or friend. Ask how loyalty has been important in that person's life. Write a paragraph about what they tell you.

THE LIFE OF GEORGE WALKER BUSH	**1946** George W. Bush is born	**1989** George W. Bush and partners buy the Texas Rangers baseball team	**1994** George W. Bush is elected governor of Texas	**2001** George W. Bush becomes the 43rd president of the United States
	1945	1960	1975	1990	2005
LIFE AROUND THE WORLD	**1945** United Nations is created	**1965** Vietnam War begins		**1993** Apartheid system ends in South Africa

PUTTING IT TOGETHER

In 1863 President Abraham Lincoln said that we have a "government of the people, by the people, for the people." His words remind us that a democracy cannot work without its citizens. The people of our country participate in government by electing representatives. Voting is our right and our responsibility. After you turn 18, you will be able to vote for national, state, and local leaders.

Senator Kay Bailey Hutchison

Candidates for office often use campaign buttons to convince people to vote for them.

Review and Assess

1. Write one sentence using each of the following vocabulary terms:

   candidate   political party

2. What are the two parts of the United States Congress?

3. Analyze the rights and responsibilities we have as Americans.

4. What qualities do you think are important in a **citizen**?

5. How can voters **make a decision** about which candidate to elect?

Activities

Draw a large triangle on a sheet of paper. Inside the triangle, write "Our Federal Government." On each point of the triangle, write the name of one of the three branches of government. Include the person or group that makes up that branch.

Government leaders should be honest and experienced in order to make decisions for our country. **Write** a paragraph describing other qualities you think a leader should possess.

345

Lesson 4 — The Western Hemisphere

Countries in the Western Hemisphere

Throughout this book you have been reading about connections with other places in the United States and with other countries of the Western Hemisphere. Use the chart to learn about the government and economy of each country in the Western Hemisphere. What is the most popular form of government? Which countries export oil?

ANTIGUA AND BARBUDA

GOVERNMENT: Constitutional Monarchy

CAPITAL★ St. John's

POPULATION: 66,000

MAJOR LANGUAGE: English

AREA: 170 sq mi; 440 sq km

LEADING EXPORTS: petroleum products, clothing, and household appliances

ARGENTINA

GOVERNMENT: Republic

CAPITAL★ Buenos Aires

POPULATION: 37 million

MAJOR LANGUAGES: Spanish, English, and Italian

AREA: 1,068,299 sq mi; 2,766,890 sq km

LEADING EXPORTS: meat, grain, hides, and wool

THE BAHAMAS

GOVERNMENT: Independent Commonwealth

CAPITAL★ Nassau

POPULATION: 295,000

MAJOR LANGUAGES: English and Creole

AREA: 5,382 sq mi; 13,940 sq km

LEADING EXPORTS: pharmaceuticals, cement, and crawfish

BARBADOS

GOVERNMENT: Democracy

CAPITAL★ Bridgetown

POPULATION: 274,000

MAJOR LANGUAGE: English

AREA: 166 sq mi; 430 sq km

LEADING EXPORTS: sugar, molasses, and electrical components

BELIZE

GOVERNMENT: Democracy

CAPITAL★ Belmopan

POPULATION: 249,000

MAJOR LANGUAGES: English and Spanish

AREA: 8,865 sq mi; 22,960 sq km

LEADING EXPORTS: sugar, citrus, clothing, and fish products

BOLIVIA

GOVERNMENT: Republic

CAPITAL★ Sucre (judicial) and La Paz (administrative)

POPULATION: 8.2 million

MAJOR LANGUAGES: Spanish, Quechua, and Aymará

AREA: 424,163 sq mi; 1,098,580 sq km

LEADING EXPORTS: metals, natural gas, coffee, and soybeans

BRAZIL

GOVERNMENT: Federal Republic

CAPITAL★ Brasília

POPULATION: 172.9 million

MAJOR LANGUAGES: Portuguese, Spanish, French, and English

AREA: 3,286,488 sq mi; 8,511,965 sq km

LEADING EXPORTS: iron ore, coffee, orange juice, and footwear

CANADA

GOVERNMENT: Confederation with Parliamentary Democracy

CAPITAL★ Ottawa

POPULATION: 31.3 million

MAJOR LANGUAGES: English and French

AREA: 3,851,798 sq mi; 9,976,140 sq km

LEADING EXPORTS: automotive products, timber, and natural gas

CHILE

GOVERNMENT: Republic

CAPITAL★ Santiago

POPULATION: 15.2 million

MAJOR LANGUAGE: Spanish

AREA: 292,259 sq mi; 756,950 sq km

LEADING EXPORTS: copper, fish, metals, and minerals

COLOMBIA

GOVERNMENT: Republic

CAPITAL★ Bogotá

POPULATION: 39.7 million

MAJOR LANGUAGE: Spanish

AREA: 439,734 sq mi; 1,138,910 sq km

LEADING EXPORTS: coffee, petroleum, coal, and bananas

COSTA RICA

GOVERNMENT: Republic

CAPITAL★ San José

POPULATION: 3.7 million

MAJOR LANGUAGES: Spanish and English

AREA: 19,730 sq mi; 50,100 sq km

LEADING EXPORTS: coffee, bananas, textiles, and sugar

CUBA

GOVERNMENT: Communist State

CAPITAL★ Havana

POPULATION: 11.1 million

MAJOR LANGUAGE: Spanish

AREA: 42,803 sq mi; 110,860 sq km

LEADING EXPORTS: sugar, nickel, shellfish, and tobacco

DOMINICA

GOVERNMENT: Parliamentary Democracy

CAPITAL★ Roseau

POPULATION: 72,000

MAJOR LANGUAGES: English and Creole

AREA: 290 sq mi; 750 sq km

LEADING EXPORTS: bananas, soap, bay oil, and vegetables

DOMINICAN REPUBLIC

GOVERNMENT: Republic

CAPITAL★ Santo Domingo

POPULATION: 8.4 million

MAJOR LANGUAGE: Spanish

AREA: 18,816 sq mi; 48,730 sq km

LEADING EXPORTS: sugar, coffee, ferronickel, cocoa, and gold

ECUADOR

GOVERNMENT: Republic

CAPITAL★ Quito

POPULATION: 12.9 million

MAJOR LANGUAGES: Spanish and Quechua

AREA: 109,483 sq mi; 283,560 sq km

LEADING EXPORTS: oil, bananas, shrimp, and cocoa

EL SALVADOR

GOVERNMENT: Republic

CAPITAL★ San Salvador

POPULATION: 6.1 million

MAJOR LANGUAGES: Spanish and Náhuatl

AREA: 8,124 sq mi; 21,040 sq km

LEADING EXPORTS: coffee, sugarcane, and shrimp

GRENADA

GOVERNMENT: Parliamentary Democracy

CAPITAL★ St. George's

POPULATION: 89,000

MAJOR LANGUAGES: English and French patois

AREA: 131 sq mi; 340 sq km

LEADING EXPORTS: nutmeg, mace, bananas, and cocoa

GUATEMALA

GOVERNMENT: Republic

CAPITAL★ Guatemala City

POPULATION: 12.6 million

MAJOR LANGUAGES: Spanish and Mayan dialects

AREA: 42,042 sq mi; 108,890 sq km

LEADING EXPORTS: coffee, sugar, bananas, and cardamom

GUYANA

GOVERNMENT: Republic

CAPITAL★ Georgetown

POPULATION: 697,000

MAJOR LANGUAGES: English, Hindi, and Urdu

AREA: 83,000 sq mi; 214,970 sq km

LEADING EXPORTS: sugar, bauxite, rice, shrimp, and molasses

HAITI

GOVERNMENT: Republic

CAPITAL★ Port-au-Prince

POPULATION: 6.5 million

MAJOR LANGUAGES: French and French Creole

AREA: 10,714 sq mi; 27,750 sq km

LEADING EXPORTS: coffee and assembled lighting products

HONDURAS

GOVERNMENT: Republic

CAPITAL★ Tegucigalpa

POPULATION: 6.3 million

MAJOR LANGUAGE: Spanish

AREA: 43,277 sq mi; 112,090 sq km

LEADING EXPORTS: coffee, bananas, shrimp, lobster, and minerals

JAMAICA

GOVERNMENT: Parliamentary Democracy

CAPITAL★ Kingston

POPULATION: 2.7 million

MAJOR LANGUAGES: English and Jamaican Creole

AREA: 4,243 sq mi; 10,990 sq km

LEADING EXPORTS: aluminum, bauxite, sugar, and bananas

MEXICO

GOVERNMENT: Federal Republic

CAPITAL★ Mexico City

POPULATION: 100.4 million

MAJOR LANGUAGES: Spanish and Náhuatl

AREA: 761,604 sq mi; 1,972,550 sq km

LEADING EXPORTS: oil, cotton, coffee, silver, and consumer electronics

NICARAGUA

GOVERNMENT: Republic

CAPITAL★ Managua

POPULATION: 4.1 million

MAJOR LANGUAGE: Spanish

AREA: 49,998 sq mi; 129,494 sq km

LEADING EXPORTS: cotton, coffee, chemicals, and foodstuffs

PANAMA

GOVERNMENT: Constitutional Republic

CAPITAL★ Panama City

POPULATION: 2.8 million

MAJOR LANGUAGES: Spanish and English

AREA: 30,193 sq mi; 78,200 sq km

LEADING EXPORTS: bananas, shrimp, clothing, and sugar

PARAGUAY

GOVERNMENT: Republic

CAPITAL★ Asunción

POPULATION: 5.6 million

MAJOR LANGUAGES: Spanish and Guaraní

AREA: 157,047 sq mi; 406,750 sq km

LEADING EXPORTS: cotton, timber, coffee, and soybeans

PERU

GOVERNMENT: Republic

CAPITAL★ Lima

POPULATION: 27 million

MAJOR LANGUAGES: Spanish, Quechua, and Aymará

AREA: 496,225 sq mi; 1,285,220 sq km

LEADING EXPORTS: oil, copper, zinc, lead, and coffee

ST. KITTS AND NEVIS

GOVERNMENT: Constitutional Monarchy

CAPITAL★ Basseterre

POPULATION: 39,000

MAJOR LANGUAGE: English

AREA: 139 sq mi; 360 sq km

LEADING EXPORTS: sugar, clothing, electronics, and stamps

ST. LUCIA

GOVERNMENT: Parliamentary Democracy

CAPITAL★ Castries

POPULATION: 156,000

MAJOR LANGUAGES: English and French patois

AREA: 239 sq mi; 620 sq km

LEADING EXPORTS: bananas, clothing, cocoa, and coconut oil

ST. VINCENT AND THE GRENADINES

GOVERNMENT: Constitutional Monarchy

CAPITAL★ Kingstown

POPULATION: 115,000

MAJOR LANGUAGE: English

AREA: 131 sq mi; 340 sq km

LEADING EXPORTS: bananas, taro, arrowroot starch, and tennis racquets

SURINAME

GOVERNMENT: Republic

CAPITAL★ Paramaribo

POPULATION: 431,000

MAJOR LANGUAGES: Dutch, English, and Hindi

AREA: 63,039 sq mi; 163,270 sq km

LEADING EXPORTS: rice, bananas, aluminum, and fish

TRINIDAD AND TOBAGO

GOVERNMENT: Parliamentary Democracy

CAPITAL★ Port-of-Spain

POPULATION: 1.2 million

MAJOR LANGUAGES: English, Hindi, and French

AREA: 1,980 sq mi; 5,130 sq km

LEADING EXPORTS: oil, chemicals, and steel products

UNITED STATES

GOVERNMENT: Federal Republic

CAPITAL★ Washington, D.C.

POPULATION: 275.6 million

MAJOR LANGUAGE: English

AREA: 3,787,319 sq mi; 9,809,156 sq km

LEADING EXPORTS: automobiles, raw materials, and consumer goods

URUGUAY

GOVERNMENT: Republic

CAPITAL★ Montevideo

POPULATION: 3.3 million

MAJOR LANGUAGES: Spanish and Brazilero

AREA: 68,039 sq mi; 176,220 sq km

LEADING EXPORTS: wool and meat

VENEZUELA

GOVERNMENT: Federal Republic

CAPITAL★ Caracas

POPULATION: 23.5 million

MAJOR LANGUAGES: Spanish and Indian dialects

AREA: 352,143 sq mi; 912,050 sq km

LEADING EXPORTS: oil, bauxite, aluminum, steel, and chemicals

SOURCE: languages, area, exports—*The CIA World Factbook*, 1994; additional information on languages—*The Europa World Book*, 1995; population, government—*The World Almanac and Book of Facts 2001*

VOCABULARY REVIEW

Number a sheet of paper from 1 to 5. Beside each number write the word or term from the list below that matches the description.

bill   **budget**

candidate **jury**

mayor

1. a plan for using taxes
2. a group of citizens selected to hear the facts of a case and make a decision
3. a citizen elected to serve as the head of a municipal government
4. a person running for office
5. a proposal for a law

CHAPTER COMPREHENSION

6. What is a city council?
7. Identify two ways citizens can take part in their local community.
8. Who was Barbara Jordan?
9. In which city is the office of our state's governor located?
10. What is the purpose of the United States Constitution?
11. How many representatives are elected from Texas to serve in the United States House of Representatives? How many senators from Texas serve in the United States Senate?
12. Who is the head of the executive branch of our national government? Describe this person's job duties.

SKILL REVIEW

13. **Reading/Thinking Skill** What is point of view?
14. **Reading/Thinking Skill** What are the steps you can take to recognize a person's point of view?
15. **Reading/Thinking Skill** Look back at the Primary Source on page 334. What is Ann Richards's point of view on government?
16. **Reading/Thinking Skill** What is the difference between facts and opinions?
17. **Reading/Thinking Skill** What is an editorial?
18. **Reading/Thinking Skill** Why is it important to understand different points of view?

USING A CHART

Levels of Government		
Local	**State**	**National**
• Mayor • City Council • Local Courts	• Governor • Texas House of Representatives • Texas Senate • Texas Supreme Court	• President • United States House of Representatives • United States Senate • United States Supreme Court

19. What is the title of the person elected to run the government on the local, state, and national levels?

20. Compare and contrast the local, state, and national levels of government.

Writing About Government Suppose you are a reporter at a local newspaper. Write an article encouraging people to vote in an upcoming election for a new mayor. Explain why it is an important responsibility for each citizen to vote.

Foldables

Use your *Foldable* to review what you have learned about government. As you look at your *Foldable*, mentally recall the responsibilities of your local, state, and national government. Think about what responsibilities you have as a citizen. Review your notes on the inside and back of your *Foldable* to check your memory and responses. Record any questions that you have on your *Foldable* and discuss them with classmates or review the chapter to find answers.

Unit 4 REVIEW

VOCABULARY REVIEW

Number a paper from 1 to 5. Beside each number write the word or term from the list below that completes the sentence.

citizen *4*   **discrimination** *1*

municipal government *3*   **elect** *5*

segregation *2*

1. Women felt the effects of _____ when they were not allowed to vote.

2. _____ kept African Americans from sharing the same schools, restaurants, and buses with white people.

3. The _____ of a city runs services such as the local police and fire departments.

4. A _____ of the United States has certain rights, responsibilities, and duties.

5. In our country, citizens have the right to _____ their leaders.

TECHNOLOGY

For more resources to help you learn more about the people and places you studied in this unit, visit **www.mhschool.com** and follow the links for Grade 4 Texas, Unit 4.

SKILL REVIEW

6. **Reading/Thinking Skill** How can drawing inferences help you understand what you read?

7. **Study Skill** Which reference source would you use to find information on *irrigation*?

8. **Study Skill** Which reference source would you use to find the definition of *technology*?

9. **Reading/Thinking Skill** Name one way that citizens can express their point of view in local government.

10. **Reading/Thinking Skill** Why is it important to recognize a person's point of view?

At community meetings people discuss issues that are important to them.

Senators and representatives work and vote on bills. Bills are proposals for laws. How does a bill become a law? It goes through a step-by-step process.

In 1977, a bill came before the Texas legislature proposing that chili be made the state dish. Ben Z. Grant and Ron Bird were two members of the House of Representatives. They wrote the bill. Some representatives argued that shrimp gumbo should be the state dish. Others wanted to vote for barbecue. After some debate, chili won the House vote. In the Senate, the bill passed without any problems.

1 You can tell from the article that—

A every state has 31 senators and 150 representatives

B some representatives eat lots of shrimp gumbo

C Texas legislators discuss bills before they vote on them

D some senators were angry that barbecue was not chosen to be the state dish

2 Based on the article which sentence above is an opinion?

A Bills are proposals for laws.

B Shrimp gumbo should be the state dish.

C A bill becomes law by a step-by-step process.

D The Texas legislature voted on a state dish.

WRITING ACTIVITIES  *TAKS Practice*

⊕ **Writing to Inform** Write a paragraph explaining how people are affected by not having the right to vote.

⊕ **Writing to Persuade** Suppose you lived during the 1960s. Write a letter or speech persuading Texans to end segregation in our state.

⊕ **Writing to Express** Write a description of how Texas helped to support our country during World War II.

The UT Institute of Texan Cultures at San Antonio

Children collect scrap metal.

LITERATURE

MAGIC WINDOWS
Ventanas mágicas
by Carmen Lomas Garza

Introduction

Cut-paper art (papel picado) has a long history in Mexico. Banners made from tree bark thousands of years ago were followed by the tissue paper cutouts you see today.

My grandmother taught me how to cut paper for **embroidery** designs when I was little. She's also the first person I saw making paper cutouts. I've been making them myself for twenty-seven years now. I started by cutting out simple designs with scissors. Later I began using a craft knife to create **intricate** designs like the pieces you see in this book.

These pieces are like magic windows. When you look through them, you can see into another world.

Introducción

El papel picado tiene una larga historia en México, desde los estandartes de amate o papel de corteza de árbol de hace miles de años hasta el papel picado que vemos hoy.

Mi abuela me enseñó cómo recortar papel para diseños de **bordado** cuando yo era pequeña. También fue la primera persona que vi hacer papel picado. Ahora ya

---

embroidery (em broi′ də rē) detailed designs on cloth or cut out on paper

intricate (in′ tri kit) very involved or complicated

bordado diseños detallados hechos en tela o papel

llevo haciéndolos yo misma por veintisiete años. Comencé recortando diseños sencillos con tijeras. Después empecé a usar un estilete con navaja para crear diseños **intrincados** como las piezas que vemos en este libro.

Estas piezas son como ventanas mágicas. Cuando miramos a través de ellas, podemos ver otro mundo.

---

intrincados diseños con mucho detalles o complejos

OFFERING FOR ANTONIO LOMAS

This is my grandfather, Antonio Lomas, watering the corn in his garden. There's also squash, garlic, chile, and **nopales**. He always had vegetables growing, and he would always share what he had grown with his sons and daughters and grandkids.

This paper cutout is big. It measures five feet by eight feet and has ten sections. I tied them to a stick, and hung the stick from the ceiling.

---

nopales (nō pə' les) prickly pear cactus

I used to love helping my grandfather water his garden at the end of the day. It gave me a chance to be really close to him. If he wanted to talk to me, I was right there to listen to him. If I wanted to ask questions, he was there for me.

Ofrenda para Antonio Lomas

Éste es mi abuelo, Antonio Lomas, regando su maizal en su jardín. También hay plantas de calabazas, ajos, chiles y **nopales.** Mi abuelo todo el tiempo plantaba verduras que cultivaba para luego siempre compartirlas con sus hijos e hijas y todos sus nietos.

Este papel picado es grande, mide cinco pies por ocho pies. Tiene diez secciones que uní al conectarlas a una vara que colgué del techo.

Me gustaba ayudar a mi abuelo a regar su jardín al final del día. Esto me daba la oportunidad de estar de veras muy cerca a él. Si él quería hablar commigo, yo estaba ahí mismo para escucharlo. Si yo le quería preguntar algo, ahí estaba él para mí.

---

nopales cactos

Write About It!

Write a paragraph that explains why you think cut-paper art is important to Carmen Lomas Garza. Then tell about a craft that you would like to learn and why it is important to you.

Texas in the 21st Century

TAKE A LOOK

What role do Texans play in the 21st century?

Texans work on projects, such as the International Space Station, with other nations.

For more about the International
Space Station, explore our Web site
www.mhschool.com

Chapter 10

THE *Big* IDEAS ABOUT...

Our Special State

How do you like to spend your free time? Maybe you like to ride your bike, play football, swim, or take long walks in the country. You might be surprised to learn how many different ways there are to enjoy and celebrate our special state. In this chapter, you will read more about the rich cultures of Texas.

A BLEND OF CULTURES

We Texans express our many cultures through our beliefs, languages, and ways of having fun.

SPORTS AND RECREATION

Our state offers a variety of activities. Texans can enjoy canoeing, camping, fishing, and sports such as football, basketball, and baseball.

LITERATURE AND THE ARTS

The arts, which are made up of all the creative things that people do, are an important part of life in Texas.

Foldables

Make this Foldable study guide and use it to record what you learn about our special state.

1. Place two sheets of paper one inch apart, forming a one-inch tab across the top.
2. Roll the bottom of the two sheets up to make three tabs the same size. Fold and staple.
3. Write the title of the chapter on the large tab, and the three lesson titles on the small equal-sized tabs.

A Blend of Cultures

Find out!

How have different cultures made Texas a special state?

Lesson Outline
- Celebrating Our Culture
- Texans One and All

READING STRATEGY

Draw a chart like this one. List four cultural groups in Texas. Write one fact about each group.

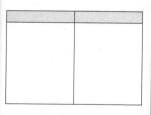

BUILD BACKGROUND

Texas is a place where different cultures live, work, and have fun together. We are lucky to live in a state where differences in heritage come together. They create a special Texan way of life.

CELEBRATING OUR CULTURE

Texans enjoy many special celebrations throughout the year. Our state hosts over 500 fairs and festivals each year. Along with events like the Scarborough Faire in **Waxahachie** and the Texas Crab Festival in **Crystal Beach**, festivals in Texas celebrate the many cultures that make our state special.

Earlier in this book you learned about June 19, or Juneteenth, when African Americans **commemorate** (kuh MEM uh rayt) freedom from slavery. To commemorate is to honor the memory of something.

Celebrations in Texas include traditional dancing at a Mexican festival (left), a Chinese New Year celebration (below), and Juneteenth (above, right). A traditional Scottish band participates in a Washington's Day parade (bottom).

On May 5, Mexican Americans celebrate Cinco de Mayo. Each spring Texans in **San Marcos**, and elsewhere in our state, learn Mexican folk dances for Cinco de Mayo. This holiday honors Mexico's victory over the French in the 1800s.

People from all over Texas enjoy Oktoberfest in **Fredericksburg**. Fredericksburg is one of the oldest German American communities in our state. At this festival people eat traditional German foods and dance and sing to German music. The polka is a popular dance here, but it's even bigger at the National Polka Festival in **Ennis**. Ennis is home to the largest Czech community in Texas.

In **Salado**, Scottish descendants come together for the Gathering of the Clans. Texans from all over enjoy music, dancing, and plenty of food at this two-day festival.

READING CHECK What things do people in Texas celebrate?

Texas Population: 2000

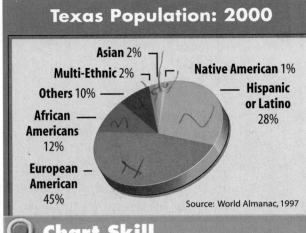

Asian 2%
Multi-Ethnic 2%
Others 10%
African Americans 12%
European American 45%
Native American 1%
Hispanic or Latino 28%

Source: World Almanac, 1997

Chart Skill

1. Which group is the largest? Which is the second largest?
2. Which two groups have the same population?

TEXANS ONE AND ALL

Today, many of our nearly 21 million Texans claim ties to over 80 countries around the world. Nearly one out of three Texans has relatives in Mexico or another Spanish-speaking country. Some Texans have relatives in places such as China, Japan, Vietnam, and Korea. As a result of our state's rich cultural diversity, many Texans are bilingual. They speak English and one other language.

Many Religions

Most Mexican Americans in Texas are Roman Catholic. Many Roman Catholic immigrants came from countries in Europe in the 1800s. Today Roman Catholics make up the fastest-growing religious group in Texas. Protestants make up the largest religious group in Texas.

Many Jews were among the European immigrants who began arriving in the 1800s. Muslims, Hindus, and Buddhists are among the other religious groups that live and worship in Texas. Texas has the eighth-largest Muslim population in the United States.

Religious holidays such as Christmas and other Christian holidays are celebrated by many Texan families. Other important religious holidays include Passover, celebrated by Jewish Texans, and Ramadan, celebrated by Muslim Texans.

Some people honor their religious heritage at mosques (left). Weddings (above) are an important part of religious heritage.

Texas Foods

Part of our culture as Texans is the huge assortment of foods we enjoy. At every celebration we are sure to find dishes ranging from guacamole to sweet potato pie and spoon bread. Look at the chart to find some festivals where you might taste some of these dishes.

One thing Texans of all backgrounds have in common is their love for Texas. On the next page you can find the words and music to "Beautiful, Beautiful Texas." What does this song celebrate?

 READING CHECK What are some religious holidays celebrated by Texan families?

Balloon racing is one thing you might see at an event in Texas.

Annual Events in Texas

Month	Event	City
January	Texas Citrus Fiesta	Mission
February	Mardi Gras	Galveston
March	Texas Independence Day Celebration	Washington
April	Fiesta San Antonio	San Antonio
May	Western Heritage Classic	Abilene
June	Tomato Festival	Jacksonville
July	Great Texas Balloon Race	Longview
August	Gillespie County Fair	Fredericksburg
September	National Championship Indian Powwow	Grand Prairie
October	Texas Rice Festival	Winnie
November	Spinach Festival	Crystal City
December	Sandhills Hereford & Quarter Horse Show & Rodeo	Odessa

Chart Skill

1. In what city is the Western Heritage Classic?

2. When is the Spinach Festival in Crystal City?

365

Beautiful, Beautiful Texas

Words and Music by W. Lee O'Daniel

Refrain:

To Beau - ti - ful, Beau - ti - ful Tex - as_____ Where the

beau - ti - ful blue - bon - nets grow _____ We're

proud of our fore - fath - ers _____ Who

fought at the Al - a - mo_____ You can

live on the plains or the moun - tain_____ Or

down where the sea - bree - zes blow_____ And you're

still in Beau - ti - ful Tex - as_____ The most

beau - ti - ful place that I know. _____

PUTTING IT TOGETHER

Texans have ancestors who were from all around the world. Many of us weren't even born in Texas. We celebrate different holidays and different traditions. Yet as Texans we also have a great deal in common. We believe in equal rights and opportunities for all. We also share the responsibility for taking care of our state, because its future is our future, too.

Square dancers perform at a Texas festival in Austin.

Review and Assess

1. Write one sentence with the following vocabulary word:

   commemorate

2. Look at the chart on page 364 and find the percentage of Texans who have ties to places such as China, Japan, and Korea.

3. Describe ways in which Texans of different cultures have contributed in making Texas a special place.

4. Roman Catholics are the fastest-growing religious group in Texas. How can **history** help us understand why this came to be?

5. **Compare** and **contrast** Cinco de Mayo and Juneteenth to Oktoberfest and the Gathering of the Clans.

Contact your local Chamber of Commerce to find out all the celebrations in your area. Create a calendar of events of your area.

· ·

Write a letter to a friend who is thinking of moving to Texas. Convince your friend to move to Texas by explaining how you benefit from living in a state with such a mix of cultures.

Sports and Recreation

Find! out!

How do Texans spend their free time?

VOCABULARY

professional
recreation
Olympic Games

PEOPLE

Lance Armstrong
Nolan Ryan

READING STRATEGY

Draw a main idea map like this one. List some places where Texans can go for outdoor recreation.

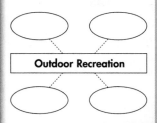

Outdoor Recreation

Lesson Outline:

• Sports in Texas
• Recreation in Texas
• Many Sports, Many Stars

BUILD BACKGROUND

In 1996 **Lance Armstrong** was ranked the number one cyclist in the world. By the end of that year, however, he was forced to stop competing because he had cancer. In 1999, after defeating the disease, he won the Tour de France, one of the most important cycling competitions in the world. In 2001 he won the race again for the third year in a row. For Lance Armstrong and many other Texans, sports and the great outdoors are some of the best reasons to live in the Lone Star State.

SPORTS IN TEXAS

From backyards to stadiums, Texans team up in almost every sport you can think of. Texas is a great place to get involved in sports.

Football fans across our state have a great deal to cheer about. Texas is the home of a **professional** football team. A professional team is made up of athletes who play the sport as a job, not just for fun. The Dallas Cowboys make their home at Texas Stadium in Irving. The Cowboys have played in more Super Bowls than any other team in the United States.

Home teams are very popular in Texas. Crowds of 20,000 or more gather each fall to watch their favorite teams play Friday Night Football. Even bigger

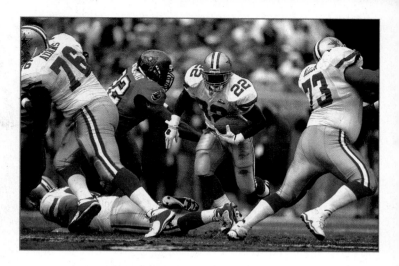

crowds pack stadiums to see college teams like the Texas A&M Aggies or the University of Texas Longhorns.

When football season ends Texas sports fans get caught up in basketball. Our state has four professional basketball teams—the Dallas Mavericks, the Houston Rockets, the San Antonio Spurs, and the Houston Comets. Texas is also home to many college basketball teams, including the Texas Tech Lady Raiders.

Football and basketball are not the only sports popular in Texas. Baseball is also a favorite. Texas has two professional baseball teams. The Texas Rangers play in the Ballpark in Arlington and the Houston Astros play at Minute Maid Park.

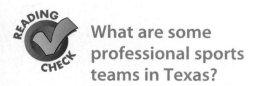

READING CHECK What are some professional sports teams in Texas?

Some of Texas's best-known athletes are Lance Armstrong (far left), a cyclist; Cheryl Swoops (left) of the Houston Comets; and Emmitt Smith (above) of the Dallas Cowboys.

RECREATION IN TEXAS

Whether you like to cycle like Lance Armstrong, swim, or read a book, our state is the perfect place for **recreation**. Recreation is what people do in order to relax and enjoy themselves. In Texas all we have to do to enjoy recreation is step outside.

Texas Outdoors

Our state and national parks are some of the best places for recreation. We have about 90 to choose from. In West Texas, you can hike through Big Bend National Park. In this rugged park you can explore huge stone canyons and old desert trails, climb mountains, and enjoy wildlife.

You'll find some of the best wind-surfing in the world along the Gulf of Mexico. If you're more interested in fishing, Corpus Christi is the perfect place to fish for speckled bass! If you simply want sun, sand, and surf, Padre Island is the place for you. Padre Island is also a good place to watch for rare sea turtles. If you prefer water sports, you have many places to go. Along the Gulf of Mexico, there are almost 400 miles of coast.

Families camp at many state parks from Galveston Island to Palo Duro Canyon State Park. Campgrounds fill up quickly, so it's a good idea to call ahead.

As you know, the bluebonnet is our state flower. We need to protect our wildflowers because they help the environment in many ways. Read the biography on the next page to learn how Lady Bird Johnson worked to preserve our environment.

What can you do at Big Bend National Park?

Texans can enjoy outdoor activities such as canoeing (left) and horseback riding (above).

BIOGRAPHY

Focus On: Responsibility

CLAUDIA TAYLOR "Lady Bird" Johnson lined the roadsides of Texas with millions of bluebonnets, reddish-orange Indian paintbrush, and purple sage wildflowers. These are native plants because they are a natural part of our state's environment. Wildflowers provide food and homes for wild birds and animals.

In 1982 Lady Bird Johnson opened the National Wildflower Research Center near Austin. At the Center, visitors can learn how to protect our environment and create their own garden with native plants. Her sense of responsibility to the environment has made Texas a better and more beautiful place.

Link to Today Interview a parent, grandparent, teacher, or friend. Ask how being a responsible citizen has been important in that person's life. Write a paragraph about what he or she tells you.

THE LIFE OF "LADY BIRD" JOHNSON	**1912** Claudia Alta Taylor is born	**1934** Claudia Alta Taylor marries Lyndon Baines Johnson	**1963** Lady Bird Johnson becomes First Lady of the United States	**1982** Lady Bird Johnson establishes the National Wildflower Research Center
	1912	1934	1960	1982	2000
LIFE AROUND THE WORLD		**1929** Stock market crash leads to the Great Depression	**1951** First color television is invented	**1963** Martin Luther King, Jr., gives his famous "I Have a Dream" speech	**1989** Spacecraft *Voyager 2* flies close to Neptune, the planet farthest from the sun

MANY SPORTS, MANY STARS

There are many famous Texans in world sports. **Nolan Ryan** of Alvin made history as one of the best baseball pitchers of all time. At least eighty-one Texans have won gold medals during the **Olympic Games**. They are held every four years and involve athletes from all over the world.

Tennis, golf, and the rodeo are also popular sports in Texas.

There are many fun and interesting places to visit in Texas. That's why many Texans spend their vacations right here in our state. Our state's diverse culture and variety of recreation have influenced many Texans.

READING CHECK Who is Nolan Ryan?

Famous Texans	Professions	Hometown
Randall Cobb	Boxer, Actor	Bridge City
Earl Campbell	Running Back	Corpus Christi
Sissy Spacek	Actress	Quitman
George Foreman	Boxer, Actor	Houston
Steve Martin	Actor, Writer, Producer	Waco
Lyle Lovett	Singer	Klein
Aaron Spelling	Film Producer	Dallas
Debbie Allen	Dancer, Actress, Producer	Houston
Dan Rather	Televison Reporter	Wharton
Michael Johnson	Olympic Runner	Dallas

◎ Chart Skill

1. Who is Lyle Lovett? Where is he from?

2. Who are two famous Texans from Dallas? What are they known for?

PUTTING IT TOGETHER

Thanks to our plentiful resources, we always have something fun to do in our great state. It provides a variety of recreational activities such as cycling, basketball, football, canoeing, hiking, and rodeo.

Michael Johnson (left) an Olympic Games gold medal winner has competed all over the world. Houston Astros pitcher Wade Miller (right) has been playing with the Astros since 1996.

Review and Assess

1. Write one sentence using each of the following vocabulary words:

   Olympic Games   professional

   recreation

2. Who is Lance Armstrong?

3. List some ways in which Texans spend their free time.

4. How does our state's geography influence the kind of recreation we enjoy?

5. What do you think Lady Bird Johnson's point of view is about our environment? Why?

Create a chart listing some types of outdoor activities available in Texas.

• •

Write a letter to a friend in another state. Describe to your friend all the different things there are to do in Texas.

Reading Road Maps

Suppose you and your family wanted to drive to Irving to watch a game at the Texas Stadium. How could you figure out how to get there? One way would be to use a **road map** to find your route. Road maps show the roads you can use to get from one place to another.

LEARN THE SKILL

Look at Map A on this page. Use it as you follow the steps below to learn more about reading road maps.

1. **Look for symbols and a map key.**
Map A shows several different kinds of roads. Look at the map key. As you can see, a heavy green line shows that a road is an **interstate highway**. An interstate highway connects two or more states. Usually these roads have at least two lanes in each direction and have a speed limit of 55 miles per hour or more.

Look again at the map key. You can see that a red line stands for a United States highway. What kind of road does a blue line stand for?

2. **Identify road numbers.**
You probably noticed that most roads on the map have numbers inside a special symbol. Those numbers are the "names" of the roads. What is the number of the road that connects San Antonio to Corpus Christi? What kind of road is it?

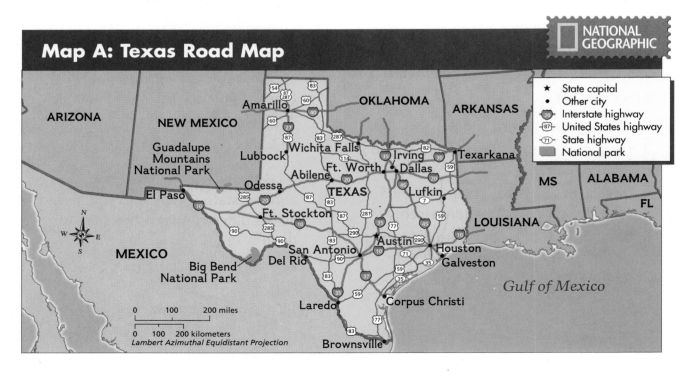

Map A: Texas Road Map

NATIONAL GEOGRAPHIC

Map key:
- ★ State capital
- • Other city
- Interstate highway
- United States highway
- State highway
- National park

If you follow some roads with your finger, you will see that they have more than one number. That's because more than one road may "share" a certain route. Follow the road from Amarillo to Lubbock, for example.

3. **Identify directions.**
Most even-numbered roads usually run east and west. Odd-numbered roads usually run north and south. This fact can help lost drivers figure out which way they're going.

4. **Identify destinations.**
Besides highways and cities, road maps can also show parks, historic sites, and other places of interest. They can help you find routes to popular locations and well-known landmarks.

TRY THE SKILL

Suppose you wanted to plan a trip from Abilene to Houston. Along the way you want to visit Austin, our state capital. Which route would you take? What kind of roads are on the route? Now use Map A to answer the following questions.

1. What does a road map show?

2. According to the map, which interstate highways connect Texas with New Mexico? With Louisiana?

3. Why do road maps usually show more than one kind of road?

4. Why is it important to be able to read a road map?

EXTEND THE SKILL

Road maps can also help you get around smaller areas. They can show not only highways but also major streets. Map B on this page shows roads in and around Irving. Study it and then answer the following questions.

- What route would you take to get from the interstate highway to Texas Stadium?

- What kind of roads would be included on a map of your city or town?

- Contact your local Chamber of Commerce to find out about major roads and highways that run through your community. Then create a road map for your area. Include a legend, scale, and a compass rose.

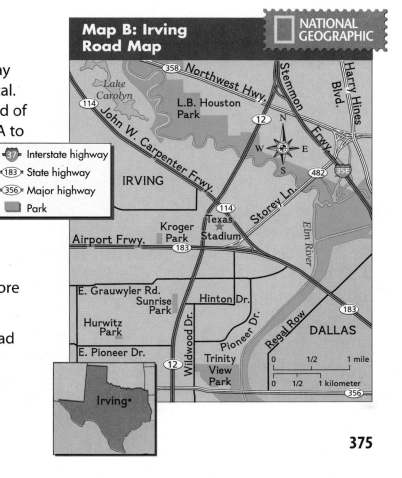

Map B: Irving Road Map

Literature and the Arts

Find! out!

How have art and literature made Texas a great place to live?

Lesson Outline
- The Arts
- Literature
- Music

BUILD BACKGROUND

The cultures in Texas have helped shape our tradition of art. Art is made up of things such as the pictures people paint, the songs they sing, and the stories they write.

READING STRATEGY

Draw a word web. List four Texan artists.

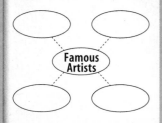

Famous Artists

Evening Star No. V, by Georgia O'Keeffe, 1917. Watercolor. Collection of the McNay Art Museum, bequest of Helen Miller Jones.

THE ARTS

No two works of art are exactly alike. Even so, artists often raise similar questions through their work. What is beautiful? What makes life fun or difficult? Texan artists have tried to answer such questions in many ways.

In 1872 **Elisabet Ney** moved here from Germany. She won fame for her sculptures of famous Texans such as Stephen F. Austin and Sam Houston.

Georgia O'Keeffe, a painter, lived in Texas for about three years in the early 1900s. Her time in the Panhandle would influence her work for years to come. This is how she described the land around her home in Canyon, Texas:

". . . There was nothing but sky and flat 'prarieland'—land that seems more like the ocean than anything else I know. . . . I love this country."

Artist **John Biggers** moved to Texas in 1949 to teach in Houston. Biggers taught his students to create art from their own experience. In 1980 he was asked to create a **mural** based on the life of Christia V. Adair, a civil rights leader in Houston. A mural is a picture painted on a wall or ceiling. The mural on the opposite page is in the Christia V. Adair Park, in Harris County.

READING CHECK

What did John Biggers teach his students?

Many of Georgia O'Keeffe's paintings (top) were influenced by the geography of the Southwest. This statue of Sam Houston (right) can be seen in the Elisabet Ney museum in Austin. Artist John Biggers (left)

LITERATURE

Throughout Texas, storytelling is a well-loved tradition. William Sydney Porter, known to most as **O. Henry**, lived in Austin during the late 1800s. He wrote short stories that ended with an unexpected twist. One of his most famous short stories is "The Ransom of Red Chief."

Ada Simond, born in Texas in the early 1900s, wrote many stories about growing up as an African American in Texas. One of her most famous books is *Mae Dee and Her Family Join the Juneteenth Celebration.* Although all of Simond's books were about Mae Dee, her books really told the stories of her own life.

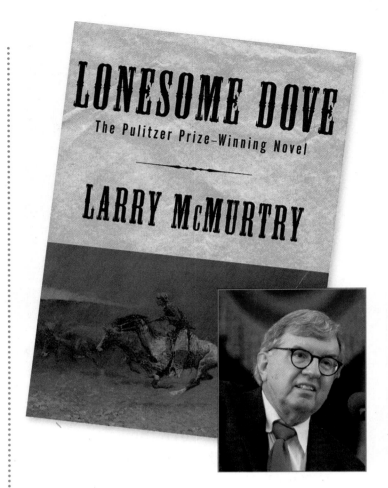

Katherine Anne Porter grew up in Indian Creek. She became well known for her short stories. In 1966 she won a **Pulitzer Prize** for her work, *Collected Stories.* Pulitzer Prizes are awarded every year for the best work in literature and newspaper writing.

Larry McMurtry was born in Wichita Falls into a family of ranchers. His experience growing up influenced his writings about the American West. He won a Pulitzer Prize for his book *Lonesome Dove.* The book told the story of a cattle drive from Texas to Montana in the 1800s.

Katherine Anne Porter (left) and O. Henry (above). Larry McMurtry (above, right) is known for his books about the West (top).

Texans Buck Ramsey (above) and Pat Mora (below) are known for their poems.

Poetry

Poems express thoughts and feelings about life. **Buck Ramsey** began writing poems after he seriously hurt his legs. He worked as a cowboy for most of his life and began writing poems about his life on the range.

Poet **Pat Mora** was born in El Paso in 1942. Her grandparents moved to Texas from Mexico. Mora, who is bilingual, worked as a teacher before she started writing. Mora's stories and poetry focus on language, tradition, and preserving culture. The following poem is from Mora's book of poems called *This Big Sky*.

READING CHECK What is Katherine Anne Porter well known for?

Primary Source:

"Twilight Choir"
— *by Pat Mora published in 1998.*

After the rain,
diamonds scattered
by some careless **duende**
glisten on willow leaves.

Butterflies and hummingbirds
flutter in the breeze.
Poppies fall in moist clusters
where they please,
and stars hum their poetry.

Kittens tease fat cats
dreaming tonguefuls of warm
honey. Trees, dark canopies,
sway melodies.

Their evening song
accompanies **cicada** *whirs*
and mockingbird's sassy,
musical originality,
after the rain.

---

duende: spirit
cicada: a loud insect

What do you think this poem is about?

MUSIC

Immigrants that came to call Texas home in the 1800s brought their own kind of folk music to our state. Often this kind of music described the beauty and hardships of everyday life. Folk singer **Nanci Griffith** of Austin has written songs about farm families struggling to survive in the Panhandle.

Country music comes from folk music and also focuses on real life experiences. Country music star **Willie Nelson**, who grew up in Abbott, is famous for songs about life in Texas.

Other Texan musicians have become famous for blending different styles of music to create a new style of their own. **Scott Joplin**, who was born in Texarkana in 1868, helped create **ragtime**. Ragtime was developed out of a mix of brassband, African American, and other sounds and rhythms. Joplin wrote and co-wrote more than 60 pieces of music. Ragtime helped give birth to jazz.

While ragtime music was becoming popular, the grandfather of **Flaco Jiménez** began using polka beats in Mexican American dance music. Today Flaco Jiménez's accordion playing has made a special style of **Norteño** (nawr TAY nyoh), or northern, music famous throughout the world.

Janis Joplin of Port Arthur, was born in 1943. Her music combined folk, country, and blues themes. Joplin became the world's first female rock music superstar.

READING CHECK What type of music did Scott Joplin help create?

Flaco Jiménez (left) and Janis Joplin (above) are two of the people that have made our state famous for music. A painting (right) by Alma Gunter shows families having dinner outdoors.

PUTTING IT TOGETHER

Art has a long history in Texas. From paintings and murals to literature and music, art is an important part of life in Texas. It is made up of all the creative things that people do. You can write songs, paint, or write stories or poems at home or at school. You don't have to be a star to create art in our state.

Review and Assess

1. Write one sentence using each of the following vocabulary words:

   mural **Norteño**

   ragtime

2. Why can painters, writers, sculptors, poets, and musicians all be called artists?

3. Describe ways in which artists, writers, and musicians have made Texas an interesting place to live.

4. How does our state's geography influence some artists?

5. Make a generalization about the importance of art in your community.

Create a two-column chart. In the column on the left, list the artists discussed in the lesson. In the column on the right list the type of art they create.

. . . .

Write a poem or short story, or paint a picture of your favorite place. Describe the land, animals, people, and anything else that is important to this place.

Recognizing Frame of Reference

In the last chapter, you learned how to recognize a person's point of view. A person's point of view is shaped by his or her **frame of reference** . Your frame of reference is your background. It includes all the things you have learned and experienced. It helps shape your thoughts, feelings, and opinions.

> **VOCABULARY**
>
> frame of reference

LEARN THE SKILL

Read the passage below. It is the point of view of Susan, a professional musician. Then follow the steps to recognize frame of reference.

Every child should learn to play an instrument. Children who study music do better in math and work well with others. I have played instruments since I was in elementary school. I started on piano, then learned bass and guitar. Music helped improve my grades. It also helped me make new friends from playing in the school orchestra. I now work as a bass player in a ragtime band.

1. **Identify the subject.**
   In the passage the subject is music education for all children.

2. **Identify the person's point of view.**
   Susan's point of view is that all children should learn to play an instrument.

3. **Examine the person's background.**
   Susan's music education has helped her a great deal.

She made better grades, gained friends, and is now a musician.

4. **Explain how the person's point of view is shaped by his or her frame of reference.**
   Susan's positive experiences with music education have shaped her point of view. It is the frame of reference that forms her opinion on the subject. She wants others to find the same success in school and life that she has.

If you recognize a person's frame of reference, you can understand why they reached their point of view. Recognizing frame of reference can also help you understand your own points of view.

3. What is Miguel's point of view?

4. How is it shaped by his frame of reference?

5. If you had attended the concert, what would your point of view have been?

6. How is your opinion of the performers shaped by your frame of reference?

TRY THE SKILL

Two fourth-graders, Claire and Miguel, each prepared a review of a concert they both attended. Willie Nelson and Flaco Jiménez were the performers. Claire is a big fan of country music. Miguel enjoys listening to Norteño. Read their reviews, and then answer the questions below.

Claire's Review: *The concert was a lot of fun. There were two performers, Willie Nelson and Flaco Jiménez. Jiménez's accordion playing was great. However, I feel Nelson put on the better show. He sang several of my favorite songs, including "On the Road Again." His performance was truly special.*

Miguel's Review: *I enjoyed the concert very much. Willie Nelson did a good job, but I believe Flaco Jiménez stole the show. Several of his songs brought the crowd to their feet. His accordion playing truly expresses the beauty of Norteño music. I would love to see him perform again.*

1. What is Claire's point of view?

2. How is it shaped by her frame of reference?

EXTEND THE SKILL

An artist's frame of reference can shape the kind of art they create. In the last lesson, you read about the poet Buck Ramsey. Ramsey worked as a cowboy for much of his life. In his poetry, he sometimes described how cowhands felt about the land they worked on. Read his poem, and then answer the following questions.

We were not told, but ours the knowing
We were the native strangers there
Among the things the land was growing—
To know this gave us more the care
To let the grass keep at its growing—
And let the streams keep at their flowing.

- What is Ramsey's point of view?

- How is it shaped by his frame of reference?

- Why is it important to recognize a person's frame of reference?

THE Big IDEAS ABOUT...

Texas, the Western Hemisphere, and the World

What future role will you play in Texas? You might be surprised to learn how your role will also affect the United States, the Western Hemisphere, and the world. In this chapter you will read more about how our state is becoming part of a global community.

GROWTH IN TEXAS

The growth of our state is tracked and studied by state and national governments to plan for the future.

NEIGHBORING COUNTRIES

Countries in the Western Hemisphere have a special relationship with Texas. These neighboring countries enjoy special rights to trade with us.

WORLDWIDE ECONOMIES

Texas reaches out beyond the Western Hemisphere. Our people work with countries all over the world.

THE WESTERN HEMISPHERE

Texans help countries in the Western Hemisphere to build stronger economies.

Foldables

Make this Foldable study guide and use it to record what you learn about Texas as a state, part of the Western Hemisphere, and the world.

1. Fold an 8 ½" x 8 ½" square of paper in half on a diagonal.

2. Open and fold in half in the opposite direction. This makes two folds that form an X.

3. Cut up one of the folds, stopping at the intersection.

4. Fold and glue one of the cut legs behind the other, forming a pyramid.

1

Texas: A Growing State

 How is the population of Texas changing?

VOCABULARY

census
decade
Sun Belt
World Wide Web

READING STRATEGY

Copy the chart you see here. Write the main idea of this lesson. Add supporting details as you read.

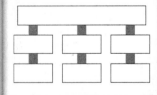

Lesson Outline

• Counting on Texas
• It's in the Numbers
• Larger Trends

BUILD BACKGROUND

As you have studied Texas history, you have read about how the population of Texas grew over time. How do we know so much about the people in our state? One way is through our nation's **census**. A census is a count of people who live in an area. The first United States census was held in 1790 to count the number of people in the newly formed country. Since then, a census has been taken every ten years so we can learn more about our country and our state.

COUNTING ON TEXAS

The United States Census Bureau is the department of our government responsible for counting the population of our country each **decade**. A decade is a period of ten years. The last census was held in the year 2000. All across the country, people received a letter and a list of questions in the mail.

Some questions were about the number of people who lived in a household, their ages, races, and how much education they've had. A few people received a longer list of questions that asked for more information about their work, income, housing, and transportation. Everyone was asked to return the answered questions to the Census Bureau.

Collecting and analyzing the results of the census takes years. Once the information is processed, it is used to plan national budgets, laws, and programs. Each state also receives information about its residents.

According to Census 2000 there are more than 20 million people living in Texas. That's enough people to fill 508 sold-out baseball games at Minute Maid Park. Compare that to just five years after Texas joined the Union with 212,592 people.

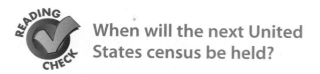

READING CHECK When will the next United States census be held?

> Every ten years, people in the United States receive **census** forms that help the government learn about our country's population.

This information can be used to decide how best to serve the people of our state.

Reading pages of numbers and percentages might not seem interesting at first. But these numbers contain important information about our state. Census numbers help businesses decide where to open new locations. Buses, trains, and airports use the information to make schedules. Community leaders use the numbers to plan for schools, voting districts, and public utilities.

IT'S IN THE NUMBERS

The census numbers tell us that Texas is the second-largest state in the country by population. Three-quarters of our 254 counties increased in population since the 1990 census. Most of the increases were around metropolitan areas such as Dallas-Fort Worth, Houston, and San Antonio.

The southwest border of Texas has also grown quickly in the last ten years. However, rural counties in the Panhandle and West Texas have had little or no growth. Some of these rural counties have fewer people in them than they did in the early 1990s.

Using information from previous censuses, the government also makes predictions about how those numbers will change by the next census.

 READING CHECK According to Census 2000, where did the population of Texas increase and decrease?

Texas events, such as rodeos (above left) and music festivals (below), reflect our state's population.

DATAGRAPHIC

Population Changes In Texas

Census 2000 showed two important changes in the population of Texas. One was the changing racial and ethnic background of Texans. The other was the movement of Texans within our state. Study the map and graph on this page and answer the questions.

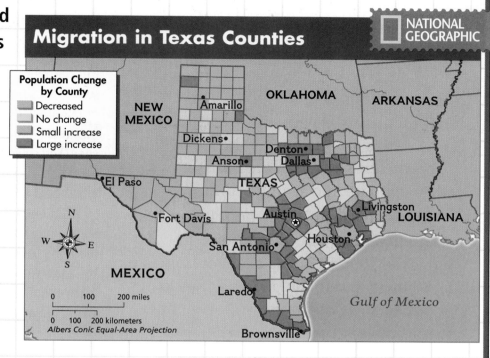

Migration in Texas Counties

NATIONAL GEOGRAPHIC

Population Change by County
- Decreased
- No change
- Small increase
- Large increase

QUESTIONS

1. What group grew the fastest in Texas between 1990 and 2000?

2. What common features are shared by the counties that increased in population?

3. What conclusion can you draw about the changes in Texas's population?

To learn more, visit our Web site:
www.mhschool.com

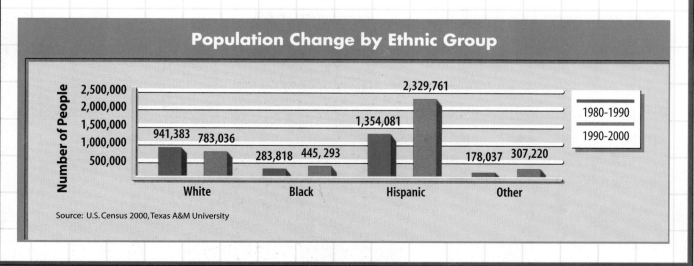

Population Change by Ethnic Group

	1980-1990	1990-2000
White	941,383	783,036
Black	283,818	445,293
Hispanic	1,354,081	2,329,761
Other	178,037	307,220

Number of People

Source: U.S. Census 2000, Texas A&M University

LARGER TRENDS

Texas is located in the Sun Belt. This is the part of the United States where the climate is warm for most of the year. The 1990 and 2000 censuses have shown states in the Sun Belt to be the fastest-growing areas of our country.

One reason Texas is so attractive to people is its central location between the two coasts of our country. This makes it easy for people to travel to other cities for business. Other reasons for Texas's growth are our state's warm climate and strong economy.

The increase in Texas's population is a sign that our state will continue to grow and change. These changes bring new challenges to the people who live in our state. Texans must work together to find ways to meet these challenges.

READING CHECK What is the Sun Belt?

Exploring TECHNOLOGY

When people are thinking of moving to Texas, they can do research using the World Wide Web. The Web is a collection of information stored on computers around the world. You can get this information from any computer with a link to the Internet. All the information from one source is called a Web site.

Many city governments, newspapers, and business organizations in Texas have Web sites. You could look for a job, find a house, and learn about schools and businesses—all without actually visiting our state!

What else might someone who was planning to move to Texas want to learn about on the World Wide Web?

The Dallas-Fort Worth area is part of the Sun Belt.

PUTTING IT TOGETHER

Every ten years, our nation's government uses a census to learn about the people in our country. Some of the people who move to our state come from other states. But many new Texans are also immigrants from other countries. One of the challenges of growth in Texas is helping people who move here to become a part of our community. To do this, Texans must work together and help each other so that our state continues to grow and change.

Welcome to Texas

DRIVE FRIENDLY - THE TEXAS WAY

Review and Assess

1. Write one sentence for the vocabulary words:

   census   **decade**

   Sun Belt

2. How often does the government conduct a census of our country?

3. Describe some of the ways the population of Texas is changing.

4. Identify some of the causes that have led to the population changes.

5. Using what you have learned in this lesson's Datagraphic, make a **prediction** about how the population of Texas will change by 2010.

Activities

Use the Atlas map and scale on page R16 to estimate the distance from Austin to the cities of New York, Chicago, and San Francisco. What is the difference between the distances to the closest and farthest cities? Draw a conclusion about how this makes Texas attractive to businesses.

∙ ∙

Write a letter to someone who is thinking about moving to your town from another state. Tell this person about your town, its history, schools, and businesses. Share any other information you think would be helpful to someone moving to Texas.

393

Points of View

Who Should Own the Water In Our State?

In Texas ranchers, farmers, and other landowners own the water underneath their land. They have the right to sell their water. But people disagree about whether buying and selling water rights is a good idea. Read the different points of view below.

KAROL PARKER
**Public Affairs Manager, El Paso Water Utilities
El Paso, Texas**
Excerpt from an interview, 2001.

❝Buying and selling water rights is a good idea. In our free-enterprise system, people have the right to decide what to do with their water rights. Our water company provides water for people in the El Paso area. Our customers have reduced water use through conservation, but the city is growing very rapidly. We need to get more water so that the city can continue to grow.**❞**

RONALD GERTSON
Rice Farmer, East Bernard, Texas
Excerpt from an interview, 2001.

❝People should be allowed to sell their water rights, but the state of Texas should make sure it buys some of these rights and reserves them for farmers. Some farmers may not be able to afford to pay for the water they need for irrigation, because they can't match the prices that cities and industries can pay. If more water is sold to cities, there will be less irrigated agriculture.**❞**

SUSAN KADERKA
Director, Gulf States Regional Office
National Wildlife Federation, Austin, Texas
Excerpt from an interview, 2001.

66 No individual really owns the water in Texas. Landowners have the right to pump water from underneath their land, and the state can grant someone the right to take water from a river. During a drought, farmers might sell their irrigation water to cities and earn as much as they would farming. But it's important to leave enough for birds, fish, and other wildlife. If we use it all up, they won't survive. 99

Thinking About the Points of View

1. Karol Parker works for the water company that provides water for El Paso. How do you think this influenced her point of view?

2. Ronald Gertson is a farmer who depends on water for irrigated farming. How do you think Gertson's job affected his point of view?

3. Susan Kaderka is the director of a group that works to protect wildlife and the environment in Texas. Do you think this may have affected her opinion? How?

4. What other points of view might people have on this issue?

 Building Citizenship

Responsibility
Water is a renewable resource. But we must use it responsibly so that all Texans have enough. In what ways might your family use water responsibly?

 Write About It!

Suppose you were the mayor of a growing Texas city. Your city has industries that use water and irrigated farms nearby. Make a list of the ways people in your community use water. Then write a speech describing the water-use issues your city faces.

Using Primary and Secondary Sources

You can get information from two different kinds of sources. One is a **primary source**. A primary source is information produced by someone who saw or took part in what he or she is describing. A primary source might be a diary, a letter, or an autobiography.

Most of the information in this textbook is from a **secondary source**. Secondary sources are written by people who were not present at the events they describe. History textbooks and encyclopedias are examples of secondary sources.

> **VOCABULARY**
>
> primary source
> secondary source

LEARN THE SKILL

Read the excerpt below. Then follow the steps to learn more about primary and secondary sources.

I moved to Houston with my family last summer. We used to live in the Northeast. Life in the Sun Belt is better. The climate here is warm and sunny most of the year. It is also the fastest growing part of our country. I hope to stay here for a long time.

1. **Look for words like "I," "we," "my," or "our."**
   In primary sources, a writer will often mention himself or herself. Writers of secondary sources do not refer to themselves. In the passage, the writer includes the word "I" several times.

2. **Identify facts and opinions.**
   Primary sources often include a writer's thoughts or feelings. Secondary sources contain more facts than opinions. The passage includes several opinions such as "Life in the Sun Belt is better."

3. **Identify if the source is primary or secondary.**

   Put all the clues together to identify if the source is primary or secondary. In this case, the passage is a primary source.

   It is important to read and study both kinds of sources. A primary source can make us feel as though "we were there." A secondary source may help us see a broader view of events.

TRY THE SKILL

Study the excerpt below. Use it to answer the questions that follow.

In the 1940s, millions of Americans began moving to an area known as the Sun Belt. The Southeast, Southwest, and parts of the West are all in the Sun Belt. The area got its name from its year-round warm, sunny climate. Popular Sun Belt cities include Houston and Dallas in Texas; Phoenix, Arizona; and Atlanta, Georgia.

1. Does the writer mention himself or herself in the passage?

2. Does the passage include more facts or more opinions?

3. Is the passage a primary source or a secondary source?

4. What is the difference between primary and secondary sources?

EXTEND THE SKILL

Write a paragraph describing how you spent last weekend. Exchange your paragraph with a classmate's. Use your classmate's paragraph to answer the following questions.

- Is the paragraph a primary source or a secondary source?

- How can you tell?

- Is a biography a primary source or a secondary source? What about an autobiography?

- How do both primary and secondary sources help us to understand history?

Lesson 2

VOCABULARY

interdependent
NAFTA
import
maquiladoras

READING STRATEGY

Copy the chart you see here. Fill in the main idea and supporting details as you read this lesson.

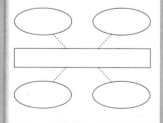

Neighbors in the Western Hemisphere

How does Texas work with countries in the Western Hemisphere ?

Lesson Outline
• Trade Agreements
• Working Across Borders
• More Trading Partners

BUILD BACKGROUND

No one state or country can produce everything its people use. The people of Texas, the United States, and other countries in the Western Hemisphere are **interdependent**. This means they depend on one another to meet their needs and wants. In this lesson you will learn how people in the Western Hemisphere reach common goals and solve shared problems.

Trade agreements let foreign countries ship goods to Texas (left) and manufacture products to sell in the United States (above).

TRADE AGREEMENTS

Countries that want to do business with each other create trade agreements. These agreements allow goods and services to be exchanged between the countries. Each country wants to make sure it will benefit from the agreement. The price, quantity, and quality of goods a country produces are just some things that affect these agreements.

Countries that are neighbors often want to trade with each other. In 1993, the United States entered into a trading agreement with Canada and Mexico. This agreement is called **NAFTA**. It stands for North American Free Trade Agreement.

The goal of NAFTA is to strengthen trading ties between North American countries. The agreement makes it easier to send exports between the three countries. The governments also agreed to get rid of taxes on **imports** between the countries. An import is something brought from one country for sale or use in another country.

Some people in the United States disagree about the effects of NAFTA. They think many factories will now choose to move to Mexico, where workers are paid less and there are fewer rules about business. They think this will leave fewer jobs for Texans and other Americans. Others think NAFTA will improve wages and working conditions in the United States, Mexico, and Canada. Over time, they think it will strengthen the economies of these countries.

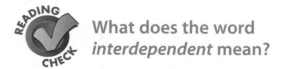

What does the word *interdependent* mean?

399

Texans export agricultural products, machine parts, and electronics to businesses in Mexico. Almost half of all exports from Texas go to Mexico. In exchange, our state imports petroleum and cars from Mexico as well as fruit, vegetables, and nuts.

Both Texas and Mexican governments watch the amount of imports and exports carefully. They want to make sure the trade relationship is working. They also want to try and predict new ways to build trade relationships that will benefit both places. Sometimes goods go back and forth across our borders more than once. For example, some factories in Texas make parts for automobiles. These parts are exported to factories in Mexico that build cars. If Texans want to buy the cars made in Mexico, they are imported to our state.

WORKING ACROSS BORDERS

Mexico and Texas have a long history between them. Today, Mexico is our state's largest trading partner. One reason Mexico is our largest partner is our shared border. Our trading relationship is also built on our shared history and culture.

Border crossings allow people to live, work, and shop in both Texas and Mexico.

Close Working Relationships

Some companies have built factories in both Texan and Mexican cities near the border. These "twin factories" are called **maquiladoras** (mah KEE lah dawr us).

Texas companies benefit from maquiladoras by paying lower taxes on goods imported from their factories in Mexico. The companies also benefit from being close to transportation systems to the United States. People in Mexico benefit from the jobs created by the maquiladoras.

Cities where maquiladoras are located become parts of the same economy. **Laredo** and **Nuevo Laredo** are two cities where many maquiladoras are located. Other popular cities for maquiladoras are **El Paso** and **Ciudad Juarez**.

The governments of Mexico and the United States have also made it easier for people to travel and trade across the Texas-Mexico border. People who live near the border might cross over it to go shopping, get to their jobs, or go out to dinner.

READING CHECK What are two reasons why Mexico is our state's largest trading partner?

Maquiladoras in El Paso and Ciudad Juarez.

MORE TRADING PARTNERS

Canada does not share a border with Texas, but it is still our second largest trading partner. In fact, only five other states in our country export more goods to Canada.

Our state exports high-tech equipment, chemicals, machinery, cars, and trucks to Canada. We import goods such as lumber, aircraft parts, and refined petroleum products.

One new way Texan and Canadian businesses are working together is by encouraging tourism. People in the tourism industry of our state and Canada meet to develop advertising, tours, and special offers for Texans and Canadians. This builds the tourism and service industries in both Texas and Canada.

Texas also trades with many countries in South America. Ranchers from Texas trade livestock with ranchers in Argentina to improve their herds of cattle. Our state also imports grapes, bananas, and pineapples from countries such as Ecuador and Chile. Look at the chart on this page to see other goods our state imports and exports in the Western Hemisphere.

 **What countries in South America does Texas trade with?**

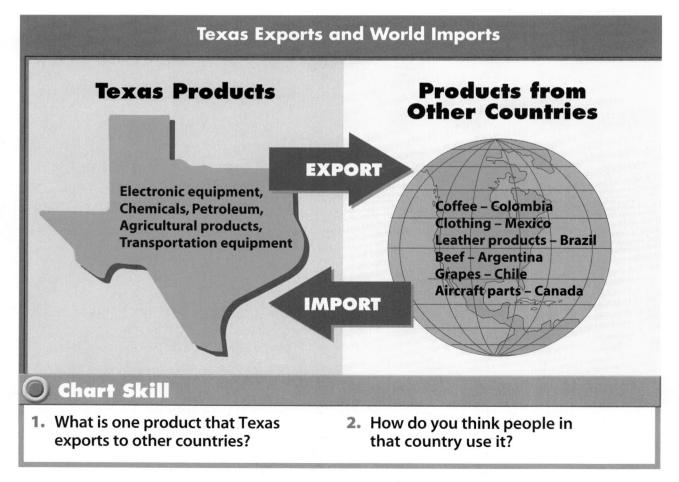

Texas Exports and World Imports

Texas Products

EXPORT

Electronic equipment, Chemicals, Petroleum, Agricultural products, Transportation equipment

IMPORT

Products from Other Countries

Coffee – Colombia
Clothing – Mexico
Leather products – Brazil
Beef – Argentina
Grapes – Chile
Aircraft parts – Canada

Chart Skill

1. What is one product that Texas exports to other countries?

2. How do you think people in that country use it?

PUTTING IT TOGETHER

Businesses in Texas produce many goods and services, but they do not supply everything that Texans want and need. Texas trades with other countries to get goods it does not produce. To make trade easier, the United States has created agreements with Mexico and Canada. Texas also trades with many other countries in the Western Hemisphere. In the next lesson you will read about how Texas works with other countries in the world.

Trucks bring timber from Canada to be used in Texas.

Review and Assess

1. Write one sentence for the vocabulary words:

   import   interdependent

   NAFTA   maquiladoras

2. What is a trade agreement?

3. Describe some ways that Texas works with countries in the Western Hemisphere.

4. Identify some reasons why Americans disagree about the effects of NAFTA.

5. How do countries solve the **problem** of not being able to make all of the goods their people want and need?

Activities

Using your school library or the Internet, find out how the maquiladoras system has changed the way Texan businesses work. List some advantages to bringing nearby Texan and Mexican cities into the same economy.

• •

Suppose you were in charge of creating trade agreements for Texas. **Write** a letter to the government of a neighboring country offering to trade goods and services. Include information about what you would like to export and import.

Drawing Conclusions

Suppose you knew the following facts. Your school's baseball team lost all the games it played in April. Rosa, a new pitcher, joined the team in May. The team went on to win the rest of the season. Based on these facts, you conclude that Rosa led the baseball team to a winning streak.

Sometimes meanings or connections are not always clear. Drawing inferences is one way to better understand what you read. Drawing **conclusions** can also help.

A conclusion is a statement you make based on several pieces of information. Then you make a statement about what they mean. A conclusion does not repeat facts. Instead, it adds them up and tells how they are connected.

VOCABULARY
conclusion

LEARN THE SKILL

Follow these steps to draw a conclusion.

1. **Identify a topic.**
   First, you must identify a topic. For example, suppose people in your area are concerned about an increase in traffic.

2. **Gather facts.**
   Next, gather facts about the topic. After reading about the traffic problem in your local newspaper, you learn the following:

   - The population in your area has increased over the last five years.

   - The roads are always crowded with traffic.

   - The city council has started construction on a new highway.

3. **Make a conclusion or a statement.**
   After looking at the facts, you make the following statement. *"The city council is building a highway to deal with the growing number of people in the community."* This conclusion connects all three facts. It finds a common idea behind them and says it in one sentence.

TRY THE SKILL

While reading a magazine article on trade, you will learn the following facts:

- A little less than one-half of all goods imported from Mexico enter our state through Laredo.

- The World Trade Bridge was built several years ago over the border into Laredo.

- Before the bridge opened, 3,500 trucks brought goods from Mexico into Laredo each day.

- Today, more than 8,000 trucks bring goods into the city daily.

Draw a conclusion about these facts. Then answer the following questions.

1. What is your conclusion?

2. How did you reach it?

3. Is the statement *"The number of trucks entering Laredo more than doubled"* a conclusion about the topic? Why or why not?

4. How can drawing conclusions help you better understand what you read?

EXTEND THE SKILL

In the last lesson, you read about trade between Texas and Mexico. Read the following passage and draw a conclusion. Use your conclusion to answer the questions below.

Texas ships auto parts to Mexico. Factories in Mexico then use the parts to make automobiles. Often, those cars are sent back to our state.

- What conclusion can you make about the facts above?

- Name some occasions when drawing conclusions can help you study.

| Trucks crossing the World Trade Bridge in Laredo.

Texas and the Global Community

Find! Out!

How is Texas connected to the rest of our world?

VOCABULARY

forecast

READING STRATEGY

Copy the chart you see here. Fill in the main idea and supporting details as you read this lesson.

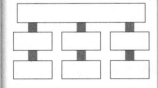

Lesson Outline

• A Global Economy
• Cooperating Countries
• Texans Make Connections

BUILD BACKGROUND

Today we see changes all around us. Some of the changes were predicted decades before they happened. Scientists and researchers spend some of their time trying to **forecast**, or predict, what life will be like in the future. Even though it is early in the twenty-first century, there are already predictions about how things will change in 50 or even 100 years.

Photo of Earth from space (left). Some of Texas's trading partners are in Japan (above).

A GLOBAL ECONOMY

Researchers predict that Texas will have even more contact with countries around the globe in the future.

One reason is that modern transportation and communication systems have improved. Bullet trains are high-speed trains that can travel up to 186 miles per hour. People today communicate more easily with cellular phones, the Internet, and even by video. They also communicate with fiber optics, which use light to transmit electronic signals over long distances. We can send E-mail in a split second. This constant communication has led some businesses to stay open 24 hours a day.

These new technologies make it easier for distant countries to trade with each other. Texas and the United States are interdependent with countries outside of the Western Hemisphere. Forecasters think we are on the way to having a global economy. Trade will take place between all the countries of the world.

Many of Texas's newest trading partners are countries on the **Pacific Rim** of Asia. These countries have ports on the Pacific Ocean. Look at the Atlas map on page R8 to locate these countries.

Texas exports many products to the Pacific Rim countries of **China, Japan**, and **South Korea**. Oil, chemicals, and packaged food are exported to these countries. Texans import automobiles from Japan, clothing from China, and electronics from South Korea.

 **What are some countries located on the Pacific Rim?**

Many people think a global agriculture market will make sure all people in the world have enough food to survive. Crops from all over the world can be sent to the places where they are needed.

COOPERATING COUNTRIES

Texas will most likely continue to be a leader in agriculture. Fruit, wheat, cotton, and beef will be exported to people in countries all over the world.

Texas farmers are sharing information and technology with farmers in less developed countries. Researchers from the Texas A&M International Agriculture program are working in countries such as Rwanda in Africa. They are developing crops that resist disease and insects. They also work to find ways to improve the size of a crop without using up valuable soil and water resources. However, some crops that are resistant to disease may kill insects that are good for the environment. So scientists must be careful about the crops they develop. They need to make sure they don't upset the balance of nature.

Scientists Working Together

American doctors and nurses often work with partners in other countries. They try to control diseases by comparing treatment programs that have been used in other countries. Some volunteer their time to help people who are sick or hungry. Lisabeth List is a nurse from Dallas. She spent a summer in Sudan, Africa, feeding young children. Read how she described one day volunteering with the group Doctors Without Borders.

READING CHECK What are some ways scientists from different countries work together?

Scientists from Texas A&M (top left) help people in Rwanda open a coffee processing center. Many countries work together to build the international space station (left).

Primary Source:

—Excerpt from a journal by Lisabeth List, Summer 1998.

6:15 A.M. The alarm in my watch goes off. I dress and crawl out of the mud hut or *tukui* that I call home and brush my teeth at a tank of filtered water.

6:45 A.M. I ride my mountain bike to the [feeding center] . . . water must be boiled . . . before high-energy milk powder can be mixed for the first feeding of the day. About 130 children and their mothers have started to arrive at the center.

7:00 A.M. We begin weighing and measuring each child. . . . Today we decide that one of the children has improved enough to leave . . . I'm very happy!

5:00 P.M. The fifth and final feeding!

6:00 P.M. I ride my bike back . . . I enjoy the ride. Instead of city traffic, I have a nice bush path . . . with people shaking my hand all the way.

8:00 P.M. Dinner time . . . Sometimes I add a piece of beef jerky from home—I'm from Texas, it's my survival gear!

8:30 P.M. A wonderful shower . . . under the stars. I pull a lever that tips a bucket from overhead.

10:00 P.M. Bedtime!

Why do you think people shook Lisabeth's hand as she rode home from work?

TEXANS MAKE CONNECTIONS

Many American cities and towns have "Sister Cities" in other countries. Southlake, Texas, for example, has a sister city relationship with Toyoma, Japan. For more than a decade people from Southlake have traveled each year to Toyoma to learn about its culture. Toyoma citizens have also come to Texas to visit.

Austin is a sister city to Adelaide, Australia. Through their special relationship, an Adelaide-based company that makes medical equipment sells its products through an office in Austin. The company earns hundreds of thousands of dollars each year, which boosts the Adelaide economy. In turn, the jobs this company produces help Austin's economy.

Business relationships can lead to growth in tourism. As a result of the Austin-Adelaide business exchange, more people from Texas are visiting Australia. And people from Australia are visiting Texas.

How do sister cities help Texans understand different cultures?

Exploring ECONOMICS

Trading with Other Countries

Most countries, including the United States, have a *market economic system*. This means that the government does not make economic decisions. Instead, buyers and sellers decide what products will be bought and sold. Businesses in Texas and throughout the United States make products that they think people in other countries will want to buy. Some of these businesses import or export goods through the Port of Houston. It is a center of international business. About $43 billion worth of goods travel to and from foreign countries each year through the Houston Ship Channel. This helps the economy of our state.

 Activity

Using your school library or the Internet, draw a chart listing three things that are *imported* through the Houston Ship Channel. Include the countries the goods come from. Which countries export the most goods to Texas?

Adelaide, Australia, is the sister city to Austin.

410

PUTTING IT TOGETHER

Scientists and researchers use what they know about our state, country, and world to make predictions about changes in the future. What do you predict Texas will be like 100 years from now?

The future depends on citizens like you. You can prepare for your future by getting an education. This is one way to learn about your community, state, country, and other countries in the world.

Astronauts from the United States and Japan travel to the International Space Station.

Review and Assess

1. Write one sentence for the vocabulary word:

   forecast

2. What countries on the Pacific Rim does Texas trade with?

3. Describe some ways in which Texas is connected to the rest of the world.

   Find Out!

4. Identify some ways Texas and the United States cooperate with other countries.

5. Summarize the main idea of this lesson and list its supporting details.

Suppose you agreed to trade with a country on the Pacific Rim. Using the Atlas map on page R4, draw a map that shows the directions and route you would take to ship your goods. Remember to include a legend, compass rose, and scale of miles.

. . . .

Write a letter to Texans in the future. Describe the changes forecasters think will happen and include any predictions of your own.

Lesson 4

The Western Hemisphere

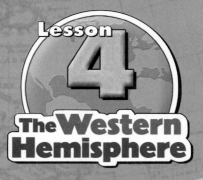

Today and Tomorrow

Find out!

What goals do countries in the Western Hemisphere share?

Lesson Outline

- Developing Economies
- From Farming to Industry

VOCABULARY

commercial farming

industrialization

READING STRATEGY

Copy the chart you see here. Write the main idea of this lesson. Add supporting details as you read.

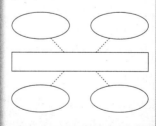

BUILD BACKGROUND

You already know about some ways the countries in the Western Hemisphere are working together. These countries all want to improve the quality of life for their people. By working together, these countries hope to find ways to reach their goals sooner. Cooperation among countries takes time, but its results can have a big effect on our world.

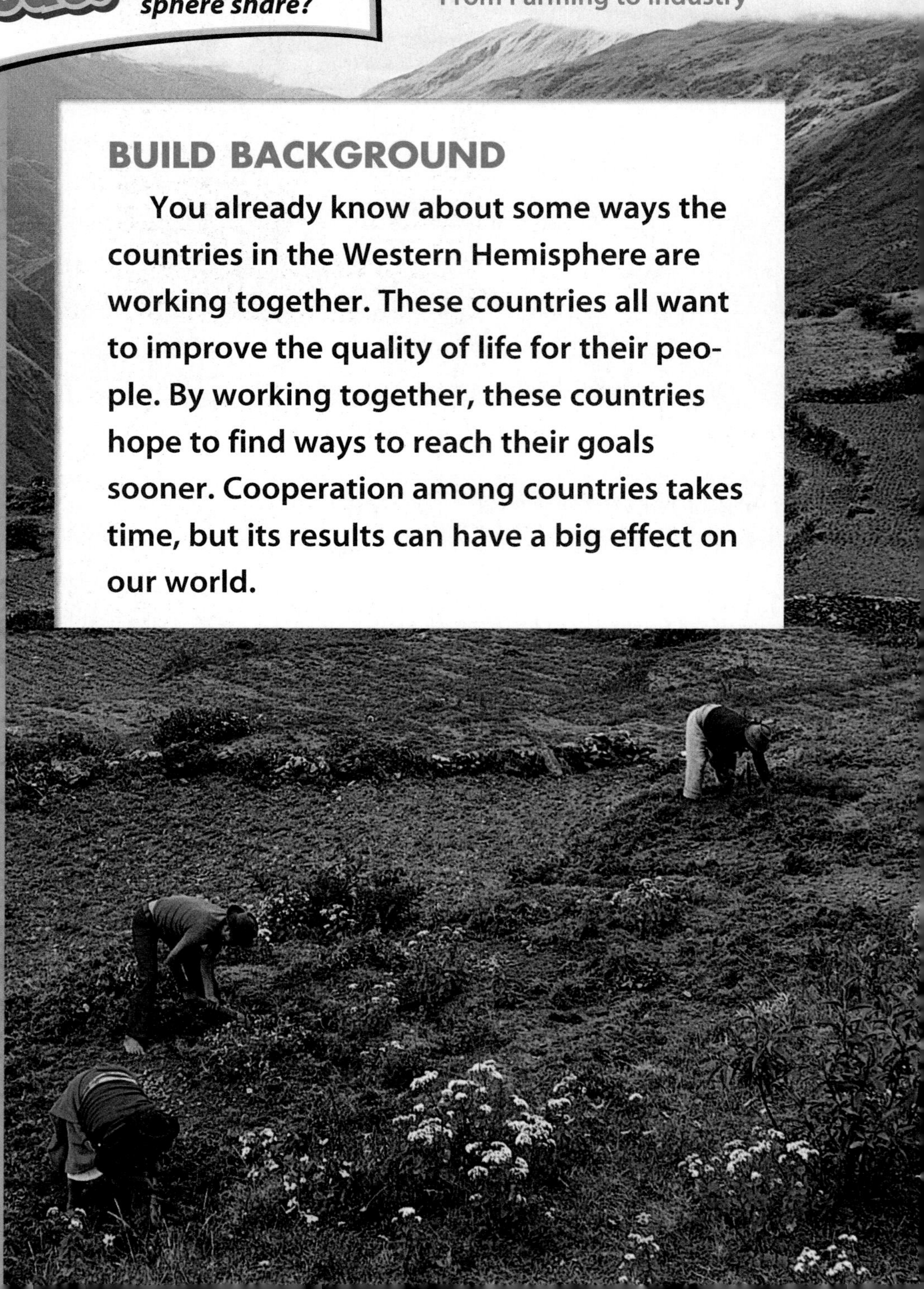

DEVELOPING ECONOMIES

In the United States our economy continues to grow stronger because of our free-enterprise system. However, many countries in the Western Hemisphere still depend on an economy of subsistence farming. As you have read, subsistence farming means people grow only enough food to live, not to sell. These countries have weak economies because people are not encouraged to start businesses to meet their needs and wants.

One way the governments of some Western Hemisphere countries are trying to improve their economies is by commercial farming. Farmers who run commercial farms raise crops and livestock to sell to people in their country and to export to other countries.

Commercial farmers in Brazil supply most of the world's coffee beans. Farmers in Peru export sugar and cotton to other countries in the Western Hemisphere, Europe, and Asia.

Do you enjoy eating grapes or berries in the middle of winter? Well, they may have come from Chile in South America. When it is winter in the United States, it is summer in countries below the equator. Trade agreements with other countries in the Western Hemisphere mean we can have a variety of fruits and vegetables all year round. These agreements also help commercial farming in other countries.

 How are commercial and subsistence farming different?

Subsistence farmers in Peru work on a potato farm (left), commercial farmers in Costa Rica cut bananas (top), women in South America pack grapes for export to the United States (below).

FROM FARMING TO INDUSTRY

Another way countries in the Western Hemisphere are trying to improve their economies is by **industrialization**, or the development of manufacturing industries. Industrialization manufactures goods less costly to make and buy, encourages trade, and improves life for people. The United States became industrialized when factories were built in the 1800s.

Today, the United States works with other countries that are trying to industrialize their economies. Companies in Venezuela and Argentina often hire Americans with manufacturing experience to build and oversee their factories. American companies also trade with these factories for materials and goods. Investors from the United States give money to some new businesses in the Western Hemisphere. If the businesses are successful, the investors will receive a share of the profits. Each new business provides jobs, income, and goods that people want and need.

Use the map on this page to find out what products are made by businesses in the Western Hemisphere.

 What is industrialization?

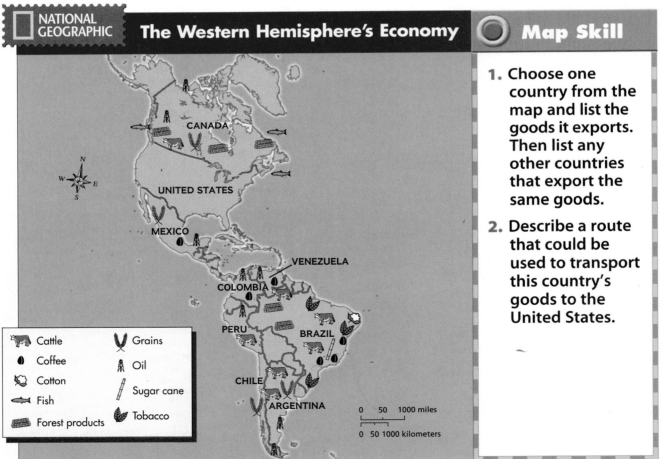

NATIONAL GEOGRAPHIC
The Western Hemisphere's Economy

Map Skill

1. **Choose one country from the map and list the goods it exports. Then list any other countries that export the same goods.**

2. **Describe a route that could be used to transport this country's goods to the United States.**

Legend:
- Cattle
- Coffee
- Cotton
- Fish
- Forest products
- Grains
- Oil
- Sugar cane
- Tobacco

0   50   1000 miles
0   50 1000 kilometers

PUTTING IT TOGETHER

When countries agree to work together, there are many challenges. Even though the countries of the Western Hemisphere are neighbors, they still have many differences, such as forms of government, economic systems, and kinds of money. Some of these countries are finding ways to work together through trading, investing, and sharing knowledge. They try to help people to make good economic decisions. This helps countries work together to meet the needs and wants of their people.

In the Western Hemisphere many different kinds of money are used. From top, currencies from Peru, Chile, and Brazil.

Review and Assess

1. Write one sentence for each of the vocabulary words:

   commercial farming   industrialization

2. What types of industries are growing in South America?

3. Describe a goal for the future that the countries of the Western Hemisphere share.

4. Identify two countries in the Western Hemisphere and their **economic** relationship to the United States.

5. Make a **prediction** about how cooperation will change the future of the Western Hemisphere.

Use the map on page R14 to help you make a table of countries above and below the equator. Find out how the seasons are different for these countries. Write the current season for each group at the top of each column in your table.

. . . .

Choose a country in the Western Hemisphere and research its economy. **Write** a letter to that country's government explaining how they might work with the United States to increase trade.

Chapter 11 REVIEW

VOCABULARY REVIEW

Number a sheet of paper from 1 to 5. Beside each number write the word or term from the list below that matches the description.

census   forecast

import   interdependent

maquiladoras   NAFTA

1. a count of the people who live in a certain place

2. relying on one another to meet needs and wants

3. agreement which has made import and export easier between the United States, Mexico, and Canada

4. something brought in from another country for sale or use

5. to predict what may happen

CHAPTER COMPREHENSION

6. What is the World Wide Web?

7. Describe some benefits that maquiladoras provide to Texas and Mexico.

8. Why do researchers predict that Texas will have more contact with countries around the world in the future?

9. What does NAFTA stand for?

10. Explain the difference between imports and exports.

11. Why are countries interdependent on each other for trade?

12. What are some ways Texas works with countries around the world?

SKILL REVIEW

13. **Study Skill** Find an example of a primary source in Unit 5.

14. **Study Skill** Read the passage below. Is it a primary or secondary source?

15. **Study Skill** Explain the difference between a primary source and a secondary source.

16. **Study Skill** Why is it helpful to understand the difference between primary and secondary sources when writing a report?

17. **Reading/Thinking Skill** What is a conclusion?

18. **Reading/Thinking Skill** Why is it important to draw conclusions about what you read?

The Indians as well as the missionaries rise with the sun, and immediately go to prayers which last for an hour. During this time three large boilers [pots] are set on the fire for cooking a kind of soup, made of barley meal.... This sort of food of which the Indians are extremely fond, is called atole.... After the meal they all go to work.... some to dig in the garden, while others are employed in domestic occupations [jobs in the house], all under the eye of one or two missionaries.

USING A CHART

19. By what amount did exports increase between 1997 and 2000?

20. What is the estimated dollar amount of exports for the year 2003?

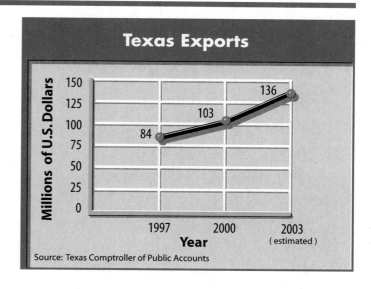

Texas Exports

Source: Texas Comptroller of Public Accounts

Activity

Learning About the Economy Using your school library or the Internet, research other economic systems in different countries. Find out who can own businesses, how the government regulates them, and whether consumers can choose where to buy goods and services. Write a report comparing and contrasting the free-enterprise system with the other systems you learned about.

Foldables

Use your Foldable to review what you have learned about Texas as a state, as part of the Western Hemisphere, and as part of the world. As you look at the three sides of your pyramid Foldable, mentally review what you learned. Look at your notes on the inside of your Foldable to check your memory and responses. Use tape and string to make your Foldable into a mobile. Hang pictures and note cards of information from each of the three sides of your Foldable.

Unit 5 REVIEW

VOCABULARY REVIEW

Number a piece of paper from 1 to 6. Beside each number write the term from the list below that best completes the sentence.

census	decade
forecast	import
Pulitzer Prize	Sun Belt

1. The _____ is the area of our country that is warm most of the year.

2. A guess based on resources about the future is a _____.

3. A _____ is a period of 10 years.

4. Each decade a _____ is performed in the United States to count the population.

5. Goods that come to Texas from other countries are known as _____(s).

6. A special award that top writers receive is the _____.

TECHNOLOGY
You learned about the World Wide Web in this unit. For more resources to help you learn about the people and places you read about, visit www.mhschool.com and follow the links for Grade 4 Texas, Unit 5.

SKILL REVIEW

7. **Geography Skill** Look at the Austin Road Map below. What is the shortest route from Ben White Boulevard to Metric Boulevard?

8. **Reading/Thinking Skill** How can recognizing a frame of reference help you understand editorials?

9. **Study Skill** Suppose you read an article in an encyclopedia about a famous athlete from our state. Would the article be a primary or secondary source?

10. **Reading/Thinking Skill** What steps should you follow when drawing a conclusion?

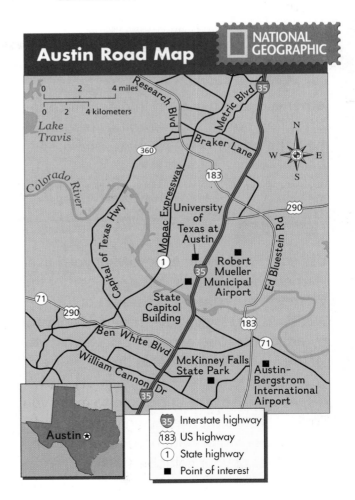
Austin Road Map

from *Magic Windows/Ventanas mágicas,* by Carmen Lomas Garza

This is my grandfather, Antonio Lomas, watering the corn in his garden. There's also squash, garlic, chile, and nopales. He always had vegetables growing, and he would always share what he had grown with his sons and daughters and grandkids.

I used to love helping my grandfather water his garden at the end of the day. It gave me a chance to be really close to him. If he wanted to talk to me, I was right there to listen to him. If I wanted to ask questions, he was there for me.

1 You can tell from the story that—
   A   Antonio Lomas sold most of the vegetables he grew
   B   the author enjoyed spending time with her grandfather
   C   Antonio Lomas lived with his children and grandchildren
   D   the author now has a vegetable garden of her own

2 Which sentence from the story tells the reader that Antonio Lomas was a generous man?
   A   It gave me a chance to be really close to him.
   B   I used to love helping my grandfather water his garden at the end of the day.
   C   If I wanted to ask questions, he was there for me.
   D   He always had vegetables growing, and he would always share what he had grown with his sons and daughters and grandkids.

WRITING ACTIVITIES *TAKS Practice*

Ⓧ **Writing to Persuade** Look at the world map on page R4. Choose a city in another country that you would like to become "Sister Cities" with. Write a letter to the leader of that country persuading him or her to help you establish a program.

Ⓧ **Writing to Inform** Choose one cultural group from Chapter 10. Using the library or the Internet, research the group and write a report to share with your class.

Ⓧ **Writing to Express** You have read about the many ways Texans express themselves in writing, art, and music. How do you best express yourself? Write a short song or poem, or draw or paint a picture showing how you feel about your community or city.

Reference Section

The Reference Section has many parts, each with a different type of information. Use this section to look up people, places, and events as you study.

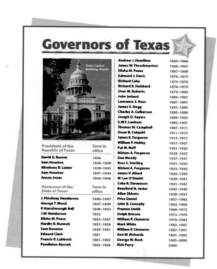

Sam Houston

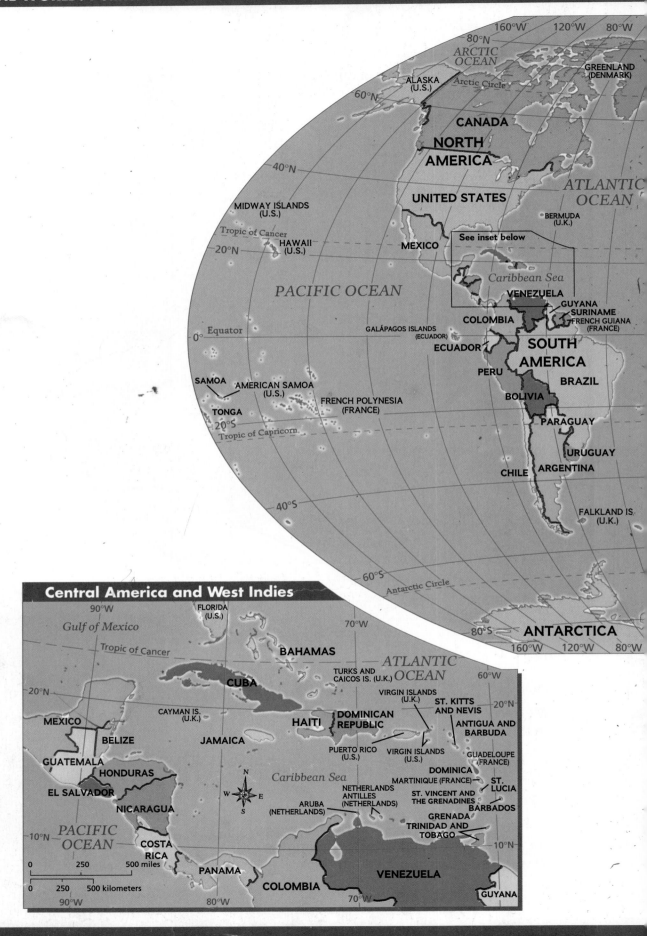

160°W   120°W   80°W

ARCTIC
OCEAN

80°N

GREENLAND
(DENMARK)

ALASKA
(U.S.)   Arctic Circle

60°N

CANADA

NORTH
AMERICA

40°N

UNITED STATES

ATLANTIC
OCEAN

MIDWAY ISLANDS
(U.S.)

BERMUDA
(U.K.)

Tropic of Cancer

See inset below

20°N   HAWAII
(U.S.)

MEXICO

Caribbean Sea

PACIFIC OCEAN

VENEZUELA
GUYANA
SURINAME
FRENCH GUIANA
(FRANCE)

COLOMBIA

GALÁPAGOS ISLANDS
(ECUADOR)

0°   Equator

ECUADOR

SOUTH
AMERICA

PERU

BRAZIL

SAMOA   AMERICAN SAMOA
(U.S.)

BOLIVIA

FRENCH POLYNESIA
(FRANCE)

TONGA

PARAGUAY

20°S

Tropic of Capricorn

URUGUAY

CHILE   ARGENTINA

40°S

FALKLAND IS.
(U.K.)

60°S

Antarctic Circle

80°S   ANTARCTICA

160°W   120°W   80°W

Central America and West Indies

90°W

FLORIDA
(U.S.)

Gulf of Mexico

70°W

BAHAMAS

ATLANTIC
OCEAN

Tropic of Cancer

TURKS AND
CAICOS IS. (U.K.)

60°W

20°N

CUBA

VIRGIN ISLANDS
(U.K.)   ST. KITTS
AND NEVIS

20°N

CAYMAN IS.
(U.K.)

HAITI

DOMINICAN
REPUBLIC

ANTIGUA AND
BARBUDA

MEXICO

JAMAICA

PUERTO RICO
(U.S.)

VIRGIN ISLANDS
(U.S.)

GUADELOUPE
(FRANCE)

BELIZE

GUATEMALA

DOMINICA

HONDURAS

N

Caribbean Sea

MARTINIQUE (FRANCE)   ST.
LUCIA

EL SALVADOR

W   E

NETHERLANDS
ANTILLES
(NETHERLANDS)

ST. VINCENT AND
THE GRENADINES

NICARAGUA

S

ARUBA
(NETHERLANDS)

BARBADOS

GRENADA

10°N   PACIFIC
OCEAN

COSTA
RICA

TRINIDAD AND
TOBAGO

0   250   500 miles

PANAMA

VENEZUELA

10°N

0   250   500 kilometers

COLOMBIA

GUYANA

90°W   80°W   70°W

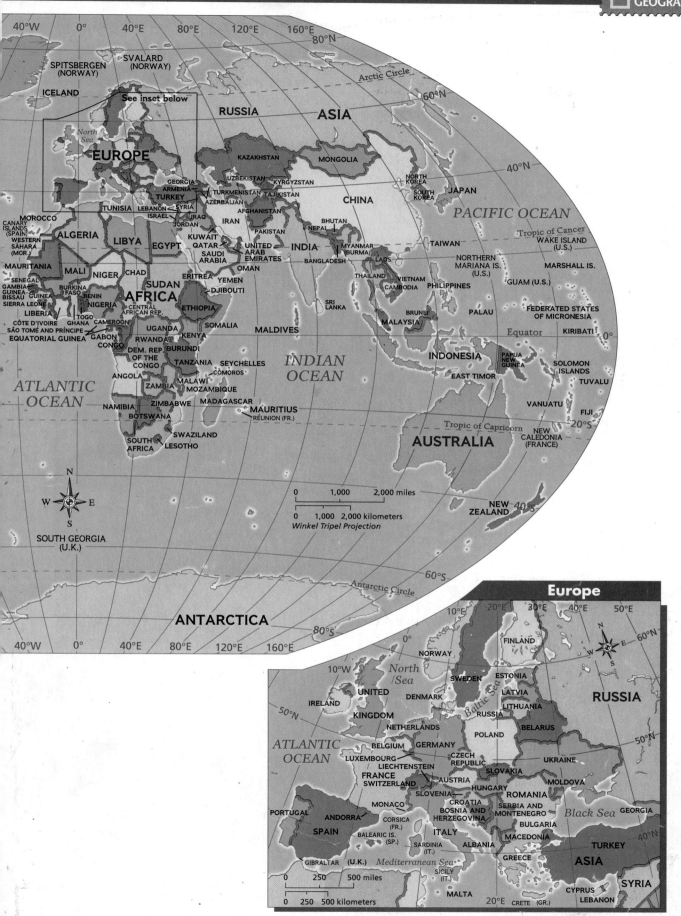

NATIONAL GEOGRAPHIC

40°W 0° 40°E 80°E 120°E 160°E 80°N

SPITSBERGEN
(NORWAY)
SVALARD
(NORWAY)
ICELAND
Arctic Circle
See inset below
60°N
RUSSIA
ASIA
North Sea
EUROPE
KAZAKHSTAN
MONGOLIA
40°N
UZBEKISTAN KYRGYZSTAN
GEORGIA
ARMENIA TURKMENISTAN TAJIKISTAN
TURKEY AZERBAIJAN
NORTH KOREA
JAPAN
TUNISIA LEBANON SYRIA AFGHANISTAN
SOUTH KOREA
PACIFIC OCEAN
MOROCCO ISRAEL
JORDAN IRAQ IRAN PAKISTAN
CHINA
CANARY ISLANDS (SPAIN)
Tropic of Cancer
WAKE ISLAND (U.S.)
WESTERN SAHARA (MOR.)
ALGERIA LIBYA EGYPT KUWAIT
QATAR
SAUDI ARABIA UNITED ARAB EMIRATES
NEPAL BHUTAN
INDIA BANGLADESH
MYANMAR (BURMA)
TAIWAN
NORTHERN MARIANA IS. (U.S.)
MARSHALL IS.
MAURITANIA MALI NIGER CHAD
OMAN LAOS
GUAM (U.S.)
SENEGAL BURKINA FASO
ERITREA YEMEN
THAILAND VIETNAM
PHILIPPINES
GAMBIA GUINEA BENIN
SUDAN DJIBOUTI
CAMBODIA
FEDERATED STATES OF MICRONESIA
GUINEA BISSAU NIGERIA
AFRICA
CENTRAL AFRICAN REP. ETHIOPIA
SRI LANKA
BRUNEI
PALAU
SIERRA LEONE LIBERIA
CÔTE D'IVOIRE GHANA TOGO CAMEROON
UGANDA SOMALIA
KENYA MALDIVES
MALAYSIA
Equator KIRIBATI 0°
SÃO TOMÉ AND PRÍNCIPE
EQUATORIAL GUINEA GABON CONGO
RWANDA
BURUNDI
DEM. REP OF THE CONGO
INDONESIA
PAPUA NEW GUINEA
SOLOMON ISLANDS
TANZANIA SEYCHELLES
INDIAN OCEAN
EAST TIMOR
TUVALU
ANGOLA COMOROS
ZAMBIA MALAWI MOZAMBIQUE
VANUATU
ATLANTIC OCEAN
NAMIBIA ZIMBABWE MADAGASCAR
MAURITIUS
Tropic of Capricorn
NEW CALEDONIA (FRANCE)
FIJI 20°S
BOTSWANA RÉUNION (FR.)
SWAZILAND
SOUTH AFRICA LESOTHO
AUSTRALIA

N
W E
S

0 1,000 2,000 miles
0 1,000 2,000 kilometers
Winkel Tripel Projection

NEW ZEALAND 40°S

SOUTH GEORGIA (U.K.)

60°S
Antarctic Circle

ANTARCTICA 80°S

40°W 0° 40°E 80°E 120°E 160°E

Europe

10°E 20°E 30°E 40°E 50°E
60°N
FINLAND
NORWAY
10°W North Sea
SWEDEN ESTONIA
IRELAND UNITED KINGDOM
DENMARK
Baltic Sea LATVIA
RUSSIA
50°N
LITHUANIA
NETHERLANDS
RUSSIA BELARUS
ATLANTIC OCEAN
BELGIUM GERMANY POLAND
LUXEMBOURG
LIECHTENSTEIN CZECH REPUBLIC
UKRAINE
FRANCE SWITZERLAND AUSTRIA SLOVAKIA
50°N
SLOVENIA HUNGARY MOLDOVA
MONACO CROATIA ROMANIA
PORTUGAL ANDORRA
BOSNIA AND HERZEGOVINA
SERBIA AND MONTENEGRO
Black Sea GEORGIA
SPAIN CORSICA (FR.)
BULGARIA
BALEARIC IS. (SP.)
SARDINIA (IT.) ITALY
MACEDONIA
ALBANIA 40°N
GIBRALTAR (U.K.) Mediterranean Sea
GREECE TURKEY
SICILY (IT.)
ASIA
0 250 500 miles
MALTA
CYPRUS SYRIA
0 250 500 kilometers
20°E CRETE (GR.) LEBANON

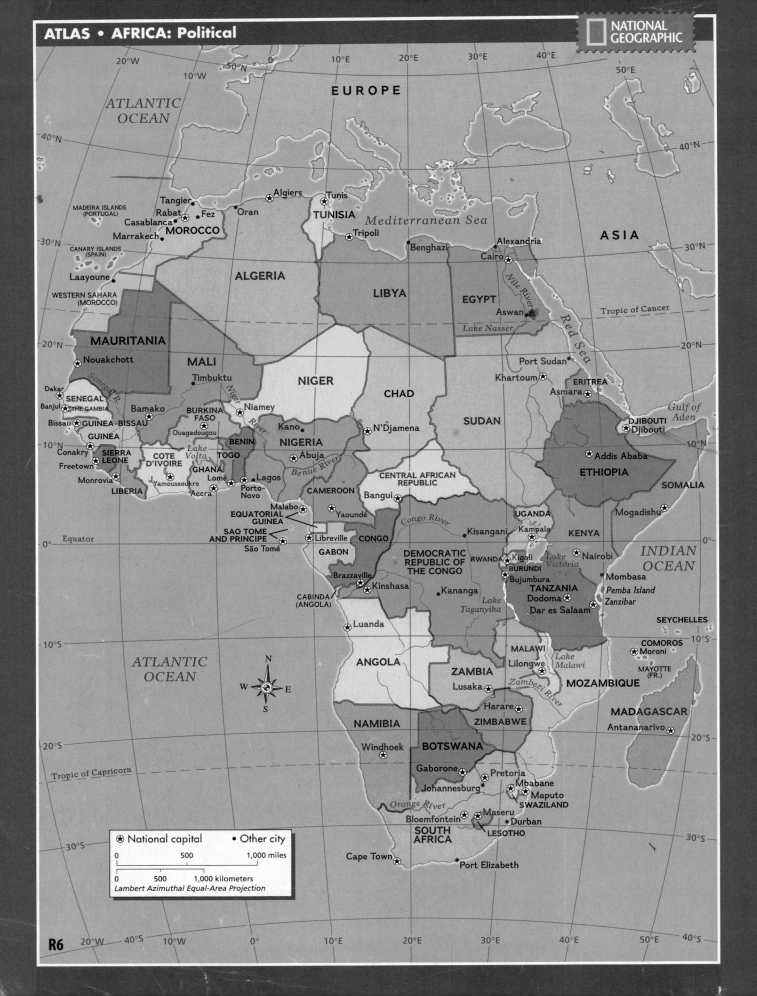

EUROPE

ASIA

ATLANTIC OCEAN

MADEIRA ISLANDS (PORTUGAL)

Tangier
Rabat • Fez
Casablanca
Marrakech
MOROCCO

Algiers
Oran

Tunis
TUNISIA

Tripoli

Benghazi

Mediterranean Sea

Alexandria
Cairo

CANARY ISLANDS (SPAIN)

Laayoune

WESTERN SAHARA (MOROCCO)

ALGERIA

LIBYA

EGYPT

Aswan
Lake Nasser

Nile River

Red Sea

Tropic of Cancer

MAURITANIA

Nouakchott

MALI

Timbuktu

NIGER

CHAD

Port Sudan

Khartoum

ERITREA
Asmara

Gulf of Aden

Dakar
SENEGAL
Banjul
THE GAMBIA
Bissau
GUINEA-BISSAU
GUINEA
Conakry
SIERRA LEONE
Freetown
Monrovia
LIBERIA

Senegal R.

Bamako
BURKINA FASO
Ouagadougou

COTE D'IVOIRE
Yamoussoukro
Accra
GHANA

Niamey
Niger River

Kano

BENIN
TOGO
Lomé
Lake Volta

Abuja
NIGERIA

Porto-Novo
Lagos

SUDAN

N'Djamena

Benue River

CENTRAL AFRICAN REPUBLIC

Bangui

CAMEROON
Yaoundé

DJIBOUTI
Djibouti

Addis Ababa

ETHIOPIA

SOMALIA

Mogadishu

Malabo
EQUATORIAL GUINEA
SAO TOME AND PRINCIPE
São Tomé

Libreville
GABON

CONGO

Congo River

Kisangani

UGANDA
Kampala

KENYA

INDIAN OCEAN

Equator

DEMOCRATIC REPUBLIC OF THE CONGO

RWANDA Kigali
BURUNDI
Bujumbura

Lake Victoria

Nairobi

Brazzaville
Kinshasa
CABINDA (ANGOLA)

Kananga

Lake Tanganyika

TANZANIA
Dodoma
Dar es Salaam

Mombasa
Pemba Island
Zanzibar

SEYCHELLES

Luanda

ATLANTIC OCEAN

N
W   E
S

ANGOLA

ZAMBIA
Lusaka

MALAWI
Lilongwe
Lake Malawi

Zambezi River

COMOROS
Moroni

MAYOTTE (FR.)

MOZAMBIQUE

MADAGASCAR
Antananarivo

Harare

Tropic of Capricorn

NAMIBIA

Windhoek

BOTSWANA

Gaborone

ZIMBABWE

Pretoria
Johannesburg
Mbabane
Maputo
SWAZILAND

Orange River

Bloemfontein
SOUTH AFRICA

Maseru
LESOTHO

Durban

⊛ National capital   • Other city

0   500   1,000 miles

0   500   1,000 kilometers
Lambert Azimuthal Equal-Area Projection

Cape Town

Port Elizabeth

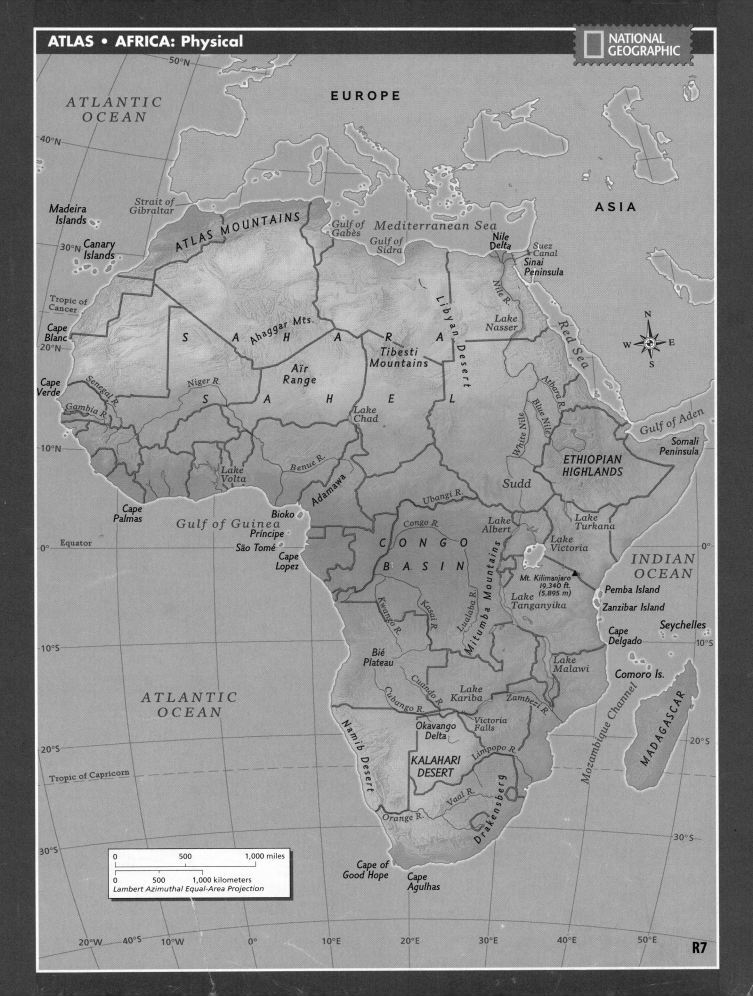

NATIONAL GEOGRAPHIC

EUROPE

ATLANTIC OCEAN

ASIA

Madeira Islands

Canary Islands

Strait of Gibraltar

Mediterranean Sea

Gulf of Gabès

Gulf of Sidra

Nile Delta

Suez Canal

Sinai Peninsula

Tropic of Cancer

Cape Blanc

ATLAS MOUNTAINS

S A H A R A

Ahaggar Mts.

Aïr Range

Tibesti Mountains

Libyan Desert

Nile R.

Lake Nasser

Red Sea

Cape Verde

Senegal R.

Niger R.

S A H E L

Lake Chad

Gulf of Aden

Somali Peninsula

Gambia R.

Benue R.

Lake Volta

Adamawa

Athara R.

White Nile

Blue Nile

ETHIOPIAN HIGHLANDS

Cape Palmas

Gulf of Guinea

Bioko

Príncipe

São Tomé

Cape Lopez

Ubangi R.

Congo R.

Sudd

Lake Turkana

Equator

C O N G O   B A S I N

Lake Albert

Lake Victoria

INDIAN OCEAN

Kwango R.

Kasai R.

Lualaba R.

Mitumba Mountains

Mt. Kilimanjaro 19,340 ft. (5,895 m)

Lake Tanganyika

Pemba Island

Zanzibar Island

Seychelles

Bié Plateau

Cape Delgado

Cuando R.

Lake Kariba

Lake Malawi

Comoro Is.

ATLANTIC OCEAN

Cubango R.

Zambezi R.

Okavango Delta

Victoria Falls

Limpopo R.

KALAHARI DESERT

Namib Desert

MADAGASCAR

Mozambique Channel

Tropic of Capricorn

Vaal R.

Drakensberg

Orange R.

0   500   1,000 miles

0   500   1,000 kilometers

Lambert Azimuthal Equal-Area Projection

Cape of Good Hope

Cape Agulhas

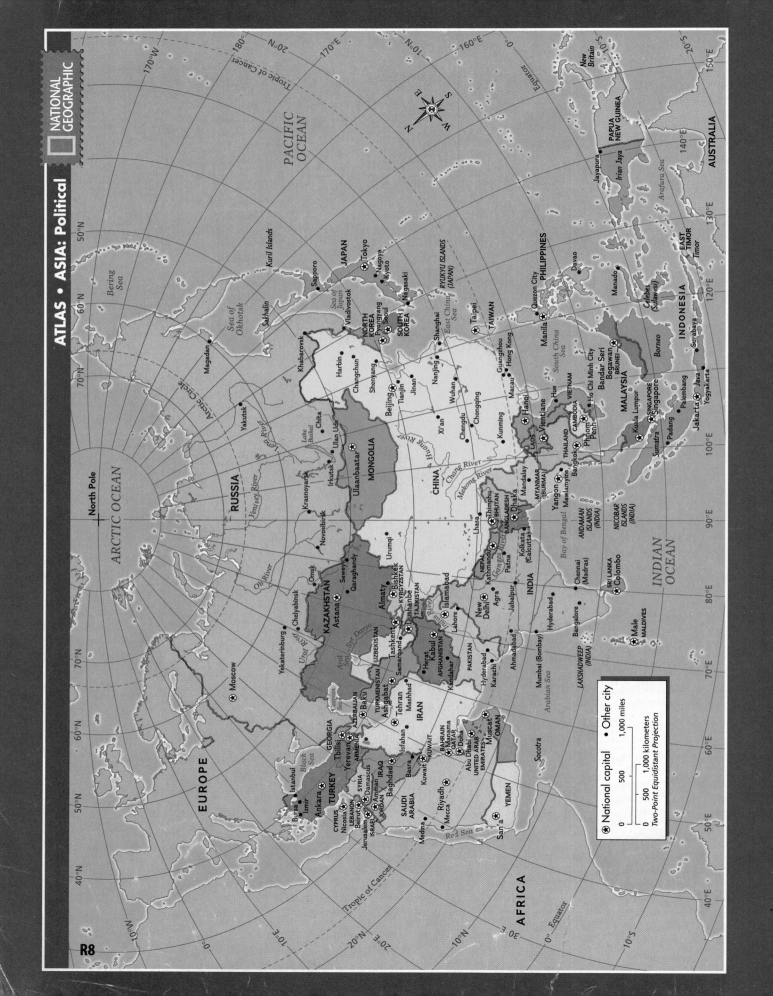

ATLAS • ASIA: Political

PACIFIC OCEAN

Tropic of Cancer

Arctic Circle

North Pole

ARCTIC OCEAN

EUROPE

RUSSIA

Moscow

Yekaterinburg

Chelyabinsk

Omsk

Novosibirsk

Krasnoyarsk

Yakutsk

Irkutsk

Ulan Ude

Chita

Khabarovsk

Magadan

Bering Sea

Sea of Okhotsk

Sakhalin

Kuril Islands

Vladivostok

Sapporo

JAPAN

Tokyo

Nagoya

Kyoto

Nagasaki

Sea of Japan

NORTH KOREA
Pyongyang

SOUTH KOREA
Seoul

Changchun

Shenyang

Harbin

Beijing

Tianjin

Jinan

Nanjing

Shanghai

Wuhan

Xi'an

Chengdu

Chongqing

Kunming

CHINA

RYUKYU ISLANDS (JAPAN)

Taipei

TAIWAN

East China Sea

Guangzhou

Hong Kong

Macau

South China Sea

Hanoi

Hue

VIETNAM

Ho Chi Minh City

Quezon City

Manila

PHILIPPINES

Davao

Manado

Celebes (Sulawesi)

INDONESIA

Borneo

Bandar Seri Begawan

BRUNEI

MALAYSIA

Kuala Lumpur

SINGAPORE
Singapore

Sumatra

Palembang

Padang

Java

Jakarta

Surabaya

Yogyakarta

EAST TIMOR

Timor

Arafura Sea

PAPUA NEW GUINEA

Irian Jaya

Jayapura

New Britain

AUSTRALIA

Equator

MONGOLIA

Ulaanbaatar

Lake Baikal

Lena River

Yenisey River

Ob River

Urumqi

KAZAKHSTAN

Astana

Qaraghandy

Semey

Bishkek

KYRGYZSTAN

Almaty

Tashkent

UZBEKISTAN

Samarqand

Dushanbe

TAJIKISTAN

Aral Sea

Syr Darya

Ashgabat

TURKMENISTAN

Herat

Kabul

AFGHANISTAN

Kandahar

PAKISTAN

Islamabad

Lahore

New Delhi

Agra

Jabalpur

INDIA

Karachi

Hyderabad

Ahmadabad

Mumbai (Bombay)

Arabian Sea

Bangalore

Hyderabad

Chennai (Madras)

Bangalore

LAKSHADWEEP (INDIA)

Male

MALDIVES

SRI LANKA
Colombo

INDIAN OCEAN

NEPAL
Kathmandu

BHUTAN
Thimphu

BANGLADESH
Dhaka

Patna

Kolkata (Calcutta)

Ganges River

Lhasa

Bay of Bengal

ANDAMAN ISLANDS (INDIA)

NICOBAR ISLANDS (INDIA)

MYANMAR (BURMA)

Mandalay

Yangon

Mawlamyine

THAILAND

Bangkok

LAOS

Vientiane

CAMBODIA

Phnom Penh

Chang River

Mekong River

Huang River

Moscow

Caspian Sea

IRAN

Tehran

Mashhad

Isfahan

Baku

AZERBAIJAN

ARMENIA

GEORGIA

Tbilisi

Yerevan

TURKEY

Ankara

Istanbul

Bursa

Izmir

CYPRUS

Nicosia

LEBANON

Beirut

SYRIA

Damascus

ISRAEL

Jerusalem

JORDAN

Amman

IRAQ

Baghdad

Basra

KUWAIT

Kuwait

BAHRAIN
Manama

QATAR
Doha

UNITED ARAB EMIRATES

Abu Dhabi

OMAN

Muscat

SAUDI ARABIA

Riyadh

Mecca

Medina

YEMEN

San'a

Socotra

Red Sea

Black Sea

AFRICA

Tropic of Cancer

Equator

Ural River

Volga

- National capital
• Other city

1,000 miles

0   500   1,000 kilometers

0   500

Two-Point Equidistant Projection

ATLAS • ASIA: Physical

NATIONAL GEOGRAPHIC

1,000 miles
500
0
1,000 kilometers
500
0
Two-Point Equidistant Projection

PACIFIC OCEAN
ARCTIC OCEAN
ATLANTIC OCEAN
INDIAN OCEAN

EUROPE
AFRICA
AUSTRALIA

SIBERIA
CENTRAL SIBERIAN PLATEAU
WEST SIBERIAN PLAIN
URAL MOUNTAINS
KIRGHIZ STEPPE
Kazakh Uplands
GOBI
Mongolian Plateau
ALTAY MOUNTAINS
TIAN SHAN
TAKLIMAKAN DESERT
Tarim Basin
Turpan Depression -505 ft. (-154 m)
ALTUN SHAN
KUNLUN MOUNTAINS
Plateau of Tibet
HIMALAYA
Mt. Everest 29,028 ft. (8,848 m)
HINDU KUSH
QIN LING
North China Plain
Manchurian Plain
GREATER KHINGAN RANGE
YABLONOVYY STANOVOY RANGE
SIKHOTE ALIN RANGE
VERKHOYANSK RANGE
CHERSKIY RANGE
KOLYMA RANGE
CHUKCHI RANGE
KAMCHATKA PENINSULA

DECCAN PLATEAU
WESTERN GHATS
EASTERN GHATS
Indian Subcontinent
Great Indian Desert
PLATEAU OF IRAN
ZAGROS MOUNTAINS
Mesopotamia
ANATOLIA (ASIA MINOR)
Syrian Desert
Nafud
ARABIAN PENINSULA
Rub al Khali

Bering Sea
Sea of Okhotsk
Sea of Japan
East China Sea
Yellow Sea
South China Sea
Gulf of Tonkin
Gulf of Thailand
Philippine Sea
Celebes Sea
Java Sea
Andaman Sea
Bay of Bengal
Arabian Sea
Gulf of Oman
Persian Gulf
Gulf of Aden
Red Sea
Mediterranean Sea
Black Sea
Sea of Azov
Caspian Sea
Aral Sea
Lake Balkhash
Lake Baikal
East Siberian Sea
Laptev Sea
Kara Sea
Strait of Malacca

Wrangel Island
New Siberian Islands
Sakhalin
Kuril Islands
Hokkaido
Honshu
Shikoku
Kyushu
Taiwan
Hainan
Philippine Islands
Borneo
Celebes (Sulawesi)
Sumatra
Java
New Guinea
Sri Lanka
Nicobar Islands
Andaman Islands
Maldive Islands
Lakshadweep
Socotra

Yamal Peninsula
Taymyr Peninsula
INDOCHINA PENINSULA

Ob R., Irtysh R., Yenisey R., Lena R., Angara R., Amur R., Huang R., Chang R., Xi R., Mekong R., Irrawaddy R., Brahmaputra R., Ganges R., Indus R., Syr Darya, Amu Darya, Ural R., Tigris R., Euphrates R.

Ustyurt Plateau

North Pole
Equator
Tropic of Cancer

R9

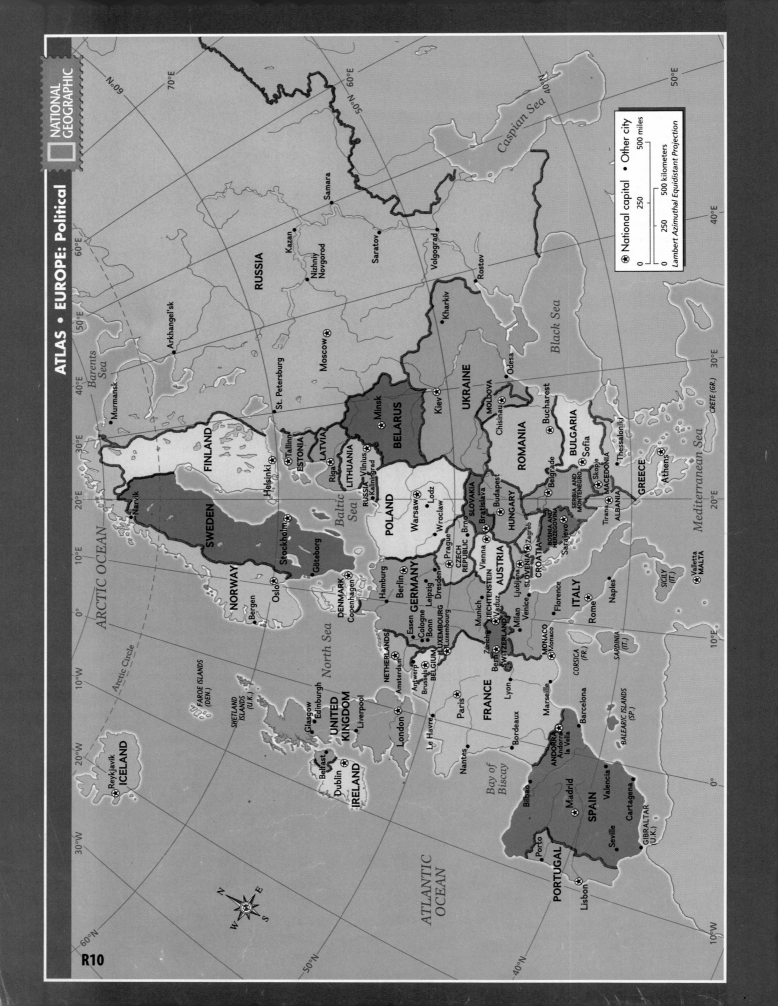

NATIONAL GEOGRAPHIC

National capital • Other city

0   250   500 miles
0   250   500 kilometers
Lambert Azimuthal Equidistant Projection

ARCTIC OCEAN

Barents Sea

RUSSIA

Murmansk

Arkhangel'sk

Caspian Sea

Samara

Kazan

Nizhniy Novgorod

Saratov

Volgograd

Rostov

St. Petersburg

Moscow

Kharkiv

Odesa

Black Sea

FINLAND

Helsinki

Narvik

SWEDEN

Stockholm

Göteborg

NORWAY

Bergen

Oslo

Baltic Sea

ESTONIA

Tallinn

LATVIA

Riga

LITHUANIA

Vilnius

RUSSIA

Kaliningrad

BELARUS

Minsk

UKRAINE

Kiev

MOLDOVA

Chisinau

ROMANIA

Bucharest

BULGARIA

Sofia

Belgrade

SERBIA AND MONTENEGRO

MACEDONIA

Skopje

Thessaloniki

GREECE

Athens

CRETE (GR.)

Mediterranean Sea

DENMARK

Copenhagen

Hamburg

Berlin

GERMANY

Essen

Cologne

Bonn

Leipzig

Dresden

Wroclaw

POLAND

Warsaw

Lodz

Prague

CZECH REPUBLIC

Brno

SLOVAKIA

Bratislava

Budapest

HUNGARY

Vienna

AUSTRIA

Ljubljana

SLOVENIA

Zagreb

CROATIA

BOSNIA AND HERZEGOVINA

Sarajevo

Tirana

ALBANIA

NETHERLANDS

Amsterdam

Antwerp

Brussels

BELGIUM

LUXEMBOURG

Luxembourg

Munich

LIECHTENSTEIN

Vaduz

SWITZERLAND

Bern

Zurich

Milan

Venice

Florence

ITALY

Rome

Naples

MONACO

Monaco

CORSICA (FR.)

SARDINIA (IT.)

SICILY (IT.)

Valletta

MALTA

North Sea

SHETLAND ISLANDS (U.K.)

FAROE ISLANDS (DEN.)

ICELAND

Reykjavik

Belfast

Dublin

IRELAND

Glasgow

Edinburgh

Liverpool

UNITED KINGDOM

London

Le Havre

Paris

FRANCE

Nantes

Bordeaux

Lyon

Marseille

Bay of Biscay

ATLANTIC OCEAN

ANDORRA

Andorra la Vella

Barcelona

BALEARIC ISLANDS (SP.)

Bilbao

Madrid

Valencia

SPAIN

Seville

Cartagena

GIBRALTAR (U.K.)

PORTUGAL

Lisbon

Porto

Arctic Circle

N

E

S

W

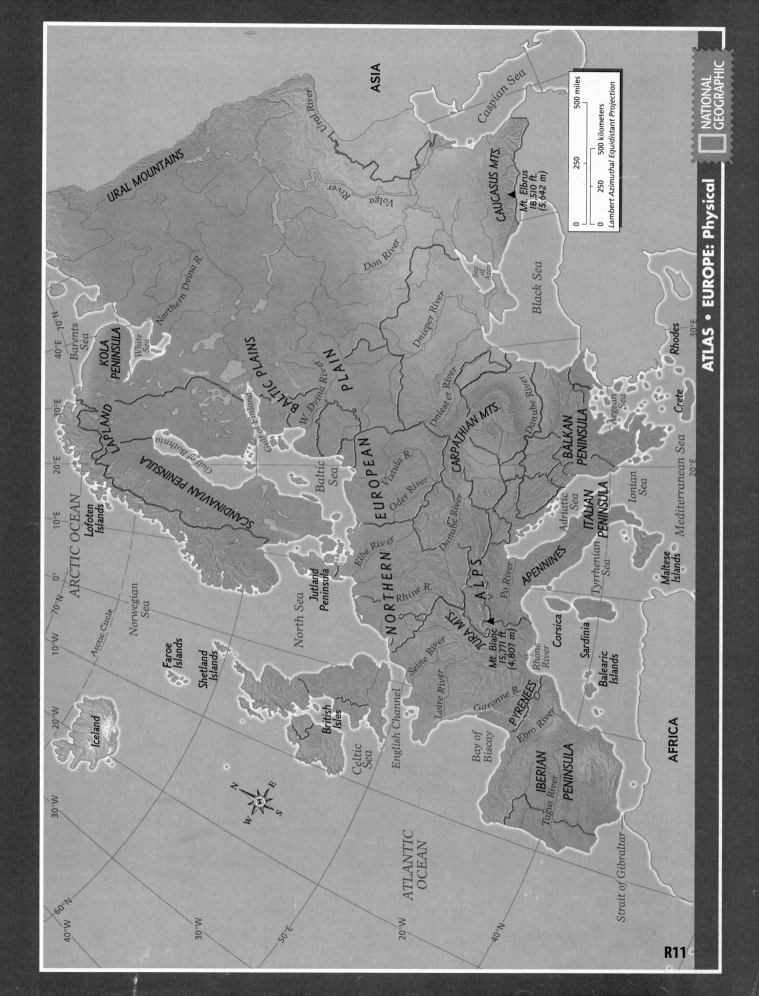

ASIA

URAL MOUNTAINS

Ural River

Volga River

Caspian Sea

CAUCASUS MTS.

Mt. Elbrus
18,510 ft.
(5,642 m)

Sea of Azov

Black Sea

Don River

Northern Dvina R.

Barents Sea

White Sea

KOLA PENINSULA

LAPLAND

Dnieper River

Gulf of Bothnia

BALTIC PLAINS

W. Dvina River

NORTHERN EUROPEAN PLAIN

Dniester River

CARPATHIAN MTS.

Danube River

BALKAN PENINSULA

Aegean Sea

Rhodes

Crete

SCANDINAVIAN PENINSULA

Gulf of Finland

Baltic Sea

Vistula R.

Oder River

Danube River

Adriatic Sea

ITALIAN PENINSULA

Ionian Sea

Mediterranean Sea

ARCTIC OCEAN

Lofoten Islands

Elbe River

Rhine R.

ALPS

Po River

APENNINES

Tyrrhenian Sea

Maltese Islands

Jutland Peninsula

Norwegian Sea

North Sea

JURA MTS.

Mt. Blanc
15,771 ft.
(4,807 m)

Seine River

Corsica

Sardinia

Balearic Islands

Faroe Islands

Shetland Islands

Loire River

Rhone River

PYRENEES

Ebro River

Iceland

British Isles

Celtic Sea

English Channel

Bay of Biscay

Garonne R.

IBERIAN PENINSULA

Tagus River

AFRICA

ATLANTIC OCEAN

Strait of Gibraltar

Arctic Circle

N E S W

500 miles
500 kilometers
Lambert Azimuthal Equidistant Projection
0   250   500
0   250   500

70°N

60°N

50°N

40°N

40°W

30°W

20°W

10°W

0°

10°E

20°E

30°E

40°E

70°N

50°N

40°N

20°E

30°E

R11

ATLAS • OCEANIA: Political

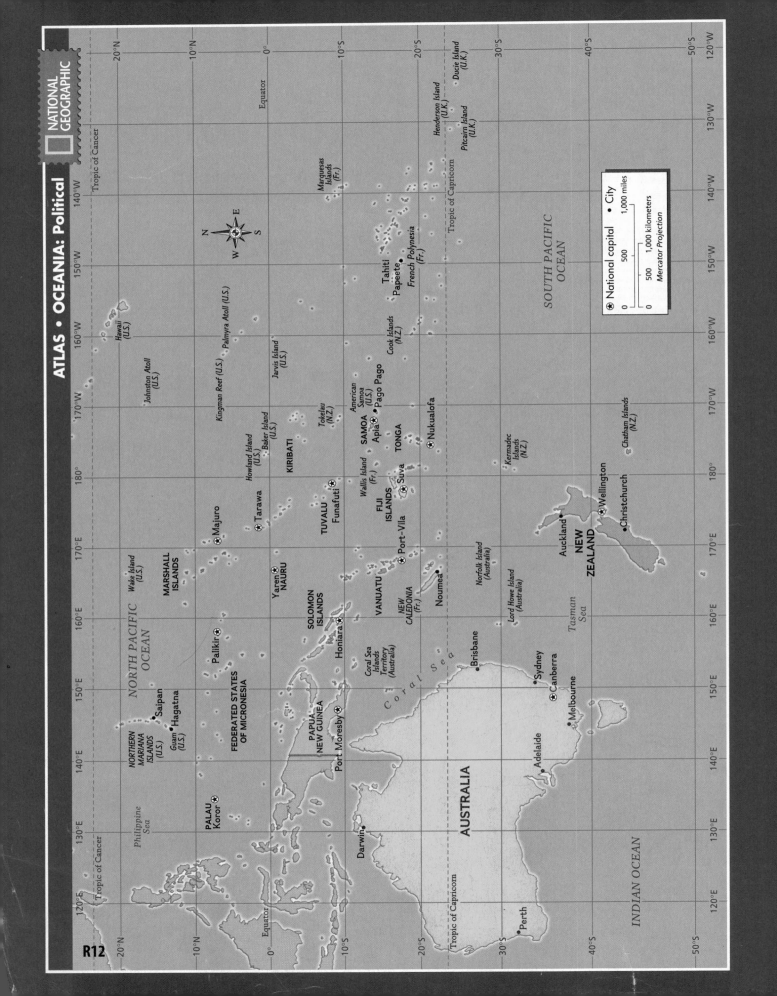

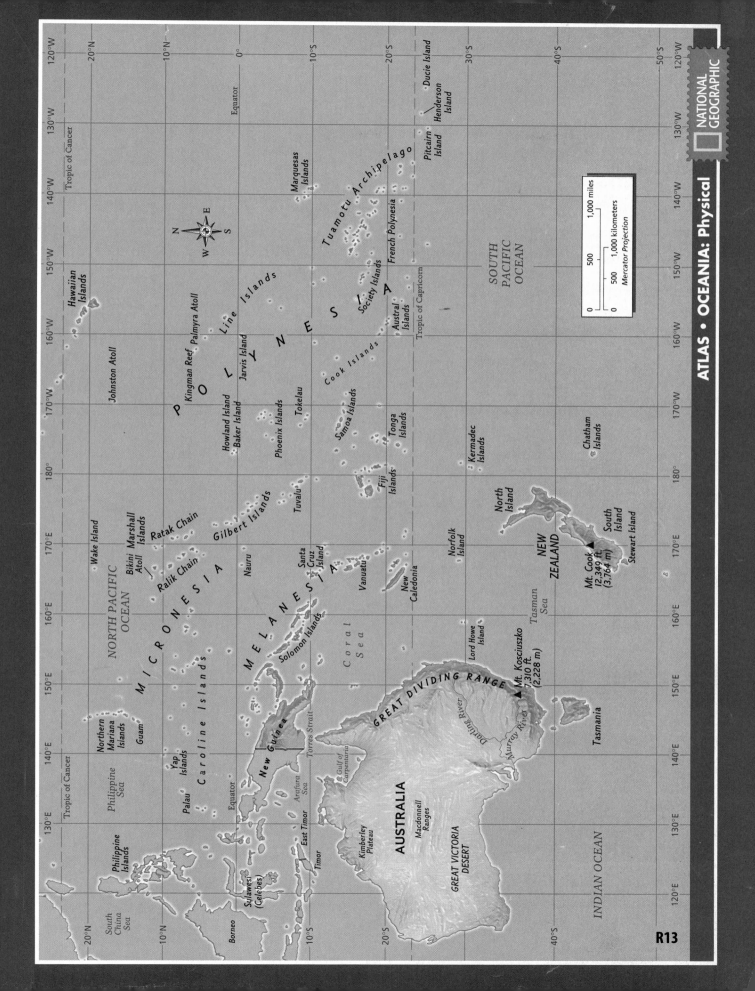

NATIONAL GEOGRAPHIC

1,000 miles
500
0
1,000 kilometers
500
0
Mercator Projection

Equator

Tropic of Cancer

Tropic of Capricorn

Tropic of Cancer

Equator

NORTH PACIFIC OCEAN

SOUTH PACIFIC OCEAN

INDIAN OCEAN

Philippine Sea

South China Sea

Coral Sea

Tasman Sea

Arafura Sea

Gulf of Carpentaria

MICRONESIA

MELANESIA

POLYNESIA

Hawaiian Islands

Johnston Atoll

Wake Island

Marshall Islands

Bikini Atoll

Ratak Chain

Ralik Chain

Caroline Islands

Northern Mariana Islands

Guam

Yap Islands

Palau

Philippine Islands

Borneo

Sulawesi (Celebes)

Timor

East Timor

New Guinea

Torres Strait

Nauru

Gilbert Islands

Tuvalu

Kingman Reef Palmyra Atoll

Line Islands

Howland Island

Baker Island

Jarvis Island

Phoenix Islands

Tokelau

Samoa Islands

Cook Islands

Society Islands

French Polynesia

Austral Islands

Tuamotu Archipelago

Marquesas Islands

Pitcairn Island

Henderson Island

Ducie Island

Fiji Islands

Tonga Islands

Santa Cruz Island

Vanuatu

New Caledonia

Solomon Islands

Kermadec Islands

Norfolk Island

Lord Howe Island

Chatham Islands

NEW ZEALAND

North Island

South Island

Stewart Island

Mt. Cook
12,349 ft.
(3,764 m)

AUSTRALIA

Kimberley Plateau

Macdonnell Ranges

GREAT VICTORIA DESERT

GREAT DIVIDING RANGE

Darling River

Murray River

Mt. Kosciuszko
7,310 ft.
(2,228 m)

Tasmania

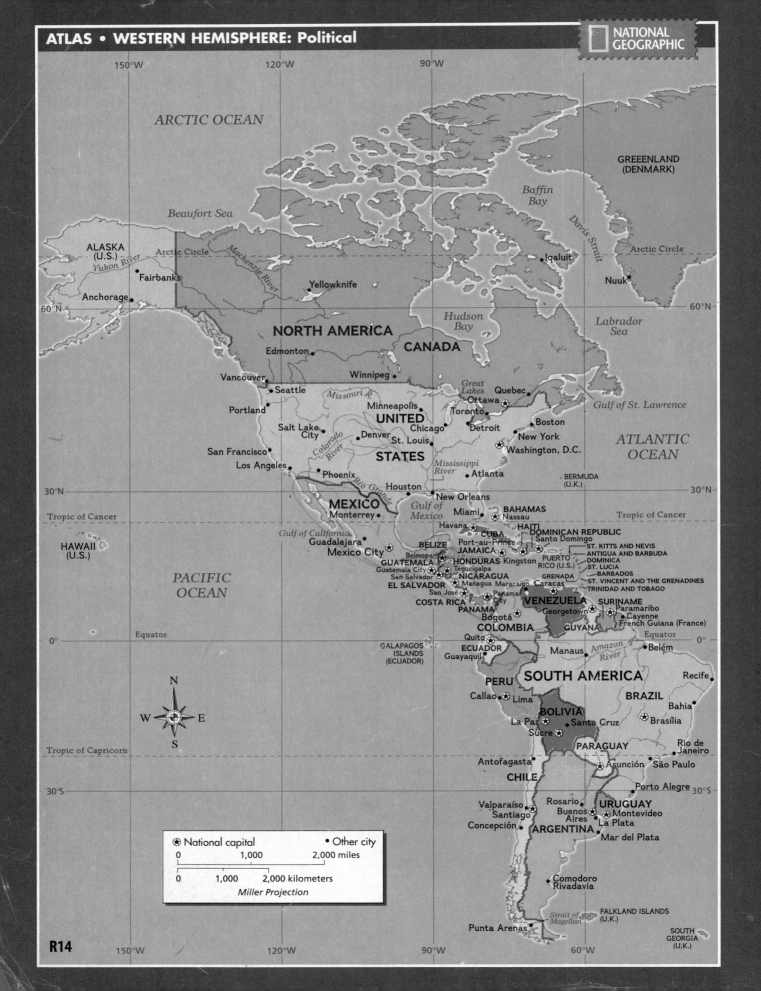

NATIONAL GEOGRAPHIC

ARCTIC OCEAN

GREEENLAND (DENMARK)

Baffin Bay

Beaufort Sea

ALASKA (U.S.)

Arctic Circle

Iqaluit

Nuuk

Arctic Circle

Yukon River

Fairbanks

Anchorage

60°N

Mackenzie River

Yellowknife

Hudson Bay

Labrador Sea

60°N

Davis Strait

NORTH AMERICA

CANADA

Edmonton

Winnipeg

Vancouver

Seattle

Missouri R.

Great Lakes

Quebec

Ottawa

Toronto

Gulf of St. Lawrence

Portland

Minneapolis

Detroit

Boston

New York

Salt Lake City

Colorado River

Denver

St. Louis

Chicago

Washington, D.C.

ATLANTIC OCEAN

San Francisco

UNITED STATES

Los Angeles

Phoenix

Rio Grande

Houston

Mississippi River

Atlanta

BERMUDA (U.K.)

30°N

30°N

New Orleans

Tropic of Cancer

MEXICO

Monterrey

Gulf of Mexico

Miami

BAHAMAS

Nassau

Tropic of Cancer

HAWAII (U.S.)

Gulf of California

Havana

CUBA

HAITI

DOMINICAN REPUBLIC

Santo Domingo

ST. KITTS AND NEVIS

Guadalajara

Mexico City

BELIZE

Belmopan

JAMAICA

Port-au-Prince

Kingston

PUERTO RICO (U.S.)

ANTIGUA AND BARBUDA

DOMINICA

ST. LUCIA

PACIFIC OCEAN

GUATEMALA

Guatemala City

San Salvador

HONDURAS

Tegucigalpa

NICARAGUA

Managua

GRENADA

Maracaibo

Caracas

BARBADOS

ST. VINCENT AND THE GRENADINES

TRINIDAD AND TOBAGO

EL SALVADOR

San José

Panama City

VENEZUELA

SURINAME

Paramaribo

Cayenne

COSTA RICA

PANAMA

Bogotá

Georgetown

French Guiana (France)

COLOMBIA

GUYANA

Equator

Quito

Equator

0°

GALAPAGOS ISLANDS (ECUADOR)

ECUADOR

Guayaquil

Manaus

Amazon River

Belém

0°

SOUTH AMERICA

Recife

N

PERU

BRAZIL

W   E

Callao

Lima

Bahia

S

BOLIVIA

La Paz

Santa Cruz

Brasília

Sucre

Tropic of Capricorn

PARAGUAY

Rio de Janeiro

Antofagasta

Asunción

São Paulo

CHILE

Porto Alegre

30°S

30°S

Valparaíso

Santiago

Rosario

Buenos Aires

URUGUAY

Montevideo

La Plata

Concepción

ARGENTINA

Mar del Plata

⊛ National capital   • Other city

0   1,000   2,000 miles

Comodoro Rivadavia

0   1,000   2,000 kilometers

Miller Projection

FALKLAND ISLANDS (U.K.)

Punta Arenas

Strait of Magellan

SOUTH GEORGIA (U.K.)

150°W   120°W   90°W   60°W

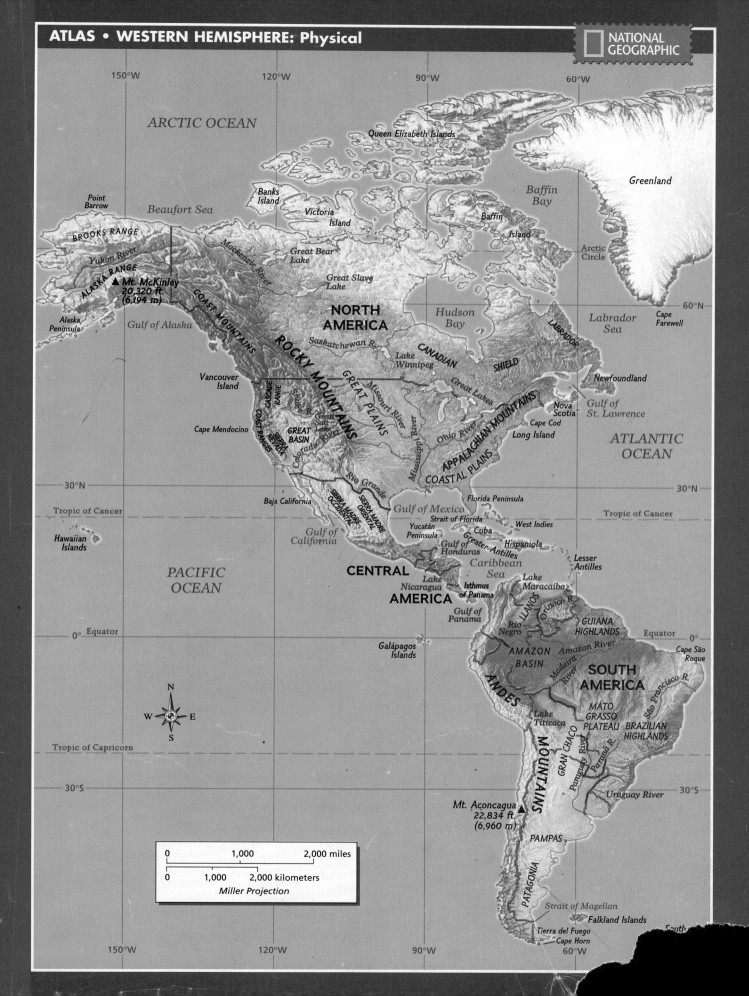

NATIONAL GEOGRAPHIC

ARCTIC OCEAN

Queen Elizabeth Islands

Greenland

Point Barrow

Beaufort Sea

Banks Island

Victoria Island

Baffin Bay

BROOKS RANGE

Yukon River

ALASKA RANGE

▲ Mt. McKinley 20,320 ft. (6,194 m)

Mackenzie River

Great Bear Lake

Baffin Island

Arctic Circle

Alaska Peninsula

Gulf of Alaska

Great Slave Lake

60°N

Cape Farewell

Labrador Sea

COAST MOUNTAINS

NORTH AMERICA

Hudson Bay

LABRADOR

Vancouver Island

Saskatchewan R.

Lake Winnipeg

CANADIAN

SHIELD

Newfoundland

ROCKY MOUNTAINS

GREAT PLAINS

Great Lakes

Gulf of St. Lawrence

CASCADE RANGE

Snake R.

Missouri River

Nova Scotia

Cape Mendocino

COAST RANGES

SIERRA NEVADA

GREAT BASIN

Great Salt Lake

Colorado River

APPALACHIAN MOUNTAINS

Ohio River

Mississippi River

Cape Cod

Long Island

ATLANTIC OCEAN

30°N

COASTAL PLAINS

30°N

Tropic of Cancer

Baja California

SIERRA MADRE OCCIDENTAL

Rio Grande

SIERRA MADRE ORIENTAL

Gulf of Mexico

Florida Peninsula

Strait of Florida

Tropic of Cancer

Hawaiian Islands

Gulf of California

Yucatán Peninsula

Cuba

West Indies

Greater Antilles

Hispaniola

Lesser Antilles

PACIFIC OCEAN

CENTRAL

Gulf of Honduras

Caribbean Sea

Lake Nicaragua

Isthmus of Panama

Lake Maracaibo

AMERICA

Gulf of Panama

LLANOS

Orinoco R.

GUIANA HIGHLANDS

0° Equator

Galápagos Islands

Rio Negro

AMAZON BASIN

Amazon River

Equator 0°

Cape São Roque

ANDES

Madeira River

SOUTH AMERICA

São Francisco R.

MATO GRASSO PLATEAU

BRAZILIAN HIGHLANDS

Lake Titicaca

N

GRAN CHACO

Paraguay River

W E

MOUNTAINS

Paraná R.

S

Tropic of Capricorn

Uruguay River

30°S

30°S

Mt. Aconcagua 22,834 ft. (6,960 m)

PAMPAS

PATAGONIA

0   1,000   2,000 miles

0   1,000   2,000 kilometers

Miller Projection

Strait of Magellan

Falkland Islands

Tierra del Fuego

Cape Horn

South

150°W   120°W   90°W   60°W

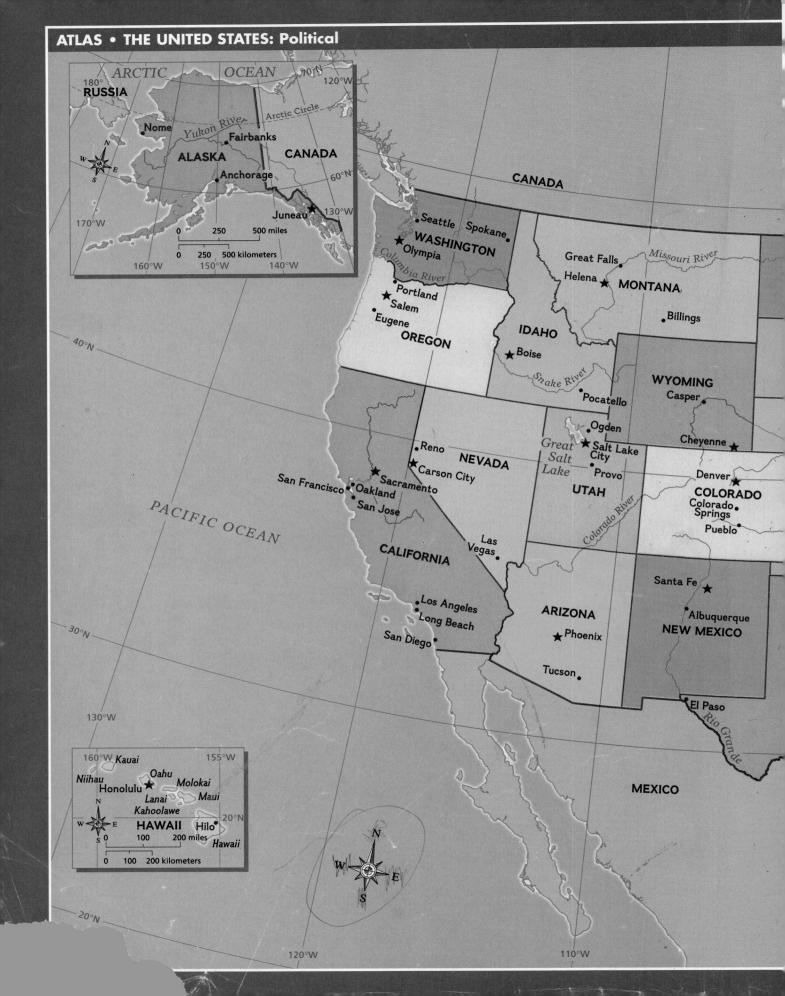

ARCTIC OCEAN

180°

RUSSIA

70°N

120°W

Arctic Circle

Nome

Yukon River

Fairbanks

ALASKA

CANADA

170°W

Anchorage

60°N

130°W

160°W

150°W

140°W

Juneau

0 250 500 miles

0 250 500 kilometers

CANADA

Seattle   Spokane

WASHINGTON

★ Olympia

Great Falls   Missouri River

Helena ★   MONTANA

Columbia River

★ Portland

Salem

Eugene

OREGON

IDAHO

★ Boise

Billings

40°N

Snake River

WYOMING

Pocatello

Casper

Ogden

Great
Salt
Lake

★ Salt Lake
City

Cheyenne ★

★ Reno

NEVADA

Provo

UTAH

★ Carson City

Denver ★

San Francisco

★ Sacramento

Oakland

San Jose

COLORADO

Colorado River

Colorado
Springs

Pueblo

PACIFIC OCEAN

Las
Vegas

CALIFORNIA

Santa Fe ★

ARIZONA

Los Angeles

★ Phoenix

Long Beach

Albuquerque

NEW MEXICO

30°N

San Diego

Tucson

130°W

El Paso

Rio Grande

160°W Kauai

155°W

Niihau   Oahu

Honolulu ★   Molokai

Lanai   Maui

Kahoolawe

HAWAII   Hilo

20°N

0 100 200 miles

Hawaii

0 100 200 kilometers

MEXICO

N

W   E

S

20°N

120°W

110°W

NATIONAL GEOGRAPHIC

CANADA

MAINE
Augusta

NORTH DAKOTA
Grand Forks
Bismarck
Fargo

VERMONT
Montpelier

NEW HAMPSHIRE
Concord

MINNESOTA
Duluth

Lake Superior

MICHIGAN

Lake Huron

L. Ontario

NEW YORK
Albany

Boston
MASSACHUSETTS
Providence
RHODE ISLAND
Hartford
CONNECTICUT

SOUTH DAKOTA
Pierre

WISCONSIN
Green Bay

Minneapolis
St. Paul

Madison
Milwaukee

Lake Michigan

Grand Rapids
Lansing
Detroit

Lake Erie

Buffalo

Cleveland

PENNSYLVANIA
Pittsburgh
Harrisburg

40°N
New York
Trenton
NEW JERSEY
Philadelphia
Dover
DELAWARE

NEBRASKA

Missouri River

Cedar Rapids

IOWA
Des Moines
Omaha

Chicago

Davenport

Gary

Toledo

OHIO
Columbus

Cincinnati

WEST VIRGINIA

Washington, D.C.
Annapolis
MARYLAND

Platte River
Lincoln

ILLINOIS
Springfield

INDIANA
Indianapolis

Charleston

KANSAS
Kansas City
Topeka

MISSOURI
Kansas City
Jefferson City

St. Louis

Louisville

Frankfort

Richmond
Norfolk

VIRGINIA

Arkansas River
Wichita

KENTUCKY
Evansville

Knoxville

NORTH CAROLINA
Raleigh

OKLAHOMA
Oklahoma City
Tulsa

ARKANSAS
Fort Smith
Little Rock

Mississippi R.

Nashville
TENNESSEE
Memphis

Tennessee R.

Charlotte

SOUTH CAROLINA
Columbia

Charleston

ATLANTIC OCEAN

Red River

MISSISSIPPI
Jackson

ALABAMA
Montgomery

Atlanta
GEORGIA
Columbus

Savannah

TEXAS
Fort Worth
Dallas

Shreveport
LOUISIANA

Biloxi
Mobile

Tallahassee

Jacksonville

30°N

Austin
San Antonio
Houston

Baton Rouge
New Orleans

FLORIDA

Corpus Christi
Laredo

Gulf of Mexico

Tampa

BAHAMAS

Miami

★ National capital ★ State capital • Other city

0   150   300 miles

0   150   300 kilometers

Lambert Azimuthal Equal-Area Projection

CUBA

100°W   90°W   80°W

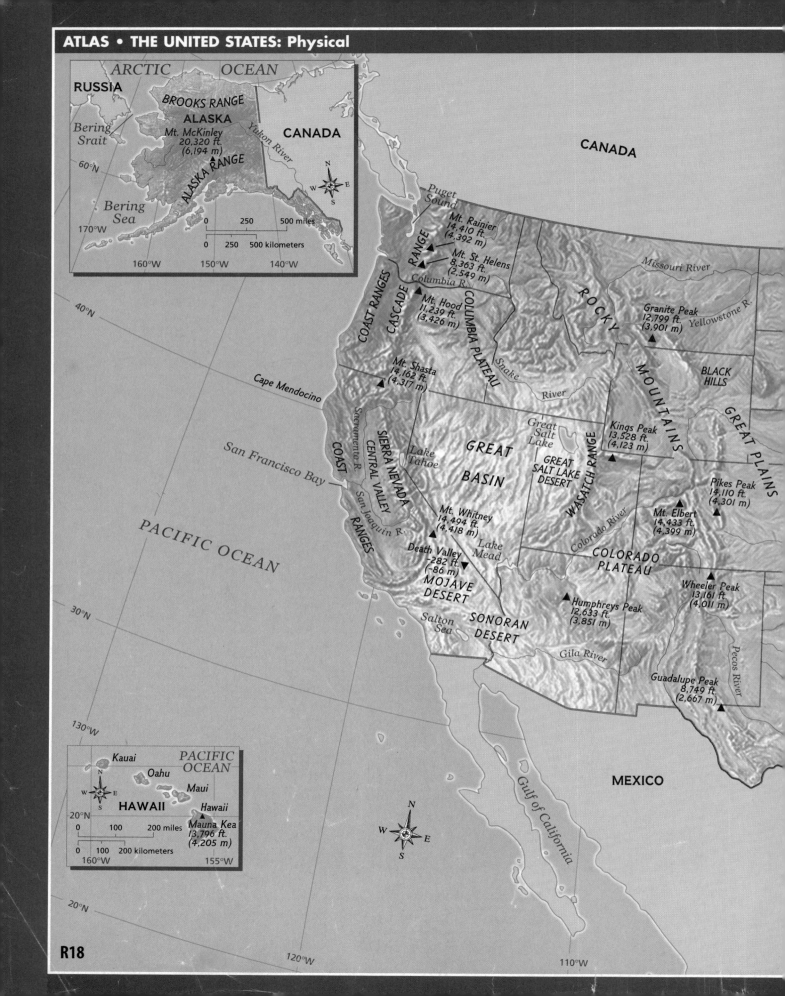

ARCTIC OCEAN

RUSSIA

BROOKS RANGE

ALASKA

Mt. McKinley
20,320 ft.
(6,194 m)

ALASKA RANGE

Yukon River

CANADA

Bering
Srait

60°N

Bering
Sea

170°W

160°W   150°W   140°W

0   250   500 miles

0   250   500 kilometers

CANADA

Puget
Sound

Mt. Rainier
14,410 ft.
(4,392 m)

Mt. St. Helens
8,363 ft.
(2,549 m)

COAST RANGES

CASCADE RANGE

Columbia R.

COLUMBIA PLATEAU

Mt. Hood
11,239 ft.
(3,426 m)

Missouri River

ROCKY

Granite Peak
12,799 ft.
(3,901 m)

Yellowstone R.

40°N

Mt. Shasta
14,162 ft.
(4,317 m)

Cape Mendocino

Snake

River

MOUNTAINS

BLACK
HILLS

GREAT PLAINS

Sacramento R.

SIERRA NEVADA

CENTRAL VALLEY

Lake
Tahoe

GREAT

BASIN

Great
Salt
Lake

GREAT
SALT LAKE
DESERT

WASATCH RANGE

Kings Peak
13,528 ft.
(4,123 m)

San Francisco Bay

COAST

Pikes Peak
14,110 ft.
(4,301 m)

PACIFIC OCEAN

San Joaquin R.

RANGES

Mt. Whitney
14,494 ft.
(4,418 m)

Death Valley
-282 ft.
(-86 m)

Lake
Mead

Colorado River

COLORADO
PLATEAU

Mt. Elbert
14,433 ft.
(4,399 m)

Wheeler Peak
13,161 ft.
(4,011 m)

30°N

MOJAVE
DESERT

Salton
Sea

SONORAN
DESERT

Humphreys Peak
12,633 ft.
(3,851 m)

Gila River

Pecos River

Guadalupe Peak
8,749 ft.
(2,667 m)

130°W

Kauai

PACIFIC
OCEAN

Oahu

Maui

HAWAII

Hawaii

20°N

Mauna Kea
13,796 ft.
(4,205 m)

0   100   200 miles

0   100   200 kilometers

160°W   155°W

Gulf of California

MEXICO

N
W   E
S

120°W   110°W

20°N

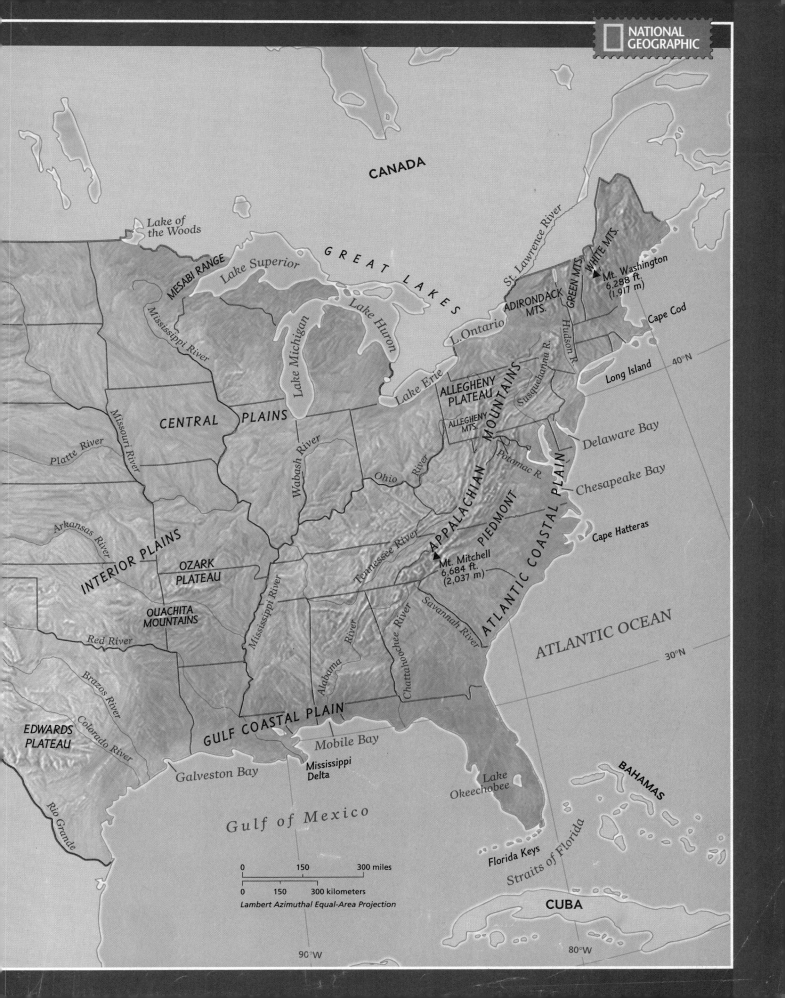

NATIONAL GEOGRAPHIC

CANADA

Lake of the Woods

MESABI RANGE

Lake Superior

GREAT LAKES

St. Lawrence River

Mississippi River

Lake Michigan

Lake Huron

ADIRONDACK MTS.

GREEN MTS.

WHITE MTS.

▲ Mt. Washington
6,288 ft.
(1,917 m)

Cape Cod

L. Ontario

Hudson R.

40°N

Lake Erie

ALLEGHENY PLATEAU

APPALACHIAN MOUNTAINS

Susquehanna R.

Long Island

CENTRAL PLAINS

ALLEGHENY MTS.

Delaware Bay

Platte River

Missouri River

Wabash River

Ohio River

Potomac R.

Chesapeake Bay

ATLANTIC COASTAL PLAIN

PIEDMONT

Arkansas River

INTERIOR PLAINS

OZARK PLATEAU

Tennessee River

▲ Mt. Mitchell
6,684 ft.
(2,037 m)

Cape Hatteras

OUACHITA MOUNTAINS

Red River

Mississippi River

Alabama River

Chattahoochee River

Savannah River

ATLANTIC OCEAN

30°N

Brazos River

Colorado River

EDWARDS PLATEAU

GULF COASTAL PLAIN

Mobile Bay

BAHAMAS

Galveston Bay

Mississippi Delta

Lake Okeechobee

Rio Grande

Gulf of Mexico

Florida Keys

Straits of Florida

CUBA

0   150   300 miles

0   150   300 kilometers

Lambert Azimuthal Equal-Area Projection

90°W

80°W

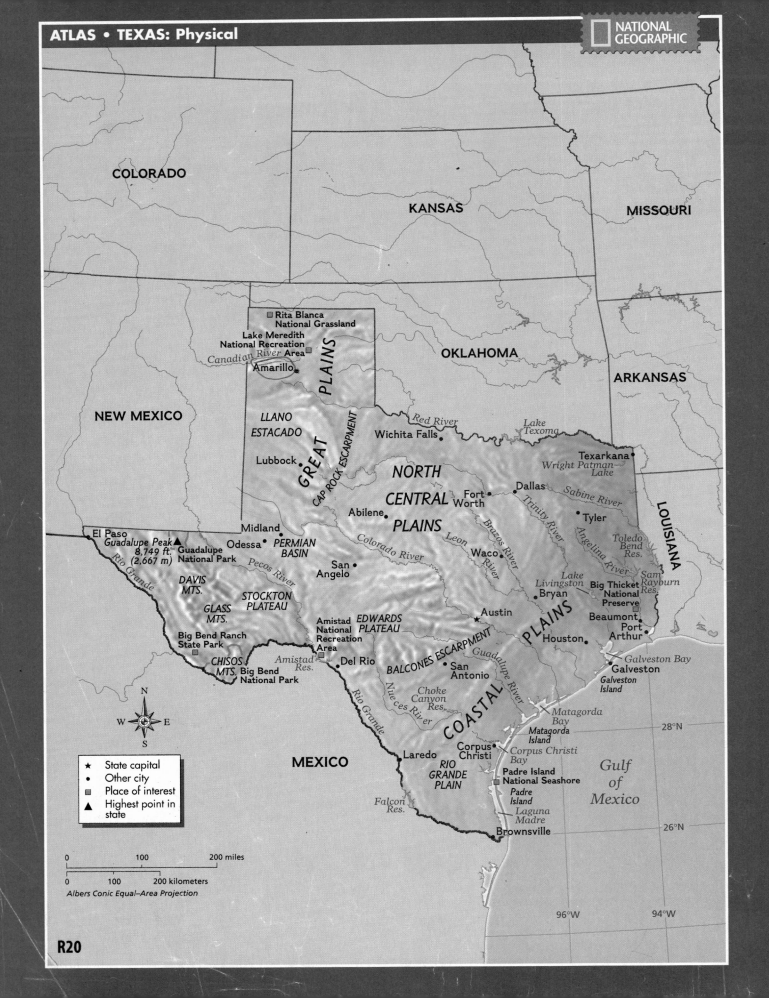

COLORADO

KANSAS

MISSOURI

NEW MEXICO

OKLAHOMA

ARKANSAS

LOUISIANA

MEXICO

Gulf of Mexico

Rita Blanca National Grassland

Lake Meredith National Recreation Area

Canadian River

Amarillo

GREAT PLAINS

LLANO ESTACADO

Lubbock

CAP ROCK ESCARPMENT

Wichita Falls

Red River

Lake Texoma

Texarkana

Wright Patman Lake

NORTH CENTRAL PLAINS

Dallas

Sabine River

Fort Worth

Abilene

Tyler

Midland

Odessa

PERMIAN BASIN

San Angelo

Colorado River

Leon River

Waco

Brazos River

Trinity River

Angelina River

Toledo Bend Res.

El Paso

Guadalupe Peak 8,749 ft. (2,667 m)

Guadalupe National Park

Pecos River

Lake Livingston

Bryan

Big Thicket National Preserve

Sam Rayburn Res.

Rio Grande

DAVIS MTS.

STOCKTON PLATEAU

Austin

COASTAL PLAINS

Beaumont

Port Arthur

GLASS MTS.

Big Bend Ranch State Park

CHISOS MTS.

Big Bend National Park

Amistad National Recreation Area

EDWARDS PLATEAU

Amistad Res.

Del Rio

BALCONES ESCARPMENT

San Antonio

Guadalupe River

Houston

Galveston Bay

Galveston

Galveston Island

Nueces River

Choke Canyon Res.

Rio Grande

Laredo

Matagorda Bay

Matagorda Island

Corpus Christi Bay

Corpus Christi

RIO GRANDE PLAIN

Padre Island National Seashore

Padre Island

Falcon Res.

Laguna Madre

Brownsville

28°N

26°N

96°W

94°W

0   100   200 miles

0   100   200 kilometers

Albers Conic Equal–Area Projection

★ State capital
● Other city
■ Place of interest
▲ Highest point in state

N   W   E   S

R20

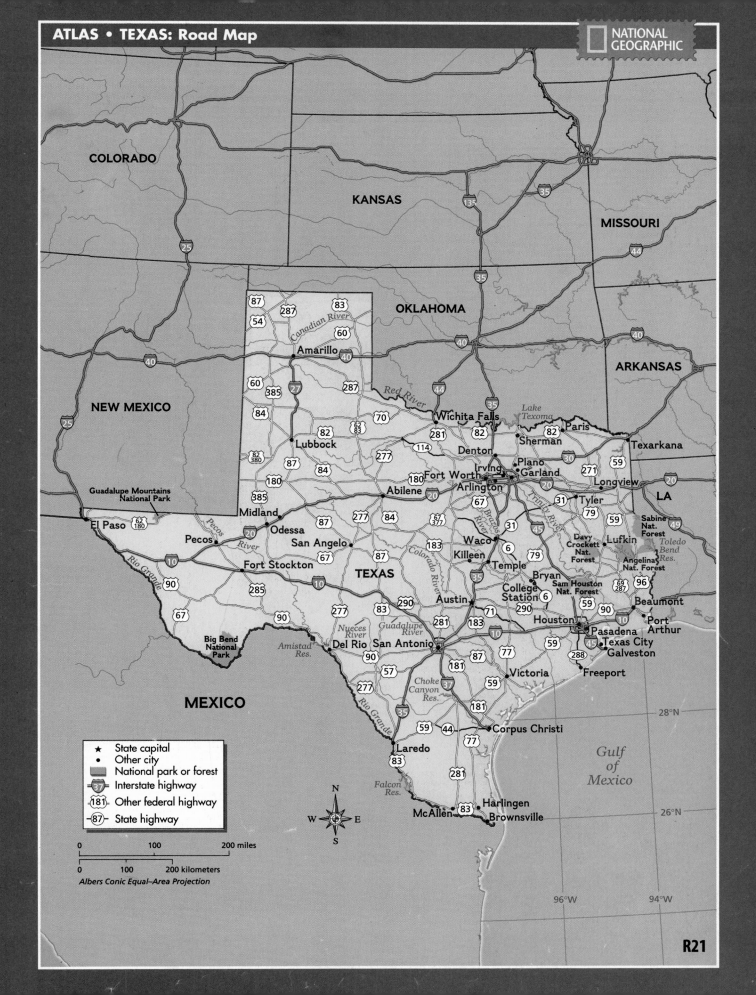

NATIONAL GEOGRAPHIC

COLORADO

KANSAS

MISSOURI

OKLAHOMA

ARKANSAS

NEW MEXICO

Canadian River

87
54
287
83
60

Amarillo

40

60
385
27
287

84

Red River

44

Lake Texoma

82
380
82

70

62
83

Wichita Falls

281
82

82

Paris

Texarkana

Sherman

Lubbock

114

Denton

30

271

Longview

59

LA

87
84

277

Plano
Garland

Irving

Fort Worth

180

Arlington

20

Tyler

79

31

59

Abilene

20

67

Sabine Nat. Forest

49

Guadalupe Mountains National Park

El Paso

62
180

Pecos River

Midland

385

180

Odessa

87

277

84

57
377

31

Brazos River

6

Davy Crockett Nat. Forest

Lufkin

Angelina Nat. Forest

Toledo Bend Res.

Pecos

20

San Angelo

67

TEXAS

Colorado River

183

Waco

Killeen

Temple

79

45

Bryan

Sam Houston Nat. Forest

69
287

96

Beaumont

Fort Stockton

10

87

College Station

6

10

90

285

Austin

290

281

183

Houston

59

90

Port Arthur

67

90

277

83

290

71

Pasadena

Texas City

Galveston

MEXICO

Nueces River

Guadalupe River

Del Rio

San Antonio

57

277

Amistad Res.

90

87

181

77

59

288

Freeport

Victoria

181

Choke Canyon Res.

37

59

Big Bend National Park

Rio Grande

Gulf of Mexico

28°N

Laredo

83

59

44

77

Corpus Christi

281

Falcon Res.

McAllen

281

83

Harlingen

Brownsville

26°N

N
W E
S

0   100   200 miles
0   100   200 kilometers
Albers Conic Equal–Area Projection

96°W

94°W

NATIONAL GEOGRAPHIC

See table for key to numbers

0   50   100 miles
0 50 100 kilometers
Albers Conic Equal–Area Projection

TEXAS COUNTIES

County	#	County	#	County	#
Anderson	133	Culberson	116	Hill	131
Andrews	97	Dallam	1	Hockley	46
Angelina	158	Dallas	86	Hood	106
Aransas	240	Dawson	76	Hopkins	69
Archer	53	Deaf Smith	16	Houston	156
Armstrong	18	Delta	68	Howard	99
Atascosa	227	Denton	65	Hudspeth	115
Austin	208	De Witt	219	Hunt	67
Bailey	27	Dickens	49	Hutchinson	8
Bandera	198	Dimmit	33	Irion	142
Bastrop	205	Donley	19	Jack	63
Baylor	52	Duval	242	Jackson	231
Bee	237	Eastland	104	Jasper	177
Bell	150	Ector	120	Jeff Davis	161
Bexar	200	Edwards	195	Jefferson	213
Blanco	185	El Paso	114	Jim Hogg	248
Borden	77	Ellis	109	Jim Wells	243
Bosque	130	Erath	105	Johnson	108
Bowie	44	Falls	152	Jones	80
Brazoria	222	Fannin	41	Karnes	228
Brazos	170	Fayette	206	Kaufman	88
Brewster	180	Fisher	79	Kendall	199
Briscoe	24	Floyd	30	Kenedy	250
Brooks	249	Foard	34	Kent	58
Brown	127	Fort Bend	210	Kerr	197
Burleson	188	Franklin	70	Kimble	183
Burnet	167	Freestone	132	King	50
Caldwell	204	Frio	226	Kinney	214
Calhoun	239	Gaines	75	Kleberg	246
Callahan	103	Galveston	223	Knox	51
Cameron	254	Garza	57	Lamar	42
Camp	72	Gillespie	184	Lamb	28
Carson	13	Glasscock	122	Lampasas	148
Cass	74	Goliad	229	La Salle	234
Castro	22	Gonzales	218	Lavaca	220
Chambers	212	Gray	14	Lee	187
Cherokee	134	Grayson	40	Leon	155
Childress	26	Gregg	94	Liberty	191
Clay	37	Grimes	172	Limestone	153
Cochran	45	Guadalupe	203	Lipscomb	5
Coke	124	Hale	29	Live Oak	236
Coleman	126	Hall	25	Llano	166
Collin	66	Hamilton	129	Loving	118
Collingsworth	20	Hansford	3	Lubbock	47
Colorado	207	Hardeman	33	Lynn	56
Comal	201	Hardin	192	McCulloch	145
Comanche	128	Harris	211	McLennan	151
Concho	144	Harrison	96	McMullen	235
Cooke	39	Hartley	6	Madison	171
Coryell	149	Haskell	60	Marion	95
Cottle	32	Hays	202	Martin	98
Crane	139	Hemphill	10	Mason	165
Crockett	162	Henderson	111	Matagorda	232
Crosby	48	Hidalgo	252	Maverick	224

County	#	County	#	County	#
Medina	216	Red River	43	Titus	71
Menard	164	Reeves	117	Tom Green	143
Midland	121	Refugio	238	Travis	186
Milam	169	Roberts	9	Trinity	157
Mills	147	Robertson	154	Tyler	176
Mitchell	100	Rockwall	87	Upshur	93
Montague	38	Runnels	125	Upton	140
Montgomery	190	Rusk	112	Uvalde	215
Moore	7	Sabine	160	Val Verde	194
Morris	73	San Augustine	159	Van Zandt	89
Motley	31	San Jacinto	174	Victoria	230
Nacogdoches	135	San Patricio	244	Walker	173
Navarro	110	San Saba	146	Waller	209
Newton	178	Schleicher	163	Ward	137
Nolan	101	Scurry	78	Washington	189
Nueces	245	Shackelford	81	Webb	241
Ochiltree	4	Shelby	136	Wharton	221
Oldham	11	Sherman	2	Wheeler	15
Orange	193	Smith	92	Wichita	36
Palo Pinto	83	Somervell	107	Wilbarger	35
Panola	113	Starr	251	Willacy	253
Parker	84	Stephens	82	Williamson	168
Parmer	21	Sterling	123	Wilson	217
Pecos	138	Stonewall	59	Winkler	119
Polk	175	Sutton	182	Wise	64
Potter	12	Swisher	23	Wood	91
Presidio	179	Tarrant	85	Yoakum	54
Rains	90	Taylor	102	Young	62
Randall	141	Terrell	181	Zapata	247
Reagan	141	Terry	55	Zavala	225
Real	196	Throckmorton	61		

Governors of Texas

State Capitol Building, Austin

Presidents of the Republic of Texas	Term in office
David G. Burnet	1836
Sam Houston	1836–1838
Mirabeau B. Lamar	1838–1841
Sam Houston	1841–1844
Anson Jones	1844–1846

Governors of the State of Texas	Term in office
J. Pinckney Henderson	1846–1847
George T. Wood	1847–1849
P. Hansborough Bell	1849–1853
J.W. Henderson	1853
Elisha M. Pease	1853–1857
Hardin R. Runnels	1857–1859
Sam Houston	1859–1861
Edward Clark	1861
Francis R. Lubbock	1861–1863
Pendleton Murrah	1863–1865

Andrew J. Hamilton	1865–1866
James W. Throckmorton	1866–1867
Elisha M. Pease	1867–1869
Edmund J. Davis	1870–1874
Richard Coke (D)	1874–1876
Richard B. Hubbard (D)	1876–1879
Oran M. Roberts (D)	1879–1883
John Ireland (D)	1883–1887
Lawrence S. Ross (D)	1887–1891
James S. Hogg (D)	1891–1895
Charles A. Culberson (D)	1895–1899
Joseph D. Sayers (D)	1899–1903
S.W.T. Lanham (D)	1903–1907
Thomas M. Campbell (D)	1907–1911
Oscar B. Colquitt (D)	1911–1915
James E. Ferguson (D)	1915–1917
William P. Hobby (D)	1917–1921
Pat M. Neff (D)	1921–1925
Miriam A. Ferguson (D)	1925–1927
Dan Moody (D)	1927–1931
Ross S. Sterling (D)	1931–1933
Miriam A. Ferguson (D)	1933–1935
James V. Allred (D)	1935–1939
W. Lee O'Daniel (D)	1939–1941
Coke R. Stevenson (D)	1941–1947
Beauford H. Jester (D)	1947–1949
Allan Shivers (D)	1949–1957
Price Daniel (D)	1957–1963
John B. Connally (D)	1963–1969
Preston Smith (D)	1969–1973
Dolph Briscoe (D)	1973–1979
William P. Clements (R)	1979–1983
Mark White (D)	1983–1987
William P. Clements (R)	1987–1991
Ann W. Richards (D)	1991–1995
George W. Bush (R)	1995–2000
Rick Perry (R)	2000–

(D) Democrat,   (R) Republican

Our Fifty States

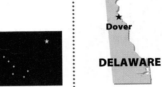

ALABAMA
★
Montgomery

Date of Statehood **1819**

Nickname **Heart of Dixie**

Population **4,447,100**

Area **52,423 sq mi;
135,776 sq km**

Region **Southeast**

★
Hartford
CONNECTICUT

Date of Statehood **1788**

Nickname **Constitution State**

Population **3,405,565**

Area **5,544 sq mi;
14,359 sq km**

Region **Northeast**

ALASKA

Juneau ★

Date of Statehood **1959**

Nickname **The Last Frontier**

Population **626,932**

Area **656,424 sq mi;
1,700,138 sq km**

Region **West**

Dover

DELAWARE

Date of Statehood **1787**

Nickname **First State**

Population **783,600**

Area **2,489 sq mi;
6,447 sq km**

Region **Northeast**

DECEMBER 7, 1787

ARIZONA

★
Phoenix

Date of Statehood **1912**

Nickname **Grand Canyon State**

Population **5,130,632**

Area **114,006 sq mi;
295,276 sq km**

Region **Southwest**

★
Tallahassee

FLORIDA

Date of Statehood **1845**

Nickname **Sunshine State**

Population **15,982,378**

Area **58,644 sq mi;
151,939 sq km**

Region **Southeast**

ARKANSAS

★
Little Rock

Date of Statehood **1836**

Nickname **The Natural State**

Population **2,673,400**

Area **53,182 sq mi;
137,741 sq km**

Region **Southeast**

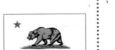
ARKANSAS

★
Atlanta

GEORGIA

Date of Statehood **1788**

Nickname **Peach State**

Population **8,186,453**

Area **58,910 sq mi;
152,576 sq km**

Region **Southeast**

CALIFORNIA

★
Sacramento

Date of Statehood **1850**

Nickname **Golden State**

Population **33,871,648**

Area **163,707 sq mi;
424,001 sq km**

Region **West**

CALIFORNIA REPUBLIC

HAWAII

★
Honolulu

Date of Statehood **1959**

Nickname **The Aloha State**

Population **1,211,537**

Area **10,932 sq mi;
28,314 sq km**

Region **West**

Denver ★

COLORADO

Date of Statehood **1876**

Nickname **Centennial State**

Population **4,301,261**

Area **104,100 sq mi;
269,619 sq km**

Region **Mountain States**

IDAHO

★ **Boise**

Date of Statehood **1890**

Nickname **Gem State**

Population **1,293,953**

Area **83,574 sq mi;
216,457 sq km**

Region **Mountain States**

ILLINOIS
★ Springfield

Date of Statehood **1818**

Nickname **The Prairie State**

Population **12,419,293**

Area **57,918 sq mi; 150,008 sq km**

Region **Middle West**

MAINE
Augusta ★

Date of Statehood **1820**

Nickname **Pine Tree State**

Population **1,274,923**

Area **35,387 sq mi; 91,652 sq km**

Region **Northeast**

INDIANA
★ Indianapolis

Date of Statehood **1816**

Nickname **Hoosier State**

Population **6,080,485**

Area **36,420 sq mi; 94,328 sq km**

Region **Middle West**

MARYLAND
Annapolis ★

Date of Statehood **1788**

Nickname **Free State**

Population **5,296,486**

Area **12,407 sq mi; 32,134 sq km**

Region **Northeast**

IOWA
★ Des Moines

Date of Statehood **1846**

Nickname **Hawkeye State**

Population **2,926,324**

Area **56,276 sq mi; 145,755 sq km**

Region **Middle West**

MASSACHUSETTS
Boston ★

Date of Statehood **1788**

Nickname **Bay State**

Population **6,349,097**

Area **10,555 sq mi; 27,337 sq km**

Region **Northeast**

KANSAS
Topeka ★

Date of Statehood **1861**

Nickname **Sunflower State**

Population **2,688,418**

Area **82,282 sq mi; 213,110 sq km**

Region **Middle West**

MICHIGAN
★ Lansing

Date of Statehood **1837**

Nickname **Wolverine State**

Population **9,938,444**

Area **96,810 sq mi; 250,738 sq km**

Region **Middle West**

KENTUCKY
★ Frankfort

Date of Statehood **1792**

Nickname **Bluegrass State**

Population **4,041,769**

Area **40,411 sq mi; 104,664 sq km**

Region **Southeast**

MINNESOTA
St. Paul ★

Date of Statehood **1858**

Nickname **North Star State**

Population **4,919,479**

Area **86,943 sq mi; 225,182 sq km**

Region **Middle West**

LOUISIANA
Baton Rouge ★

Date of Statehood **1812**

Nickname **Pelican State**

Population **4,468,976**

Area **51,843 sq mi; 134,273 sq km**

Region **Southeast**

MISSISSIPPI
★ Jackson

Date of Statehood **1817**

Nickname **Magnolia State**

Population **2,844,658**

Area **48,434 sq mi; 125,444 sq km**

Region **Southeast**

Our Fifty States
Missouri • Oregon

MISSOURI
★
Jefferson City

Date of Statehood **1821**

Nickname **Show Me State**

Population **5,595,211**

Area **69,709 sq mi;
180,546 sq km**

Region **Middle West**

NEW YORK
Albany ★

Date of Statehood **1788**

Nickname **Empire State**

Population **18,976,457**

Area **54,475 sq mi;
141,090 sq km**

Region **Northeast**

MONTANA
★
Helena

Date of Statehood **1889**

Nickname **Treasure State**

Population **902,195**

Area **147,046 sq mi;
380,849 sq km**

Region **Mountain States**

**NORTH
CAROLINA**
Raleigh ★

Date of Statehood **1789**

Nickname **Tar Heel State**

Population **8,049,313**

Area **53,821 sq mi;
139,396 sq km**

Region **Southeast**

NEBRASKA
Lincoln ★

Date of Statehood **1867**

Nickname **Cornhusker State**

Population **1,711,263**

Area **77,358 sq mi;
200,357 sq km**

Region **Middle West**

**NORTH
DAKOTA**
Bismarck
★

Date of Statehood **1889**

Nickname **Peace Garden State**

Population **642,200**

Area **70,704 sq mi;
183,123 sq km**

Region **Middle West**

NEVADA
★ Carson City

Date of Statehood **1864**

Nickname **Silver State**

Population **1,998,257**

Area **110,567 sq mi;
286,369 sq km**

Region **West**

OHIO
★
Columbus

Date of Statehood **1803**

Nickname **Buckeye State**

Population **11,353,140**

Area **44,828 sq mi;
116,105 sq km**

Region **Middle West**

NEW HAMPSHIRE
Concord
★

Date of Statehood **1788**

Nickname **Granite State**

Population **1,235,786**

Area **9,351 sq mi;
24,219 sq km**

Region **Northeast**

OKLAHOMA
★
Oklahoma City

Date of Statehood **1907**

Nickname **Sooner State**

Population **3,450,654**

Area **69,903 sq mi;
181,049 sq km**

Region **Southwest**

NEW JERSEY
★
Trenton

Date of Statehood **1787**

Nickname **Garden State**

Population **8,414,350**

Area **8,722 sq mi;
22,590 sq km**

Region **Northeast**

NEW MEXICO
★
Santa Fe

Date of Statehood **1912**

Nickname **Land of Enchantment**

Population **1,819,046**

Area **121,598 sq mi;
314,939 sq km**

Region **Southwest**

★ Salem

OREGON

Date of Statehood **1859**

Nickname **Beaver State**

Population **3,421,399**

Area **98,386 sq mi;
254,820 sq km**

Region **West**

PENNSYLVANIA
Harrisburg ★

Date of Statehood **1787**

Nickname **Keystone State**

Population **12,281,054**

Area **46,058 sq mi; 119,290 sq km**

Region **Northeast**

RHODE ISLAND
Providence ★

Date of Statehood **1790**

Nickname **Ocean State**

Population **1,048,319**

Area **1,545 sq mi; 4,002 sq km**

Region **Northeast**

SOUTH CAROLINA
★
Columbia

Date of Statehood **1788**

Nickname **Palmetto State**

Population **4,012,012**

Area **32,007 sq mi; 82,898 sq km**

Region **Southeast**

Pierre ★
SOUTH DAKOTA

Date of Statehood **1889**

Nickname **Mount Rushmore State**

Population **754,844**

Area **77,121 sq mi; 199,743 sq km**

Region **Middle West**

TENNESSEE
★ Nashville

Date of Statehood **1796**

Nickname **Volunteer State**

Population **5,689,283**

Area **42,146 sq mi; 109,158 sq km**

Region **Southeast**

TEXAS
Austin ★

Date of Statehood **1845**

Nickname **Lone Star State**

Population **20,851,820**

Area **268,601 sq mi; 695,677 sq km**

Region **Southwest**

★
Salt Lake City
UTAH

Date of Statehood **1896**

Nickname **Beehive State**

Population **2,233,169**

Area **84,904 sq mi; 219,901 sq km**

Region **Mountain States**

VERMONT
★
Montpelier

Date of Statehood **1791**

Nickname **Green Mountain State**

Population **608,827**

Area **9,615 sq mi; 24,903 sq km**

Region **Northeast**

VIRGINIA
Richmond ★

Date of Statehood **1788**

Nickname **Old Dominion**

Population **7,078,515**

Area **42,769 sq mi; 110,772 sq km**

Region **Southeast**

★ Olympia
WASHINGTON

Date of Statehood **1889**

Nickname **Evergreen State**

Population **5,894,121**

Area **71,303 sq mi; 184,675 sq km**

Region **West**

WEST VIRGINIA
★ Charleston

Date of Statehood **1863**

Nickname **Mountain State**

Population **1,808,344**

Area **24,231 sq mi; 62,758 sq km**

Region **Southeast**

WISCONSIN
Madison
★

Date of Statehood **1848**

Nickname **Badger State**

Population **5,363,675**

Area **65,503 sq mi; 169,653 sq km**

Region **Middle West**

WYOMING
Cheyenne ★

Date of Statehood **1890**

Nickname **Equality State**

Population **493,782**

Area **97,818 sq mi; 253,349 sq km**

Region **Mountain States**

Sources: Population — U.S. Bureau of Census, 2000; Area — U.S. Bureau of Census, 2000.

Dictionary of Geographic Terms

GULF (gulf) Part of an ocean that extends into the land; larger than a bay.

RESERVOIR (rez'ər vwär) A natural or artificial lake used to store water.

PLATEAU (pla tō') A high, flat area that rises steeply above the surrounding land.

DAM (dam) A wall built across a river, creating a lake that stores water.

CANYON (kan'yən) A deep, narrow valley with steep sides.

MESA (mā'sə) A hill with a flat top; smaller than a plateau.

BUTTE (būt) A small, flat-topped hill; smaller than a mesa or plateau.

OASIS (ō ā'sis) A fertile area in a desert that is watered by a spring.

HILL (hil) A rounded, raised landform; not as high as a mountain.

VALLEY (val'ē) An area of low land between hills or mountains.

DESERT (dez'ərt) A dry environment with few plants and animals.

COAST (kōst) The land along an ocean.

BAY (bā) Part of an ocean or lake that extends deeply into the land.

ISLAND (ī'lənd) A body of land completely surrounded by water.

PENINSULA (pə nin'sə lə) A body of land nearly surrounded by water.

VOLCANO (vol kā′nō) An opening in Earth's surface through which hot rock and ash are forced out.

MOUNTAIN (moun′tən) A high landform with steep sides; higher than a hill.

HARBOR (här′bər) A sheltered place along a coast where boats dock safely.

PEAK (pēk) The top of a mountain.

GLACIER (glā′shər) A huge sheet of ice that moves slowly across the land.

CANAL (kə nal′) A channel built to carry water for irrigation or transportation.

LAKE (lāk) Body of water completely surrounded by land.

TRIBUTARY (trib′yə ter ē) A smaller river that flows into a larger river.

PORT (pôrt) A place where ships load and unload their goods.

SOURCE (sôrs) The starting point of a river.

TIMBERLINE (tim′bər līn) A line above which trees do not grow.

WATERFALL (wô′tər fôl) A flow of water falling vertically.

PLAIN (plān) A large area of nearly flat land.

RIVER BASIN (riv′ər bā′sin) All the land that is drained by a river and its tributaries.

MOUNTAIN RANGE (moun′tən rānj) A row or chain of mountains.

RIVER (riv′ər) A stream of water that flows across the land and empties into another body of water.

BASIN (bā′sin) A bowl-shaped landform surrounded by higher land.

DELTA (del′tə) Land made of soil left behind as a river drains into a larger body of water.

MOUNTAIN PASS (moun′tən pas) A narrow gap through a mountain range.

MOUTH (mouth) The place where a river empties into a larger body of water.

OCEAN (ō′shən) A large body of salt water; oceans cover much of Earth's surface.

R29

Gazetteer

This Gazetteer is a geographical dictionary that will help you to pronounce and locate the places discussed in this book. Latitude and longitude are given for cities and some other places. The page numbers tell you where each place appears on a map or in the text.

A

Abilene (ab'ə lēn) City located in northwestern Texas; 32°N, 100°W. (m. 31, t. 31)

Africa (af'ri kə) A continent south of Europe and between the Atlantic and Indian Oceans. (m. xxv, t. xxiv)

Alamo (al'ə mō) Also known as the San Antonio de Valero mission. In 1836 it was the site of the most famous battle in Texas history. (m. 103, t. 105)

Amarillo (am ə ril'ō) City in northwestern Texas; 35°N, 102°W. (m. 33, t. 32)

Anáhuac (änä'wäk) Town in Mexico that was the site of the first conflict which led to the Texas Revolution. (t. 135)

Antarctica (ant ärk'ti kə) Continent located in the Southern Hemisphere. (m. H12, t. H11)

Appalachian Mountains (ap ə lā'chē ən moun'tənz) Chain of mountains in the eastern United States. (m. 22)

Arctic Ocean (ärk'tik ō'shən) Ocean surrounding the North Pole. (m. H12, t. H11)

Argentina (är jən tē'nə) Country in South America. (m. R4, t. 414)

Asia (ā'zhə) The largest continent, located in the Eastern and Northern hemispheres. (m. H12, t. H11)

Atlantic Ocean (at lan'tik ō'shən) Ocean that borders eastern North and South America and western Europe and Africa. (m. H12, t. H11)

Austin (ôs'tən) Capital of Texas, located in the south-central part of the state; 30°N, 98°W. (m. xxvi, t. 29)

Australia (ôs trāl'yə) Continent and country located in the Eastern and Southern hemispheres. (m. H12, t. H11)

Austria-Hungary (ôs'trē yə hung'ə rē) Large empire that once combined several countries in central Europe. (t. 277)

B

Bahama Islands (bə hä'mə ī'ləndz) A group of islands in the Atlantic Ocean south of Florida making up the Commonwealth of the Bahamas. Columbus was the first European to arrive on the islands in 1492. (m. R4, t. 83)

Balcones Escarpment (bal kō' nəs e skärp'mənt) Steep cliff that cuts across part of Texas from north to south. (m. H17, t. 8)

Beaumont (bō'mänt) City in southeastern Texas, that was the site of an early oil boom; 30°N, 94°W. (m. H13, t. 268)

Bering Strait (bə'ring strāt) Body of water that separates North America from Asia. (t. 49)

Beringia (bə rin'jē ə) A land bridge believed to have connected Asia with North America for about 2,000 years during the Ice Age. (m. 49, t. 49)

pronunciation key

a	at	ī	ice	u	up	th	thin
ā	ape	îr	pierce	ū	use	th	this
ä	far	o	hot	ü	rule	zh	measure
âr	care	ō	old	ù	pull	ə	about, taken,
e	end	ô	fork	ûr	turn		pencil, lemon,
ē	me	oi	oil	hw	white		circus
i	it	ou	out	ng	song		

Big Bend National Park (big bend nash'ən əl pärk) National park in western Texas on a bend of the Rio Grande. (m. 35, t. 370)

Brazil (bra sil') Country along the northeast coast of South America. (m. 108, t. 109)

Brownsville (brownz'vil) Port city in southern Texas; 26°N, 98°W. (m. H13, t. 210)

Canada (kan'ə də) Country bordering the United States to the north. (m. 5, t. 4)

Caribbean Sea (kar ə bē'ən sē) Tropical sea between North and South America. (m. R4, t. 83)

Castroville (kas' trō vil) A town settled by French immigrants to Texas in the 1800s; 29°N, 99°W. (m.186, t. 184).

Central America (sen'trəl ə mer'i kə) Part of North America between Mexico and South America made up of a number of countries. (m. 5, t. 4)

Central Plains (sen'trəl plānz) Part of the Interior Plains of the Middle West, an area of gently rolling hills where much corn is grown. (m. 22, t. 6)

Chapultepec (chə pul'tə pek) A rocky hill in Mexico City, Mexico. Site of a fortress captured by United States forces during the Mexican War; 19°N, 99°W. (t. 177)

Chihuahuan Desert (chə wä'wun dez'ərt) Flat dry area stretching from western Texas to northern Mexico. (m. 35, t. 34)

China (chī'nə) A country in eastern Asia, the most populous country in the world. (t. 407)

Chisholm Trail (chiz'əm trāl) Cattle drive route in 1880s stretching about 800 miles from San Antonio, Texas, to Abilene, Kansas. (m. 238, t. 238)

Chisos Mountains (chē'sôs moun'tənz) Mountain range in western Texas. (m. 35, t. 34)

Ciudad Juarez (sē'ü dad hwär'əs) Mexican city across the Rio Grande from El Paso; 32°N, 106°W. (m. 34, t. 35)

Clear Lake (klir lāk) A suburb of Houston which is home to the Johnson Space Center. (t. 308)

Coastal Plain (kōs'təl plān) Low plain along the Atlantic Coast from Massachusetts to Texas. The Coastal Plain forms the easternmost region of Texas. (m. 29, t. 7)

Colorado River (kôl ə rad'ō riv'ər) River that flows from the Rocky Mountains to the Gulf of Mexico. (m. H13)

Columbia (kə lum' bē ə) Town on the Brazos River that was the first capital of the Republic of Texas; 29°N, 96°W. (t. 159)

Corpus Christi (kôr' pəs kris' tē) Port city in southern Texas; 28°N, 98°W. (m. 12, t. 29)

Corpus Christi Bay (kôr' pəs kris' tē bā) Narrow body of water leading to the Gulf of Mexico, located in southern Texas. (m. 12, t. 29)

Cross Timbers (krôs tim' bərz) One of three geographical areas in the North Central Plains of Texas. (m. 31, t. 30)

Crystal Beach (kris' təl bēch) Town in the Bolivar Peninsula in Galveston County. (t. 363)

Dallas (dal'əs) City in northeastern Texas; 33°N, 97°W. (m. H13, t. 29)

Davis Mountains (dā'vəs moun'tənz) One of three groups of mountains located in western Texas. (m. 69, t. 34)

Dolores (dō lō'res) Town in central Mexico. (t. 152)

Eastern Hemisphere (ēs'tərn hem'i sfîr) The half of Earth east of the prime meridian. (m. H12, t. 4)

Edwards Plateau (ed'wərdz pla tō') One of three geographical areas on the Great Plains of Texas. (m. 33, t. 32)

El Capitan (el kap ə tan') One of the Guadalupe Mountains of western Texas; 32°N, 105°W. (m. 35, t. 3)

El Paso (el pas' ō) City in westernmost Texas on the Rio Grande; 32° N, 106° W. (m. 35, t. 35)

England (ing' lənd) Island country in Europe which began establishing colonies in North America in the 1500s. England is part of the United Kingdom of Great Britain. The United States fought against Great Britain in the American Revolution. (m. R5, t. 106)

Ennis (en'əs) City in north central Texas and home of the largest Czech community in Texas; 32°N, 97°W. (t. 363)

Europe (yûr'əp) Continent located in the Eastern and Northern hemispheres. (m. H12, t. H11)

F

Fort Sumter (fôrt sum'tûr) Union fort in South Carolina where the first Civil War battle took place; 33°N, 80°W. (m. 211, t. 213)

Fort Worth (fôrt wərth) City located in the North Central Plains of Texas; 33°N, 98°W. (m. 31, t. 31)

France (frans) Country in western Europe which began establishing colonies in North America in the 1500s. (m. R5, t. 106)

Fredericksburg (fre' dər iks bûrg) Town in the Texas Hill Country founded by German immigrants; 30°N, 99°W. (t. 184)

G

Galveston (gal' və stən) Port city in southeastern Texas; 29°N, 94°W. (m. H13)

Goliad (gō'lē ad) Southern Texas town that was the site of a massacre of 300 Texans in 1836, 29°N, 97°W. (m. 137, t. 136)

Gonzales (gôn sa'ləs) Southern Texas town near San Antonio. Site of the first battle in the Texas Revolution; 29°N, 97°W. (m. 137, t. 136)

Grand Canyon (grand kan'yən) Large canyon on the Colorado River in northwestern Arizona. (t. 22)

Great Lakes (grāt lāks) Chain of five large freshwater lakes between the northern United States and Canada. (m. R18)

Great Plains (grāt plānz) Part of the Interior Plains of the Middle West, an area of dry grassland where much wheat is grown. The Great Plains form one of the regions of Texas. (m. 22, t. 6)

Guadalupe Mountains (gwäd a lüp'ā moun'tənz) Mountain range in southern New Mexico and south-western Texas. (m. 35, t. 9)

Guadalupe Mountains National Park (gwäd a lüp'ā moun'tənz na'shə nəl pärk) National park in south-western Texas. (m. 35, t. 3)

Guadalupe Peak (gwäd a lüp'ā pēk) Highest moun-tain in Texas and a peak of the Guadalupe Mountains. (m. 35, t. 9)

Gulf of Mexico (gulf əv mek'si kō) A gulf of the Atlantic Ocean bordering Mexico and five states of the United States, including Texas. (m. H13, t. 28)

H

High Plains (hī plānz) One of three geographical areas on the Great Plains of Texas, located in the Panhandle. (m. 33, t. 32)

Houston (hūs'tən) Port city in southeastern Texas and a major oil-refining center; 30°N, 95°W. (m. H13, t. 18)

Houston Ship Channel (hūs'tən ship chan'əl) A 50-mile-long body of water that connects Houston with the Gulf of Mexico. (m. 28, t. 307)

Huntsville (hənts' vil) City near Houston where Melinda Rankin taught and wrote about Texas. (t. 210)

I

Indian Ocean (in'dē ən ō'shən) An ocean between Africa, southern Asia, and Australia. (m. H12, t. H11)

Indian Territory (in'dē ən ter'ə tôr ē) Area set aside for Native Americans in what is now the state of Oklahoma. (t. 253)

Interior Plains (in tir'ē ər plānz) The large plain in the central part of the United States that includes the Central Plains and the Great Plains. (m. 22, t. 6)

J

Jamestown (jāmz'toun) The first permanent English settlement in America, established in the colony of Virginia in 1607; 37°N, 77°W. (m. 107)

Japan (jə pán) Country of eastern Asia made up of islands in the Pacific Ocean. (m. R5, t. 407)

Johnson Space Center (jon'sən) An important center for the United States space program. It is located in Clear Lake, a suburb of Houston. (t. 308)

K

Killeen (ki'len) City in the central part of Texas north of Austin. (t. 285)

L

Lake Texcoco (lāk tā skō′kō) A lake in what is now Central Mexico on which the Aztec built Tenochtitlán. (t. 159)

Laredo (lə rā′ dō) City in westernmost Texas on the Rio Grande. (t. 401)

Louisiana Territory (lü ē′sē an ə ter′ə tôr ē) The area stretching from the Mississippi River to the Rocky Mountains claimed by French explorer La Salle and purchased in 1803 by the United States for $15 million. (m. 123, t. 123)

Lubbock (lub′ək) City in northwestern Texas; 34°N, 102°W. (m. H13, t. 33)

M

Massachusetts (mas ə chü′sits kol′ə nē) One of the 13 English colonies, founded in 1620; later became the state of Massachusetts. (m. 107, t. 107)

McAllen (mə ka′lən) Town in southern Texas near the Mexican border. (t. 326)

Metroplex (met′rō pleks) Metropolitan area made up of two large Texas cities, Dallas and Fort Worth. (t. 31)

Mexico (mek′si kō) Country bordering the United States to the south. (m. H13, t. 4)

Mexico City (mek′si kō sit′ē) Capital and largest city of Mexico, built as a Spanish settlement on the ruins of Tenochtitlán; 19°N, 99°W. (m. 92, t. 101)

Middle West (mid′əl west) A region of the United States made up of the Great Lakes states of Illinois, Indiana, Michigan, Minnesota, Ohio, and Wisconsin, and the Plains states of Iowa, Kansas, Missouri, Nebraska, North Dakota, and South Dakota. (m. 22, t. 22)

Midland (mid′lənd) City on the Great Plains of Texas; 32°N, 102°W. (m. 33, t. 33)

Millsap (mil′sap) Town in north-central Texas; 33°N, 98°W. (m. 31)

Mississippi River (mis ə sip′ē riv′ər) The second longest river in the United States. (m. 7, t. 7)

Mountain (moun′ tən) A region of the United States made up of the Mountain states of Colorado, Idaho, Montana, Nevada, Utah, and Wyoming. (m. 22, t. 22)

Mountains and Basins (moun′tənz and bā′sinz) Westernmost region of Texas. (m. 69, t. 22)

N

Nacogdoches (nakə do′chez) City in East Texas; 32°N, 95°W. (t. 204)

New Braunfels (nü brôn′felz) Town in the Texas Hill Country founded by German immigrants; 30°N, 98°W. (m. 186, t. 184)

New Spain (nü spān) Area of the Aztec empire renamed by its conqueror, Hernando Cortés. New Spain included Mexico and what is now Texas. (m. 108, t. 86)

North America (nôrth ə mer′i kə) Continent in the Western hemisphere. (m. H12, t. H11)

North Central Plains (nôrth sentral plānz) Region of Texas that is part of the Interior Plains of the United States. (m. 31, t. 30)

Northeast (nôrth ēst′) A region of the United States made up of the New England states of Connecticut, Maine, Massachusetts, New Hampshire, Rhode Island, and Vermont, and the Middle Atlantic states of Delaware, Maryland, New Jersey, New York, and Pennsylvania. (m. 22, t. 22)

Northern Hemisphere (nôr′thərn hem′i sfir) The half of Earth north of the equator. (m. H12, t. H12)

North Pole (nôrth pōl) The most northern place on Earth. (m. H12, t. H12)

Nueces River (nwā′sāz ri′ver) River in southeastern Texas involved in border dispute during the Mexican War. (m. H17, t. 175)

Nuevo Laredo (nwe′vō lə rā′dō) Mexican city across the Rio Grande from Laredo. (t. 401)

---

pronunciation key

a **at**; ā **ape**; ä **far**; âr **care**; e **end**; ē **me**; i **it**; ī **ice**; îr **pierce**; o **hot**; ō **old**; ô **fork**; oi **oil**; ou **out**; u **up**; ū **use**; ü **rule**; ù **pull**; ûr **turn**; hw **white**; ng **song**; th **thin**; th **this**; zh **measure**; ə **about, taken, pencil, lemon, circus**

O

Odessa (ō des'ə) City on the Great Plains of western Texas; 32°N, 102°W. (m. H13, t. 33)

P

Pacific Ocean (pə sif'ik ō'shən) Ocean that borders western North and South America and eastern Asia. (m. H12, t. H11)

Padre Island (päd'rā ī'lənd) Barrier island in the Gulf of Mexico off the south Texas coast. (m. 29, t. 370)

Palmito Ranch (pal mēt'ō ranch) Site of the final battle of the Civil War. (m. 220, t. 218)

Palo Duro Canyon (pal'ô dür'ô kan'yən) Canyon along the Red River in northwestern Texas. (t. 265)

Panama Canal (pan'ə ma kə nal') Canal through the country of Panama that links the Atlantic and Pacific oceans; 9°N, 80°W. (t. 4)

Panhandle (pan' han dəl) An arm of land that extends like the handle of a pan in northwestern Texas. (m. 33, t. 9)

Panna Maria (pa'na ma rē'ə) Village in Texas that is believed to have the oldest Polish Roman Catholic church in the United States. (m. 186, t. 184)

Permian Basin (pər'mē ən bā'sin) One of the world's largest oil-producing areas, located in the Great Plains of Texas. (m. 33, t. 33)

Philippines (fil'ə pēnz) A group of islands off the coast of southeast Asia making up the country of the Philippines. (t. 407)

Piney Woods (pī'nē wüdz) The wettest of the five areas that make up the Coastal Plain of Texas. (m. 29, t. 28)

Plymouth (pli'məth) Settlement in what is now Massachusetts, established by Pilgrims sailing from England on the Mayflower in 1620; 42°N, 71°W. (m. 107, t. 107)

Port Arthur (pôrt är'thər) City in Southeast Texas on Sabine Lake and southeast of Beaumont. (m. 29, t. 272)

Portugal (pôr'chə gəl) Country in southwestern Europe which began establishing colonies in South America in the 1500s. (m. R5, t. 109)

R

Republic of Colombia (ri pəb'lik əv kə lum'bē ə) Country in South America. First became a republic under Simón Bolívar in 1819. (t. 151)

Rio Grande (rē'ō grän'dē) The longest river in Texas, it forms part of the border between the United States and Mexico. (m. 9, t. 9)

Rio de Janeiro (rē'ō dā zhə nā'rō) Port city in southeastern Brazil; 23°S, 43°W. (m. R14)

Rocky Mountains (rok'ē moun'tənz) Mountain range that stretches from Canada through the western United States into Mexico. (m. 22, t. 4)

Round Rock (raünd räk) Town located in the south central part of Texas near Austin. (t. 290)

S

Sabine Pass (sə bēn' pas) Where Sabine Lake opens into the Gulf of Mexico in eastern Texas. It was the site of an important battle during the Civil War; 30°N, 94°W. (m. 220, t. 216)

Sabine River (sə bēn' riv'ər) River in eastern Texas. (m. 29, t. 197)

Salado (se läd'ō) Town located in the south central part of Texas. (t. 363)

San Antonio (san an tō'nē ō) Third largest city in Texas; 29°N, 99°W. (m. H13, t. 21)

San Antonio de Béxar (san an tō'nē ō dā bā'här) Fort built to protect the San Antonio de Valero mission. (m. 103, t. 105)

San Antonio de Valero (san an tō'nē ō dā va lār'ō) Mission on the San Antonio River whose church later became known as the Alamo; 29°N, 99°W. (m. 103, t. 105)

San Antonio River (san an tō'nē ō riv'ər) River in South Texas which flows into the Gulf of Mexico. (t. 237)

San Felipe de Austin (san fə lē' pā də ô'stin) Town chosen by Stephen F. Austin as the capital for his colony; 30°N, 96°W. (m. 137, t. 126)

San Jacinto River (san jə sin'tō riv'ər) River in southeastern Texas. The battle that won independence for Texas was fought at the mouth of this river. (t. 147)

San Jose Mission (san hō zā′ mish′ən) A mission built in 1721 near the Alamo. (m. 103, t. 105)

San Marcos (san mär′kəs) City in South Texas northeast of San Antonio. (t. 363)

South America (south ə mer′i kə) Continent in the Western Hemisphere. (m. H12, t. H11)

Southern Hemisphere (suth′ərn hem′i sfir) The half of Earth south of the equator. (m. H12, t. H12)

Southeast (south ēst′) A region of the United States made up of Alabama, Arkansas, Florida, Georgia, Kentucky, Louisiana, Mississippi, North Carolina, South Carolina, Tennessee, Virginia, and West Virginia. (m. 22, t. 22)

South Pole (south pōl) The southernmost place on Earth. (m. H12, t. H12)

Southwest (south west′) A region of the United States made up of Arizona, New Mexico, Oklahoma, and Texas. (m. 22, t. 22)

Spain (spān) Country in southwestern Europe which began establishing colonies in North and South America in the late 1400s and early 1500s. (m. R5, t. 83)

Spindletop (spin′dəl top) A hill near Beaumont, Texas, where oil was discovered. (t. 269)

T

Tenochtitlán (te nōch tē tlän′) Capital of the ancient Aztec empire, on the site of present-day Mexico City; 19°N, 99°W. (m. 59, t. 59)

Texas (tek′səs) A state of the Southwest region. (m. H13, t. 3)

U

United States (ū nī′tid stātz) Country in North America, made up of 50 states. (m. H16, t. 6)

V

Velasco (və läs′kō) Town where the treaty that ended the Texas Revolution was signed. (t. 149)

Venezuela (ven ə zwä′lə) Country in northern South America. (m. R4, t. 151)

Victoria (vic tôrē ə) Town founded by Don Martín and Patricia de la Garza de León; 29°N, 97°W. (t. 126)

W

Washington, D.C. (wô′shing tən dē sē) Capital of the United States; 39°N, 77°W. (t. 342)

Washington-on-the-Brazos (wô′shing tən on thə braz′əs) Town where the Texas Declaration of Independence was signed; 30°N, 96°W. (m. 137, t. 142)

Waxahachie (wak sə hach ē) The county seat of Ellis County, 30 miles south of Dallas. (t. 363)

West (west) A region of the United States made up of the Pacific states of Alaska, California, Hawaii, Oregon, and Washington. (m. 22, t. 22)

Western Hemisphere (wes′tərn hem′i sfir) The half of Earth west of the prime meridian. (m. H12, t. 4)

Wichita Falls (wich′ə ta falz) City in north central Texas; 34°N, 98°W. (m. 31, t. 31)

Y

Ysleta Mission (ē slā′tə) First Spanish mission in Texas, built in 1681 near what is now El Paso; 32° N, 106° W. (m. 103, t. 101)

---

pronunciation key

a at; ā ape; ä far; âr care; e end; ē me; i it; ī ice; îr pierce; o hot; ō old; ô fork; oi oil; ou out; u up; ū use; ü rule; ù pull; ûr turn; hw white; ng song; th thin; <u>th</u> this; zh measure; ə about, taken, pencil, lemon, circus

Biographical Dictionary

The Biographical Dictionary tells you about the people you have learned about in this book. The Pronunciation Key tells you how to say their names. The page numbers tell you where each person first appears in the text.

A

Adair, Christia (a dâre′), 1893-1990 Fought segregation during the 1950s and 1960s. (p. 288)

Armstrong, Lance (ärm′strong), 1971- Cyclist and three-time winner of the Tour de France. (p. 368)

Arnold, Hendrick (ärn′əld, hen′drik), ?-1849 Free African American who acted as a scout and soldier during the Texas Revolution. (p. 147)

Austin, Moses (au′stin), 1761-1821 Planned the first colony of United States settlers in Texas. (p. 123)

Austin, Stephen F. (au′stin), 1793-1836 Established the first colony of United States settlers in Texas. (p. 122)

B

Biggers, John (bi′gərz), 1924-2001 Artist who taught his students to create art from their own experience. (p. 377)

Bolívar, Simón (bō lē′vär, sē mōn′), 1783-1830 Venezuelan leader who helped South American countries fight for independence. (p. 151)

Bonham, James (bon′əm), 1807-1836 Fought for Texas during the Battle of the Alamo. (p. 139)

Borden, Gail, Jr. (bôr′dən), 1801-1874 Invented a new way to produce milk. (p. 279)

Borginnis, Sarah (bôr gin′nis), ?-1866 Helped the United States army during the Mexican War. (p. 176)

Bowie, Jim (bü′ē, bō′ē), 1796-1836 Led a group of volunteers who fought at the Alamo. (p. 139)

Bowles, Philip (bōlz′), ?-1839 Cherokee chief who signed a peace treaty with Sam Houston. (p. 160)

Burnet, David G. (bûr net′), 1788-1870 The first president of the Republic of Texas. (p. 142)

Bush, George (bush), 1924- Texan President of the United States from 1989 to 1993. (p. 343)

Bush, George W. (bush), 1946- Elected the 43rd President of the United States in 2000. (p. 343).

C

Cabeza de Vaca, Alvar Núñez (ka bā′sa dā va′ka, al′vär nün′yāz), 1490?-1560? Spanish explorer who was shipwrecked and enslaved by the Karankawa in Texas. (p. 92)

Cabral, Pedro Álvares (kə bräl′, pä′dro äl′vä räs), 1460?-1526? First Portuguese explorer to land in area that is now Brazil. (p. 109)

Castro, Henri (kas′trō, on rē′), 1786-1865 Frenchman who settled the town of Castroville. (p. 184)

Cazneau, Jane McManus (kaz nō′, jān mək ma′nus), 1807-1878 Served during the Mexican War. Was the only female to report from behind enemy lines. (p. 177)

Cisneros, Henry (sis ne′rōs), 1947- In 1993, he became United States Secretary of Housing and Urban Development. (p. 292)

Clark, Edward (clärk), 1815-1880 Governor of Texas under the Confederacy. (p. 212)

Cockrell, Sarah (kok′rəl), 1819-1892 Dallas businesswoman. (p. 249)

Columbus, Christopher (kə lum′bəs), 1451-1506 Italian explorer working on behalf of Spain who arrived in the Americas in 1492. (p. 83)

Coronado, Francisco Vásquez de (kôr ô nä′dô, fran sēs′kô vas käs dā), 1510-1554 Spanish explorer who led an army into Texas in search of the Seven Cities of Gold. (p. 94)

pronunciation key

a	at	ī	ice	u	up	th	thin
ā	ape	îr	pierce	ū	use	th	this
ä	far	o	hot	ü	rule	zh	measure
âr	care	ō	old	u̇	pull	ə	about, taken,
e	end	ô	fork	ûr	turn		pencil, lemon,
ē	me	oi	oil	hw	white		circus
i	it	ou	out	ng	song		

Cortés, Hernando (kôr tes', er nän'dô), 1485-1547 Spanish conquistador who defeated the Aztec empire. (p. 84)

Cos, Martín Perfecto de (kôs, mär'tēn pär fek'tô də), 1800-1854 Mexican general during the Texas Revolution. (p. 136)

Craft, Juanita (krâft, hwa nē'tə), 1902-1985 Fought for civil rights. Was the first African American woman to vote in Dallas County. (p. 290)

Crockett, David (kro'kət), 1786-1836 Led a group of volunteers from Tennessee who fought at the Alamo. (p. 139)

Cuney, Norris Wright (kyü'nē), 1846-1897 African American businessman who served in Texas and national governments. (p. 247)

 D

Davis, Jefferson (dā'vis), 1808-1889 President of the Confederate States of America. (p. 208)

de León, Don Martín (də lə ôn', dôn mär tēn'), 1765-1833 A Tejano empresario who brought 200 families to Victoria in 1824. (p. 126)

de León, Patricia de la Garza (də lə ôn', pa trē'sya də la gär'sa), 1760s-1849 Tejano who helped found Victoria. (p. 126)

de Narváez, Pánfilo (när vā'es, pan'fi lô də), 1478-1528 Spanish explorer who died in a shipwreck off the Texas coast. (p. 91)

de Piñeda, Alonso Alvarez (də pin yə'da, a lôn'zô al'va rəs), late 1400s-early 1500s Spanish explorer who may have been the first European to see present-day Texas. (p. 91)

de Soto, Hernando (də sô'tô, er nän'dô), 1500?-1542 Spanish explorer of what is now the southeastern United States. (p. 96)

Dickenson, Suzanna (dik'ən sən), 1820-1883 Alamo survivor who helped spread word of the battle throughout Texas. (p. 142)

Doña Marina (dô'nya mə rē'nə), c.1501-1550 Mexican Indian who helped Cortés communicate with Indian groups. (p. 85)

 E

Eisenhower, Dwight D. (ī'zən how ər), 1890-1969 Texan who was Allied commander in Europe during World War II and President of the United States from 1953 to 1961. (p. 285)

Esparza, Gregorio (as pär'zə), 1802-1836 Fought for Texas at the Battle of the Alamo. (p. 139)

Estevanico (es tə va nē'kô), ?-1539 Enslaved Moroccan scout for Fray Marcos. (p. 92)

 F

Fannin, James W. (fan'ən), 1804-1836 Texan commander who was killed with 300 soldiers in the Goliad Massacre. (p. 143)

Ferguson, Miriam (fûrg'ə sən), 1875-1961 First woman governor of Texas. (p. 289)

Flipper, Henry O. (flip'ər), 1856-1940 African American who served in the Texas Cavalry. (p. 257)

 G

Gallegos, Mario (go yā'gôs), 1950- Elected to Texas Senate in 1994. (p. 293)

Glidden, Joseph F. (glid'ən), 1813-1906 Iowa farmer who invented barbed wire. (p. 241)

González, Henry B. (gon so'ləs), 1916-2000 United States Representative from Texas. (p. 292)

Goyens, William (goi'əns), 1794-1856 Free African American businessman and interpreter for Sam Houston. (p. 204)

Grant, Ulysses S. (grant, ūlis'ēz), 1822-1885 Union general during the Civil War. (p. 218)

Griffith, Nanci (grif'əth), 1953- Texan folk singer and songwriter. (p. 380)

 H

Henderson, James Pinckney (hen'dər sən, jāmz pink'nē), 1808-1858 First governor of Texas. (p. 169)

Henry, O. (hen'rē, ō), 1862-1910 Pen name of short-story writer William S. Porter, who lived in Austin during the late 1800s. (p. 378)

Hidalgo, Miguel (ē dal'gô, mē gel'), 1753-1811 Mexican priest who helped Mexico begin to fight for independence. (p. 152)

Higgins, Pattillo (hig'ənz, pa til'yô), 1863-1955 Texas mechanic who discovered oil at Spindletop in 1901. (p. 268)

Hobby, Oveta Culp (ho'bē, ō vēt'ə kulp), 1905-1995 Organized and commanded the Women's Army Corps during World War II. (p. 285)

Hogg, James S. (hog), 1851-1906 Texas governor from 1891 to 1895. (p. 250)

Hood, John Bell (hüd), 1831-1879 Leader of Hood's Texas Brigade, which fought in several major battles during the Civil War. (p. 215)

Houston, Sam (hū'stən), 1793-1863 A general during the Texas Revolution, he later served as president of the Republic of Texas and governor of Texas. (p. 134)

Idar, Jovita (ē'där, hŏ'vē ta), 1885-1946 Formed the League of Mexican Women. (p. 292)

Iturbide, Agustín de (ē tür'bē də, a güs tēn' də), 1783-1824 Mestizo leader who won Mexico's independence from Spain. (p. 153)

Jefferson, Thomas (jef'ər sən), 1743-1826 President of the United States from 1801 to 1809. (p. 123)

Jemison, Mae (jem'i sən), 1956- First African American woman to go into space. (p. 309)

Jiménez, Flaco (hē men'ez, fla'kŏ), 1939- Accordionist and popularizer of Norteño music. (p. 380)

João, Dom (jô ow', dôm), 1769-1826 Ruler of Portugal who put his son, Prince Pedro, in charge of Brazil. (p. 230)

Johnson, Andrew (jon'sən), 1808-1875 President of the United States from 1865 to 1869. (p. 224)

Johnson, Lady Bird or Claudia Taylor (jon'sən), 1912- First Lady from 1963-1969. Worked to protect Texas wildlife. (p. 361)

Johnson, Lyndon B. (jon'sən), 1908-1973 Texan who was President of the United States from 1963 to 1969. (p. 291)

Jones, Anson (jōnz, an'sən), 1798-1858 Last president of the Republic of Texas. (p. 169)

Joplin, Janis (jä'plən), 1943-1970 First female rock music superstar. (p. 380)

Joplin, Scott (jop'lən), 1868-1917 Ragtime composer born in Texarkana. (p. 280)

Jordan, Barbara (jôr'dən), 1936-1996 Texan who served in the United States House of Representatives from 1973 to 1979. (p. 336)

Karnes, Henry (kärnz), 1812-1840 Scout for Sam Houston's army who helped win the Battle of San Jacinto. (p. 148)

King, Martin Luther, Jr. (king), 1929-1968 Civil-rights leader who worked to gain equal rights for African Americans. (p. 291)

King, Richard (king), 1824-1885 Founder of King Ranch in South Texas, one of the largest working ranches in the United States. (p. 319)

Lamar, Mirabeau B. (lə mär', mir'ə bō), 1798-1859 President of the Republic of Texas from 1838 to 1840. (p. 161)

La Salle, René Robert Cavelier, Sieur de (lə sal', re nā' rō bâre' ka vəl yā', sir de), 1643-1687 French explorer who helped establish Fort St. Louis in Texas. (p. 96)

Lee, Robert E. (lē), 1807-1870 Confederate general during the Civil War. (p. 215)

Lincoln, Abraham (ling'kən), 1809-1865 President of the United States from 1861 to 1865. (p. 210)

Long, Jane (long), 1798-1880 One of the old Three Hundred. Often called the "Mother of Texas." (p. 124)

Lucas, Anthony (lū' kus), 1855-1921 A mining expert who struck oil at Spindletop. (p. 270)

Lucchese, Josephine (lü ka'zē), 1901-1974 Opera singer from San Antonio. (p. 280)

MacKenzie, Ranald S. (mə ken'zē), 1840-1889 United States Army colonel in the Battle of Palo Duro Canyon. (p. 254)

Martínez, Antonio (mär tē'nez), (?-1823) Spanish governor who allowed United States citizens to settle in Texas. (p. 124)

Matthews, Sallie Reynolds (ma'thūz), 1861-1938 Daughter of Texas settlers who wrote about how colonists lived. (p. 130)

McMurtry, Larry (mək mûr'trē), 1936- Texan writer who won a Pulitzer Prize. (p. 378)

Moctezuma II (mok tə zü'mə), 1480?-1520 Last ruler of the Aztec empire. (p. 84)

Mora, Pat (mô'rə), 1942- Writer whose stories and poems focus on language, tradition, and the preservation of culture. (p. 379)

Morelos, José María (mô rə'lôs, hô sə' ma rē'a), 1765-1815 Priest who helped lead the struggle for Mexico's independence. (p. 153)

Moscoso de Alvarado, Luis de (môs kôs' ô də al va ra'dô, lü ēs' də), 1505-1551 Spanish explorer who led Southeast expedition after the death of de Soto. (p. 96)

Murphy, Audie (mûr'fē, ô'dē), 1924-1971 Most decorated American soldier during World War II. (p. 285)

Nelson, Willie (nel'sən), 1933- Country music star from Abbott. (p. 380)

Ney, Elisabet (nā, ə lis'a bet), 1833-1907 Sculptor of Sam Houston and Stephen F. Austin statues in the Texas Capitol. (p. 377)

O

O'Keeffe, Georgia (ō kĕf', jôr'jə), 1887-1986 Painter who taught briefly in Texas and was influenced by the prairie landscape. (p. 377)

Osterman, Rosanna (ös'tər min, rō zan'na), 1818-1866 Created Galveston army hospital during the Civil War. (p. 217)

P

Parker, Cynthia Ann (pär'kər), 1827-1864 Daughter of white settlers who was captured and adopted by Comanche. Mother of Quanah Parker. (p. 254)

Parker, Quanah (pär'kər, kwän'ə), 1845-1911 Comanche chief who led his people against the Texas Rangers in the Red River campaign. (p. 254)

Pedro I, Dom (pā'drô, dôm), 1798-1834 Declared Brazil's independence and became king in 1821. (p. 230)

Pedro II, Dom (pā'drô, dôm), 1825-1891 Ruler of Brazil who ended slavery there in 1888. (p. 230)

Polk, James K. (pōlk), 1795-1849 President of the United States who helped make Texas the 28th state in 1845. (p. 169)

Porter, Katherine Anne (pôr'ter), 1890-1980 Pulitzer Prize-winning writer who grew up in Indian Creek. (p. 378)

R

Ramsey, Buck (ram'zē), 1937-1998 Cowboy poet from Amarillo. (p. 379)

Rankin, Melinda (rang'kən), 1811-1888 Christian missionary, writer, and abolitionist. (p. 210)

Richards, Ann (ri'chərdz), 1933- Governor of Texas from 1991 to 1995. (p. 334)

Rodriguez, Cleto (rod rē'gez), 1923-1990 Mexican American staff sergeant who served during World War II and received the Medal of Honor. (p. 285)

Roosevelt, Franklin Delano (rōz'velt, frang'klən del'ə nō), 1882-1945 President of the United States from 1933 to 1945. (p. 284)

Ruby, George T. (rü'bē), 1841-? African American elected to 1869 Texas Senate. (p. 227)

Ruiz, Francisco (rü îs'; fran sîs' kō), 1783-1840 Signer of the Texan Declaration of Independence. (p. 142)

Ryan, Nolan (rī'ən, nō'lən), 1947- Baseball player from Alvin. (p. 372)

S

Santa Anna, Antonio López de (san'ta an'a, an tô'nē ō lô'pəs də), 1795-1876 President of Mexico and general who led attack on the Alamo. He was defeated at San Jacinto. (p. 135)

Satanta (sə tan'te), 1807?-1878 Kiowa chief who fought the relocation of Native Americans to reservations. (p. 252)

Scott, Winfield (skot, win'fēld), 1786-1866 United States general who captured Mexico City during the Mexican War. (p. 177)

Seguín, Juan (sə gēn', hwan), 1806-1889 Tejano leader who fought for Texas at the Battle of San Jacinto. (p. 139)

Sherman, William Tecumseh (tə küm'sə), 1820-1891 Civil War general sent to Texas in 1871. (p. 253)

Simond, Ada (sī'mənd), 1903-1989 Writer of short stories that tell of growing up as an African American in Texas. (p. 378)

Smith, Erastus Deaf (smith, ə ras'təs def), 1787-1837 Army scout during the Texas Revolution. (p. 147)

Stinson, Marjorie (stin'sən), 1896-1975 and **Katherine** 1891-1977 Sisters who were pioneers of aviation. (p. 278)

T

Taylor, Zachary (tā'lər, zak'ə rē), 1784-1850 United States general during the Mexican War and President of the United States from 1849 to 1850. (p. 175)

Terry, Benjamin Franklin (ter'ē), 1821-1861 Leader of Eighth Texas Cavalry unit, also known as Terry's Texas Rangers during the Civil War. (p. 215)

Travis, William B. (tra'vəs), 1809-1836 Commander of the Texans at the Alamo. (p. 135)

Tucker, Sara Martínez (tu'kər), 1955- President of the Hispanic Scholarship Fund, which helps Latino students pay for their college education. (p. 304)

W

Washington, George (wô'shing tən), 1732-1799 Commander of the American army during the American Revolution and first President of the United States. (p. 150)

Williams, Lizzie Johnson (wil'yəmz), 1843-1924 Known as the "Cattle Queen of Texas." (p. 238)

Z

Zavala, Lorenzo de (sa va'la, lô rən'sô dä), 1788-1836 Mexican who established a colony in eastern Texas and became the first vice president of the Republic of Texas. (p. 142)

Glossary

This Glossary will help you to pronounce and understand the meanings of the vocabulary in this book. The page number at the end of the definition tells where the word first appears.

A

abolition (ab ə lish'ən) Ending or doing away with completely; often used in reference to slavery. (p. 209)

adobe (ə dō bē) Brick made from clay and straw that has been dried in the sun. (p. 71)

agribusiness (ag'rə biz nis) A large farm or ranch which is combined with other businesses. (p. 318)

agriculture (ag'ri kul chər) The business of growing crops and raising animals. (p. 317)

Allied Powers (al'īd pow'ərz) Countries who fought in World War I on the side led by England, France, Russia, the United States and Italy. (p. 277)

Allies (al'īz) Countries who fought in World War II on the side led by England, France, Russia, and the United States. (p. 284)

amendment (a mend'mənt) Addition to the United States Constitution. (p. 225)

American Revolution (ə mer'i kən rev ə lü'shən) The war fought by the American colonies to end British rule, 1775-1783. (p. 150)

ancestor (an'ses tər) A person in your family, starting with your parents, who was born before you. (p. 18)

annexation (an ek sā'shən) Incorporating a territory into a country. (p. 167)

Anglo-American (an'glō ə mer'ə kən) A person with English or Northern European anscestors. (p. 126)

aquifer (ak'wə fər) A layer of rock or gravel that absorbs rainfall and keeps it flowing underground. (p. 15)

archaeology (ar kē ol'ə jē) The study of the way people lived in the past, including prehistoric times. (p. 51)

artifact (ar'tə fakt) Object made by people who lived in the past, often found and studied by archaeologists. (p. 51)

assembly line (ə sem'blē līn') A line of workers and machines along which a product is moved to be put together. (p. 300)

Axis Powers (ak'sis pow'ərz) Countries who fought in World War II on the side led by Germany, Italy, and Japan. (p. 284)

B

band (band) Small family group to which some Native Americans belonged. (p. 68)

barbed wire (bärbd wīr) Wire with sharp metal points that is used to fence off areas of land. (p. 241)

barter (bärt'ər) To trade things for other things without using money. (p. 130)

basin (bā'sin) A low, bowl-shaped landform surrounded by higher land. (p. 9)

Battle of the Alamo (al'ə mō) One of the most important battles of the Texas Revolution. (p. 140)

Battle of Boyaca (boi a'ka) Battle that freed the territory of New Grenada. (p. 151)

Battle of San Jacinto (san jə sint'ō) Last battle of the Texas Revolution. Santa Anna's troops were defeated. (p. 148)

bilingual (bī ling'gwəl) People who are able to speak two languages. (p. 133)

bill (bil) A proposal for a law. (p. 335)

Black Codes (blak kōdz) Laws passed by Southern states, including Texas, that restricted the rights of African Americans. (p. 225)

blockade (blo kād') Shutting off of an area to prevent supplies from entering or leaving. (p. 216)

pronunciation key

a	at	ī	ice	u	up	th	thin	
ā	ape	îr	pierce	ū	use	th	this	
ä	far	o	hot	ü	rule	zh	measure	
âr	care	ō	old	u̇	pull	ə	about, taken,
e	end	ȯ	fork	ûr	turn		pencil, lemon,
ē	me	oi	oil	hw	white		circus
i	it	ou	out	ng	song		

boom town (büm'town) A community that grows at a rapid rate. (p. 270)

branch (branch) A part of government. (p. 334)

brand (brand) A design that cowboys burned into an animal's hide to identify the ranch to which it belonged. (p. 237)

brazilwood (brə zil'wud) A tree in Brazil used to make a popular red dye. (p. 229)

budget (buj'it) Plan for using an amount of money for specific purposes. (p. 333)

butte (būt) A flat-topped hill, smaller than a mesa. (p. 30)

C

canal (kə nal') A waterway dug across land for transportation or irrigation. (p. 4)

candidate (can'di dāt) A person running for office in an election. (p. 341)

canyon (can'yən) A deep valley with steep sides. (p. 9)

cardinal direction (kär'də nəl di rek'shən) One of the main directions of the globe—north, south, east, and west. (p. xxvi)

cash crop (kash krop) A crop that is grown to be sold for money rather than to be used on the farm where it is grown. (p. 130)

cattle drive (cat'əl drīv) A journey in which cowboys herded cattle north to railroad depots in the late 1800s. (p. 238)

cause (kôz) An event that makes something else happen. (p. 88)

cavalry (ka'vəl rē) A group of soldiers who fight on horseback. (p. 215)

CD-ROM (sē dē rom') A reference source used with a computer that may include writing, pictures, sounds, or short movies. (p. 314)

 census (sen'səs) A count of the people who live in a place. (p. 388)

Central Powers (sen'trəl pow'ərz) Countries that fought in World War I on the side which included Germany, Austria-Hungary, Turkey and Bulgaria. (p. 277)

checks and balances (cheks and bal'ən səs) The idea that each branch of government keeps watch over the others. (p. 334)

circle graph (sûr'kəl graf) A graph in the shape of a circle that shows the sizes of different parts of a whole; also called a pie graph. (p. 172)

citizen (sit'ə zən) A person who is born in a country or who has earned the right to become a member of that country by law. (p. 327)

city council (sit'ē kown'səl) Group of people elected to make laws for and help run a city or town. (p. 328)

city manager (sit'ē man'a jər) Person hired by the mayor and city council of a large city to run its daily business. (p. 328)

civilization (siv əl ə zā'shən) A culture that has developed systems of government, education, and religion. (p. 58)

civil rights (siv'əl rīts) The rights of people to be treated equally under the law. (p. 290)

Civil War (siv'əl wôr) The war in the United States between the Union states of the North and the Confederate states of the South, 1861-1865. (p. 213)

climate (klī'mit) The pattern of weather of a certain place over many years. (p. 12)

coast (kōst) The land next to an ocean. (p. 7)

colony (kol'ə nē) A place that is ruled by another country. (p. 84)

Columbian Exchange (kə ləm'bē ən iks chānj') The movement of people, food, and diseases from Europe, Asia, Africa, and the Americas in either direction following the voyages of Columbus. (p. 84)

commercial farming (kə mūr'shəl fär'mēng) The raising of crops and livestock to sell in one's own country and for export. (p. 413)

communications (kə mū ni kā'shənz) The exchange of information between people, often using the latest technology. (p. 281)

compass rose (kum'pəs rōz) A small drawing on a map that shows directions. (p. H13)

Compromise of 1850 (käm'prə mīz) Agreement whereby Texas agreed to give up land that is now part of New Mexico in exchange for $10 million. (p. 178)

conclusion (kən klü'zhən) A statement that pulls together several pieces of information and gives them a meaning. (p. 404)

Confederacy (kən fed'ər ə sē) The government formed by 11 Southern states that seceded from the United States, 1861-1865. (p. 211)

congress (kong'ris) The legislative, or law-making, branch of a state or national government. (p. 159)

conquistador (kon kēs'tə dôr) The Spanish word for a conqueror, one who takes ownership by force. (p. 84)

consequence (kän'sə kwents) A result. (p. 26)

conservation (kon sər vā'shən) The careful use of a natural resource. (p. 15)

constitution (kon sti tü'shən) A document that has the basic rules to govern a state or country. (p. 142)

Glossary

consumer (kon sü′mər) Person who buys a product or uses a service. (p. 301)

continent (kon′tə nənt) One of Earth's seven great bodies of land—Africa, Antarctica, Asia, Australia, Europe, North America, and South America. (p. H11)

convention (kən ven′shən) A formal meeting held for a special purpose. (p. 134)

county (kown′tē) One of the sections into which a state is divided. (p. 329)

cradleboard (krā′dəl bōrd) A wooden frame covered with deerskin which holds a baby. (p. 68)

crop rotation (krop rō tā′shən) Method of planting a different crop each year on the same soil. (p. 72)

crude oil (krüd oil) Petroleum that lies near the surface of the ground. (p. 272)

custom (kus′təm) The special way a group of people does something. (p. 15)

D

Davis Guards (dā′vis gärdz) Texas Confederate soldiers stationed at Fort Griffin. They turned back the Union Army at the Battle of the Sabine Pass. (p. 216)

debt (det) Amount of money owed. (p. 160)

decade (de′kād) A period of ten years. (p. 389)

decision (di sizh′ən) A choice that helps you reach a goal. (p. 144)

degree (di grē′) A unit for measuring distance on Earth's surface; also a unit for measuring temperature represented by the symbol °. (p. 54)

delegate (del′i git) A person who is chosen to speak for a group. (p. 134)

democratic republic (dem ə krat′ik ri pub′lik) A government in which citizens elect representatives to run the government. (p. 341)

desert (dez′ərt) A dry area that gets less than 10 inches of precipitation each year. (p. 34)

dictator (dik′tā tər) A leader with complete control of the government. (p. 135)

dictionary (dik′shə ner ē) A book that explains the meanings of words and shows how to pronounce and spell them. (p. 314)

discrimination (dis kri mi nā′shən) Unfair difference in the treatment of people. (p. 290)

distribution map (dis trə byü′ shən map) Map which shows how something is spread out over an area. (p. 180)

dugout (dug′out) A home dug out of the side of a hill. (p. 130)

E

editorial (ed i tôr′ē əl) A newspaper article that gives opinions, rather than facts. (p. 331)

effect (i fekt′) An event that happens as a result of another event. (p. 88)

elect (i lekt′) Choose by voting. (p. 327)

elevation (el ə vā′shən) The height of land above sea level. (p. 10)

Emancipation Proclamation (i man sə pā′shən prok lə mā′shən) Announcement by President Lincoln in 1863 that all enslaved people living in Confederate states were free. (p. 218)

empire (em′pī ər) A large area of different groups of people ruled by one country or leader. (p. 59)

empresario (em prəs är′ē ō) A person given a large piece of land by a government and allowed to sell the land to settlers. (p. 126)

encyclopedia (en sī klə pē′dē ə) A book or set of books that gives facts about people, places, things, and events. (p. 314)

entrepreneur (än trə prə nûr′) Person who organizes and runs a business. (p. 270)

environment (en vī′rən mənt) The surroundings in which people, plants, or animals live. (p. 14)

equator (i kwā′tər) An imaginary line that lies halfway between the North Pole and the South Pole, at 0° latitude. (p. H12)

ethnic group (eth′nik grüp) A group of people whose ancestors are from the same country or area. (p. 18)

evaluates (i val′ yə wāts) Judges the value of something. (p. 26)

executive branch (eg zek′yə tiv branch) The branch of government that carries out laws. (p. 334)

expedition (eg spə dish′ ən) A journey of exploration. (p. 91)

explore (ek splôr′) To travel in unfamiliar places in order to find out and learn about them. (p. 84)

export (ek′spôrt) Something sold or traded to another country. (p. 229)

F

fact (fakt) A statement that can be checked and proven true. (p. 330)

food processing (füd pros′es ing) Any of hundreds of ways of turning crops and livestock into different food products. (p. 307)

forecast (fôr′kast) To predict what may or will happen. (p. 406)

frame of reference (frām əv ref′rents) All the things learned or experienced that help shape thoughts, feelings, and opinions. (p. 382)

Freedmen's Bureau (frēd′menz byu̇′rō) Organization which helped former slaves build new lives for themselves, established by the government during Reconstruction. (p. 222)

free-enterprise system (frē en′tər prīz sis′təm) The economic system that allows people to own and run their own businesses. (p. 298)

frontier (frun tîr′) The edge of a settled area. (p. 124)

G

generalization (jen ər ə lə zā′shən) A statement that ties together several different examples, showing how they are connected by a single concept or idea. (p. 244)

geography (jē og′rə fē) The study of Earth and the way people, plants, and animals live on and use it. (p. 4)

glacier (glā′shər) A huge sheet of ice that moves slowly across the land. (p. 49)

global grid (glō′bəl grid) The crisscrossing lines of latitude and longitude found on a map or globe. (p. 56)

Goliad Massacre (gō′lē ad mas′ə ker) A brutal event of the Texas Revolution in which surrendering Texans were murdered by Santa Anna. (p. 143)

Grange (grānj) An association formed by farmers in the late 1800s. Grange members worked to make life better for farmers by sharing information about crops, prices, and supplies. (p. 250)

graph (graf) A diagram that shows information in a picture. (p. 172)

Great Depression (grāt di presh′ən) Period of widespread economic hardship in the 1930s. (p. 282)

guide word (gīd wûrd) One of the words at the top of each page of a reference book that shows the first and last entries on that page. (p. 314)

gusher (gush′ər) An oil well that gives forth a lot of oil without being pumped. (p. 273)

H

hemisphere (hem′i sfîr) Half a sphere; one of the four hemispheres of Earth—Northern, Southern, Eastern, and Western hemispheres. (p. H12)

heritage (her′i tij) The history and traditions that a group of people share. (p. 18)

high-tech industry (hī tek in′dus trē) The use of advanced scientific ideas and special skills and tools to meet people's needs. (p. 308)

historical map (his tor′i kəl map) A map that shows information about past events and where they occurred. (p. xxxi)

history (his′tə rē) The story of what happened in the past, usually as preserved in written records. (p. 51)

Hood's Texas Brigade (hu̇dz tek′səs bri gād′) A brigade of Texas Confederate soldiers led by General John Bell Hood. (p. 215)

hunters and gatherers (hən′tərz and ga′thər ərz) People who hunt and collect fruits and other goods. (p. 50)

I

Ice Age (īs āj) A period of time when glaciers covered much of Earth's surface. (p. 49)

import (im′pôrt) Something brought in from another country for sale or use. (p. 399)

industrialization (in dus trē əl ə zā′shən) Development of manufacturing industries. (p. 414)

industry (in′də strē) All the businesses that make one kind of product or provide one kind of service. (p. 29)

inference (in′fə rənts) Something figured out based on clues and information. (p. 274)

interdependent (in tər di pen′dənt) Relying on one another to meet needs and wants. (p. 25)

intermediate direction (in tər mē′dē it di rek′shən) Any direction in between two cardinal directions— northeast, southeast, southwest, northwest. (p. H13)

Internet (in′tər net) A network of computers that connects people around the world. (p. 314)

interstate highway (in′tər stāt hī′wā) A road that connects cities in two or more states, with at least two lanes of traffic in each direction. (p. 374)

invention (in ven′shən) A newly created product. (p. 279)

investor (in ves′tər) Someone who puts money into a business and expects a share of the profit. (p. 300)

irrigation (ir i gā′shən) The use of ditches or pipes to bring water to fields. (p. 32)

J

judicial branch (ju̇ dish′əl branch) The branch of government that interprets, or explains, laws. (p. 335)

---

pronunciation key

a **at**; ā **ape**; ä **far**; âr **care**; e **end**; ē **me**; i **it**; ī **ice**; îr **pierce**; o **hot**; ō **old**; ô **fork**; oi **oil**; ou **out**; u **up**; ū **use**; ü **rule**; u̇ **pull**; ûr **turn**; hw **white**; ng **song**; th **thin**; <u>th</u> **this**; zh **measure**; ə **about, taken, pencil, lemon, circus**

jury (jùr′ē) A group of citizens in a court of law who must decide if someone accused of a crime is innocent or guilty. (p. 327)

K

kerosene (ke′r ə sēn) A colorless liquid made from petroleum that is used as a fuel. (p. 269)

L

landform (land′fôrm) Any of the shapes that make up Earth's surface. (p. 4)

landform map (land′fôrm map) A map that shows the landforms of an area. (p. H17)

large-scale map (lärj skāl map) A map that shows a lot of detail on a smaller area. (p. 220)

latitude (lat′i tüd) A measure of distance on Earth north or south of the equator. (p. 54)

legislative branch (lej′is lā tiv branch) The branch of government that makes laws. (p. 334)

line graph (līn graf) A graph that shows how a piece of information changes over time. (p. 172)

locator (lō′kāt ər) A small map or globe set onto another map that shows where the main map is located. (p. H15)

longhorn (lông′hôrn) One of a breed of cattle having very long horns. (p. 237)

longitude (lon′ji tüd) A measure of distance on Earth east or west of the prime meridian. (p. 55)

Louisiana Purchase (lü ē zē an′ə pûr′chəs) The purchase of the Louisiana Territory in 1803 by President Thomas Jefferson. (p. 123)

Louisiana Territory (lü ē zē an′ə ter′itôrē) The land that stretched from the Mississippi River west to the Rocky Mountains. (p. 123)

lowland (lō′land) Land with an elevation just above sea level. (p. 29)

M

Manifest Destiny (man′ə fest des′tə nē) Idea popular around the 1840s that the United States would grow as far west as the Pacific and as far south as the Rio Grande. (p. 167)

maquiladoras (mə kē′lə dōr əs) Factories that are owned by the same company that are built on either side of the Texas and Mexican border (p. 401)

manufacturing (man yə fak′chər ing) The making of goods by machinery. (p. 307)

map key (map kē) An explanation of what the symbols on a map represent. (p. H14)

map scale (map skāl) A line divided into units of measurement, such as inches, used to represent a real distance on Earth. (p. 220)

map symbol (map sim′bəl) A small drawing that stands for something else on a map. (p. H14)

marsh (märsh) An area of low wet land covered mostly with tall grasses. (p. 52)

mayor (mā′ər) Elected head of the government of a city. (p. 328)

meridian (mə rid′ē ən) A line of longitude. (p. 55)

mesa (mā′sə) A flat landform that rises steeply above the surrounding land; smaller than a plateau. (p. 30)

mestizo (me stē′zō) Person who is part Spanish and part Mexican Indian. (p. 102)

metropolitan area (met rə pol′i tən âr′ē ə) A city and its suburbs together. (p. 29)

Mexican War (mek′sə kən wôr) The war fought between Mexico and the United States between 1846 and 1848 over Texas. (p. 176)

mineral (min′ər əl) A nonrenewable natural resource that is found in the ground and does not come from plants or animals. (p. 15)

mission (mish′ən) A settlement where Europeans taught Native Americans the Christian religion. (p. 100)

missionaries (mish′ən âr ēz) People who teach their religion to others who have different beliefs. (p. 100)

monarchy (mon′är kē) Nation or state that is led by a king, queen, or other ruler. (p. 230)

mouth (mouth) The place where a river empties into an ocean or another large body of water. (p. 7)

municipal government (mū nis′ə pəl) Having to do with the running of a city. (p. 327)

mural (myur′əl) A picture painted on a wall or ceiling. (p. 377)

N

NAFTA (naf′tə) North American Free Trade Agreement, which has made import and export easier between the United States, Mexico, and Canada. (p. 399)

natural feature (nach′ər əl fē′chər) Any part of Earth's surface formed by nature. (p. 8)

natural resource (nach′ər əl rē′sôrs) Something found in the environment that people can use. (p. 14)

New Deal (nü dēl) Government programs introduced during the Depression by President Franklin D. Roosevelt. (p. 284)

nonrenewable resources (non ri nü′ə bel rē sôr′sez) Resources that are available in a limited supply. When used they are gone forever. (p. 14)

Norteño (nôr tā′ nyō) Mexican American dance music. (p. 380)

O
---

ocean (ō′shən) One of Earth's four largest bodies of water—the Atlantic, Arctic, Indian, and Pacific oceans. (p. H11)

Old Three Hundred, The (ōld thrē hun′drid) The first three hundred families to settle in San Felipe de Austin in 1825. (p. 124)

Olympic Games (ō lim′pik gāmz) International athletic contests held every four years. (p. 372)

opinion (ə pin′yən) A personal feeling or belief. (p. 330)

outline (out′līn) A plan for organizing written information about a subject. (p. 16)

P
---

parallel (par′ə lel) A line of latitude. (p. 54)

petrochemical (pet rō kem′i kəl) One of various substances produced in refineries from petroleum. (p. 272)

petroleum (pə trō′lē əm) A thick, black liquid found underground, commonly called oil. (p. 15)

physical map (fiz′i kəl map) A map that shows natural features of Earth. (p. H17)

pilgrim (pil′grəm) A person who travels to a place for religious reasons. (p. 107)

pioneer (pī ə nīr′) A person who leads the way. (p. 123)

plain (plān) A large area of flat or nearly flat land. (p. 4)

Plan of Iguala (i gwa′lə) Agustín de Iturbide's plan for Mexican independence from Spain in 1821. (p. 153)

plantation (plan tā′shən) A large farm where cash crops such as cotton or corn were grown. (p. 201)

plateau (pla tō′) A high, flat area that rises steeply above the surrounding land. (p. 8)

point of view (point əv vyü) A way of looking at or thinking about something. (p. 330)

political (pə li′ti kəl) Of or having to do with politics, politicians, or government. (p. 183)

political map (pə lit′i kəl map) A map that shows information such as cities, capitals, states, and countries. (p. H16)

political party (pə lit′i kəl pär′tē) Group of people who share similar ideas about government. (p. 341)

pollution (pə lü′shən) Result of carelessly using resources, such as chemicals, that make air, water, or soil dirty. (p. 15)

port (pôrt) A place where ships load and unload their goods. (p. 29)

prairie (prâr′ē) Flat or gently rolling land thickly covered with grasses and wildflowers. (p. 29)

precipitation (pri sip i tā′shən) The moisture that falls to the ground as rain, snow, sleet, or hail. (p. 12)

presidio (pri sid′e o) A fort where soldiers lived to protect nearby Spanish settlements. (p. 101)

prehistory (prē his′tə rē) The time before written records. (p. 51)

primary source (prī′mer ē sôrs) Information that comes from someone who observed or took part in what he or she is describing. (p. 394)

prime meridian (prīm mə rid′ē ən) The line of longitude, marked 0°, from which other meridians are numbered. (p. 55)

professional (prə fesh′ə nəl) A person who gets paid for an activity usually done for fun, like sports. (p. 369)

profit (prof′it) The money a business earns after it pays for tools, salaries, and other costs. (p. 299)

pueblo (pweb′lō) "Village" in Spanish; any of several Native American groups that live in adobe and stone houses. (p. 70)

Pulitzer Prize (pul′it sər prīz) Award given every year for the best work in literature and news reporting. (p. 378)

R
---

ragtime (rag′tīm) A type of music which mixes brass band, African American, and other sounds and rhythms. (p. 380)

ranch (ranch) A large area of land used to raise cattle, sheep, or horses. (p. 31)

Reconstruction (re kon struk′shən) Time period following the Civil War in which the Southern states were brought back into the Union. (p. 224)

---

pronunciation key

a **at**; ā **ape**; ä **far**; âr **care**; e **end**; ē **me**; i **it**; ī **ice**; îr **pierce**; o **hot**; ō **old**; ô **fork**; oi **oil**; ou **out**; u **up**; ū **use**; ü **rule**; ù **pull**; ûr **turn**; hw **white**; ng **song**; th **thin**; th **this**; zh **measure**; ə **about, taken, pencil, lemon, circus**

recreation (rek rē ā′shən) What people do for relaxation or enjoyment. (p. 370)

recycle (rē sī′kəl) To use something again instead of discarding it. (p. 15)

reference source (ref′ər əns sôrs) A book or any form of information that contains facts about many different subjects. (p. 314)

refinery (ri fī′nə rē) A place where a raw substance such as crude oil or sugar is separated into parts to be used. (p. 272)

reform (rē fôrm′) A change designed to make things better. (p. 250)

region (rē′jən) An area with common features that set it apart from other areas. (p. 22)

relative location (re′lə tiv lō kā′shən) The location of one place in relation to another. (p. H13)

religion (rē lij′ən) The way people worship God, a god, or gods they believe in. (p. 60)

renewable resource (ri nü′ə bəl rē′sôrs) A natural resource that can be replaced for later use, such as a forest. (p. 14)

republic (ri pub′ lik) A form of government in which people choose leaders to represent them. (p. 149)

reservation (rez ər vā′shən) Land set aside by the United States government for a purpose, such as for Native Americans to live on. (p. 253)

reservoir (rez′ər vwär) A natural or artificial lake used to store water. (p. 35)

resolution (rez ə lü′shən) Decision stated in a formal way. (p. 169)

revolution (rev ə lü′shən) A sudden change of government. (p. 169)

road map (rōd map) A map that shows travelers which roads to use to get from one place to another. (p. 374)

Roaring Twenties (rôr′ing twen′tēz) What people often call the 1920s, a decade of many exciting changes. (p. 278)

Runaway Scrape (run′ə wā skrāp) The flight of Texans from the advance of Mexican troops during the Texas Revolution. (p. 147)

rural (rùr′əl) Of the countryside. (p. 18)

S

scale (skāl) The relationship between the distance shown on a map and the real distance on Earth. (p. H15)

secede (sə sēd′) To withdraw or formally leave an organization such as a government. (p. 211)

secondary source (sek′ən der ē sôrs) Information written by someone who was not present at the events described. (p. 394)

seeds of change (sēdz əv chānj) Five things included in the Columbian Exchange that changed many lives around the world. (p. 84)

segregate (seg ri gā′t) To keep two groups separate. (p. 290)

senator (se′nə tər) A member of Congress. (p. 171)

service industry (sûr′vis in′də strē) Businesses or jobs in which people help others. (p. 310)

sharecropper (shâr′krop ər) A person who grows crops on someone else's land, then pays a part of that crop to the owner. (p. 226)

slavery (slā′və rē) The practice of making one person the property of another. (p. 18)

small-scale map (smol skāl map) A map that shows few details on a larger area. (p. 220)

source (sôrs) The place where a river begins. (p. 7)

special district (spe′shəl dis′trikt) Group of people elected for a special purpose, such as overseeing schools. (p. 328)

specialize (spe′shə līz) To know a great deal about one particular thing. (p. 318)

stampede (stam pēd′) Herd of cattle running wild. (p. 239)

states' rights (stāts rīts) Belief that the people of each state have the right to decide laws for themselves. (p. 209)

stock (stok) A share, or part, of ownership in a company. (p. 283)

subsistence farming (səb sis′təns fär′məng) Growing only enough food to live, not to sell. (p. 130)

suffrage (suf′rij) The right to vote. (p. 289)

Sun Belt (sun belt) Those parts of the United States that have a warm, sunny climate all or most of the year. (p. 392)

T

tax (taks) Money people pay to a government (p. 135)

technology (tek nol′ə jē) The use of skills, ideas, and tools to meet people's needs. (p. 306)

teepee (tē′pē) A cone-shaped tent that can be put up and taken down quickly. (p. 66)

Tejanos (te hän′ōz) Mexican people who live in Texas. (p. 126)

temperature (tem'per ə chər) A measurement of how hot or cold something is. (p. 12)

term (tərm) A limited period of time. (p. 162)

Terry's Texas Rangers (ter'ēz tek'ses rān'jerz) A group of cavalry soldiers, led by Colonel Benjamin Franklin Terry, who fought for the Confederacy. (p. 215)

Texas Declaration of Independence (tek'səs dek lə rā'shən uv in di pen'dəns) A document declaring Texas's separation from Mexico. (p. 142)

Texas Railroad Commission (tek'səs rāl'rōd ko mi'shən) Organization created to stop the railroad companies' unfair practices. (p. 250)

Texas Rangers (tek'ses rān'jerz) A group of volunteers formed to defend the Republic of Texas in 1835. Today they are part of the state police force. (p. 159)

Texas Revolution (tek'ses rev ə lü'shən) The fight for Texas's independence from Mexico. (p. 136)

time line (tīm līn) A diagram that shows a series of events in the order in which they happened. (p. 98)

time zone (tīm zōn) A region in which all the clocks are set to the same time. (p. 35)

tornado (tôr nā'dō) A destructive, swirling funnel of wind that moves over the ground at high speeds. (p. 13)

tourist (tùr'əst) A person who travels for the fun of seeing new sights. (p. 310)

trade (trād) Buy and sell goods. (p. 12)

transportation (trans pər tā'shən) Moving people or goods from one place to another. (p. 25)

transportation map (trans pər tā'shən map) A map that shows how to travel from one place to another. (p. H17)

treaty (trē'tē) A formal agreement between countries. (p. 149)

Treaty of Guadalupe Hidalgo (trē'tē uv gwa də lü'pə hi dol'gō) Agreement signed by the United States and Mexico in 1848 ending the Mexican War. (p. 178)

Treaty of Medicine Lodge Creek (trē'tē uv med'ə sin loj crēk) Treaty of 1867 that said that some Native Americans would move their people to reservations in what is today Oklahoma. (p. 253)

Treaty of Velasco (trē'tē uv vəl as' kō) The agreement of 1836 which ended the Texas Revolution. (p. 149)

tributary (trib'yə ter ē) Any river that flows into another, larger river. (p. 7)

tribute (trib'yūt) Payment in the form of valuable goods and services, usually demanded by a foreign ruler. The Aztecs demanded tribute from the people they conquered. (p. 62)

trotline (trot'līn) A long heavy fishing line that has several baited hooks on it. (p. 72)

tundra (tun'dra) A huge plain that is frozen for most of the year. (p. 4)

Union (ūn'yən) The states that make up the United States. Used during the Civil War to refer to the government of the Northern States. (p. 210)

United States Congress (kong'ris) The legislative branch of our national government. (p. 342)

United States Supreme Court (sə prēm' kôrt) The highest court of the United States. (p. 342)

urban (ûr'bən) Of a city. (p. 18)

vegetation (vej ə tā'shən) The plant life of an area. (p. 28)

vegetation map (ve jə tā'shən map) A map which shows different kinds of plant areas (p. 36)

veto (vē'tō) The power of the executive branch to reject a bill passed by the legislative branch. (p. 335)

World War I (wûrld wôr wun) The first war between countries from around the world, fought mostly in Europe from 1914 to 1918. The Allied Powers fought against the Central Powers. (p. 277)

World War II (wûrld wôr tü) War fought mostly in Europe, North Africa, and the Pacific from 1939 to 1945. The Allies fought against the Axis Powers. (p. 284)

World Wide Web (wərld wīd web) A collection of information stored on computers around the world. (p. 392)

pronunciation key
a **a**t; ā **a**pe; ä f**a**r; âr **ca**re; e **e**nd; ē m**e**; i **i**t; ī **i**ce; îr p**ie**rce; o h**o**t; ō **o**ld; ô f**o**rk; oi **oi**l; ou **ou**t; u **u**p; ū **u**se; ü r**u**le; ù p**u**ll; ûr t**u**rn; hw **wh**ite; ng so**ng**; th **th**in; th **th**is; zh mea**s**ure; ə **a**bout, tak**e**n, penc**i**l, lem**o**n, circ**u**s

Index

This index lists many topics that appear in the book, along with the pages on which they are found. Page numbers after an *m* refer you to a map, and after a *p* refer you to photographs or artwork.

Acknowledgments (continued from page ii)

From **Magic Windows, Ventanas Magicas** by Carmen Lomas Garza. Copyright © 1999 by Carmen Lomas Garza. Children's Book Press, San Francisco, California. Used by permission. Texas State Song, "Texas, Our Texas." Words by Gladys Yoakum Wright and William J. Marsh. Music by William J. Marsh. Copyright © 1925 by William J. Marsh. Copyright © renewed 1953 by William J. Marsh. Southern Music Company. Used by permission. "Beautiful, Beautiful Texas," printed in **Texas: Great Songs of the Lone Star State.** Words and Music by W. Lee O'Daniel. Copyright © 1985 CPP/Belwin, Inc., Miami, Florida. Copyright © MCMXXXIII renewed and assigned by W. Lee O'Daniel. Copyright © renewed by Shapiro, Bernstein & Co., Inc., New York. Used by permission. Quote from **Conquest, Montezuma, Cortés, and the Fall of Old Mexico** by Hugh Thomas. Copyright © 1993 by Hugh Thomas. Simon & Schuster, New York. Used by permission. Excerpt from **Interwoven** by Sallie Reynolds Matthews. Copyright © 1988 by Macmillan Publishing Collier Books, a division of Macmillan Publishing Company, New York. Used by permission. From **The Alamo Remembered: Tejano Accounts and Perspectives** by Timothy M. Matovina. Copyright © 1955 University of Texas Press, Austin, Texas. Used by permission. From **The Raven** by Marquis James. Copyright © 1929 by Marquis James. Copyright © renewed 1956 by Jacqueline Mary Parsons James. University of Texas Press, Austin, Texas. Fifth University of Texas Press printing, 1999. Used by permission. From **Texas and Texans** by Adrian Anderson, Ralph Wooster, David G. Armstrong, Jeanie R. Stanley. Copyright © 1993 by the Glencoe Division of Macmillan/McGraw-Hill School Publishing. All rights reserved. Used by permission. From **American Indian Leaders: Studies in Diversity**, edited by R. David Edmunds. Copyright © 1980 by the University of Nebraska Press. University of Nebraska Press, Lincoln and London. Used by permission. From **Texas Cowboys: Memories of the Early Days**, edited by Jim Lanning and Judy Lanning. Copyright © 1984 Texas A & M University Press, College Station. Used by permission. From **Texas Women Who Dared to Be First** by Jean Flynn. Copyright © 1999 by Jean Flynn. Eakin Press, Austin, Texas, An imprint of Sunbelt Media, Inc. Used by permission.
Inaugural Address by former Texas Governor Ann Richards from **Governor Ann Richards and Other Texas Women** by Ruthe Winegarten. Copyright © 1993 Eakin Press, Austin. Used by permission. Quote by Barbara Jordan. Taken from **Brave Black Women** by Ruthe Winegarten and Sharon Kahn. Copyright © 1997 University of Texas Press, Austin. Used by permission. From **Woody Guthrie: American Balladeer** by Janelle Yates. Copyright © 1995 Ward Hill Press, Staten Island, New York. Used by permission. From "Twilight Choir" from **This Big Sky** by Pat Mora. Text copyright © 1998 by Pat Mora. Scholastic Press, a division of Scholastic Inc., New York. Used by permission. From **As I Rode Out on the Morning** by Buck Ramsey. Copyright © 1993 by Texas Tech University Press. Used by permission. From **Georgia O'Keeffe: A Life** by Roxana Robinson. Copyright © 1989 by Roxana Robinson. Harper & Row, Publishers, Inc. Used by permission. List, Lisabeth. From "A Day in the Life of a Doctors Without Borders Nurse." Summer 1998. http://www.refugeecamp.org/learnmore/nutrition/tfc_day.htm Used by permission.

Credits